THE GODDESS AND THE NATION

Sumathi Ramaswamy

THE **GODDESS AND THE NATION**

MAPPING MOTHER INDIA

Duke University Press

Durham and London

2010

© 2010 Duke University Press

Printed in Canada on acid-free paper ♾

Designed by Heather Hensley

Typeset in Warnock Pro by Tseng Information Systems, Inc.

Library of Congress Cataloging-in-Publication Data appear on the
last printed page of this book.

Duke University Press gratefully acknowledges the support of
the Trinity College of Arts and Sciences at Duke University,
which provided funds toward the production of this book.

Frontispiece: Mother India with Gandhi, Bose, Patel, and Nehru.
Print by Oriental Calendar, Calcutta, circa 1948. (Courtesy of Erwin
Neumayer and Christine Schelberger, Vienna); Facing page 1: P. T.
Velu, Cutantira Devi, 15–8–47 (Goddess of freedom). Print from
Erode, 1947. (Author's collection)

For my two mothers,

KAUSALYA AND PATRICIA,

in gratitude and with love

The fundamental event of the modern age is the
conquest of the world as picture.

MARTIN HEIDEGGER, "THE AGE OF THE WORLD PICTURE"

The Geography of a country is not the whole truth.
No one can give up his life for a map.

RABINDRANATH TAGORE, *THE HOME AND THE WORLD*

CONTENTS

ILLUSTRATIONS

ACKNOWLEDGMENTS

Walter Benjamin—the consummate guru for many of us who work on matters visual and more—once wrote about his method of cultural analysis, "I have nothing to say. Only to show. I will purloin nothing valuable and appropriate no ingenious turns of phrase. But the shards, the trash: I do not wish to inventory them, but simply give them their due in the only possible way: by putting them to use" (qtd. in Richter 2006, 136–37). As with all of Benjamin's aphoristic pronouncements, these words have been variously interpreted by scholars, but for me, they offer the inspiration for undertaking this particular analysis of a constellation of mass-produced images from a specific part of the world—with the conviction that cultural artifacts that have been dismissed as ephemera or trash can be historically constitutive and profoundly illuminating. In reaching this conviction, I have received encouragement and support from many individuals and institutions over the years, and it is a pleasure to acknowledge in print my debts to them.

The idea for this book emerged quite out of the blue—as is frequently the case with enticing projects—in an invitation I received in fall 1997 from Richard Davis to join a panel on Indian popular visual culture and nationalism for the annual South Asia conference in Madison, Wisconsin. To him and to my fellow panelists Ron Inden and Sandy Freitag, and to the audience at that event, especially Carla Petievich, I owe my first words of gratitude for their encouraging response to my preliminary thoughts. An early written attempt to take stock of the relationship between the map of India and Mother India followed in my essay in *The Blackwell Companion to Hinduism* (2002), and I thank its editor Gavin Flood for his invitation to contribute to that volume.

To many in the transnational scholarly community of visually minded South Asianists scattered across the globe I am enormously grateful for their work and for their thoughts, not to mention their fantastic collection of images. Their numbers may be small, but they more than make up for it by their generosity of spirit and quality of intellect, without which I could not have progressed in my own foray into this emergent field. The members of this group include Christiane Brosius, Robert Del Bonta, Richard Davis, Sandy Freitag, Joerg Gengnagel, Jyotindra Jain, Kajri Jain, Philip Lutgendorf, Erwin Neumayer, Christopher Pinney, Christine Schelberger, Yousuf Saeed, Kavita Singh, Gayatri Sinha, and Patricia Uberoi. In addition, from my Tasveerghar colleagues and good friends—Chris, Yousuf, Manishita, and Shuddha—I have learned to appreciate the sheer fun of getting entangled in the vibrant world of popular visual culture, as we put our heads and energies together to build a virtual "picture home" at www.tasveerghar.net. Since the time I first got interested in Indian maps and the history of cartography over a decade ago, Matthew Edney's scholarship has spurred on my own endeavors, and his diligent advice on critical sources has been invaluable. Over the years I have known her, Urvashi Butalia has continued to be a source of inspiration in so many regards, and her early faith in this project helped nurture my own excitement about it. At critical moments when I was puzzling over the theoretical orientation of this work, my wonderful conversations with Geeta Kapur, Vivan Sundaram, and Tanika and Sumit Sarkar helped me think through thorny issues, and I am very grateful to them for their time and good thoughts.

Numerous librarians, bibliographers, and archivists across the world have helped me to track down elusive pictures and maps, and in the process they frequently brought to my attention images that I did not even know existed. In particular I would like to mention Leena Mitford and Andrew Cook at the British Library; Abhijit Bannerjee at the Center for Studies in Social Sciences, Calcutta; G. Sundar at the Roja Muthiah Research Library, Chennai; Kamala at the Mahakavi Bharatiyar Museum cum Research Centre, Puducheri; Jaya Ravindran at the National Archives of India, New Delhi; Uttam Sinha at the National Gandhi Museum, New Delhi; Jim Nye at the University of Chicago; Ray Lum at Harvard; Avinash Maheshwary at Duke; Sunita Vaze at the New York Public Library; and Tim Utter and Karl Longstreth, the dedicated map librarians at the University of Michigan, Ann Arbor.

Priya Paul, a truly avante garde hotelier, welcomed me into her lovely home in New Delhi and generously shared her wonderful collection of images as well as her own thoughts on their importance. Milind Sabnis, a schoolteacher in Pune, willingly sent me copies of Mother India pictures that he himself had been collecting over the years, and he took time to talk to me about them. I was only able to dare into the world of Bangla literary texts and poems because of Mandira Bhaduri's diligent translation skills, and I thank her for her skillful assistance and loving friendship.

In this volume I take you into the world of maps and mother/goddesses in India through a number of amazing paintings by Maqbool Fida Husain, and I am grateful to him for the time he took to speak to me about them as well as for graciously granting me permission to reproduce them. Prati-bha Umashankar, a Dubai-based journalist, facilitated my discussion with Husain as well as shared her own thoughts about him, as did Sharon Apparao in Chennai. For their help with tracking down high-resolution images as well as elusive copyright holders, I also want to especially thank Susan Bean, Esa Epstein, Tapati Guha-Thakurta, Mrinalini Sinha, and Rosie Thomas.

I have been enormously fortunate in the financial and institutional sup-port I have received over the decade that it has taken for this project to come to fruition. A Fredrick Burkhardt Fellowship from the American Council of Learned Societies enabled me to relocate to Chicago in 2001–2002 to immerse myself in the fascinating interdisciplinary world of the history of cartography at the Newberry Library. In particular, I thank Jim Akerman and

Bob Karrow at the Herman Dunlop Smith Center for the History of Cartography at the library for many good conversations—not to mention goodwill—during my tenure there. Grants from the American Philosophical Society and the American Institute of Indian Studies funded archival and field trips to India. A Guggenheim fellowship enabled me to complete this book in 2007–2008 in the hallowed and inspiring reading rooms of the British Library in London and the Bodleian at Oxford. For a generous subvention that underwrote the production of this volume, I am grateful to Duke University and especially to Bill Reddy and Sally Deutsch. I am also very appreciative of Ken Wissoker and Mandy Earley at Duke University Press for their cheerful guidance and unwavering encouragement of this book from the start.

I began serious work on this project when I was a faculty member at the University of Michigan, an institution to which I owe an immense debt for giving me the time and space, not to mention funds, to pursue my interests. Many affiliates of Ann Arbor's intellectual community—my colleagues, students, and especially members of Lee Schlesinger's precious Kitabmandal—helped ask tough questions as well as sustained me with their own scholarly passions: Barbara and Tom Metcalf, Tom Trautmann, Farina Mir, Will Glover, Donald Lopez, Bhavani Raman, Frank Cody, Chandan Gowda, Danna Agmon, Anshuman Pandey, Avani Taylor, and not least Lee Schlesinger. In the course of this project I took a long leave of absence from Michigan to work for the Ford Foundation in its New Delhi office as program officer for education, arts, and culture. I am very grateful to the many talented grantees of the program whose own dedicated creativity only furthered my conviction of the importance of arts education and humanist scholarship.

Over the years I have been involved in this project, my inner circle of *sahelis* (some of them scholars in their own right) cheered me on with their friendship, good humor, and most of all their love across time zones and in spite of work pressures. For this I thank Ruqayya Khan, Michelle Maskiell, Vathsala Aithal, Chris Brosius, Neena Uppal, Shalini Urs, and the late Papiya Ghosh. From Steve Lawry I have relearned the value of maintaining meaningful relationships amid the maddening swirl of modern life. When my spirits were flagging and I was ready to throw in the towel, he reminded me of Aeschylus's precious words:

He who learns must suffer,
And, even in our sleep, pain that cannot forget falls drop by drop upon
    the heart,
and in our own despair, against our will,
comes wisdom to us by the awful grace of God.

My husband Rich Freeman has lived with every word in this book in more ways than even he would care to remember. As he well knows, I could not have done "my map book," or anything else in my life, without his unconditional love, equanimity and steadiness of purpose, wisdom and wit, and dedicated commitment to a life of the mind. Neither could I have finished this work without the love of the two special women to whom I dedicate this book. To them all I can say is thank you for being in my life and for your nurture and care over the years I have known you.

Prologue YEARNING FOR FORM

Yearn. *Intr. v.* To have a strong desire or longing; . . .
to have an appearance as of longing.

Form. *n.* The visible aspect of a thing, now usually in narrower sense,
shape, configuration; . . . a body considered in respect to its outward
shape and appearance, especially that of a living being, a person.

OXFORD ENGLISH DICTIONARY, 2ND ED.

In the closing decades of the nineteenth century in a land already thronging with all manner of gods and goddesses there surfaced a novel deity of nation and country who at some moments in the subsequent years seemed to tower over them all. Invoked in English as "Mother India," and most usually in various Indian languages as "Bharat Mata" (literally "India Mother"), she was over time imagined as the substantial embodiment of national territory—its inviolable essence, its shining beacon of hope and liberation—and also as a powerful rallying symbol in its long hard struggle for independence from the modern world's largest empire.[1] Over the course of the next half century and more, as the subcontinent itself was transformed from Britain's most important colony into the free states of India and Pakistan, she gathered together in common celebration and devotion large sections of the region's vast population fissured by caste, language, ethnicity, and local and regional sentiments even as she came to be perceived as escalating the irrevocable rupture catastrophically developing between its two dominant religious communities, Hindu and Muslim.[2]

This book is about this new and unusual mother/goddess and her complicated entanglement in the Indian nation's attempts to create for itself a visible and tangible form over the course of a century that began in the 1880s. Specifically, in these pages I analyze the myriad ways in which Mother India has been visualized in painting, print, poster art, and pictures, with a view toward developing a key proposition. Despite the garb of venerable antiquity in which Bharat Mata has been presented to her (Indian) beholders, she is a tangled product of charged encounters between the new and the old and of a fraught and conflicted modernity that is India's late colonial and postcolonial experience of history.[3] Mother India's hesitant novelty and ambiguous modernity only becomes apparent, however, if we consider her diverse pictorial appearances, for much of the abundant poetry and prose utterances on the goddess contrarily clothe her in the archaic and root her in an immemorial past.

This pictorial history of Mother India seeks to understand why a nation striving to be secular, diverse, and modern would also resort to the timeworn figure of a Hindu goddess in its yearning for form.[4] What is at stake in drawing such a tendentious female form to picture a sovereign national territory that has also sought to project itself as a culturally and religiously plural body politic? This study also explores how the divinized Mother India becomes a focal point for many of the developing nation's contentious debates between authenticity and imitation, between tradition and modernity and religion and science, and between being essentially Hindu but aspiring simultaneously to secularity and pluralism, to name the most urgent. How do such struggles leave their traces on this embattled embodiment of the nation? Not least, against the ingrained anti-visualism of the social sciences, in this book I insist that pictures, too, have stories to show and arguments to manifest, and that images are not just illustrative and reflective but also constitutive and world-making rather than world-mirroring.[5] How do such visual displays and pictorial revelations relate to verbal histories and prosaic narratives? What are the points of convergences, and as important, how do we account for the differences? This, then, is a book about pictorial ways of learning the nation and visually coming to know it and live with it—and ultimately to die for it.[6]

It is fitting to begin this pictorial history in 1997 with a triptych published in one of the country's leading English-language dailies, the *Times of India*, to commemorate the fiftieth anniversary of Indian independence from colonial rule on August 15, 1947. In the middle panel of this triptych, as the accompanying text states, the "contours of our great country transform into the image of Mother India sprinkling Ganga [Ganges] water from one hand, the other releasing the bird of freedom, Ganesha perched on her arm like Bhujbal [the strong-armed]" (figure 1).[7] As the sun rises over the jagged Himalayan peaks alongside a crescent moon, Mother India appears as a youthful woman whose torso and limbs are playfully arranged to approximate an outline map of India, the heartland of whose terrain is occupied by the emblematic spoke wheel, most familiar to Indian readers of the newspaper from their national flag. The figure of Mahatma Gandhi (1869–1948), arguably the most iconic Indian of the twentieth century and one of Bharat Mata's favorite sons, moves out of the first panel of the triptych to occupy the bottom of the centerpiece (albeit outside the mapped form of India) and leads his fellow citizens on one of his marches, his trademark staff in hand.

Another work by the same artist, also dated 1997, reiterates this pictorial commemoration of Mother India (figure 2). Here as well the female shape partially outlines the cartographic form of India, but with some significant differences. The single faceless head of the triptych is joined by two others, possibly aligning Mother India more closely with some of the multi-headed divinities that the artist imaginatively, playfully, and reverentially engaged from the late 1950s. Added to the picture is an airplane flying off into the distant skies, perhaps taking the country along with it on its new global adventures. Strikingly, parts of the woman's body and her attire, and the map of India she suggestively outlines, are painted in the saffron, white, and green colors of the national flag, while Ganesha nestles in her brown scarf that gracefully sweeps across the heartland of India.

Almost a decade later in 2005—the intervening years being a period dur-

Contours of our great country transform into the image of Mother India sprinkling Ganga water from one hand, the other releasing the bird of freedom, Ganesha perched on her arm like Bhujbal

FIGURE 1 Maqbool Fida Husain, Center panel of *50 Years of Emerging India: A Triptych*. Illustration for the *Times of India* (Bombay), special supplement, August 15, 1997. (Reproduced with permission of M. F. Husain)

ing which the artist found himself increasingly embattled for daring to visualize Hindu goddesses in the nude—Bharat Mata made her appearance again on his canvas (although he left the painting unnamed). In this later work, the many colors of the female body in figure 2 give way to a monochromatic red, and the former frontal appearance of the goddess is replaced by a partly scarred face that turns away, refusing to meet our eyes (figure 3). Still, the jagged peaks of the lofty Himalayas are drawn, as is the wheel emblem of the national flag. Further, as in the earlier pictures, the woman's torso and limbs (albeit revealingly amputated) are arranged to approximate parts of the mapped image of India. In this case, however, her body is inscribed in English with the names of representative cities and symbolically important places: Cochin, Chennai, Bangalore, Goa, Hyderabad, Kolkata, Mumbai, Jai-

FIFTY YEARS OF INDEPENDENCE

FIGURE 2 Maqbool Fida Husain, *50 Years of Independence*. Print, 1997. (Reproduced with permission of M. F. Husain)

pur, Banaras, Delhi, and Srinagar. Two other names appear as well on this bodyscape: Gujarat on the right breast, and Bhopal under the left, two ignominious sites of genocide and of death from corporate negligence. Most consequentially for the fate of this particular painting the woman appears in the nude before the citizen's eyes (although not for the first time, as I note later), with her unclothed body reproducing in part the cartographic shape of a territory of which she is the skeletal embodiment. Both woman and country stand stripped at a time in the nation's history when religious intolerance and ultranationalist ideologies had scaled a new height.

Soon after the painting was revealed to the public in the course of a high-profile art auction in the nation's capital early in 2006 (figure 4), it raised a violent outcry among Hindu nationalist groups in India and abroad who attacked the artist for daring, especially as a Muslim, to "disrobe our Beloved Bharat Mata."[8] The painting was withdrawn from the auction, and the art-

5

FIGURE 3 Maqbool Fida Husain, Untitled [*Bharat Mata*]. Acrylic on canvas, 2005. (Reproduced with permission of M. F. Husain. Courtesy of Apparao Gallery, Chennai)

ist himself issued an apology even as multiple cases were brought against him in several Indian courts for "hurting the religious sentiments, displaying obscenity at public places, defaming Bharat Mata, and conspiring to cause communal unrest and disunity in the country."⁹ A putatively modern and rational civil society has been left to contend with hefty rewards offered by his detractors to anyone willing to kill the artist, chop off his hands, or gouge out his eyes. In the wake of the global controversy surrounding the publication of offending cartoons of the Prophet Muhammad in the European press, an ostensibly liberal and secular national government in India also felt compelled to investigate the artist's work on the grounds that "there should be limits to an individual claiming immunity in the name of artistic freedom."¹⁰

I have chosen to begin this pictorial history of Mother India with these works by Maqbool Fida Husain (b. 1915) because they demonstrate that even

FIGURE 4 "Art for Mission Kashmir." Auction advertisement, Apparao Art Gallery, Chennai, 2006. (Courtesy of Apparao Gallery, Chennai)

one of the most famous of India's artists occupying the very pinnacle of its national and international circuit of fine art has felt persuaded to visualize Indian national territory by turning to the female form—highly stylized though it may appear on his canvases.[11] Just as tellingly, the undertow of Hindu symbolism pulls at the creations of this most self-consciously secular, pluralist, and modernist of Indian artists, as does the weight of archetypal imagery and colors.[12] Most saliently, though, for a key proposition of this book, in Husain's pictures of Bharat Mata her body is conspicuously carto-graphed to approximate the scientifically mapped shape of India, itself a product of recent colonial history.[13] In turn, the map of India—that proud creation of a self-consciously rational and modern science—is deeply gendered and divinized through its occupation by the figure of a Hindu goddess, its cartographic space filled up with her anthropomorphic presence.[14] "For me, India's humanity is what is important, not its borders," the flamboyant artist once declared. His carto-graphed Bharat Mata is exemplary of this sentiment.[15]

I will return to Husain's creations in subsequent pages, but for now I close this introduction to Bharat Mata and her carto-graphed form by noting that the incorporation into her visual persona of the map of India (sometimes clearly identifiable as such with remarkable attention to detail, at other times caricatured as a rough and indeterminate, even spectral, outline) sets her apart from the myriad other Hindu goddesses to whom she otherwise bears a close resemblance, as I discuss in chapter 2. In turn, the map of India with which she comes to be associated is possibly the most telltale sign of Mother India's complex and complicated modernity, of her novel appearance on the Indian visual landscape, and of the indebtedness of the imaginations that produce and sustain her to cartographic science and its protocols for interpreting and representing place and space. This pictorial history of the convergence of the form of the mother/goddess with the mapped form of the nation—its "geo-body"—demonstrates how this coming together simultaneously anthropomorphizes the map of India, even while it carto-graphs the figure of Bharat Mata.[16] In this process, it also reveals another important truth not as readily apparent from verbal and textual histories. Simply put, there are heterogeneous ways of imagining and seeing the country in twentieth-century India, of creating a tangible and visible form for the new nation. In this study I focus upon two such ways of pictorially and patriotically investing in the territorial idea of India, with each in turn complexly evolving and changing over time as they also coexist, challenge, and converge with the other. I characterize these regimes of patriotic visualization as the scientific-geographic and the anthropomorphic-sacred. In the pages of this book, as indeed in the visual work of the patriot, the scientific-geographic manifests itself in the outline map form of India, itself a highly condensed cartographic outcome of nearly two centuries of colonial rule starting in the 1760s when a place called India (or "Hindoostan") began to be progressively reconfigured and spatially stabilized on the earth's surface as a geo-body through empirical observation, terrestrial survey operations, triangulation, and inscription. Concurrently, maps of a scientifically measured, delimited, and self-contained India soon start to be printed and then begin to circulate both in Europe and across the subcontinent.[17]

The mapped image of India as a measured whole stretching with a peninsular form across a more-or-less fixed grid of latitudes and longitudes (itself a mathematized product of the science of geometry, "the measurement of earth") is among the proudest achievements of a rationalizing colonial state that professed to wean its subjects away from the stranglehold of their irrational traditions in order to make them modern (figure 5, for example). Many of these subjects—especially those who went to colonial schools and those who became part of the state's evolving bureaucratic regime—did become good learners, and to this day the scientific empire of mathematical geography and cartography holds sway in the subcontinent long after colonial rule has formally ended. The geographical image of India does indeed come to prevail but not without struggles and transformations, especially as it circulates outside the realms of science and state. Indeed, one of my principal reasons for writing this book is to document *one* manner in which *some* Indian patriots challenged the seizing of their lived space by the modern scientific imperative to measure, map, and dominate the land cartographically. And their challenge also found expression in the embracing of another vision and version of the same territory as an anthropomorphic being imagined as Mother India written, recited, *and* pictured with filial affect. From the 1880s some Indians thus sought to persuade their fellow citizens to (continue to) relate to the colonized land called India with filial love and care regardless of its increasingly hegemonic presence as a "geo-coded" country.[18] This book is an account of how these individuals created and mobilized pictures to conduct their politics of persuasion by turning as well to the idiom of the anthropomorphic-sacred, a regime of visual imagination in which the nation appears also as a "sensuously qualified place-world" instead of just gridded lines of power.[19] "The program of the Enlightenment," wrote Theodor Adorno and Max Horkheimer, "was the disenchantment of the world; the dissolution of myths and the substitution of knowledge for fancy" (1972, 3). Yet the images that I present and analyze here show how the European Enlightenment project is undone at one (post)colonial address by the recuperation of old myths and the return of fancy. The fact that modern secular and scientific mapped knowledge is hijacked to assist in this unraveling is one of the many ironies of an Indian visual and patriotic modernity that I hope will become apparent in these pages.

FIGURE 5 *Hindoostan.*
Published according to Act
of Parliament by J. Rennell,
London, 1782. (© British
Library Board, V 51)

FIGURE 5A *Hindoostan*
(detail)

My analysis in this volume has been informed by recent scholarship on colonialism and the postcolonial condition that has persuaded me to conclude that the response to the program of disenchantment unleashed by the colonial state does not take the route of straightforward rejection or unilateral opposition. Instead, it is a much more ironic process that is laden with ambivalences and contradictions—as colonialism itself was in practice in the colonies—in which empire's gifts and artifacts are both disavowed and desired (Bhabha 1994). The images I consider in this book are very much a product of this condition of desiring-while-disavowing and disavowing-while-desiring, as they show the entanglement of the scientific-geographic with the anthropomorphic-sacred in complex and contradictory ways that I disclose through the course of this book. What is clear though is that the measured and mathematized geo-body of India and the anthropomorphic form of Mother India vitally implicate each other in patriotic visual labor as that work creates and cultivates devotion toward a territory called India. Their coexistence and convergence reveals the extent to which the form of the mother/goddess and the mapped form of the country are deemed mutually indispensable yet apparently inadequate on their own for visually investing in the territorial idea of India.[20] As I document over the course of these pages, the map of India time and again seems to seek out Bharat Mata's body in the work of her artists, just as the mother/goddess reaches for the map form in order to transform the geo-body into a homeland and motherland to live and die for. As a result of their mutual implication, while Mother India is carto-graphed the map of India stands anthropomorphized. In recent years we have been reminded many times of the mutual implication of nation and gender, with one influential anthology even characterizing this implication as a "dangerous liaison" (McClintock, Mufti, and Shohat 1997). This study demonstrates the entanglement of the secular sciences of modern cartography and geography in this dangerous liaison, and it charts the salience of visual productions in the reproduction of nation's territory as a deeply gendered, divinized, and affect-laden place.

FORMAL CONCERNS

1

Maqbool Fida Husain is one among a long line of artists and illustrators who since the early years of the twentieth century have felt persuaded to visualize India as a carto-graphed mother/goddess.[1] They have turned to oil and watercolor, pen and ink, and even rough drawing to portray her on canvas and paper; in posters, calendars, and book wrappers; on mastheads and covers of newspapers, magazines, and journals; in advertisements, street hoardings, manufacturers' labels, and on walls and as murals; as clay figurines, marble statues, and icons in temples, schools, and civic gardens; and as a figure on the movie screen. These images are products of visual labor that I gloss as patriotic, although many of them also participate in other pictorial regimes of late colonial and postcolonial India. While I hope to make apparent the complexities and transformations of patriotic visual work over the course of the twentieth century, I should also note that my primary concern is to underscore the pictorial investment, in the age of mechanical reproduction and mass replication, in the territorial idea of India as it is variously configured and imagined. In particular I wish to draw attention to the interested, motivated, and sustained deployment of the mapped configuration of India and the anthropomorphic form of Mother India in printed pictures, sometimes each by itself but more often than not in each other's company. How and what these forms are doing with one another is my dominant interest in this chapter and in those that follow.

While some visual votaries of the carto-graphed mother/goddess are well-known artists with a body of work not necessarily limited to patriotic themes, the majority are relatively unknown or completely anonymous. Correspondingly, many of their works are difficult to date with precision and occasionally are mass produced under different production banners whose circulation contexts are frequently elusive and indeed "profoundly recursive" (Pinney 2005, 265). The creators of these images have at times been products of the various art schools set up in colonial India from the 1850s, but they have also been the unschooled who have nevertheless been moved to participate in a dynamic new patriotic habit of picturing nation and country. Almost all of the known artists have been men (with the few exceptions that I discuss in chapter 6) and the vast number have been nominally Hindu, with many hailing from the upper and artisanal castes of the subcontinent. Novel though Bharat Mata might have been when she first became manifest in the closing years of the nineteenth century, by the 1930s a visual standard for the mother/goddess emerges across the land as a consequence of such efforts, which few have questioned or caricatured. The stabilization of a familiar look does not mean, however, that her image is free of contradictions or traces of the struggles that have gone into her shaping as embodiment, symbol, and sign of the emergent nation and its territory. Symbolic representations, the feminist scholar Joan Landes reminds us, "are counters in symbolic actions" that are "risked" as they are deployed (2001, 9). In this chapter I analyze how Mother India's look is formalized, mobilized, and risked as she is fashioned under the pressures of an evolving visual patriotism. In the course of this analysis I consider as well how and why the mapped form of India becomes an intimate part of her familiar look.

Almost exactly a century before Husain produced his controversial nude, Bharat Mata appeared in a watercolor painting—arguably for the first time, in a new technique referred to as "wash"—in a completely contrary guise (for a slightly later mass-produced version, see figure 6).[2] Its creator was one of late colonial India's best-known artists, if not the most illustrious of them all, Abanindranath Tagore (1871–1951).[3] The historical context in which he painted Bharat Mata was the nativist *swadeshi* ("of one's own country") movement sparked off in 1905 around the territorial partitioning of Bengal, British India's largest presidency.[4] Probably completed around 1905 Abanindranath's *Bharat Mata*, albeit envisioned in the throes of unrest produced around a catastrophic territorial event, does not incorporate the mapped image of India. Instead it followed the protocols of an emergent "neo-Bengal" revivalist style of depicting the female form as ethereal and austere, even wispy. A well-known admirer of one version of this painting—the Irish-born Sister Nivedita (1867–1911), whom I discuss in greater detail in chapter 6—responded to it in 1906 soon after it was printed in a local magazine with the caption title *The Spirit of the Motherland*: "In this picture—which would need to be enlarged and printed . . . in two or three bright but delicate colours—we have a combination of perfect refinement with great creative imagination. Bharat-Mata stands on the green earth. Behind her is the blue sky. Beneath the exquisite little feet is a curved line of four misty white lotuses. She has the four arms that always, to Indian thinking, indicate the divine power. Her sari is severe, even to puritanism, in its folding lines. And behind the noble sincerity of eyes and brow we are awed by the presence of the broad white halo. Shiksha-Diksha-Anna-Bastra[,] the four gifts of the Motherland to her children, she offers in her four hands."[5]

Modeled though she clearly was on the everyday Bengali woman—even possibly the young girls of the artist's aristocratic family—Bharat Mata's divine stature in this painting is most obvious from her four arms and from the delicate halo that rings her head. Goddess though she may be, nothing indicates that she is indeed a new deity of country, even if the artist apparently first named her Banga Mata (Mother Bengal) and only later called her Bharat Mata.[6] The tricolor banner and the mapped form of India that

FIGURE 6 *Bharat Mata*. Chromolithograph of Abanindranath Tagore's watercolor *Bharat Mata* (dated to 1904–1905), published by the Indian Press, Allahabad, circa 1910. (OSIAN's Archive, Research and Documentation Centre, Mumbai)

most obviously signal her pictorial appearance as novel goddess of nation and country are nowhere present. Indeed, even as a female deity her ethereal ascetic air sets her apart from the "poster" goddesses that were becoming increasingly visible in the glossy chromolithographs and colorful calendars of the subcontinent's burgeoning popular art industry, as well as apart from the sensuous deities in oils painted in the illusionist academic style and even from the long-established divinities who adorned the sanctums and walls of the innumerable Hindu temples, high and low, across the country.

Bharat Mata was used as a mobilizing artifact—enlarged and transferred to a silk banner by a Japanese artist—during the anti-partition processions of 1905–1906 in Bengal, and in its own time and since, it has been appreciated by art critics for inaugurating a new "nationalist" aesthetic. Nonetheless, Abanindranath's picturing of the goddess has had minimal impact on her subsequent visualizations.[7] Sister Nivedita may have fervently hoped that she would publish the painting, "by tens of thousands, and scatter it broadcast over the land, till there was not a peasant's cottage nor a craftsman's hut between Kedarnath and Cape Comorin, that had not the presentment of *Bharat-Mata* somewhere on its walls," but this has not been its fate despite the early attempt to print it as free-standing poster (figure 6) (1967, 3: 61). Instead, in the mass-produced images of her artists, Mother India wears a very different look. Frequently flanked by one or more ferocious lions, she is armed and in turn, she arms her sons to battle for her; she is variously attired and adorned but certainly not in the garb of a virginal ascetic; and most importantly for the argument of this book, she appears as a carto-graphed form associated with the mapped configuration of the nation. For the large majority of her visual votaries Bharat Mata is a worldly mother/goddess, and her rootedness in the mundane politics of the terrestrial earth is suggested fairly early in her pictorial career by the incorporation of the mapped configuration of the country into her visible persona. In fact, roughly around the same time that Abanindranath attempted his otherworldly *Bharat Mata*, fellow artists had begun to place the new mother/goddess in the company of the map of India. A confidential government report records that in the course of a raid in November 1908 on the premises of the Dacca-based Anushilan Samiti (a secret society notorious for its violent militancy) the colonial police recovered a "framed" and "glazed" picture, apparently in a prominent place at the entrance to the building, of "Bharat Mata—the map of India represented by a woman in flowing garments."[8] This is possibly the first time that the carto-graphed Mother India leaves a trace (albeit fleeting) in the official archive of the colonial state.

Nagendranath Sen Gupta, who was a school child during these momentous years, retrospectively offers a graphic description of one such carto-graphed image that has unfortunately not survived. He writes, "A celebrated artist of Western India painted an adorable picture of the Mother within a map of India which brought out beautifully the idea of the living Mother India. The head and halo around it covered the Punjab and Kashmir; the feet touched the southernmost parts of Madras; one hand stretched towards Gujarat and the other through Central India towards Bengal; the hair swept the region of the Himalayas; Ceylon formed a lotus at the feet of the Mother. We gazed at the picture and saw the soul" (Sen Gupta 1974, 27). The power of printed images such as this to move young patriots is apparent from Sen Gupta's passionate declaration in his memoir tellingly titled *Repentant Revolutionary*, "I remember seeing that picture over and over again and every time having my heart filled with emotion and hope. There was nothing I could desire more than to be a solider in the army of such a Mother. What was the use of life unless it could be dedicated to this service?" (28).

MOTHER INDIA IN TAMIL INDIA

Elsewhere Bengal's swadeshi protests incited the appearance of the cartographed form of the mother/goddess in the distant southern Indian presidency of Madras, which around the same time was "awakened" from its much-talked about state of stupor by the political journalism of the Tamil poet-patriot Subramania Bharati (1882–1921).[9] In the Tamil newsweekly *Intiya*, which he founded and edited from 1906 to 1910 first in Madras and then in exile in the neighboring French colony of Pondicherry, Bharat Mata appears, possibly for the first time in southern India, in the company of the mapped configuration of India. Inspired by the fiery oratory of Bipan Chandra Pal (1858–1932) and the devotional fervor of Sister Nivedita, Bharati's *Intiya* featured a number of political pictures visually proclaiming the new religion of swadeshi nationalism sweeping across the country that in turn consolidated the adulation, even worship, of the new mother/goddess. On April 20, 1907, the paper printed on its cover an illustration of a sari-clad seated woman with one arm resting in a proprietary manner on a terrestrial globe displaying only the rough outline of an unnamed India and with the other arm extended to bless a group of men—variously attired possibly to signify the diverse communities of the Indian geo-body—who pay homage to her (figure 7). The picture was meant to commemorate the start of the Tamil New Year, and although the woman is identified as the "Goddess of the New Year" she could very well be Bharat Mata, with her association with the map form of India and the accompanying editorial supporting this possibility.

By the time this picture was published in *Intiya* Bharati was already intensely involved through his writings in spreading the message of swadeshi nationalism, for which in Tamil he composed poems on India as a sacred female personage and mother figure. Indeed, *Happy New Year's Day* is accompanied by one of his poems that eventually would become famous in

[handwritten annotations:] "Golden of the New Year" (Tamil New Year)

[handwritten annotation:] Globe featuring India

FIGURE 7 *Happy New Year's Day: Putu Varushapirappu Naal.* Illustration in *Intiya* (Pondicherry), April 20, 1907. (Courtesy of Ceeni Viswanathan)

the Tamil country because of its attempt to harmonize pride in a regional identity with devotion to the newly forged idea of India:

> Long live glorious Tamil, long live the fine Tamil people!
> Long live the auspicious precious Bharata country!
> The troubles that plague us today, may they vanish!
> May goodness gather among us! All that is evil should wither!
> Virtue should grow among us! All that is sinful should disappear!
> The manly efforts of the noble inhabitants of this country, may they
>   excel day by day!
> May my fellow citizens flourish forever!
> *Vande Mataram! Vande Mataram!*[10]   *[handwritten annotation:]* ("I bow to thee, Mother")

The April 20 edition of *Intiya* was not the only time that it featured India as female. From September 1906 until 1910 when the newsweekly ceased

publication, the image of a feminized country appeared on a fairly routine
basis, including as a fecund cow milked dry by the British;[11] as a woman
wasting away while her children played about unheedful of her plight, or
while her home was being plundered by outsiders; and most often, as a
Hindu goddess.[12] Such visual imaginings took another cartographic detour
on April 10, 1909, when the paper published an advertisement for a new
Tamil daily called *Vijaya* (which Bharati hoped to launch in Madras) that
featured Bharat Mata as a four-armed figure occupying the outline map of
India (figure 8). While the crown adorning her head sketches the rough outline of Kashmir, her feet peep out from under the folds of her sari to rest at
the southern end of the peninsula and her body masks the heartland of the
Indian geo-body. Although Bharati's proposed daily was named after the
Hindu goddess of victory Vijaya, the female form used to advertise the new

venture is unambiguously named (in the north Indian Devanagari script, but with Tamil spelling) Bharata Mata.

The image in the advertisement also proclaims Bharati's pluralistic vision of Indian national territory as the patrimony of the several communities that occupy it, symbolized by the figures of the four men who stand embracing each other in elaborately carved boats at Bharat Mata's feet. Their clothing visually marks them as Hindu and Muslim, and their banners declare (in Tamil and Telugu) that disunity had to be resisted. Overtures to India's two dominant religious communities are also made in the two slogans inscribed in the picture: Bharat Mata might look like a Hindu goddess in her visual appearance, but in one of her four hands she carries a banner proclaiming in Urdu script "Allahu akbar" (God is great). This conventional nod to Islam is graphically complemented not with a phrase from the Hindu scriptures but by a new phrase that had recently become the rallying call for swadeshi patriots in Bengal and elsewhere—namely "vande mataram" (I worship the mother) inscribed in Devanagari (itself in the process of being stabilized as the "national" script). As I discuss in chapter 3, this signature salutation and slogan, originating in Bengal and mobilized to propagate the new religion of Bharat Mata, is itself rooted in a nationalized Hindu sensibility. It is used here (as elsewhere and at other times), however, to stand in for an emergent *Indian* patriotism, thereby betraying not just the undertow of Hinduism in Bharati's thought and practice (as indeed in that of almost all votaries of Bharat Mata) but also the easy convergence of "India" with "Hindu" from nationalism's earliest moments on the subcontinent. The graphic subordination as well of "Allahu akbar" to "vande mataram" and "Bharata Mata" in the picture is a visual reminder that twentieth-century India's vaunted pluralism rarely escapes entirely from the sensibilities and aesthetics (however varied) of its numerically most dominant religious community.

An intriguing story told in later days by the Tamil poet Bharatidasan (1891–1964), one of Bharati's ardent young followers from those heady years, recalls an incident, probably around 1911, when the poet and some of his associates, ostensibly inspired by a Bengali picture of the mother/goddess (possibly Abanindranath's *Bharat Mata*), commissioned a clay figurine of Bharat Mata from a local potter. In Bharatidasan's recollection, when the potter noted that the goddess in the Bengali picture wore no jewels one of Bharati's associates, the fiery London-returned barrister V. V. S. Iyer (1881–1925) who was bred on a growing expatriate penchant for political radicalism, apparently agreed with such a visual rendering when he stated, "What does India have now? Foreigners have plundered its wealth. Is it appropriate to adorn our Bharat Mata with jewels when she languishes away amid the famine and poverty that surrounds her?" Bharati, however, is believed to have demurred and then retorted, "What indeed have the foreigners taken away? Have the Ganga and the Yamuna been rolled up and taken away? Have the Himalaya and Venkatam [Tirupati] mountains been borne away on their heads? And [what of] our culture, heroism, and religion . . . ? Our Bharat Mata is indeed an Empress . . . Go forth and adorn her with jewels" (Ilavarasu 1990, 53–54). The clay images were accordingly cast, and then were put to an astonishing subversive use: hidden in their hollow cores were small revolvers smuggled into British India by revolutionaries traveling from French Pondicherry (Ramalingam 1995). Apocryphal though the story might be, it is worth noting that in the surviving replicas of these clay dolls Bharat Mata is an explicitly carto-graphed figure: she is a four-armed goddess whose sari is arranged to roughly outline a map of India that includes British Burma. Sri Lanka is transformed into a floral bud at her feet, and even the sovereign (Hindu) kingdom of Nepal is claimed by her flowing tresses (figure 9). It is important to underscore that Bharati's territorial nationalism as it finds expression in his poetry and prose is far less ambitious and imperialistic in its reach than in such a material expression in clay.

There is another striking singularity about the carto-graphed Bharat Mata who appeared in *Intiya* in 1909, for despite her name and her status as "mother" there are few pictures that explicitly visualize Mother India engaged in acts generally associated with maternality. Yet this pictorial advertisement is unusual in this regard because Mother India holds not one but four infants in her arms, two of which are suckling at her discreetly exposed breasts. In Husain's controversial *Bharat Mata* (figure 3), the mother's exposed breasts are provocatively associated with the words *Gujarat* and *Bhopal*, now widely recalled as sites of ignominious carnage. In contrast the *Intiya* illustration is not threatening because the breasts, partly concealed by

includes Burma, Sri Lanka, Nepal.

FIGURE 9 *Bharat Mata.*
Terra-cotta figurine attributed
to Subramania Bharati, circa
1911. Photograph by Kota
Noble. (Bharatidasan Museum
cum Research Centre,
Puducheri)

the folds of the mother's sari and the infants she holds, are engaged in a task
that reaffirms the woman's primary identity as child bearer and nurturer. As
such the partial nudity of Bharat Mata in this earlier picture does not seem
to have given offense, in contrast to Husain's painting.[13]

THE PICTORIAL DILEMMAS OF MATERNALITY

ca. 1911 – Terracotta murtis of "Mother India" hide small revolvers, bullets, etc. to smuggle the weapons into British India from French Pondicherry.

(may be propagate.)

lly through suckling her breasts as she occupies the map of the country. ᴜᴇ̱ᴇʀ, it is through suckling the shared mother's milk that the four infant-citizens are conjoined in a web of sibling intimacy that may be characterized as patriotic milk kinship.[14] Most artists, however, rarely show Mother India breastfeeding the infant-citizen, although every now and then a picture surfaces in which she is in her child's company.

Such was the case in 1885 when an illustration in the Bengali children's magazine *Balak* introduced the new deity to Bengal's young readers. The illustration accompanied the publication of the poem featuring the signature slogan "vande mataram," and showed the *mataram* in the familiar guise of their own flesh-and-blood mothers. She appears seated in a densely planted grove with a naked infant on her lap, and other babies at play around her (figure 10).[15] About two decades later, on November 20, 1909, Bharati's *Intiya* carried a print of "Bharata Devi" holding a male child in her arms (as well as a trident), while the goddess Lakshmi blesses her from the heavens. Another example—an untitled painting in oil possibly completed around 1917 by the academic painter Pandit Shripad D. Satwalekar (1867–1968), a graduate of Bombay's prestigious J. J. School of Arts—features an older woman holding a large naked infant in her arms (figure 11).[16] Seated in a scenic glen on a rock surrounded by flowing water, she is unusually clad in a drab white sari that is arranged around her to approximate peninsular India, with its southern tip flowing into the waters of the stream and a small metal pot marking the place on which the island of Sri Lanka would occupy in modern maps. In dramatically lighting the mis-en-scéne the sun struggles to emerge from the menacing dark clouds, which are sprinkled with demonic shapes. As in Abanindranath's *Bharat Mata*, the woman holding the child is unadorned, even possibly a widow. She wears a pensive look and refuses to meet the eyes of the child (the future citizen of India?) who looks up at her and presumably seeks to rescue his enslaved "mother" from the demons of colonialism.

In another untitled painting from about a decade later a sari-clad woman stands on a partly visible terrestrial globe, on which is drawn a rough outline of the southern half of India and the island of Sri Lanka; the woman herself stands on the southwestern part of the peninsula. She too carries an infant, while other (celestial?) women gather around her with garlands and trays bearing lamps, possibly waiting to offer worship (figure 12). This painting, in-

FIGURE 10 Hurish Chunder Haldar, *Bande Matarang* (I worship the mother). Illustration in *Balak*, Calcutta, 1885. (Courtesy of Tapati Guha-Thakurta)

FIGURE 11 Pandit Shripad D. Satwalekar, Untitled [Bharat Mata and Child]. Oil on canvas, circa 1917. (Courtesy of Asha Kirloskar)

sri Lanka

terpreted as one of Bharat Mata, has been attributed to Ustad Allah Bukhsh (1895–1978), a self-taught commercial artist of Kashmiri origin via Punjab, and possibly one among only a handful of Muslim artists drawn to picturing the mother/goddess.[17] More recently, in an oil on canvas that I discuss in greater detail in chapter 3, Bharat Mata is seated within the shadowy outlines of a map of India, with one of her hands resting on a male child who looks up at her (figure 13). Multiple arms and a crown are painted in a spectral manner to suggest her supra-mundane status, but the dominant idea that the Maharastrian commercial artist Sachin Joshi seeks to convey is of Mother India's gentle (and genteel) human maternality, so much so that his own mother modeled for this painting.

In spite of these images, in the first few decades of Mother India's appearance as a carto-graphed deity it was more likely than not that beholders would see her not as a nurturing maternal figure occupying the map of India but as a potential warrior. This is perhaps not surprising when we recall that for a number of years prior to 1920 when Indian nationalism, at least officially, took a nonviolent Gandhian turn it was largely propelled by a militant patriotism that celebrated the mother/goddess in her activist incarnation as a fierce combatant who demanded blood and heads to "assuage her hunger" rather than as a quiescent woman dependent on others, especially her sons, to defend her. It was the combative Bharat Mata who was the presiding deity of many clandestine organizations that covertly sprang up in the opening years of the twentieth century, including the so-called Yugantar Party and the Anushilan Samiti in Bengal, the Bharat Mata Society in Punjab, the Bharat Mata Association in the Madras presidency, and the Matravedi Sanstha ("The society of those who are prepared to sacrifice their lives for the motherland") in the United Provinces. A number of organizations above ground also embraced such a vision. Thus it was in 1919, in what is possibly her earliest appearance as a carto-graphed "calendar" goddess, that "Bharat Mata," portrayed as an armed woman wearing a crown and occupying a roughly drawn outline map of India, was featured on the February page of an almanac published in the north Indian city of Faizabad (figure 14). While the lower part of her body merges into the peninsular half of the nation's geo-body, Sri Lanka is transformed into a lotus bud at her feet. She holds a sword in one hand inscribed with the polyvalent Sanskrit word *shakti*

FIGURE 12 Untitled [Bharat Mata], attributed to Ustad Allah Bukhsh. Oil on mountboard, late 1920s. (OSIAN's Archive, Research and Documentation Centre, Mumbai)

His own mother modelled for this painting

FIGURE 13 Sachin Joshi, *Rastrabhakti Prema Ka Gaan Vande Mataram* ("Vande Mataram," song of national devotion). Oil on canvas, commissioned by Milind Sabnis, 1999. (Courtesy of Milind Sabnis)

FIGURE 14 Page from the Hindi almanac *Om Arya Kailendar*, published by Somadeva Sharma, Faizabad, 1919. (© British Library Board [APAC: Proscribed Publications Collection], PP Hin F 10)

(literally power, but also female energy), while in her other hand she holds knowledge, or *vidya*. This picture of Mother India is flanked on either side by messages in Hindi that verbally reaffirm her visual appearance as a goddess poised for battle: "Awake, brave Indians, look at your present condition and advance, and show the foreigners that you have become fit to achieve liberty, your birth right." And "Youths! The burden of uplifting India is on you. To whom are you looking? Arise and through the protection of the Motherland, show again to the world the grandeur of your past."[18]

Such a message was popularized by nationalist leaders like Bal Gangadhar Tilak (1857–1920) of Maharashtra and Lala Lajpat Rai (1865–1928) of Punjab, whose portraits also appear on the almanac page alongside Bharat Mata. A later page for the month of November confirms that her loyal sons did indeed respond to her call—at least in the pictorial realm—with the words,

FIGURE 15 Cover page of *The Bande Mataram: Monthly Organ of Indian Independence*, March 1913. (Courtesy of the New York Public Library)

"Arise, Mother India! Awake, Mother! Wipe the tears from your face! Do not be anxious. Your sons have determined to give even their lives for your sake, if you require it." Predictably, an anxious colonial state proscribed the "seditious" calendar. [19]

DIASPORIC TRAVELS

The calendar from Faizabad is not the first appearance of Bharat Mata as an armed woman in the company of a map of India. A few years earlier, in 1913, she was featured as such on the cover page of an expatriate newsmagazine (banned in British India) called *The Bande Mataram: Monthly Organ of Indian Independence*, which was published in Geneva with the financial support of a fascinating Parsi woman, Bhikhaiji Cama (1861[?]–1936) (figure 15). In the image a youthful-looking woman stands under a banner inscribed with the magic words "vande mataram," which is held aloft by two cherubs. Her sari is tautly wrapped around her legs, and her body and streaming hair roughly outline the cartographic shape of India. As is often the case the island of Sri Lanka is transformed into a flower bud. Instead of looking directly at us—as is routine in later visualizations—the figure faces west, her sword drawn ready to do battle. Her willingness to go to war is confirmed by the inscription printed in Devanagari below her poised figure: "This war has offered itself to you as your duty. If you refuse to fight this righteous war [*dharmyam samgraamam*], you will ruin your life's duty [*swadharma*] and fame [*kirti*], and incur sin [*paapa*]."[20] These words are visually echoed in the dramatic assemblage of weapons—cannons, rifles, and spears—that frames the carto-graphed form.

That the visual persona of a territorial goddess like Mother India should receive attention outside the putative borders of the emergent nation and through the interventions of expatriates and long-distance patriots is one revealing outcome of this pictorial history. It is also instructive that Bharat Mata's form is not as explicitly Hindu as it appears within the nation's borders, thereby possibly visually iterating the plural constituencies of many early diasporic organizations. In recent years scholarly analyses have attended to the role played in the imagination of the Indian nation by cross-border exchanges as well as the interventions of the diaspora of Indians scattered across the colonial world, with Gandhi being only the most globally prominent example from among a number of expatriate men and some women.[21] Yet these studies have not yet critically examined the visual patriotism of the diaspora, especially the deployment of the map form of the nation or the hallowed body of Mother India. In fact, the banner of the most enduring of such extraterritorial nationalisms, the Punjabi- and Sikh-dominated Ghadar ("mutiny") movement that flourished in parts of North America from around 1913 into the 1940s, was inscribed with a map of (British) India with its principal internal divisions and places clearly identified.[22] And the carto-graphed Bharat Mata is a staple icon that recurs in its numerous publications printed between 1914 and the 1920s in Punjabi (in both the Persian and Gurmukhi scripts), Urdu, Hindi, and English that celebrate Indian martyrs and that call for armed battle and revolution to overthrow the colonial regime

FIGURE 16 Title page of the Hindi book *Deshabhakti ke Geet* (Songs of National Devotion). Hindustan Ghadar Press, San Francisco, 1916. (© British Library Board [APAC: Proscribed Publications Collection], PP HIN F 43)

(in an idiom that is inflected by the tradition of Sikh martyrdom). For instance the title page of the Hindi anthology *Deshbhakti Ke Geet* (Songs of national devotion), published in San Francisco in 1916, features a roughly drawn illustration framed by the words "Swatantrata ke Liye Bharat ke Kara Mein Kadak" (Steadiness in the Service of Indian Independence) (figure 16). It shows a female figure—most likely Bharat Mata—in the act of drawing out her sword from its scabbard, and the map of India that her sari-clad body occupies also incorporates the head of a lion. While the verses that flank the carto-graphed woman urge India's patriots to live up to their manhood and arm themselves with the sword in order to fight for freedom, it is clear from the rifles in the illustration that the battle against a modern colonial state would be fought with modern weapons. Not surprisingly such publications, however crudely assembled, were proscribed in India (although produced

FIGURE 17 Title page of *The United States of India.* Pacific Coast Hindustani Association, San Francisco, 1923. (© British Library Board [APAC: Proscribed Publications Collection], EPP 2/24)

in distant America), given that the association of the map of India with a woman brandishing a weapon produced considerable colonial alarm.[23]

In the 1920s as the Ghadar movement sought to assimilate itself into the North American mainstream in response to racial and ethnic prejudice against Indian immigration the image of the militant Bharat Mata was replaced, in some of its official publications, by a nymph-like figure whose appearance is vaguely Caucasian. In the image she safely blows the horn of "independence" rather than wielding the sword of bloody revolution, and her body posture approximates the cartographic shape of India that in turn appears as a spectral outline on the terrestrial globe on which she stands (figure 17). Tamed and docile, the figure in this illustration—reprinted in some Ghadar publications into the 1930s—echoes the neoclassical female bodies of Western illustrated magazines, and it is only her sari and the map of India that it outlines that betrays its inspiration elsewhere.

We know practically nothing about the artists who produced some of the early carto-graphed visions and versions of Mother India. Bharati, for instance, closely collaborated with local artists, whom unfortunately he does not name, in order to transform his prosaic and poetic patriotism into visual form. The fact that his illustrations in *Intiya* are invariably accompanied by extensive explanatory commentaries, or that images of Bharat Mata have inevitably needed to be verbally identified as such even many years after her appearance on the Indian patriotic landscape, reminds us that visual literacy is as much learned knowledge as is verbal literacy.[24] That early nationalists such as those associated with the swadeshi movement and Bharati, Cama, or the expatriates of the Hindustan Ghadar Party, were aware that the visual media was essential for educating Indians to become patriotic was a lesson not lost on the colonial state, which from the early years of the twentieth century frequently censored "seditious" pictures for their "mischievous" content and for their potential to foment trouble. An unintended consequence of such censorship was the preservation of this material in a rich official archive, thereby ensuring its availability to the historian of visual patriotism.[25]

Even a cursory analysis of the archive demonstrates that all manner of amateur and unnamed artists and illustrators took to drawing the carto-graphed form of Bharat Mata, which from the first decade of the twentieth century begins to appear in lithographs, on title pages of patriotic anthologies and sundry publications in most major Indian languages, and on mastheads of nationalist newspapers (figure 27), as well as on items such as patriotic letterheads (figures 60 and 61) and merchandise labels advertising swadeshi products (figure 24), with the colonial strictures on such publications notwithstanding. The persistence of the figure of Bharat Mata in these mass media may not be surprising given the general popularity of all manner of female divinities across India from which she obviously benefited. Her association, however, with scientific cartographic devices like maps and terrestrial globes is an innovation indeed. As historians of cartography insist, mapped knowledge is "hard won knowledge"—a product of sustained cultural, ideological, and pedagogic work (Wood and Fels 1992, 5). The fact that even the relatively unlettered and unschooled frequently used the map image of the nation—its geo-body—to picture Bharat Mata at a time when literacy rates in the colony were appallingly low is remarkable testimony to the emergence of what I refer to as barefoot cartography—that is, a set of demotic practices and techniques whose primary creative influence and aesthetic milieu is the art of the bazaar.

Patricia Uberoi defines calendar or bazaar art as "a particular style of popular color reproductions, with sacred or merely decorative motifs . . . The art style extends beyond calendars and posters. In fact, it is a general 'kitsch' style which can be found on street hoardings, film posters, sweet boxes, fireworks, wall paintings, and advertising, and in the knick-knacks sold in fairs" (1990, 46).[26] In this wider sense bazaar art is ubiquitous across the nation, providing it with a visual vocabulary shared by regions and communities otherwise divided from each other, as Sandria Freitag has shown in her work.[27] The art historian Kajri Jain notes that the term captures "a set of expectations on the part of consumers and critics of a specific range of subjects and their visual treatment and to a set of imaginings on the part of producers of who these consumers are and what they want" (2007, 15). Jain has brilliantly documented the social, moral-ethical, and commercial networks within which bazaar images have been produced, evaluated, disseminated, and consumed from the later years of the nineteenth century to the present.[28] Further, Jyotindra Jain has usefully shown how this art form uses "a visual language of collage and citation which, in turn, act[s] as a vehicle of cultural force, creating and negotiating interstices between the sacred, the erotic, the political, and the colonial modern" (2003, 13). Most influentially, the anthropologist Christopher Pinney has insightfully analyzed the visual politics of the deployment of bazaar imagery that are enormously revealing of the "corpothetic" sensibility that undergirds its anticolonial impulses.[29]

My own work builds on this scholarship while focusing on the use of the scientific map form of the country in and by that sector of bazaar or calendar art that I identify as patriotic because of its investment in the territorial idea of India (albeit variously configured, as is apparent from these pages). My conceptual analytic of barefoot cartography is meant to distinguish bazaar art's investment in the map form from the state's command mapmaking ventures conducted with scientific instruments of surveillance, measurement, and inscription by trousered-and-booted men of secular science.[30] As others have shown, the modern state's deep involvement in mapping is instrumental and regulative in order to make land visually legible for rule and resource management and for determining sovereignty and policing borders. In such readings the scientific map is a classic example of a "state simplification," and as such it attempts to systematize and demystify the state's terrain in the dispassionate interest of command and rule (Scott 1998; Biggs 1999). In contrast barefoot cartography in India, even while cheekily reliant on the state's cartographic productions, also routinely disrupts them with the anthropomorphic, the devotional, or the maternal. This is so much the case that in its productions the integrity of the mother/goddess's form takes precedence over the fidelity or accuracy of the mapped image of the nation.

Undoubtedly the barefoot is in contested intimacy with command cartography, as it dislodges the state's highly invested map form from official contexts of production and use and then reembeds it—sometimes to the point of only faint resemblance—in its own pictorial productions. In doing this, barefoot cartography reveals its own corpothetic and worshipful investment in national territory in contrast to command cartography's geometrical grids of certitude and lines of power. In particular, barefoot cartographic work suggests that at least for some Indians the map of India—that symptomatic scientific artifact used to delimit a measured territory called India—is not an adequate representation in and of itself for mobilizing patriots to the point of bodily sacrifice, indispensable though it might be for bestowing a credible form upon the emergent nation. As such it has to be supplemented by something else, which more often than not is the gendered divinized form of Mother India. I want to remind my reader that barefoot mapmaking is not antagonistic or antithetical to state and scientific cartography in a simplistic manner. Rather, after the fashion of so much else in colonial India where the artifacts of empire and science were simultaneously disavowed and desired, patriotic popular mapmaking takes on the cartographed form of the nation but also pushes it in directions not intended for it by either science or state.

India's barefoot mapmakers are almost always male and not always the products of formal schools or art education. Even with no obvious training in map use or in the science and aesthetics of cartographic production these men play no small role in popularizing what Benedict Anderson refers to as the "logo" form of the national geo-body such that it becomes recognizable and familiar and not in need of the crutch of naming or identification (1991, 175). If we follow John Pickles, such men are exemplary of "the legion of map-makers and map users that is not part of the professional cadre of expert cartographers" (2004, 60). Regardless of the various social, economic, regional, religious, and ideological differences that might prevail among these artists or the changes they might undergo over time, they warrant being treated as a unified field in terms of their inexpert, undisciplined, and informal relationship to the science of cartography and its mathematized products to which they turn for various purposes. Their lack of specialist cartographic expertise should not, however, be read to mean that they are naive or apolitical. On the contrary, my goal is to demonstrate the highly complex and competent ways in which a specialized artifact—one of the most prized inventions of Europe, and consolidated by colonial surveyors and their Indian assistants through many decades of triangulation, measurement, and inscription—is dislodged from its official circles of circulation and use and put to purposes that exceed those of science or state.

In fact, I would even venture to say that in the late colonial period when few Indians went to school and studied geography books or encountered maps and globes in their classrooms, it was through the mass media that the mapped image of the nation was rendered familiar to the average citizen as it traveled—albeit in a highly condensed and even caricatured form—across the subcontinent and was incorporated into newspaper mastheads and cartoons, merchandise labels and advertisements, god posters and calendars, and the like. As it has circulated in this manner the accuracy of the mapped form of the nation has varied, ranging from rough-and-ready sketches of the Indian geo-body to highly specific renderings with an astonishing attention to physiographic detail (for example, see the frontispiece and figures 21 and 85). From such a diverse range of barefoot cartographic creations spanning the twentieth century I have identified five different ways in which the anthropomorphic form of the mother/goddess is thrown into the company of the nation's geo-body represented by the map of India, and vice versa. The result of this convergence is that the map form of India is "anthropomorphized" while the gendered body of Mother India comes to be "cartographed."

First and most commonly Bharat Mata literally occupies the map of India by partly or substantially filling up cartographic space with her anthropomorphic form, as seen in figure 8. There are many ingenious ways in which her body blurs or undoes the carefully configured boundaries and borders of command cartography. This is particularly true of the contested land of Kashmir, parts of which have been lost to Pakistan and China in the years since Indian independence, which is frequently claimed by the strategic placement of Mother India's head, her crown, or her halo. Such is also the case with Pakistan, which may have become independent in 1947, but is still very often incorporated into Bharat Mata's body in the inventive sweep of her saree, the flow of her long tresses, or the reach of an arm. Instructive in this regard is a rare picture in color of Bharat Mata that appeared in a Tamil textbook published in 1958 for elementary school students. It shows her as a two-armed goddess with a halo around her head, surprisingly clad in the clinging garments worn by the coquettish beauties of commercial art starting from the late nineteenth century. Her body curves suggestively toward a space that on world maps would be occupied by the independent state of West Pakistan, while her green scarf also flows out to claim parts of this sovereign space as that of India and hence its citizens (figure 18). Her body substantially masks the geo-body of India created by state cartography, with the large halo around her head covering the disputed territory of Kashmir. Although the textbook was published a decade after the catastrophic territorial and political events of 1947, the picture appears to deny the partition of British India by presenting Bharat Mata as the occupier of a land stretching from the distant snow-capped Himalayan ranges of the north to the ocean to the south.

Another illustration, also published in a Tamil textbook dated 1948, similarly denies the historical fact of the subcontinent's partition. Bharat Mata's toe also reaches out and claims Sri Lanka, a country that had never been part of British India (figure 19; see also figure 34). The poem accompanying this black-and-white illustration—which the young reader was expected to memorize—praises Bharat Mata for her beauty, achievements, compassion,

FIGURE 18 Frontispiece to the Tamil schoolbook *Putiya Aarampakkalvit Tamil (Moonram Puttakam)* (New elementary Tamil: Book three) by V. Lakshmanan. Shri Shanmugha Publishing House, Mannargudi, 1958.

and the wealth of her rivers and fields.[31] Although there is nothing particularly cartographic about the poem, the accompanying carto-graphed image of the mother/goddess—possibly recycled from an earlier decade when British India had not yet been partitioned—is pictorially useful to deny history and to visualize a new nationalist geography that is subtly expansionist. That such images appeared in Tamil textbooks is also worth underscoring, given the ambivalent participation of the Tamil region in the hegemonic project of Indian nationalism that I have documented elsewhere.[32] They also offer testimony, if only fleetingly, of the extent to which such picturing had become part of a patriotic common sense in late colonial and postcolonial India.

While the inclusion of such images in ostensibly secular textbooks is troubling in itself, their adoption by Hindu nationalist parties with irredentist claims shows their continued political efficacy. So perhaps the most ubiq-

8. பாரதத் தாய் (பாட்டு)

ராஜராஜ ராஜராஜ ராஜன் வாழ்கவே என்ற மெட்டு.

1. எங்கள் அன்னே பாரதத்தாய் எழில் மிகுந்தவள்
   இசைநலமும் மொழிநலமும் இனிது வாய்ந்தவள். (எங்)

2. நீர்வளமும் நிலவளமும் நிரம்பப் பெற்றவள்
   சேர்மையும் தயாளமுமே மிகவும் உற்றவள். (எங்)

3. பொங்குபல கைத்தொழிலும் புரியத் தேர்ந்தவள்
   பொருளநியில் பலகலையில் புனிதம் வாய்ந்தவள். (எங்)

4. அன்னியர்க்குப் பஞ்சதவும் அரிய காரணி
   அண்டினேரை யாதரிக்கும் ஆதி காரணி. (எங்)

5. கடல்கடந்தும் பொருள் திரட்டும் கண்ய வர்த்தகி
   உடல்செழிந்த படையினரை ஈன்ற சித்தகி. (எங்)

6. உழவுதொழில் வளர்க்கமிக ஊக்கம் உள்ளவள்
   உலகம்எலாம் புகழவரும் அன்னே நல்லவள். (எங்)

குறிப்பு : இப்பாட்டு மனனத்திற்கு மட்டும் கொடுக்கப்பட்டது.

FIGURE 19 Illustration of Bhaaratat Taay (Mother India) with accompanying poem in the schoolbook *Malait Tamil Vaacakam (Moonravatu Puttakam)* (Tamil reader: Book three) by Kuppuswamy Das. C. Coomaraswamy Naidu and Sons, Madras, 1948.

uitous current visual image of the mother/goddess to which most Indians today are exposed—circulated as it has been through picture postcards, wall posters, calendar art, processional pictures, and the Worldwide Web—is of Bharat Mata as a gloriously bejeweled goddess whose body occupies a substantial part of the Indian geo-body, with her haloed head placed on that part of the country that in normative maps would be occupied by the contested land of Kashmir, and with the critical postcolonial borders demarcating India from its neighbors (Pakistan, Nepal, and Bangladesh) completely dissolved. Significantly, the monochromatic saffron flag associated with Hindu nationalism replaces the more inclusive tricolor national flag (figure 20; see also figures 23 and 39).[33] A doggerel verse from a fabricated Sanskrit source printed below the image declares that the goddess's divinely created domain stretches from the Himalayas to the southern ocean. Such a geographical vision is more explicitly enunciated in another incarnation of this persistent

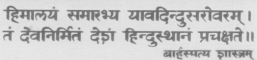

image in which the following statement in Hindi is printed: "I am India. The Indian nation is my body. Kanyakumari is my foot and the Himalayas my head. The Ganges flows from my thighs. My left leg is the Coromandel coast, my right is the Coast of Malabar. I am this entire land. East and West are my arms. How wondrous is my form! When I walk I sense all India moves with me. When I speak, India speaks with me. I am India. I am Truth, I am God, I am Beauty."[34]

If in such pictures the body of the mother/goddess, distinct from the outline map of the nation, anthropomorphizes the map by moving in to occupy it, there are others in which parts of Bharat Mata merge with the Indian geo-body so that the two are in parts undistinguishable. The *Om Arya Kailender* from 1919 (figure 14) in which the lower extremities of the female form disappear into the peninsular contours of the map of India is an early emergent example, as is the Ghadar picture *The United States of India* (figure 17).

FIGURE 21 *Bandhan Mein Bharata Mata Ki Bhent: Lahore Conspiracy Case Decision—Sentenced to Death, No. 1403.* Single leaf, 50 × 36 cm, published by Anarkali, Lahore, circa 1931. (National Archives of India, New Delhi, No. 1789 [Proscribed Literature: Hindi])

Another striking illustration is offered by a proscribed black-and-white lithograph from possibly around 1931 entitled *Bandhan Mein Bharata Mata Ki Bhent: Lahore Conspiracy Case Decision—Sentenced to Death, No. 1403* (figure 21). In chapter 5 I will discuss various details in this complex picture, but for now I wish to draw attention to the manner in which the lower half of Bharat Mata's body disappears into the map of India (extending toward and including Burma) on which are delineated the country's rivers, mountain ranges, and other features of its terrain. The use made by demotic barefoot cartography of statist mapped knowledge is clearly on display here, as is the fact that the latter is not simply taken on board without adjoining it with the anthropomorphic form of Mother India.

Sometime in the late 1920s or early 1930s, Roopkishore Kapur (1893–1978), whose work I examine in greater detail in chapter 5, painted a picture that was published as a dramatic black-and-white lithograph titled *Bharat-Mata* in both Hindi and English (figure 22). Here, the partly visible geo-body of

भारत-माता.   *Bharat-Mata.*

Published by
BABULAL BHARGAVA,
Glass & Picture Merchant
Bagla Mani Ram, Cawnpore.

Ramdass Press, Cawnpore.

प्रकाशक:—बाबूलाल भार्गव,
ग्लास एण्ड पिक्चर मर्चेन्ट,
बगला मनि राम, कानपुर ।

FIGURE 22 Roopkishore Kapur, *Bharat-Mata*. Printed by Babulal Bhargava, Glass and Picture Merchant, Cawnpore, circa 1931. (Courtesy of Urvashi Butalia, New Delhi)

India (which includes within its borders British Burma) is transformed into a hive of industrious activity and prosperity: farmers plough their land, boats ply their trade off the coast, a train makes its way down the east coast of the mapped land, and lofty mansions reach to the sky while the sun rises above the mountains to the north. Temple, churches, and mosques are scattered across this busy landscape, over which towers the four-armed figure of the mother/goddess with the lower part of her body literally merging into the geo-body so that she seems to virtually spring out of the land.

The persistence of this visual motif in subsequent decades is suggested in a recent book illustration, printed by a Hindu nationalist publishing house in New Delhi, that shows the mother/goddess leaping out of a fiery orange map of India in flames (figure 23). In this image her arms reach out to the viewer as she "summons" her children, presumably to save her and the national territory into which she partly merges. Images like these pictorially connect with an important suggestion that was made by several key intellectuals at

FIGURE 23 Cover of the Hindi
book *Ma ka Aahvaan* (The mother
summons) by Dinanath Batra.
Published by Suruchi Prakashan,
New Delhi, 1996. (Courtesy of
Christiane Brosius, Heidelberg)

the start of the nationalist century that there is no distinction between the
country named India by colonial geography and Bharat Mata who resides in
all its constituent parts. As one such thinker, Aurobindo Ghose (1872–1950),
insisted rhetorically in 1905: "For what is a nation? What is our mother-
country? It is not a piece of earth, nor a figure of speech, nor a fiction of the
mind. It is a mighty Shakti, composed of the Shaktis of all the millions of
units that make up the nation" (2002, 83).

In a third configuration Bharat Mata, rather than occupying the cartographic space of India or merging with it, stands on a map of the nation
whose outline is sketched on a terrestrial globe that is sometimes shown
partially and at other times is seen as a whole sphere gridded by latitudes
and longitudes (figure 24). There are a few early appearances of the mother/
goddess in the company of the globe (for example, figures 7 and 17), but
such a carto-graphed vision of Mother India appears to gain in popularity

as the nationalist movement became increasingly confident as the decades wore on, and as freedom from British rule seemed imminent: the map of the nation is literally at her feet and Indian national territory at her bid and command.

A typical example created sometime after Indian independence in 1947 and Gandhi's passing in 1948 is *Message of Love* by T. B. Vathy, an artist from the south Indian town of Nagerkovil (figure 25).[35] This lithograph—printed by several publishers—shows Bharat Mata as a two-armed goddess standing at the center of a map of India whose partial outline is drawn on a partly visible globe. She holds the recently instituted orange, white, and green official flag of the new nation-state in one of her hands, and she is surrounded by a host of male characters, including Jesus and the Buddha. While Gandhi beams down upon her, almost as if blessing her (and the map of India), other men—her "sons" who had come to occupy important positions in the new independent government—stand smiling on the globe, seemingly pleased with their recently hard-won struggle for freedom.[36] In another example printed in Calcutta around the same time, a poster titled in English *Free India*, a jeweled and crowned goddess with a halo around her head and a pleasant smile on her face sits on a partly visible gridded globe covered by the partial outline of a map of India. On the globe the words "independent Bharat" are inscribed in Bengali and Hindi across the geo-body of the country (figure 26). The chains of servitude that shackled India to Britain have now been broken, with the former state of enslavement possibly echoed in an earlier incarnation of the mother/goddess in her captive state pictured above her new victorious self.

In such pictures Mother India appears as the mistress of a carto-graphed world, with her crowned head reaching into the firmament as the national territory that she embodies on the globe on which she rests is visually rendered as the only one that matters on the face of this earth. The conceit of the modern terrestrial globe is that it seemingly privileges no specific point on the earth's surface, "spreading a non-hierarchic net across the sphere," as Denis Cosgove notes. The dispassionate and disenchanted goal of the science of cartography in this regard is to generate "uniform global space" (2001, 105–6, 114). Yet India's barefoot mapmakers betray their patriotic and worshipful predilections by appropriating the normative terrestrial globe and

ভারত মাতা

KESORAM COTTON MILLS LTD. CALCUTTA

भारत माता

FIGURE 24 Merchandise label for Kesoram Cotton Mills, Ltd., Calcutta. Printed by the Indian Photo Engraving Company, Calcutta, circa 1940. (Urban History Documentation Archive, Centre for Studies in Social Sciences, Calcutta)

putting it to a very different purpose by virtually erasing the presence of other lands and other nations from the surface of the earth, so that frequently only "India" looms large and visible as it is anthropomorphized and sacralized by the body of Bharat Mata perched perkily on it.

The fourth configuration is also possibly the most consequential as the barefoot cartographer entirely dispenses with the map of India as ground and as prop. In its place, Mother India's anthropomorphic form literally comes to stand in for the map of India, outlining in this process the cartographic shape of the country. In such pictures, even without a map form, the mapped image of the country is presumed. Emergent instances of this development may be seen in expatriate publications from the first few decades of the twentieth century (figure 17), as well as in Pandit Satwalekar's painting in oil around 1917 (figure 11), and in the surviving clay dolls possibly fashioned under Subramania Bharati's inspiration (figure 9). The masthead

FIGURE 25 T. B. Vathy, *Message of Love*. Printed by Bhagavati Industries, Trivandrum, and by Ravi Varma Press, Malavli, circa 1948. (Author's collection)

শ্বাধীন ভারত   Free India

FIGURE 26 *Svadhin Bharat: Free India*. Chromolithograph published by S.N.S., Calcutta, circa 1947. (Courtesy of Erwin Neumayer and Christine Schelberger, Vienna)

FIGURE 27 Sarma Bros., banner of the Tamil newspaper *Kutiaracu*. Erode, 1925.
(Roja Muthiah Research Library, Chennai)

of a nationalist newspaper in Tamil in 1925—which under the editorship of
the iconoclastic leader of the Dravidian movement E. V. Ramaswami Naicker
(1879–1973) would soon turn radically against Indian nationalism—incorporated the carto-graphed form of a four-armed goddess, with her billowing
sari and posture approximating the cartographic shape of India, beneath
which the tiny island of Sri Lanka is turned into a floral bud (figure 27).[37]

A mature instance of this pictorial development is a chromolithograph
titled *Vande Mataram*, which was printed in 1937 in the south Indian city of
Coimbatore, possibly to celebrate the recent victories of the Indian National
Congress in the countrywide elections. In this image Bharat Mata is clad in
the flag of the party as espoused by Gandhi in the 1920s, and the contours
of her body sketch out the mapped outline of India as her tricolor sari (with
the spinning wheel drawn along its border as a decorative motif) billows out
to claim the territorial spaces of the emergent nation (figure 28). Around the
time of Indian independence a few years later, the same artist, P. S. Ramachandra Rao, painted "Bharath Devi," "Goddess Bharata," in a work titled

FIGURE 28 P. S. Ramachandra Rao, *Vande Mataram* (I worship the mother). Chromolithograph published by Rao Brothers, Coimbatore, 1937. (Courtesy of Erwin Neumayer and Christine Schelberger, Vienna)

The Splendour that Is India (figure 29). Once again the artist dispenses with the map of India, and the body of the mother/goddess, draped in the official Indian flag, is carefully arranged to resemble what is quite identifiable as the cartographic shape of the new nation-state. Contrary to many other such pictures, this particular sartorial arrangement leaves the newly created state of (east and west) Pakistan *outside* India's geo-body. As is usual for pictures produced in Tamil India, Sri Lanka is claimed as part of Bharat Mata's domain.

These examples and others like them suggest that by the middle decades of the twentieth century the geo-body of the country and the mother/goddess are interchangeable, with one standing in for the other. The measured and mapped configuration of the country was replaceable by the anthropomorphic form of the nation, and vice versa. As I discuss in great detail in chapter 4, this mutuality becomes critical to the very first temple to Mother India that opened in the north Indian city of Banaras in 1936, which housed not an image of the mother/goddess but rather a marble relief map of India, made to scale, with its topographic features shown in great detail (figure 64).

THE SPLENDOUR THAT IS INDIA

FIGURE 29 P. S. Ramachandra Rao, *The Splendour that Is India*. Printed by P. S. R. Rao, Madras, circa 1947. (Author's collection)

The indebtedness to colonial cartographic surveys is evident in this novel shrine of and to the nation named after the anthropomorphized form of the country but without her idolatrous presence. Such a move was possible because the work of visual patriotism and barefoot cartography over a number of decades had made Mother India and the map of India so intimate as to be indistinguishable, especially to the patriotic eye.

Finally, in a fifth alignment of the map with the mother's form, Bharat Mata moves out of the mapped outline of the country to either sit or stand in front of the map as it appears as a shadowy silhouette in the background. An interesting instance of this particular arrangement is a painting, later transformed into a chromolithograph, by the prolific Maharastrian artist Vishnu Sapar based in Sholapur (figure 30).[38] Printed possibly in the mid-1960s (when the Indian republic engaged in yet another war with its neighbor Pakistan), the image shows the mother/goddess in a pose reminiscent of

FIGURE 30 Vishnu Sapar, *Bharat Mata*. Publications details not available, acquired around 1967 in Delhi. (Courtesy of J. P. S. and Patricia Uberoi, Delhi)

Britannia, another national embodiment tested by the fires of battle. While she looks straight at her viewer, trident in hand and roaring lion by her side, parts of the map of India spectrally appear in the shadowy background, with the disputed territory of Kashmir (large chunks of which at the time were in reality not under Indian control) the most visible portion of the nation's geo-body.

Similarly in a recent poster printed by the famous calendar publisher Brijbasi of Delhi Bharat Mata stands smiling, wearing a sari in the colors of the Indian flag with the words "vande mataram" written across it in Devanagari (figure 31). Her body partly masks a clearly delineated map of independent India silhouetted in the background. Such pictures offer an important contrast to the dominant representation in the early decades of the nationalist century of the carto-graphed Bharat Mata. It is as if with freedom from British rule Mother India's claim on India's geo-body is secure enough to not have her occupy it or merge into it as her votaries obviously felt compelled to do during the colonial period. The map of India continues to be necessary to her visual persona because it establishes, along with the national flag, her

FIGURE 31 Appu, Untitled [Bharat Mata wearing a *Vande Mataram* sari]. Printed by Brijbasi, Delhi, circa 2005. (Author's collection)

distinctiveness as a territorial deity of the country. All the same, as the freedom movement draws to a close and India's independence from colonial rule is secured, the map of India can be relegated to the background as a shadowy prop into which the mother/goddess can move in times of national crisis or threat (for other examples of this configuration, see figures 13 and 36).

INDISPENSABLE BUT INADEQUATE

While such pictures confirm that no single or homogeneous visualization of national territory prevails in twentieth-century India, there is also consistent recourse over a century of barefoot cartographic practice and patriotic visuality to the imaginaries that I have characterized as the scientific-geographic and the anthropomorphic-sacred as these find expression in the outline map of the country (however caricatured) and the corporeal figure of Bharat Mata (however varied). I have found it useful to turn to the concept of the supplement to understand the range of associations established between these two protagonists of pictures such as these, and I want to argue that only a pictorial history—and not a history solely based on words and texts—makes visible the recurring process of supplementarity through which these imaginaries are mutually implicated. So implicated, neither seems dispensable or adequate in and of themselves for patriotic mobilizations.

The *Oxford English Dictionary* defines the supplement as "something added to supply a deficiency; an addition to anything by which its defects are supplied." It is a part that is added "to complete" or to make good "what is wanting." In Jacques Derrida's productive reading there is a double logic at work in the process of supplementarity—that is, the supplement adds and substitutes at the same time. On the one hand the supplement adds something: it is "a surplus, a plenitude enriching another plenitude, the *fullest measure* of presence. It cumulates and accumulates presence. It is thus that art, techne, image, representation, convention, etc. come as supplements to nature and are rich with this entire cumulating function" (1976, 144). In the later half of the nineteenth century the mapped form of India—its geo-body—circulated as one such visual plenitude, bolstered by the powers of European science, the colonial state, and modern pedagogy. As a product of more than a century of colonial survey activity, the geo-body displayed India as a measured delimited place, and as knowable, manageable, and governable. Through its mediation, the country appears seemingly complete, thus making visible something that is otherwise only intuitively present. For, most consequentially, the mapped form enables the whole country to be seen at one glance in its entirety and synoptically, thus allowing the citizenry to take "visual and conceptual possession" of the entirety of land that they imagine they inhabit as a collective (see, for example, figure 71).[39] That many Indians in the colonial and postcolonial period succumbed to the lure of the map form that enables their India to be presented as whole and complete is quite clear from the hold of the science of cartography on official practice and in some measure on the popular imagination as well, even after British rule ends in the subcontinent.

Yet to many others the map of India in and of itself was not an adequate representative device for picturing their country as *homeland* and *motherland*. As some dissenting voices from early in the century began to remind their fellow citizens, India was more than "a mere bit of earth," more than "the dust of some map-made land," and more than the lines and contours on a map of the influential colonial sciences and pedagogic disciplines. Instead, it was *as well* a divine presence, a "living mother" (Ramaswamy 2003, 183–84). The scientific map form of the country is indispensable, for after all it gives concrete shape to India following the precise protocols of mathematical cartography, it provides the basis for rule and governance, and it demarcates what belongs within its borders and what does not. In other words, it gives tangible form to a nation yearning for form. But nonetheless from the start of nationalist mobilization doubts surfaced about this novel device that magically gave form to the ephemeral abstraction that is the nation: Could one reverence such an image, or die for what were after all lines drawn on a piece of paper? Indispensable it might be, but in and of itself it seemed inadequate to adopt a worshipful attitude and especially to compel the patriot to sacrifice life and limb. This inadequacy was to be countered and compensated by supplementing it with something else, and this something else was the gendered, divinized (Hindu) form of Mother India, which is deployed—poetically, prosaically, and pictorially—to anthropomorphically (re)claim an India seized and enframed as map by scientific geography and cartography. To paraphrase Derrida, Mother India is a plenitude enriching another plenitude. [over-determined]

On the other hand, as Derrida also reminds us, the supplement "supplements. It adds only to replace" (1976, 145).[40] The supplementation of the map of India by the anthropomorphic form of Mother India in the many ways that I have identified above—occupying it and filling up cartographic space; merging partly with it; seated or standing on it; vacating it in order to relegate it to a shadowy silhouette; and most destabilizing of all, dispensing with it entirely—reveals that for the barefoot mapmaker who produced such pictures the scientific map of the country was merely a set of dashes and dots drawn between various mathematically determined coordinates on the earth's surface. What and where is the divinity or intimate earthiness of the land that these lines putatively enclose and bound? How could mere dots and dashes chart out "home" and "homeland"? Once brought into proximity with the country's map form, the plenteous, bejeweled divine female form shows up the insufficiency of one of the Enlightenment's and colonial science's most consequential inventions.[41] Not surprisingly, as the anthropomorphic, divine form of the mother/goddess supplements another supplement—namely, mathematical cartography's geo-coded image of Indian territory—it also replaces the map by standing in and for it and frequently taking its place, as is apparent from pictures such as *Vande Mataram* (1938) and *The Splendour that Is India* (1947) (figures 28 and 29).

At the same time, this pictorial history also shows that Mother India herself is revealed as not self-sufficient by the mapped form of the country, once the latter is adjoined to her form. Although patriotic visuality does generate images of Bharat Mata sans map (for example, figures 37, 102, and 121), it is also the case that Mother India needs the outline map form to set her apart from other female divinities in order to assure her status as a special deity of national territory and so that she is indeed regarded as an adequate and appropriate representation, embodiment, and symbol of a legitimate and authentic modern nation. As I discuss in the next chapter, around the time the mapped image of India progressively takes hold from the early decades of the nineteenth century—as a small but growing number of Indians begin to use modern maps for learning, work, and pleasure—there is a persistent anterior imagination among the numerically dominant Hindu population of land and the earth as a divine female presence that it is never able to lay to rest. In fact, it is the prevalence of this prior imagination that makes any mapped representation of the new national territory inadequate in and of itself. At the same time, this anterior imagination of land as female and divine cannot pass into national modernity unscathed and untransformed, once the maps of the newly measured geo-body begin to circulate as authoritative knowledge. In other words, the anthropomorphic-sacred also has to contend with the newly visualized mapped form of the land.

This is why Bharat Mata is fundamentally a novel, even unorthodox, goddess. Although her artists might model her on other goddesses of antiquity, as I elaborate in the next chapter, the very intervention of the map of India into her visual persona—as product of modern mapped knowledge, as an artifact of the colonial and scientific West, and as supplement—discloses how the female divine form, however sacred and sensuous, is no longer adequate in and of itself in embodying territory once the scientific map form arrives on the scene. The former plenitude is rendered wanting, lacking, and insufficient. Just as the map of India alone cannot adequately serve patriotic purposes, this pictorial history demonstrates why Bharat Mata has to necessarily be visualized as a carto-graphed form. For once the world is carto-graphed—transformed into a product of mathematized mapped knowledge—*all* discourses of territory, especially nonscientific, sentimental, and sacral ones, have to necessarily contend, one way or the other, with the scientific map form.

SUBTERFUGES OF ANTIQUITY

As many scholars have demonstrated, nations across the world have gone to great lengths to conceal their recent origin, their relative youthfulness, and even their inauthenticity by resorting to all manner of what Sudipta Kaviraj adroitly characterizes as "subterfuges of antiquity" (1993, 13). While the verbal discourses on Bharat Mata show that patriotism in India is not an exception in this regard either, it is a pictorial analysis that is most revelatory of the extent to which her devotees cover Mother India in the garb of antiquity. So much so that it is commonplace for her followers—and some scholars—to be taken in by the subterfuge and assume that she is one among the many time-honored goddesses of the region. Yet she is not one, and even the subterfuges of antiquity to which her pictures resort are unable to shake off the telltale traces of her novelty and modernity, as is one of my goals to demonstrate.

As Mother India's persona progressively took shape from the 1880s, her visual votaries work with and adapt long-standing Sanskritic conventions for representing the divine form, including codes of frontality for direct engagement with the viewer. Using the example of *Cutantira Devi, 15–8–47* (Goddess of freedom, August 15, 1947) by the artist P. T. Velu (figure facing page 1), if we look at Mother India's appearance almost every element of her visual persona—with the striking exception of the map form of the country in which her throne is placed as well as the large national flag fluttering behind her—would be familiar to any Hindu accustomed to offering worship to enshrined images. She is seated on a golden lotus pedestal (*padma asana*) and her legs are arranged following a convention called *lalita asana*, with one leg dangling and the other flexed at the knee.[42] Her right hand is held in what is characterized in iconographic texts as the *abhaya mudra*, the "fear-not gesture," which is the most prevalent of the divine hand gestures (*mudra*s) and signifies "the assurance of fearlessness, tranquility, and protection given by the deity to his worshipper" (Banerjea 1956, 251). On her head is a jewel-encrusted crown resembling the *kirita makuta* generally worn by the supreme god Vishnu. The ensemble is completed by a bright halo along the lines of the *prabhamandala* prescribed by the texts to surround all divine beings (but also possibly updated in imitation of Christian sacred pictures). This is indeed a figure fashioned to meet the demands of conventional Hindu consecration and worship.

All the same, and without a doubt, Mother India's artists also respond to the new demands of naturalism ushered in from the West that brought in techniques such as perspective, the rendering of shadow and light, the detailing of anatomy, and so on.[43] In this regard, they responded intervisually to each other as over time a pictorial look for Bharat Mata was cobbled together from diverse sources scattered across various media including illustrated magazines and books, the proscenium theater, studio photographs, and the early movies. Her visual persona, assembled through pictorial techniques of collage and citation, was also responsive to the changing imperatives of Indian nationalism. This was especially the case as the anticolonial struggle took a nonviolent Gandhian turn in the early 1920s away from the more militant stance of the early swadeshi movement to which it somewhat reverted in the 1940s under the heady influence of men like Subhas Chandra Bose (1897–1945). Notwithstanding the emergence by the 1930s of a nationwide visual profile for the goddess, many pictures are also marked by local and regional peculiarities and influences (this is certainly the case for the image facing page 1, which shows the influence of south Indian iconographic conventions). In addition, and crucially, while the production of pictures of Bharat Mata was fairly constant during the twentieth century it appears to spike around charged moments such as occurred in the early 1930s in the massive mobilization during the course of the so-called civil disobedience movement, and then again in the mid-1940s with the countdown to independence and freedom.[44] More recently, with the resurgence of a virulent form of Hindu nationalism and its political consolidation in the late 1990s, Bharat Mata—and the visual program around her image—has received renewed attention and artistic interest, which has been carefully documented by the anthropologist Christiane Brosius (2005, 2006). Even amid all these shifts and changes certain key visual elements are enduring, the most telltale of which reveal Mother India's relative novelty on the Indian visual landscape.

Despite the interventions of practitioners of fine art like Abanindranath Tagore or M. F. Husain in picturing Bharat Mata, and notwithstanding the weight of inherited Hindu iconographic demands for fashioning deities, in her visual incarnation she is fundamentally a poster mother/goddess—a product of the age of mechanical reproduction and industrial print techniques. Her pictorial persona essentially follows the newly formulated canons of the "god-poster" industry for representing the divine female as sensuous but untouchable, blandly generic and anonymous. She is ethnically indeterminate and not readily associable with women of any particular region or locale, although the (unnatural) fairness of her complexion would appear to her Indian viewer as that of an upper-caste female.[45] Invariably, as a deity deemed fit for devotion and worship she looks at her viewers with a full frontal gaze in order to directly engage their attention with her prominently figured eyes. In the anthropologist Christopher Pinney's important characterization of the aesthetic of "embodied corpothetics" that underlies such poster images, "the beholder is a worshipper, drinking the eyes of the deity that gazes directly back at him" (2004, 23).[46] As observed by many who have written on the glossy chromolithographs and the colorful calendars that flood the public arenas and domestic spaces of colonial India from the closing decades of the nineteenth century, the mechanical reproduction of deities did not rob them of aura, authenticity, or authority. On the contrary, the gods continue to be perceived as immanent and involved in the lives of their devotees through (and in spite of) the interventions of the new mass media. Bharat Mata's visibility and spread as a new goddess certainly benefited from such new technological, commercial, and artistic developments, partly because her visual votaries consciously modeled her on familiar female divinities, some of whom we will encounter in greater detail in the next chapter.

Thus, as with these other goddesses, Bharat Mata's body is generally covered with jewels from head to toe, with a shining crown on her haloed head, gold necklaces with encrusted gems adorning her throat, waist ornaments, bangles, armlets, and anklets completing the ensemble. As revealed in the exchange, discussed earlier, between Subramania Bharati and V.V. S. Iyer over the fashioning of a terracotta figurine of the goddess, Bharat Mata might have emerged as the embodiment of an enslaved and impoverished territory but she was nevertheless pictured, despite the verbal discourses on her to the contrary, as sumptuous and well-endowed. And especially in the years since 1947, and in recent times when a powerful sense of the emergence of India as an imminent superpower has seized the (middle-class) Indian imagination, she is rarely if ever depicted as anything but a glorious haloed figure decked out in all her finery. Even while her bejeweled visual appearance confers on her the status of an exceptional personage—a goddess no less—it also bestows on her an aura of timelessness comparable to that worn by the time-honored deities of the land.

More often than not her visual votaries place a spear, trident, sword, and even occasionally a club (figure 33) in one of her many hands, clearly aligning her persona with the warrior goddesses of the Hindu pantheon, such as Durga, rather than with the unarmed consorts in the company of their divine husbands, such as Sri, Sita, or Parvati. However, in contrast to modern pictures of these warrior goddesses that visually cast them as agents of the destruction of demons and other malignant forces (figures 53 and 54), Bharat Mata is rarely ever shown as such, and the weapons she carries are only suggestive of her destructive potential. The expatriate prints from the early decades of the twentieth century in which she appears poised for battle are exceptional in this regard (see figures 15 and 16), but even in these she is not shown actively engaged in combat and the enemy is left unspecified and unpictured.[47] As I discuss in chapter 5, in some surviving pictures from the 1930s and the 1940s Mother India is shown arming the more militant among her sons with swords, thus visually echoing a theme in the many verbal discourses in which she urges them to battle her foes on her behalf rather than heading off into combat on her own (figures 32 and 102). To this extent, such pictorial productions are not all that different from the verbal discourses of Indian nationalism, with their bourgeois squeamishness and patriarchal anxieties visible in their hesitancy over overt female militancy. Although

FIGURE 32 J. B. Dixit, *Bharat Mata.*
Oil on canvas, 1975. (Raja Dinkar Kelkar
Museum, Pune)

মায়ের শৃঙ্খল মোচন   J. P. Co. /R. 115   नाला का बन्धन मोचन

FIGURE 33 *Mata ka Bandhan Mochan*
(Mother's liberation from enslavement).
Printed by Rising Art College, Calcutta,
circa 1950. (Courtesy of Christopher
Pinney)

Indian nationalism did take a nonviolent turn from the 1920s under Gandhi's influence, the struggle against colonial rule reverted time and again to the use of modern weapons, including bombs and explosives (outmoded though these often were). I have yet to see Mother India armed with a revolver or a rifle; instead, she invariably carries archaic weapons, which in turn add to the aura of the timelessness that surrounds her persona.

And yet for her devotees Bharat Mata is rarely just a warrior, potential or actual. For, after all, her predominant identity is that of a compassionate and nurturing mother figure who gave birth to the millions who were her children, nourished them on her milk, and raised them into patriotic citizens of India. And this is where the multiple arms with which she is frequently endowed become pictorially useful, for in each of her hands are placed objects that reaffirm various aspects of her persona.[48] In Abanindranath Tagore's *Bharat Mata*, where she arguably appears for the first time in the pictorial realm with four arms, the goddess is shown holding objects that bestowed upon her devotees the blessings of clothing, food, learning, and spiritual grace (figure 6). And since that time other artists have put her multiple arms to similar uses. At the height of Gandhi's influence on Indian nationalism and its patriotic visual labors, she was often depicted holding one of his penchants—the spinning wheel (charka) with which he urged his fellow Indians to produce homespun cloth in order shake off their dependency on British imports (see figures 32; 34–35).[49] One picture published in the Hindi heartland even seems to suggest that Bharat Mata had slain her (white) conquerors with the power of the spinning wheel rather than with the sword; their suited and hatted figures lie strewn around the map of India from whose territorial space they have apparently been cast out (figure 34).

Most commonly Bharat Mata holds her flag in all its various configurations ranging from the changing banners of Congress (figures 26 and 35) to the new nation's standard (figure 25) to the orange pennant of Hindu nationalism (figure 20). When she has more than four arms they are shown holding various objects that alert the viewer not only to her fecundity, her learning, and her compassion for her children but also to her potential for violence (see, for example, the frontispiece and figure 13). In an untitled print possibly dating from the early 1980s, an anonymous artist has painted a cartographed Mother India as a ten-armed goddess with a large halo around her

FIGURE 34 Cover illustration of the Hindi pamphlet *Bharat Mata Ki Lataad* (Bharat Mata's exhortation) by Jaitapura Kalam. Babu Ram Sharma, Agra, 1930. (© British Library Board [APAC: Proscribed Publications Collection], PP HIN B 263)

भारत माता

FIGURE 35 *Bharat Mata.* Chromolithograph published in Delhi, circa 1920s. (Courtesy of Priya Paul, New Delhi)

FIGURE 36 Untitled [Bharat Mata]. Published by Coronation Litho, Shimla, acquired in 1983. (Courtesy of J. P. S. and Patricia Uberoi, Delhi)

head that casts a glow on the spectral outline of the contested territory of Kashmir (figure 36). In addition to a trident, she holds a sword and shield in two of her hands. Water flows out of small pots held in two other hands, presumably to nourish the outline map of India against which she is silhouetted. The fecundity of the country she embodies is also possibly suggested by the sheaf of grain and sickle that she holds in yet another hand. Additional hands hold a lotus (a symbol of fertility, purity, and spiritual exaltation) and a rosary (indicating the benediction of spiritual grace), as well as a manuscript signifying her status as a goddess of learning. This is indeed an all-purpose deity, and her capacities are apparent from the range of objects she holds. In customary Hindu iconography to which the pictorial crafting of Bharat Mata is undoubtedly indebted, the possession of multiple arms by deities points toward their supranormal powers and their capacity for independent action, even universal rulership. In contrast, the consort goddesses, when they are in the company of their divine husbands, are only shown with two arms. Bharat Mata might be a mother but she is no one's obvious consort,

62

and the country she embodies is imagined as an immanently powerful entity. Not surprisingly, she is frequently endowed with numerous arms, however interested her visual votaries might be in also presenting her as a figure akin to their own (human) mothers. This is especially true for images made in recent years when a growing sense of pride in (Hindu) Indian identity and India's rightful place in the global world is displaced onto images of an all-powerful territorial mother/goddess triumphing over all.

Possibly the most striking presence in figure 36 is the mighty lion that the all-purpose goddess rides. As I note in the next chapter, the lion is the chosen bestial companion of Durga, the warrior goddess whom Mother India most closely mimics in attributes, powers, and visual persona. But the lion is also associated with Britannia and hence with the British Empire (see, for example, figures 5a and 40). There is arguably an element of mockery and sub-version in *painting back* in response to the colonizing power when her artists incorporate the lion into Bharat Mata's visual appearance, especially when there is a striking resemblance to the Britannia imagery as in Vishnu Sapar's painting of the mother/goddess discussed earlier (figure 30). Similarly, in a poster with the title *Bharat Mata* (published sometime around or after 1950 with the signature of Sobha Singh [1901–1986]), the roaring lion—frequently associated with Britannia in *her* prints—now appears flanking the mother/goddess as she stands draped in the Indian tricolor (figure 37).[50] This is indeed, as Ashis Nandy has suggested in another context, an intimate enemy whose leonine strength has to be made one's own. The lion—always male and generally large with a powerful torso and a glorious mane—plays no small role in building a particular kind of visual persona for the carto-graphed mother/goddess, so much so that in some pictures its head or body even blends into the map of India that Bharat Mata occupies (for example, figures 15, 16, and 60).

In the early years of her visual presence Bharat Mata was generally accompanied by just one lion, but increasingly as the nationalist movement gained in self-confidence, and as her artists are convinced about the imminence of independence and about the capacity of the nation to become a global superpower, they frequently paint multiple lions, roaring lions, lions about to spring into action, and so on to visually mark the eventual triumph of the

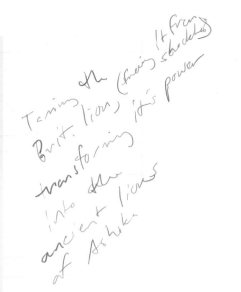

Taming the (freeing it from shackles) Brit. lion) transforming it's power into the ancient lions of Ashoka

FIGURE 37 Sardar Sobha Singh, *Bharat Mata*. Print by Mehta Art Press, New Delhi, circa 1950. (Courtesy of Erwin Neumayer and Christine Schelberger, Vienna)

nation (figures 30–31, 37–38, and 55). In other words, the lion appears to be Bharat Mata's alter ego, even possibly the masculine aspect of herself. As the years wear on the lion is not just a feature of the patriotic visual landscape flanking Bharat Mata's carto-graphed form, but instead it assumes a more active role as she sits on it, a smile on her face and sword or spear in her hand (see figure 36). Roaring lions pulling a chariot on which Bharat Mata rides to freedom and to victory are also scattered across the visual landscape. The most striking example of this image is a trilingual poster called *March to Independence* in English, printed possibly around the time of Indian independence, in which Gandhi acts as her charioteer, while other sons and two of her daughters accompany her (figure 38). Mother India—and her victorious children—may be headed toward a modern Parliament to assume power in this picture, but that she does so in a chariot pulled by two roaring lions is a telltale sign of the subterfuges of antiquity that accompany her visual look.

स्वराज मन्दिर

handwritten note: Gandhi as charioteer

Publishers :—SUDARSHAN STUDIO,
60, McLEOD ROAD,
LAHORE.

MARCH TO INDEPENDENCE
राहे आज़ादी

(All Rights Reserved)

VIR MILAP PRESS, LAHORE.

COPY RIGHT

Brij Lal

FIGURE 38 Brij Lal, *March to Independence: Raahe Aazaadi*. Printed by Sudarshan Studio, Lahore, circa 1947. (Courtesy of Urvashi Butalia, New Delhi)

MODERNITY'S REVELATIONS

Like the majority of the mechanically reproduced goddesses of Indian modernity, Bharat Mata is generally modestly clothed with barely a sense that she might have large swelling breasts, one of the requirements of the Hindu iconographic tradition for the divine female.[51] Every now and then she is presented as forlorn or destitute (see, for example, figure 11), but more commonly she appears clad in lush colored silks and draperies. Once in a while she appears in the garb of a classical heroine in a fitted bodice and draped garments—a pan-Indian style that became visible from the late nineteenth century in Ravi Varma's canvases of female bodies, and in the calendar art that commercialized his many innovations (see figures 18 and 33). However, in a vast number of her images, as befitted her dominant persona as a homely matron, Mother India is shown demurely clad in a sari in the national style (sometimes called *nivi*) increasingly associated with the respectable middle-class, upper-caste Hindu woman. Although this manner of wearing the sari accompanied by a stitched and sleeved blouse is deemed "traditional," it was itself fashioned in the later half of the nineteenth century through the joint interventions of European missionaries and modernizing Indians.[52] Newly wrought though it might have been in late-colonial India, the sari worn in this particular manner soon became the sartorial sign of the authentic and well-bred Indian woman. Thus it is not surprising that Bharat Mata, the mother of them all, is invariably draped in this style.

But the sari is doing much more than affirming Bharat Mata's essential identity as an *Indian* goddess. As I have already noted, the very manner in which it is arranged in many of these pictures visually enables her identity as the anthropomorphic form of this particular geo-body, its folds and flows suggesting the cartographic shape of India (see, for example, figures 11, 17, and 35). Her distinctiveness, further, as a goddess of Indian territory is also established frequently for her by the artists who clothe her in a sari in the colors of the flag of the emergent nation, itself progressively systematized from the 1930s, as saffron, white, and green (see figures 28, 29, and 31). Husain's flamboyant painting of 1997 (figure 2) in which a carto-graphed Mother India is draped in the tricolor Indian flag thus has major precedents in the barefoot cartographic labors of the preceding decades.

Indeed, if there is any single object that rivals the mapped form of India in conferring distinction on Mother India it is the flag of the nation with which she is associated, thereby setting her apart from other goddesses as a deity of a distinctive country. In traditional Hindu iconography goddesses are not generally shown carrying a banner, yet the flag is certainly one of Mother India's signature possessions. Its increasingly familiar colors clearly identify her with the emergent nation (and with a particular party that presented itself as spearheading the anticolonial charge) and also, after 1947, with the newly constituted republic. The poster *Svadhin Bharat: Free India* (figure 26), published in Calcutta, offers a synoptic (albeit nonlinear) history of the flag's many mutations between 1906 and 1947, when its final official colors and look were fixed.[53] From the 1920s, when Gandhi's influence on Congress politics was on the rise, his spinning wheel became visible on the flag, and Mother India frequently appears carrying a tricolor banner (in various configurations) with the charka inscribed on it, thus implicitly suggesting that she had extended her blessings to his project and his party (see, for example, figures 35, 86, 102, and 105). Her flag also became the subject of innumerable patriotic poems, songs, and worship to the point of idolatry. Patriots began to express their willingness to die for it from 1923 when the Nagpur "flag satyagraha" was staged. Secular rituals such as the "flag day" were instituted soon after, and a documentary film commemorating its virtues was produced by the Congress party in 1934 (Virmani 2008). The map of India, by contrast, has not been the recipient of this sort of praise and adulation *in and of itself*. Indeed, other than the expatriate Ghadar Party which adopted for its banner the outline map of India, the cartographic form of the country was never a serious contender as a national emblem, in the late colonial period or since. The map of India is not even statutorily covered under either the Emblems and Names (Prevention of Improper Use) Act (1950) or the Prevention of Insults to National Honor Act (1971), which regulate the symbolic economy of the republic.

In this light, the attempts by Mother India's artists to supplement the outline map of India in the very many ways that I have documented in this chapter stand out. In their many visual productions more than her anthropomorphic presence supplements the map. Frequently the gridded cartographic space of the official map is transformed into a lush landscape of plenitude and promise that is filled with the snow-capped Himalayan mountains in the north and with gushing streams and waterfalls, verdant grasslands, and a brimming ocean to the east, west, and south (see, for example, the frontispiece, the figure facing page 1, and figures 22, 29, and 106). Incongruously reminiscent though these landscapes sometimes are of the Swiss or English countryside—themselves re-presented in contemporary pictures as bucolic scenarios of serenity and calm order—they are pictured essentially through an aesthetic that I would characterize as patriotic pastoral. Through the operations of such an aesthetic the national territory of India is transformed from the mere dust of a map-made land into the "richly watered, richly fruited" landscape described in the most influential song written in honor of Bharat Mata (see chapter 3). The topographic is thus visually transformed into the topopoetic. As the phenomenologist Edward Casey writes, "In topography, one measures the terrain whereas in topopoetry one *contemplates* the form of this same terrain."[54] Topography is disenchanted, utilitarian, realist, prosaic, measured; it offers "the path of instruction." On the other hand, topopoetry, or "the poetry of place," transforms the nation's territory into the sensuous, the elemental, the fecund, and the productive—like the mother herself. "To move to the topopoetic is to move to a deeply psychical dimension of the painterly field: it is to move to a place from which the world is viewed not only with one's physical eyes but with 'the eye of the soul'" (Casey 2002, 71). The patriotic topopoetic "moves" the artist to view national territory with the eye of the patriot and then re-present it as an object of love and piety. In her analysis of Indian calendar art, Kajri Jain notes, "The nation as geography, as body, as present, is curiously absent, giving way instead to a mythical, undifferentiated foreign" (1995, 77). For the patriotic Indian artist concerned with producing pictures of the country rather than the generic poster, one strategy for countering this risk of producing "a mythical, undifferentiated foreign" landscape is by placing Mother India in the foreground. As such both any place and no place are at once converted into a particular place—the Indian national territory she embodies. Another revealing device is the outline map of India into which the idealized place-world of plenitude is reinstated; the danger of confusing India with any or no place at all is thus muted (for striking examples, see the frontispiece, the figure facing page 1, and figure 22). In such instances "mapping itself becomes a mode of praise" by visually enacting in picture form the adulation of the nation's territory by countless patriotic poems and nationalist prose.[55] Poetry, prose, and picture all converge to transform the geo-body of the nation into a place of plenitude and promise that one was drawn to defend—at the risk of giving up one's life, if need be, as I discuss in a later chapter.

THE MOTHER AND HER MAP-MADE LAND

But even more so than poetry and prose, Bharat Mata's pictures reveal the many fissures in the patriotic imagination of the mother/goddess as a territorial embodiment. Like many other female allegories and national embodiments that I describe in the next chapter, Mother India in her pictures generally wears an air of "mute remoteness" and "emptiness of expression," to use terms created by the feminist scholar Madelyn Gutwirth. Indeed, Gutwirth argues that such female icons of the nation have to appear to be untouchable because they cannot become the objects of competitive sexual attraction

FIGURE 39 *Bharat Mata,*
signed by the Studio E. Jesudass.
Published and printed by SPP,
acquired circa 1997. (Courtesy
of J. P. S. and Patricia Uberoi,
Delhi)

a Kerala christian -

among their followers, especially their "sons" or the male citizens of the nation (see Gutwirth 1992, 256). If that were to happen, their very purpose of
serving as a unifying symbol would be defeated. So even though Mother India
is supposed to embody a hospitable, even vulnerable, motherland for whom
one should be willing to give up one's life, this is not what is readily projected
by such visual representations in which her appearance over the years has
been formalized, depersonalized, and emptied of expression (through the
sustained interventions of mechanical reproduction, I might add). In other
words, even though the empty cartographic space of the map-made land
might be enlivened by supplementing it with Bharat Mata's anthropomorphic presence, such a supplementation does not resolve the representational
dilemma of fashioning a deity who has to appear approachable even while
being untouchable, human but also emphatically divine.

A pictorial history of Bharat Mata's image foregrounds as well the contradiction between her verbal naming as "mother" and the relative invisibility of signs of her motherhood, especially the absence of babies in her arms.[56] I will return to this theme in chapter 5 when I consider how attempts to show the filial piety of Mother India's citizen-sons pose a problem for pictorially emphasizing her maternality. Here I note that attempts at visualizing her as a mortal mother—and there are several of these, as we have seen, from early on in her pictorial career to the present—are overshadowed by the more dominant habit of divinizing her, with her suprahuman and godly status revealed by the large halo that rings her head, the multiple arms her body bears, and the abhaya mudra "fear-not" gesture her hand generally assumes. In other words, human motherhood is almost consistently displaced by supernal divinity. It can be rightly argued that since the line between motherhood and divinity is rather thin across South Asia, especially (but not exclusively) among its Hindu inhabitants, her artists are only visually reiterating a dominant belief about mothers when they endow her with a divine appearance. Nonetheless, this very act of pictorial translation reduces the visual capacity of Mother India to serve as *just* a mother, and moves her into the realm of (Hindu) idolatry.

For most consequentially the possibility of bringing about the unity of the citizenry through such means founders on the obvious contradiction that Mother India's manifest form is so visibly Hindu as betrayed by so many of the elements that have gone into fashioning her pictorial self. In the verbal discourses of nationalism it is easier to reiterate that she is the mother of us all, and that all of India's citizens—be they Parsi, Sikh, Christian, Muslim, or Hindu—are equal in her eyes. In the course of picturing Mother India, however, her visual votaries (even when they are Muslim, Christian, Sikh, or Parsi) turn again and again to the iconographic practices of *saguna* Hinduism (updated through recent bazaar art) almost as if they are unable to escape its reach and hold, with the result that there is no mistaking her visibly Hindu form (for example, see figure 39 whose creator Jesudass is a Kerala Christian).[57] So, what happens to her capacity to unite all her children around her stable maternal body if these same citizens do not share Hindu sensibilities, and in fact have a tradition of opposing what is deemed idolatrous? As we will see as we move further into this study, this is a problem that even the most pluralist or secular of her devotees have been unable to overcome.

Bharat Mata's anthropomorphic form, deployed visually to transform "the dust of some map-made land" into a "living mother," at the same time undermines attempts to secure a plural and religious diverse body politic, and the rational science of cartography itself ironically becomes complicit in picturing India as essentially and eternally Hindu.

OTHER WOMEN, OTHER MOTHERS

In spite of the insistence by Mother India's loyal followers of her uniqueness and singularity, she shares many elements of her persona with other figures in the world who like her have been imagined and then function as embodiments of modern nations. Indeed, in some of her pictures there are shades of Britannia, herself a personage from classical antiquity who found renewed visibility in the resurgence of a modern English-British national imperialism (see, for example, figure 30). Even more striking, Bharat Mata's visual persona is powerfully reminiscent of the numerous goddesses (*devi*) who have populated the divine landscape of the subcontinent over the millennia. In the course of my research I encountered many individuals in India who told me that there is nothing surprising about the divinization of the country as mother, for after all, they say, have we not *always* thought of India as a divine mother, and indeed, have we not *always* declared "Janani janmabhumischa svargadapi gariyasi" (Mother and motherland are greater than heaven)?[1] One goal of my work in this chapter is to demonstrate that there is nothing natural, timeless, or obvious about the maternalization of India as Mother India. She may look like many other devis, especially in the manner in which they have been visualized in bazaar art over the last century and a half. However as I will argue over the course of the following pages there are historically specific reasons for the feminization of *national territory* as mother/goddess that are a product of the contingent politics of colonial modernity as these play out over the course of the half century and more from the 1870s. Contrary to patriotic wisdom and common sense, the ready glossing of *janmabhumi* as motherland in this widely invoked nationalist phrase is a novel outcome of (divinized and maternalized) territorial nationalism rather than a resonant residue of a venerable tradition.

Not least, Bharat Mata also pictorially resembles her human surrogate, the flesh-and-blood sari-clad Indian woman, especially the mother who presides over the home as a sentient nurturing presence. As Anne McClintock notes, "Despite their myriad differences, nations are symbolically figured as domestic genealogies" (1995, 357). Correspondingly, nationalist discourse across the modern world is saturated with familial imagery, or what Lynn Hunt in the context of her discussion of French revolutionary politics has termed "family romance."[2] The country is thus imagined as a homeland with its language(s) recast as mother tongue(s) and its citizens constituting a brotherhood and fraternity, and the nation itself is incarnated as parent—sometimes a father figure but more often than not a mother. As Mrinalini Sinha writes, the familial imagery offers "the invented nation a powerful legitimizing language of naturalization" (2004, 187–88). Inhabitants of the national territory are conceived—and perceive themselves—through the optic of family romance as organically and timelessly connected with each other in "natural" bonds of affect and intimacy that are placed above history and politics. In late colonial India, as in so many other countries of an industrializing world, the nuclear hetero-bourgeois family becomes progressively the productive and reproductive norm. The woman at the heart of this reconfiguration is over time recast as modern yet modest, with her essential difference from a hegemonic West (as well as vulgar populism within the country) ensured by her rootedness in a selectively appropriated "Indian" tradition, itself (discreetly but) invariably modeled on Hindu, upper-caste, and Sanskritic-Aryan norms (Sinha 2004, 193). Like her human surrogate, Bharat Mata is a "new woman," appearances to the contrary.³ She is the inviolable essence of the nation in the making, and as such she is imagined as the cherished and venerable mother who presides over her home that is deemed the last bastion of autonomy and authenticity in a world that has been made over by the work of empire and colonialism. Yet rather than remain out of sight and contained within the domestic realm, Mother India is all too visible and conspicuous as the artistic labors of visual patriotism render her as a public woman for all to behold and revere.

Therefore, to craft a distinctive visual personality for their special woman in such circumstances, even while borrowing all that was desirable from available models of idealized femininity (Indic, Western, divine, human, maternal), is the pictorial challenge with which Mother India's artists and illustrators wrestled from the 1880s. And this struggle leaves its mark in the visual archive where we simultaneously encounter Bharat Mata as divine and human; as "Indian" but also reminiscent of female figurations of the nation from other parts of the world, especially the imperial West; as invincible but also vulnerable; as benevolent but also blood thirsty; as comely maiden but also ageless matron. As we now recognize after a few decades of revisionist scholarship, the nation is a "fragile social achievement" and as such it remains "ephemeral unless hard and regular work is undertaken to produce and maintain its materiality."⁴ Cultural workers for the nation attempt to transform this abstraction into a tangible and enduring entity that can be seen, affectively experienced, and even touched and felt. My goal in this chapter is to explore why in making palpable through pictures the abstraction that is India, the nation's artists turn to the figure of the woman, especially one of a particular sort.

To begin, I suggest that they do so because across the modern world as bourgeois norms of domesticity, proprietorship, and citizenship are put into place, the (middle-class) female body comes to be burdened with the maintenance of authenticity, originality, purity, and virtue, even as men assume for themselves the powers of the public and the visibility of the political.⁵ In the symptomatic words from 1865 of John Ruskin, one representative Victorian at the height of the century that stabilized such divisions: "The man's power is active, progressive, defensive. He is eminently the doer, the creator, the discoverer, the defender. His intellect is for speculation and invention; his energy for adventure, for war, and for conquest . . . But the woman's power is for rule, not for battle, and her intellect is not for invention or creation, but for sweet ordering, arrangement and decision . . . Her great function [is] praise . . . By her office and place, she is protected from all danger and temptation. The man, in his rough work in [the] open world, must encounter all peril and trial . . . but he guards the woman from all this, within his house, as ruled by her."[6]

As the world itself is carved up in the age of nationalism into the bounded places that are sovereign nation-states, this gendered division of values—and privileges and burdens—finds tangible expression in transcendent figures such as Britannia, Marianne, Erin or Hibernia, Columbia, Guadalupe, Mother Iran, Misr (Egypt), and other such exceptional women who embody the country as motherland, much in the manner that the woman as mother is the gentle custodian of the nuclear family home. From Afsaneh Najmabadi's fine work on gendered nationalism in modern Iran, we learn that the geo-body of a nation cannot be only a mathematically inscribed outcome of scientific cartography. Nor is it ever gender-neutral. A feminist analysis of modern territorial nationalism underscores instead the constitutive role of the female body in partitioning the world into sovereign spaces "to love and possess, to protect and defend, to protect and die for" (1997, 450). Mother India is one among such female bodies that are emblematic of the bourgeois fetishization of property and propriety in an age that witnessed the transformation of national territories into enclosed objects of possession and protection. How she and others like her across the modern world are products of evolving nationalist ideals of possession and propriety is my concern in this chapter.[7]

ANTHROPOMORPHIZING INDIA

Characteristically, like so much else in British India that mimed the master's culture, some of the earliest images of India as an anthropomorphized female (although not carto-graphed) appeared in and from contexts that we can recognize as European and colonial. In 1777 the East India Company—which after nearly a hundred and fifty years had recently graduated from its formal role as a trading firm to that of a territorial ruler of newly acquired lands in Bengal and on the Coromandel Coast—commissioned from the

FIGURE 40 Spiridione Roma, *The East Offering Its Riches to Britannia*. Allegorical ceiling piece commissioned by the East India Company for the Revenue Committee Room in East India House, London. Oil on canvas, 1778. (© British Library Board [India Office Select Materials Print and drawings F 245])

little-known artist Spiridione Roma (c. 1737–1781) a painting for the ceiling of its Revenue Committee Room at its headquarters in London (figure 40). This was roughly the same time that the company was also gearing up to bring the authority of scientific cartography to bear on the mapping of India, as Matthew Edney (1997) has documented. While the cartographic assault on the subcontinent began to progressively transform land into colonial property and visually consolidate India as a measured geo-body occupying a mathematically determined grid, Roma's allegorical painting continues an older European habit of anthropomorphizing the same territory as a delectable, even eager, female. His allegory centers on a youthful Britannia sitting atop a rock, holding a string of pearls that she has obviously picked out from a basket of riches offered to her by a dark, comely woman most likely signifying India. As we would expect from a colonial visual culture that is already color conscious, Britain's paleness stands in stark contrast to the dark form of India, but a suggestive equivalence between both women is established in their bare breasts—or nearly so, for Britannia's bosom is partially covered by her flowing garments.[8]

Roma's painting in turn echoes a marble bas-relief executed between 1728 and 1730 by the sculptor John Michael Rysbrack (1694–1770) that adorned the chimneypiece at the old East India House in London. In this piece Britannia sits regally on a globe by the seashore, with one hand resting on her trademark shield as she benevolently looks at "India" who, one breast bared, hands her a casket filled with various riches.[9] While Britannia herself is fully clothed, other bare-breasted female bodies personifying Asia and Africa also pay homage to the British nation at the start of a century that was to establish its worldwide dominion, especially over the seas—as signified in both Roma's and Rysbrack's artistic efforts by sailing ships on the horizon. Barbara Groseclose notes in a rare study of such artistic productions that "conventions of allegorical art in the eighteenth century easily lent themselves to the idealization of a relationship between Orient and Occident in which a compliant, ingratiating East hands over jewels and other costly goods to a receptive, passive Britannia" (1995, 50). Although it was conventional in Europe at this time, as many feminist scholars have shown, to monumentalize various virtues and values as nude and partially covered females, the bare breasts of "India" are particularly important to note because in the charged colonial context of its deployment the naked female body suggests vulnerability and availability, even an "invitation to conquest."[10] The bare-breasted "India" of this early colonial art also stands out in contrast with the Bharat Mata of patriotic art who is almost never shown as such. And as in the case of M. F. Husain, when someone dares to reveal her breasts it is deemed sacrilegious, even a cause for extreme public censuring.

As Britain progressively consolidated its proprietary control over the subcontinent—a process that was increasingly reflected in the many maps that were produced by the new science of cartography from the 1780s—India came to be paradoxically clothed by the colonizer's artists, with her naked breasts covered by loosely draped fabric, even as she continued to become more and more abject and obsequious—a humble shadow of the bejewelled woman who had once offered her riches to the West.[11] For instance, in a marble relief fashioned around 1818 to memorialize a Calcutta merchant named Alexander Colvin, the sculptor Richard Westmacott includes a seated India with her head and breasts demurely covered, her body unadorned by jewels, and her hand resting on what looks like an empty pot rather than a brimming basket. Her material riches, the relief seems to suggest, have already been transferred from one territory to another. And around the same time, in a monument mounted in distant Penang to memorialize the achievements of one of the company's more interventionist governor-generals, the Marquess Cornwallis, India is reduced to a weeping female while a helmet-wearing Britannia takes one of her young men under her wings and introduces him to his new master.[12] Indeed, in British fine and popular art over the course of the imperial nineteenth century, India invariably appears as a figure of deprivation and desolation, or as a dusky maiden whose fate rests with others who are stronger than she is. In such images, by contrast, Britannia is a powerful even martial woman who wears an air of authority and command and lords over her Indian subjects.[13]

BRITANNIA TRAVELS TO INDIA

In what might be her first appearance in an Indian cartographic context, Britannia appears in an elaborate cartouche affixed to James Rennell's important map titled *Hindoostan*, which was printed in December 1782 and reprinted in 1785 (figures 5 and 5a).[14] On this map, which Rennell declared would be "highly interesting to every person whose imagination has been struck by the splendor of our victories, or whose attention is rouzed by the present critical state of our affairs, in that quarter of the globe," Britannia is described by the English cartographer as "receiving into her Protection, the sacred Books of the Hindoos, presented by the Pundits, or Learned Bramins" (1783, i, xii). At her feet lie what look like the tools of the surveyor, and behind her on a pedestal stands a lion with its foot resting on a sphere, possibly a terrestrial globe. Engraved on the pedestal are "the Victories, by means of which the British Nation obtained, and has hitherto upheld, its Influence in India" (xii). This complex cartouche has been variously interpreted, but for the purposes of my argument the geo-body of India (albeit only partly a product as yet of mathematically produced knowledge) is associated with the feminized body of Britain in a colonial economy of exchange: in return for the sacred textual knowledges of the East, symbolized by the "Shaster" (sacred books) that the Hindu pundits give to Britannia, she gives to them

FIGURE 41 *Bharat Bhiksa* (India begging). Lithograph published by Calcutta Art Studio, Calcutta, circa 1878. (Courtesy of Christopher Pinney)

Rennell's map of their land, the cartographic exemplar of the new rational, scientific ordering of India.[15]

Almost a century later and at the height of the colonial period, an Indian illustrator appears to acknowledge that it is not just the sacred books of India that need Britannia's safekeeping but the country itself (figure 41). In one of the earliest extant prints of the then recently established Calcutta Art Studio, dated to sometime in the late 1870s, a haggard, even grotesque India (clad possibly in widow's garb) is incongruously but revealingly paired with a youthful and lovely Britannia, trident in hand. The object of transaction between them is a large (naked) male child sitting between them, his gaze toward Britannia and his back to India, as both "mothers" seek to hold him. The Bengali title of the print is *Bharat Bhiksha*, which has been variously translated as "India Begging," or "the Begging of India." In the words of Christopher Pinney, "If the directionality of the 'gift' of the child is unclear, the child's identity as a newly reformed—Romanized—India is not all that opaque."[16] In a contemporary allegorical Bengali narrative from 1873 called *Dasamahavidya* (Ten aspects of the goddess), India strikingly resembles the haggard crone of *Bharat Bhiksha*: "*Bharat Mata* is now Dhumabati—the widow. In her state of widowhood, she lacks food to nourish her body and clothes to cover herself. Her hair is rough from the lack of oil and unkempt. She has lost her teeth and suffering has made her gaze intense and piercing."[17]

As Indira Chowdhury has suggested in her fine analysis of songs and plays of these decades in Bengal written by the bhadralok elite of the region, Bharat Mata (already named as such from around 1873) appears not as an all-powerful goddess but as a dispossessed and destitute woman robbed of her luster and reduced to begging. Consider a verse from 1873 composed by Dwijendranth of the influential Tagore family, many of whose members imagined Mother India in a completely different guise in the following few decades:

> Oh Bharat your countenance is like the fading moon,
> By day or night your tears flow incessantly;
> Accustomed as I am to your glowing beauty,
> How can I look upon this pale image [?][18]

This verse opened a play titled *Bharat Mata* by Kiran Chandra Bandopadhyay in which the mother/goddess laments to her "sons," "The plundering robbers have taken away all my ornaments. I have no oil for my hair and how much longer will I have to wear these dull and tattered rags?"[19]

On the one hand, such utterances verbally echo *Bharat Bhiksha*. On the other hand, the Calcutta Art Studio print also appears to be responding to another sentiment in the Bengali air of the 1860s and 1870s. For, as Chowdhury has shown, Queen Victoria herself appears in some songs and plays of the period, patriotic though they might be in their apparent intent, as a rival mother who would rescue India and Indians from their sorry plight: "The great Queen is not only the empress of India, but the most suitable mother to her Hindu children."[20] And Bharat Mata herself appears to have endorsed the more powerful mother who now competed with her for her children's affections and allegiance:

Are my darlings not yours as well? . . .
They live or die according to your will.
And regard you as a goddess.
Oh do not despite these sons of your maid!
Think of your own situation, mother!
The weight of your grief when you'd lost a son
And here I am suffering the loss of so many![21]

In Kiranchandra's earlier *Bharat Mata*, staged around 1873, Victoria in turn promises to bring an end to the woes of the aggrieved mother/goddess (Sarkar 2006, 3965).

It is not Victoria alone who is a rival mother to India but Britannia as well, as is apparent from a "huge" painting apparently commissioned by the journalist Nabagopal Mitra and prominently put on display in the proto-patriotic annual gathering called Hindu Mela (the Hindu fair) held in 1877 in Calcutta. The painting apparently showed "Indians sitting with folded hands before Britannia," and it was disturbing enough to cause one prominent visitor to burst out, "Turn it [a]round, turn it [a]round."[22] From around the time of the Hindu Mela painting or the Calcutta Art Studio's *Bharat Bhiksha*, anthropomorphized images of Britain and India as female figures (either jointly or on their own) appear in various English-language periodicals published by Anglo-Indians and Indians alike, such as *Indian Charivari* and *Mookerji's Magazine* from Calcutta, *Oudh Punch* from Lucknow, and most regularly and elaborately in *Hindi Punch* from Bombay.[23] To invoke just one example from a whole host of such images that regularly appeared in the pages of *Hindi Punch* from the 1880s, a cartoon titled *Churning!* shows Britain and India as women who together churn in a pot the recently established Indian National Congress's annual meeting (along with a good amount of "loyalty," "contentment," "Western culture," "national aspirations," and "peace" thrown in) under a banner that announces "God save the queen" (figure 42). Hind, as she is generally referred to in the pages of this magazine (with the qualifiers "Madame," "Lady," "Sister," or occasionally even "Mother") is a respectable matronly figure. She wears her sari, hair, and jewels in a regional Maharastrian style, and she is frequently shown with a trident as her distinguishing insignia in one of her hands. She is clearly a special personage, but she is not

CHURNING!
THE INDIAN NATIONAL CONGRESS, ELEVENTH SESSION - POONA. 27th, 28th, AND 30th DECEMBER. 1895.
[*Hindi Punch, Dec., 1895.*]

FIGURE 42 *Churning! The Indian National Congress, Eleventh Session: Poona 27th, 28th, and 30th December 1895.* Cartoon in *Hindi Punch*, December 1895. (© British Library Board, 1876.b.61)

explicitly marked as a divinity.[24] The anonymous artists of *Hindi Punch* generally visualized her as Britannia's principal female companion in India, but she is clearly subordinate to Britannia in demeanor and forms of address. In turn Britannia, invariably shown as an armor-clad Amazon, is for Hind an amiable elder sister, occasionally even a mother (and hence to her children as well).

Modeled as it was on the parent magazine in England whose title as well it echoed, *Hindi Punch* often resorted to visual idioms and images popularized in the West, including the use of female bodies to represent nations and countries, virtues and values, activities and movements. Maps, globes, and carto-graphed bodies also appear in its pages from the 1890s, and such images are among the earliest emergent examples of what I have termed barefoot cartography. Thus in November 1904, on the occasion of the Industrial and Agricultural Exhibition, the magazine published a cartoon showing two

FIGURE 43 *Duo-in-Uno.* Cartoon in *Hindi Punch*, November 1905. (© British Library Board, London, SV 576)

sari-clad women—representing Agriculture and the Congress—standing on a gridded globe on which is drawn a rough physical map of India. In another cartoon published in the same issue, a female figure representing the Hindu festival of Divali sprightly perches on a gridded terrestrial globe (on which some parts of the map of India are visible) and wishes the children of Mother Hind the very best of the season (Nowrosjee 1904, 93–94). Less frivolously, in *Duo-in-Uno* (1905), Britannia and Hind occupy a framed picture in which both sit on a partly visible terrestrial globe, holding hands under the watchful eyes of a cherub (figure 43). The cartoon commemorates the recent Indian visit of the Prince of Wales and his wife, who are shown being handed over by Britannia to the able care of her "sister Hind" for the duration of their stay.

The reach of such images would have been highly limited given their appearance in English-language illustrated magazines whose circulation was generally restricted to the big cities and the educated urban male elite. Nonetheless, it is important for this history to note their presence, because they allow me to locate some Victorian-era precedents for the barefoot cartographic practice of the twentieth century that is my focus, and also to mark points of departure from it. For as anti-British nationalism gained in strength in various parts of the subcontinent from the 1890s, and as the patriotic artist's confidence in its eventual outcome grew, such images of condescension or alliances across the imperial-racial line fade, and India rarely appears as either an abject figure of destitution or an obsequious woman kowtowing to British might. Britannia as well recedes into the background, rarely putting in an appearance in the company of Mother India. Instead Bharat Mata—now invariably pictured as a glorious mother/goddess in the many guises I discussed in chapter 1—becomes hypervisible as the undisputed mother of the patriotic citizenry, although elements of her iconography such as the trident or the lion, and even the stance of her body, are sometimes vaguely reminiscent of Britannia. Indeed, in prints such as Sardar Sobha Singh's *Bharat Mata*, published possibly after 1950 when the newly independent nation-state was officially declared a republic, even her sari (one of her more unambiguously "Indian" markers) is draped in a Roman fashion (figure 37). Further, a slender arm reaches down to casually stroke the mane of a powerful lion as it snarls at a toppled (British) crown and breaks apart its shackles. In many elements of its visual program—the snarling lion, the robe-cum-sari, the overturned crown—it is possible to interpret Sobha Singh's *Bharat Mata* as signaling the end of the (pictorial) reign of the other (British) mother that had begun two centuries before. [25]

CONTENDING WOMEN

Joan Scott, among others, has argued that in modern times "power relations among nations and the status of colonial subjects have been made comprehensible (and thus legitimate) in terms of the relation between male and female" (1988, 48). In other words, Britain's mastery over India in the age of worldwide empires was as natural and as deserved as the mastery of man over woman in the logic of the patriarchal sex/gender system. The visual evidence from and about India, however, shows that the colonial exercise of sovereignty and power, and the proprietary takeover of one land by another, can also find expression in contending female bodies. This happens, I suggest, because of the manner in which the female and the maternal were configured to express notions of property and propriety in India, Europe, and Britain in recent centuries.

Turning first to Europe, many scholars have traced to at least the Renaissance the prevalence of a European habit of corporealizing countries and continents, when from around the 1540s in royal spectacles and theatrical productions Asia, Europe, Africa, and the newly "discovered" America were represented as women—the former two clothed in sumptuous glory. As John Higham observes, "It was an age of exuberant display . . . an age in which everything seemed to teach a lesson and invite a wondrous analogy" (1990, 46). Such analogies were systematized in print in Cesare Ripa's *Iconologia* (first published in 1593 and then with woodcut illustrations in 1603), an expansive manual that for several centuries following became the touchstone for European artists interested in representing abstract ideas as well as continental formations in visual terms. Higham notes that Ripa's view suggests that Europe should be shown as a grandly dressed matron surrounded by "trophies, books, and musical instruments at her feet, to denote her superiority above all other parts of the world . . . Her crown should show that Europe has always been esteemed the queen of the world" (46–47).[26] Her status as "queen of the world" did not lead Ripa in 1603 to present her with a terrestrial globe, although there was precedence for this in the sumptuously engraved frontispiece that adorns Abraham Ortelius's *Theatrum Orbis Terrarum* (Theater of the world), arguably the world's first atlas, published in 1570 (figure 44).[27] Ortelius's frontispiece shows five variously adorned female figures placed around the title words inscribed in Latin. Valerie Traub observes in her analysis of this image: "The crowned queen of Europe—holding a scepter in one hand and in the other, a Christianized T-in-O-globe—lords over her supposedly less civilized sisters. Asia with her censer is on the left; Africa, her head surrounded by a fiery halo, is on the right; and America reclines below with her hammock and bow and arrow, brandishing a severed head. At her feet, a bust of the fabled continent of Magellanica suggests the possibility of discovery of another new world. In the spatial iconography of Ortelius's title page, Europe enthroned contrasts explicitly to the cannibalis-

FIGURE 44 Engraved frontispiece to Abraham Ortelius's *Theatrum Orbis Terrarum*. Apud Aegid. Coppenium Diesth, Antwerp, 1570. (Library of Congress, Washington, D.C.)

tic America lolling on the ground, while Asia and Africa provide subservient if statuesque support to the edifice of European dominion" (2000, 53).

As the influential commentator Giovanni Botero (1544–1617) wrote in 1591, Europe, though the smallest of the continents, "was born to rule over Africa, Asia and America," and the new science of cartography as well as the older arts proudly displayed this worldly truth in their various productions.[28] Ortelius inaugurates a practice that continues well into the next century in which bodies (female and male, variously clothed and unclothed) are associated with gridded territories in numerous European maps and atlases. With "the stable binary of a feminized personification of territory contrasted to the particular men who chart and conquer it," these maps of the later sixteenth and seventeenth centuries deploy a new spatializing strategy in their use of the human form to map places (Traub 2000, 46). The domination of

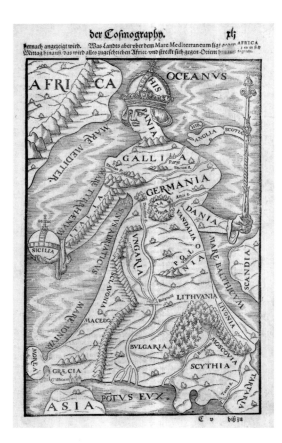

FIGURE 45 *Europa Regina*. Engraving on wood attributed to Johann "Bucius" Putsch, circa 1537. (University of Michigan Map Library, Ann Arbor)

one part of the world—Europe—over others is also visually condensed in the figures of contending women, with the superiority of one over the other marked literally on their bodies.

This anthropomorphizing strategy also led some illustrators and print-makers from the sixteenth century to clothe the feminized form of the continent in the map of Europe, parts of which were coming under cartographic surveys commissioned by early modern states for the first time.[29] An early expression of this convergence of map and female form is the Tyrolese engraver Johann ("Bucius") Putsch's *Europa Regina* (figure 45).[30] As Darby Lewes notes, engraved around 1537 "the entire image is one of orderliness: Spain, the queen's crown, is firmly settled upon her head, and any wanton ringlets of hair are neatly bound beneath a snood. Her crown, orb (Sicily), and heart (Bohemia) form a triangle that directs the viewer's eye away from eastern Europe toward the west, the scene of Spanish triumph in America.

Surrounding territories are indistinct, negligible bits of real estate that in no way distract from the central image. A blob of British Isles perches parakeet-fashion near Europa's shoulder; similar clumps of vague African and Norwegian terrain float shapelessly at her head and hip. Her skirt is composed of the Baltics and Greece; Turkey and Russia are beneath her feet" (2000, 134). This carto-graphed Europe, placid and orderly, was a much-copied image that later works by Sebastian Munster, Heinrich Bunting, and Mathias Quad reiterated with some modifications over the course of the sixteenth century and into the early seventeenth in several languages. "Indeed," Lewes writes, "the Europa Regina figure was so popular that she became a genre of sorts" (134).

Lewes uses the neologism "visual somatopia" to refer to such images in which "places are simultaneously composed of female bodies and designed for male bodily satisfaction" (2000, 3, 129–64).[31] In one of the few scholarly studies of such images that historians of cartography have tended to dismiss as "curiosities" and "oddities," Lewes argues that "the somatopic ordering of Europe took the form of maps representing the continent as a female figure, an image that must have offered some comfort to men caught in the tumultuous conflicts of their age. Reducing Europe to a woman allowed one to reduce treacherously shifting geographic/religious margins and thresholds to a comfortably familiar cliché: land could be perceived as a domestic goddess, for example, serene and secure; an enticing virgin awaiting her lover; a threatened mother, desperately in need of male protection; a whore, property of any male who wished to use her; or a mannish unnatural harridan, whose power was illusory. In any case, she was a male construct, whose future was determined by male power" (2000, 133). Such visual somatopias in turn are pictorial manifestations of a recurrent textual habit in many European languages of analogizing land to a woman, an early modern expression of which in English are the numerous narratives of "exploration," "discovery," "conquest," and "settlement" that are peppered with sexual tropes as exemplified, for instance, by Walter Raleigh's revealing statement, "Guiana is a countrey that hath yet her maydenhead."[32] In remarking on this comment, Louis Montrose observes that "the ideology of gender hierarchy sanctions the Englishmen's collective longing to prove and aggrandize themselves upon the feminine body of the New World; and, at the same time, the emergent hierarchical

FIGURE 46 Marcus Gheeraerts the Younger, *Queen Elizabeth I* (the Ditchley portrait). Oil on canvas, circa 1592. (National Portrait Gallery, London, NPG 2561)

discourse of colonial exploitation and domination reciprocally confirms the hegemonic force of the dominant sex/gender system" (1992, 154).

That the visual and verbal analogizing of land and the female form could as well be used to aggrandize a woman when she is the sovereign is apparent from the so-called Ditchley portrait of Elizabeth I dated to circa 1592 (figure 46). This much-discussed painting that, according to Montrose, "realizes the tropological equivalence of land and woman in the conjunction of a carto-graphic image with a royal portrait," shows the queen of England standing, "like some great goddess or glorified Virgin Mary, with her feet upon the globe and her head amidst the heavens." Critically, in terms of anticipating a similar conjunction in India's patriotic art, Elizabeth "stands upon a car-tographic image of Britain, deriving from Christopher Saxton's collection of printed maps. Like Saxton's 1583 map, the painting divides England into counties, each separately colored, and marks principal towns and rivers . . .

This representation of Queen Elizabeth as standing upon her land and sheltering it under her skirts suggests a mystical identification of the inviolate female body of the monarch with the un-breached body of her land, at the same time that it affirms her distinctive role as the motherly protectoress of her people"(1992, 156).

At a time when Christopher Saxton's maps, based on new but as yet rudimentary mathematical techniques and instruments of survey, were beginning to "magisterially" generate a "new visual image of England," the Ditchley portrait powerfully supplements the cartographic with the corporeal, and vice versa (Morgan 1979, 135, 144).[33] As the emergent science of cartography begins to mathematically fashion for England a geo-body, the painting identifies "her virginal female body with the bounded body of her island realm" (Montrose 1992, 175–76). Most saliently, this portrait points to how the map of the realm can be visually deployed to suggest that "Elizabeth is England, woman and kingdom are interchangeable" (Strong 1987, 136).

By the time the Ditchley portrait was completed, other paintings, illustrations, and engravings had consolidated the idea that the queen's body and her realm were inseparable. Thus the frontispiece to Saxton's *Atlas* (1579) centered on a crowned Elizabeth carrying an orb and a scepter and flanked by two men representing Astronomy and Geography, both holding globes. Elizabeth looks straight at us while below her, on the bottom left-hand side of the page, a cartographer is hard at work, measuring and mapping his monarch's island realm. In Roy Strong's estimation of this frontispiece, "to all intents and purposes looking at an image of Elizabeth was looking at England" (1987, 99).[34] A few years later a series of sumptuous royal portraits reveal the symbolic salience of cartographic instruments in the emergent "cult" of the Virgin Queen.[35] The large so-called "Armada" portrait, for instance, shows a resplendent Elizabeth standing with her hand resting on a terrestrial globe on which unnamed territories are clearly marked. By 1588, when George Gower completed this painting, the New World territory of Wingandacoa had been claimed and renamed "Virginia" in honor of the Virgin Queen. In Louis Montrose's nuanced reading of this act of dispossession, appropriation, and renaming, "the Virgin Queen verbally constitutes the land as a feminine place unknown to man; and by doing so, she also symbolically effaces the indigenous society which already physically and culturally inhabits

and possess that land. In this royal renaming of Wingandacoa as Virginia
. . . the discursive power of the inviolate female body serves as an emergent
imperialist project of exploration, conquest, and settlement" (1992, 148.).
Virginia also provides a precedent for an enduring European practice in the
New World of associating land with female bodies that produced such iconic
entities as America and Columbia.[36]

Richard Helgerson in his insightful analysis of "forms of nationhood" that
emerged in Elizabethan and early Stuart England has drawn upon such pictures to argue that just as the monarchical cult of Elizabeth had replaced
the prior cult of the Virgin on which it had drawn, "the cult of Britain" now
assumes shape, and it is helped by images of the newly drawn map of the
country that Saxton's *Atlas* had helped popularize. Thus, the frontispiece
of William Camden's *Britannia* from 1600 (originally published in Latin in
1586), as well as of the chorography's first English edition in 1610, is centered
on a map of Britain above which Britannia appears with one of her arms
resting on a spiked shield.[37] Even more suggestive is the appearance in 1612
of "Great Britain" as a female figure, one breast bared, on the front page of
Michael Drayton's *Poly-Olbion* (figure 47). Reminiscent of Elizabeth as she
had appeared on the earlier cover page of Saxton's *Atlas*, this is nevertheless
not the flesh-and-blood monarch but instead *the land itself* made to assume
the female form. This new figure was clearly inspired by the work of England's new army of cartographers and chorographers diligently going around
mapping the realm. Most strikingly, the figure appears clothed in the very
map that is the fruit of their diligent labors. As Helgerson observes, albeit
with some hesitation, "even the ugly distortion in the drawing of Britain, the
squat lower limbs and the elongated torso, may have been intended. This
distortion allows Britain's gown to assume a shape roughly approximating
the outline of England and Wales, as one sees it on Saxton's map" (1986, 83).[38]
While the four male bodies flanking her (representing rival monarchs) warily
eye each other and the figure of Britain, "this new figure gazes serenely out,
a confident source of identity and continuity. Edgy and mutually destructive male rivalry is theirs; power and plenty remain always with her. While
they are mere artifacts of stone, 'trophies,' as Drayton calls them, raised to
adorn her triumphal arch, she, holding the fruits of her bounteous womb in
the position traditionally reserved for the Madonna's divine child, is a living

FIGURE 47 Title page of *Poly Olbion* by Michael Drayton. Engraved and signed by W. Hole. Printed by Humphrey Lownes, London, 1612. (Reproduced by permission of the Huntington Library, San Marino, California, No. 59144)

embodiment of nature" (Helgerson 1986, 64). Drayton's frontispiece caused "a conceptual revolution," the culmination in a series of pictorial efforts, exemplified in Saxton's frontispiece and in that of Camden, which enabled the progressive transfer of allegiance and attachment "from universal Christendom to dynastic state to land-centered nation" (1986, 62, 64).

The female figure at the heart of this conceptual revolution, Britannia, is critical to my analysis, especially because of her subsequent entanglement in the pictorial history of Mother India that I chart in this volume. As the few scholars who have worked on the figure have noted, Britannia first emerged in the Roman Empire to celebrate the conquest of Britain in first century BCE. In commemorative reliefs dating from the first century CE in Aphrodesias in Turkey she appears in a short tunic with one breast bared, and she is about to be carried off by a male figure signifying possibly the Roman emperor (Dresser 1989, 26–28; Warner 1985, 45–46). About a century later she is featured on Roman coins from the time of Hadrian and Antoninus Pius in a form that largely endures to this day. Herbert Atherton describes her as "a classically-draped figure, seated three-quarters left; a spear held out in her right hand; her left forearm resting on her shield; her feet against the rocks; her head adorned with a plumed helmet" (1974, 89). Although she is not of any particular significance after the end of the Roman Empire, Britannia resurfaces in 1600 on the title page of Camden's chorographic work *Britannia* in the company of a map of the island-nation. Her increasing popularity in popular print as well as fine art from then on, especially in the eighteenth and nineteenth centuries, has been attributed to the growing territorial transformation of "England" into "Great Britain" and the progressive creation of a worldwide empire that was symbolically heralded in James Thomson's patriotic ode, "Rule, Britannia!" (1740). From the middle of the nineteenth century she frequently graces the pages of the popular English periodical *Punch* in at least four different capacities, including "the vulnerable virgin courted and/or threatened by the powers of the day; the compassionate weeping Madonna who mourns national tragedies and cares for the helpless; 'She Who Must be Obeyed,' the slightly ridiculous but rather formidable nanny figure, whose commanding power . . . endures to this day; and the war-like Athena who is the most conventionally emblematic and stylized of the four types, but who now exhorts rather than participates directly in battle."[39] Over the course of the Victorian period, appearing on coins as well as public statuary, Britannia looms large as the very embodiment of a global sea-borne empire. Instead of flagrantly bare breasted she is modestly clothed, and with a trident in her hand and a lion by her side she confidently and imperiously looks out on her domains. In this capacity she frequently appears in the company of the maps of the British Empire (either in its whole or parts of it). Among the earliest (if not the first) of such appearances is in an emblematic cartouche on a map of Barbados in the so-called Blathwayt Atlas (which, commissioned in the mid-seventeenth century, is sometimes described as the first atlas of the British Empire). A spectacular later example is *Imperial Federation: Map of the World Showing the Extent of the British Empire in 1886*, which is attributed to the well-known Victorian illustrator Walter Crane.[40] At the bottom center of the world map laid out on a grid, with the British colonies

LOOK FOR THE NAME **GENATOSAN**, LTD.

YOUR NEW
BRITISH
POSSESSIONS—
GENUINE
Sanatogen
AND
Formamint

MAKERS OF SANATOGEN, FORMAMINT, GENASPRIN, ETC.

FIGURE 48 Advertisement by Genatosan, Ltd. for its products Sanatogen and Formamint. Color process print after E. F. Skinner, 27 x 20.9 cm. Glasgow and London, circa 1914–1915. (Wellcome Library, London, L0023921)

tinted pink, Britannia sits on a terrestrial globe (borne on the shoulders of Atlas). Carrying her trademark trident, her other hand resting on her shield, she is surrounded by other figures—men and women (some bare breasted)—who represent various imperial possessions. Clearly a decorative map, it was also invested in publicizing the serious business of empire: statistical details regarding major British colonies, including the amount of trade, shipping, imports, and exports are enumerated on the map. Hallowed figure though she might be in some regards, Britannia is also drawn into selling or endorsing products of the empire to her children at home or to her subjects in the colonies, frequently using maps and globes to make her case, as was done in an advertisement used by a British trading firm sometime around 1914–1915 (figure 48).[41]

But possibly the most striking example of the convergence between the

ENGLAND.

Beautiful England,—on her Island throne,—
Grandly she rules,—with half the world her own;
From her vast empire the sun ne'er departs:
She reigns a Queen—Victoria, Queen of Hearts.

FIGURE 49 *England.* Lithograph from *Geographical Fun: Being Humorous Outlines of Various Countries,* by William Harvey ("Aleph"). Vincent Brooks, Day and Son, London, 1868. (Courtesy of Library of Congress, Washington, D.C.)

cartographic and the corporeal in the visualizing of Britain and Britannia appears in a children's book called *Geographical Fun: Humorous Outlines of Various Countries* (figure 49). Published in London in 1868 as the Victorian empire was poised to expand even further, and on the eve of the world-wide scramble for territories among various European nations, the book is a series of twelve sketches, apparently drawn by a teenage girl to amuse her bedridden brother, with accompanying verses by "Aleph," a pseudonym for William Harvey (1796–1873) who was an author and popular contributor to London newspapers. The opening sketch, "England," shows Britannia-cum-Victoria clothed in a dark robe. Facing east she partly occupies a map of England, with her back resting on a castle placed in the western part of her island realm. Her hand is placed on a shield at her side, and a ship at her knee is ready to set sail. Printed below the sketch is a short poem:

Beautiful England—on her island throne,—
Grandly she rules,—with half the world her own;
From her vast empire the sun ne'er departs:
She reigns a Queen—Victoria, Queen of Hearts.

Such examples notwithstanding, it has to be said that the map of Britain (or of its global empire) does not appear as a consistent or consequential part of Britannia's visual persona as is the case, as I have argued, for the map of India and for Mother India. The same observation holds as well for other female embodiments of the nation across the modern world that, in existing scholarly analyses, show a curious lack of sustained reliance on the map form. For instance, Afsaneh Najmabadi in her fascinating work on the "matriotic" discourse that runs through Iranian nationalism from the closing decades of the nineteenth century includes a print from the 1920s of a carto-graphed Mother Iran who stands on the geo-body of Iran, drawn on a terres-trial globe, triumphantly holding the Iranian flag (2005, 130). All the same, in Iran as in nearby Egypt as the historian Beth Baron has discussed (2005, especially chapter 3), even while the emergent nation is frequently repre-sented in popular prints and visual culture as a woman (variously configured at different times as pleasant and smiling or ailing and distressed; as maiden or matron; and as traditional or modern), these works do not point to the reliance by the female embodiment on the map form of the country.

Moving back in centuries and across the continents, John Higham's analy-sis reveals the ways in which American artists sought to create a distinctive persona for Liberty so that even as she drew strength from her classical and European origins she was progressively invested with unambiguous symbols of American nationality such as the flag, the shield emblazoned with the stars and stripes, the bald eagle, and the presence of George Washington. Higham does not list the map of the nation, however, as one of the elements to which these artists turned in order to invest Liberty "with the corporeal reality of a place" (1990, 66). Similarly, in David Brading's comprehensive analysis of the development of Our Lady of Guadalupe as an enduring sym-bol over five centuries of Spanish colonialism and Mexican nationhood the map of Mexico does not appear necessary for "the nationalization" of that Virgin. Maurice Agulhon's pioneering study of the many configurations of

Marianne, imagined as the embodiment of the modern French nation from the 1790s, shows that she too did not apparently need the map of the country as a visual crutch.[42] In her analysis of Mother Ireland, Belinda Loftus makes note of Sarah Trench's Gaelic League poster of 1920 that features a carto-graphed Eire occupying a map of Ireland. Typically in her analysis, however, the feminized Ireland (variously imagined as Hibernia, the Maid of Erin, Cathleen-ni-Houlihan, and the Virgin Mary) is associated with objects such as the harp, the shamrock, or the Irish flag rather than the map of the home-land that so many were giving up their lives for in their bloody struggles with the English.[43]

THE HINDU GODDESS AND THE INDIAN NATION

Given the evidence (or lack thereof) from comparable contexts, what can be said about the specific conjuncture of historical and cultural obligations that leads artists and illustrators in late colonial and postcolonial India to use the mapped configuration of the nation as a signature feature in the visual persona created over time for Bharat Mata? What is the logic of the obliga-tion to present her as a carto-graphed personage? In order to address these questions I turn now to the hegemonic form of the Hindu goddess (devi) in whose awe-inspiring shade her artists labored, many of whom also doubled as painters of deities and divinities of the vast Hindu pantheon. Influential scholars have proposed that the political, economic, cultural, and psycho-logical dislocations and destabilizations caused by the arrival and consoli-dation of British rule in regions like Bengal resulted in a resurgence of god-dess cults and beliefs among a "matri-focal" people who viewed all physical and material reality (*prakrti*) as feminine.[44] If we follow this argument, the turn to feminizing India as a once-powerful but now vulnerable devi under duress was culturally (and psychologically) enabled by an environment in which new goddesses were emerging and old devis were being revamped as the hope for a subject population that had been effectively emasculated with the colonial conquest of the land. Bharat Mata obviously benefited from the company of these old and new goddesses alike whom she strikingly re-sembles in both the verbal and visual productions of her devotees.

Yet it was also necessary—if nationalism had to succeed and the new project of India to gain votaries of its own—to chart a different course for

Bharat Mata so as to distinguish her from these other goddesses even while relying on their influence and powers. And this is where significantly but ironically the mapped image of the country—that proud outcome of the imperial science of cartography—is useful, for it enables the visual transformation of the generic devi into the nation's goddess. The political theorist Sudipta Kaviraj observes that there is "something similar but fundamentally different" about Bharat Mata (1995 140). The historian Sabyasachi Bhattacharya similarly notes that in the figure of Bharat Mata we see traces of something that belonged to the past but also is a revelation of something new (2003, 93). However, neither of these scholars explicitly identifies what is "different" or "new" about Mother India. I suggest that it is the arrival and consolidation of a novel modality of conceptualizing the country as a delimited and named geo-body that is also imagined as the collective property of its citizen-inhabitants. Maps of the nation that proliferate across the modern world in the age of nationalism, India included, enable the nation's citizens to take visual and conceptual possession of the land that they imagine they inhabit as a collectivity, so that the visualized geo-body is "their" country that belongs to them and to which they in turn belong. Bharat Mata is no generic earth, warrior, or mother goddess (although she is also all of these); instead she is a very specific kind of territorial deity, one who embodies and presides over a delimited, nameable, identifiable geo-body. The incorporation into her pictorial persona of the map of the nation (as well as the flag that comes to be increasingly associated with her realm) signals a novel way of relating to land—as a measured geo-body rendered visible at one glance to the citizen-devotee's eye through (command and barefoot) cartographic practices. The map of India also distinguishes her and sets her apart from other goddesses on whom she is modeled and whose powers and potencies she mobilizes in order to convert land into motherland. It is at the cusp of the "same but different" and the "old but also new" that we can identify the forces and pressures inducing the (re)conceptualization of India as a cartographed Mother India. And it is an analysis of her many pictures, rather than the hundreds of thousands of words as well that have accrued around her, that really enables us to grasp this sense of same but different—her fundamental unorthodoxy.

Who are some of these devis with whom Bharat Mata could be confused, especially visually, but yet not readily conflated? First, there are those goddesses most clearly associated with earth, land, and soil, among the most ancient of whom is Prithvi ("the Extended"), who is also known, especially in southern India, as Bhu Devi or Bhumi Devi ("Earth Goddess-Queen") (Kinsley 1987, 8–9, 178–81). In a print published in Madras that bears the date 1953 (figure 50), M. Ramaiah presents Prithvi in a manner that is at significant odds with the dominant manner in which she has been visualized in monumental art, votive images, and manuscript illuminations from the middle centuries of the first millennium CE. In such works she is generally shown as a demure, two-armed, seated female figure in the company of her lord and master Vishnu, who frequently dwarfs her by the sheer size of his massive (and virile) presence. Indeed, in the monumental sculptures created to commemorate the primeval rescuing of Earth from the clutches of a demon by Vishnu in his incarnation (*avatara*) as the boar Varaha—possibly the most important context in which Prithvi appears visually—she is generally shown clinging to him, a diminutive figure entirely dependent on his strength and will (figure 51).[45] In Ramaiah's print, on the other hand, we see an autonomous standing goddess with four arms, looking directly at her viewer. She carries insignia associated with Vishnu himself, the conch and the discus. Most critically, her body looms over a partially visible gridded globe that she appears to be blessing, centered on the partly delineated geo-body of India.

Ramaiah's artwork brings together two incommensurable imaginations relating to Earth—the anthropomorphic-sacred and the scientific-geographic—within the frame of the poster revealingly titled in English as *Bhoodevi*. In this picture, however, Bhu Devi is not just the goddess Earth but also the geo-body of India, left unnamed but quite obvious from the partial outline of its mapped form with the island of Sri Lanka off its southeastern tip. If the figure had not been named as such, Ramaiah's carto-graphed Bhoodevi could well have been confused by the devoted (cartographically minded) viewer—and by others—with Mother India herself, a confusion that the artist might have intended in order for the novel goddess of territory to benefit from the powers that over three thousand years had accrued to the ancient goddess of earth. In fact, almost fifty years before the creation of this poster an illustration published in 1908 in Bharati's *Intiya* unequivocally hails Bhu Devi as Bharat Mata.[46] Around the same time, a confidential colonial report

FIGURE 50 LEFT M. Ramaiah, *Bhoodevi* (Goddess Earth). Printed by R. Ethirajiah and Sons, Madras, 1953. (Author's collection)

FIGURE 51 RIGHT Vishnu as the boar-god Varaha rescuing the earth goddess Prithvi. Sandstone standing figure, Eran, Madhya Pradesh, circa sixth century CE. (Photograph courtesy American Institute of Indian Studies, Gurgaon, Accession No. 6768)

also comments as much when in the small north Indian town of Meerut, tableaux (*chauki*) of Bharat Mata were cleverly interjected into religious processions featuring the major Hindu god Rama and his wife Sita. As the report notes: "With regard to Meerut a chauki of Bharat Mata is shown there along with the procession of Rama's marriage. Pandit Nand Kishore, who recites verses from the Ramayana and who conducts the performances of the Ramlila, stated that a chauki of Prithvi Mata [Mother Earth] is shown in the above procession along with those of other gods . . . Prithvi Mata is exhibited as being the mother of Sita. . . . *The educated classes probably call it or will call it Bharat Mata, whatever it may be called by the pandits*." The colonial police in particular took note of such "undesirable forms of novelty," since they "are calculated to excite resentment against the British Government." [47]

Some of Hinduism's most ancient ritual texts from as early as the middle of the second millennium BCE are filled with expressions of the awe in which

Earth is perceived and praised for its stability, its fecundity, and its life-sustaining capacity. The anthropomorphization of Earth as sentient female and as Prithvi is also as old as Hinduism (although not unique to it, as we know from scholarly work on other parts of the world). Her marital association with male gods is also confirmed by these early texts, as it is apparent from some later accounts that accumulate around her in the sacred Sanskrit Puranas from the early decades of the first millennium CE in which she is rescued from the clutches of a wicked demon by Vishnu, who subsequently marries her (in some versions of the legend). Not surprisingly, Prithvi is useful for mortal sovereigns as well who, as gods on earth, claimed her as their symbolic consort through the privilege of acting as her protector. A royal stone inscription from the middle of the first millennium CE even likens specific features of her body to topographic elements from the monarch's domain: her "marriage-string is the verge of the four oceans, [her] large breasts are (the mountains) Sumeru and Kailasa; [and her] laughter is the full-blown flowers showered forth from the borders of the woods."[48]

Some scholars have drawn upon such evidence to suggest a seamless transition from Prithvi to Bharat Mata. The historian of art Vidya Dehejia thus writes, "Since the land itself is spoken of in Sanskrit as Prithvi or goddess earth, it is perhaps not surprising that kingdoms, cities, districts, and boroughs are gendered feminine. India is Bharat Mata or Mother India" (1997, 14–15). The historian of religion David Kinsley similarly posits that "the fundamental conviction that the earth itself, or the Indian subcontinent itself, is a goddess, indeed, that she is one's mother, pervades the modern cult of Bharat Mata (Mother India)" (1987, 181).[49] While the imagination of Earth and its constitutive elements as sacred, feminine, and maternal undoubtedly fuels the persona of Bharat Mata, there are critical differences between the two goddesses including the fact that Mother India appears to have no known consort at all and that Prithvi appears in most of her visual representations as a deferential appendage to a more powerful lord rather than an autonomous deity in her own right. But most saliently, Mother India is imagined as the embodiment of a specifically delineated piece of territory rather than the entire Earth personified. This is a fundamental shift that is reflective of a new patriotic fact: Prithvi as a sentient female divinity has to make room for another mother/goddess who looms large(r) as the hallowed embodiment of one's own country. In fact, I would even venture that not-withstanding Ramaiah's *Bhoodevi*—and it *is* a rather singular image—Prithvi recedes into the background in the patriotic Indian imagination with the arrival of Bharat Mata on the scene.[50]

Another Hindu goddess who helps consolidate the new imagination of India as a deity is Sati, "the virtuous one" (Kinsley 1987, 35–41). As the story goes in the sacred Puranas, Sati, the wife of the fierce lord Shiva, immolates herself to avenge her husband who is slighted by her father. Learning of her death, Shiva arrives at the gory scene: "He picks up her body and, racked with grief, begins to wander the cosmos. He is so distraught by Sati's death and so grieved by the presence of her corpse that he completely ignores his divine responsibilities. His sobbing and grief threaten the stability of the world. Vishnu is called upon to remedy the situation. He enters Sati's body by yoga, or else slices pieces of her body off bit by bit, but in one way or another he disposes of her body a bit at a time. Where the parts of Sati's body fell, sacred places called *pitha*s [literally, altar or seat] were then established"(1987, 186).[51] For the history I narrate here the importance of this gruesome tale of female self-immolation and dismemberment is in David Kinsley's interpretation as follows: "According to this myth, then, the Indian subcontinent has been sacralized by the remains of Sati. India is in effect her burial ground. The subcontinent is sown with the pieces of Sati's body, which make the land especially sacred . . . Each *pitha* represents a part of Sati's body or one of her ornaments; taken together, the *pitha*s found throughout India constitute or point toward a transcendent (or, perhaps better, a universally immanent) goddess whose being encompasses, underlies, and unifies the Indian sub-continent as a whole. In short, the Indian subcontinent *is* the goddess Sati" (1987, 187).[52]

Fast forward to the middle of the nineteenth century, and to the fertile imagination of Bhudev Mukhopadhyay (1827–1894), the Bengali litterateur, thinker, and protonationalist. As Bhudev tells his readers: "When I was a student of Hindu College [in Calcutta], a European teacher told [us] that patriotism was unknown to the Hindus, for no Indian language had any word to express the idea. I believed his word and was deeply distressed by the thought. I knew then . . . the mythical account of . . . Sati's death, but that knowledge did not help me refute the teacher's statement or console myself. *Now I know*

that to the descendants of the Aryans the entire motherland [matribhumi]
with its fifty-two places of pilgrimage is in truth the person of the Deity."[53] In
the face of a powerful official-colonial disavowal of the sacred knowledges
of his "motherland," Bhudev took refuge in an old myth and charged it with
new meaning, as the historian Tapan Raychaudhuri has noted. In his subsequent writings Bhudev went on to name the deity that is the motherland, or
matribhumi, as Adibharati (literally, First India), and he narrated her many
sufferings under the "alien" rule of the British. I have found no pictorial representation of Adibharati, but in Bhudev's literary imagination the Puranic
once again comes to the service of the patriotic, and ancient myths are recycled to sustain the new mother/goddess of territory (Raychaudhuri 1988,
26–102).

As we know, there is no seamless recuperation of the archaic into modernity, and as the sacred-sectarian landscape is transformed into secular-
national territory, the territory retains, like a palimpsest, traces of the
mythic, the vestigial, and the redundant. For a striking exemplar of a pictorial
palimpsest that discloses the Puranic layered into the patriotic, I turn to an
untitled painting by M. F. Husain dated to around 1976, which has the word
Parvati inscribed on the back of the canvas in another hand (figure 52).[54] As
an evocative precursor to his *Bharat Mata* of 2005 (figure 3), the painting
shows an unclad female form with three arms. Her body and hair suggestively approximate what is quite identifiable as the outline map of India, the
tall snowcapped mountains to the north a riot of glorious colors. This is
further confirmed by the visual fact that sprinkled across this bodyscape in
the official Devanagari script are the first initials of the names of individual
states that constitute the modern republic. Finally, the official Indian flag
that appears at the bottom left of the picture rounds off the visual program.

Much can be said about this complex painting, but here I limit myself to
the association established between the female form and the Indian geo-body,
however spare they might both appear on the canvas. On the one hand, if we
assume that the painting is a portrait of Parvati then it is suggestive because
she is deemed to be a manifestation of Sati in her incarnation as Shiva's second spouse and her mythology is, as Kinsley notes, "almost always treated as
the ongoing story of Sati" (1987, 35). In Husain's transformative recuperation,
the Puranic once again comes to the aid of the patriotic, as the *sakta pitha*s

FIGURE 52 Maqbool Fida Husain, Untitled, [inscribed with the name Parvati on reverse in another hand]. Oil on canvas, circa 1976. (The Chester and David Herwitz Collection, Peabody Essex Museum, Salem, Massachusetts, E301023)

(power places) of the Hindu *Bharatavarsha* morph into the secular states of the Indian republic. This recuperation is particularly noteworthy given that the work is by an artist who consciously presents himself as both secular and Muslim. On the other hand, an equally interesting possibility is that this untitled painting could be of Bharat Mata herself. The presence of the official flag as well as the map of the republic point to this, and three-quarters of a century of barefoot cartographic practice has laid the pictorial groundwork for it. In either case I contend that such a visualization is triggered by the stirring up of a sedimented memory of the land now named "India" as having been formerly constituted through a primeval act of dismemberment of a divine female body, and its subsequent re-aggregation through devotional practice. Such a subterranean memory may no longer be active or conscious in the imaginations of disenchanted secular Indians, but Husain's civilizational obligation surfaces it, and brings it into alignment with a modern

FIGURE 53 Nirmala, The goddess Durga. Printed by Jothi, acquired circa 1995. (Courtesy of J. P. S. and Patricia Uberoi, Delhi)

cartographic imagination of the national territory as geo-body. In doing so, he clears a space to accommodate the memory of an archaic dismembered woman, so that even as the sacred-sectarian landscape of a Puranic past gives way to the secular-national territory of the modern present, she returns to exuberantly—if nakedly—lay claim to "her" geo-body.

In some readings, Parvati/Sati is the docile and domesticated manifestation or version of Durga, the paradigmatic warrior goddess of the Hindu pantheon, and undoubtedly the most important source of inspiration for Mother India. Prior to her taming through marriage and motherhood Durga is a three-eyed, multi-armed, and multiply armed goddess wielding weapons of all sorts. Resolutely unattached to any male, she rides a fierce lion, is invariably victorious in battle, and is a fearless slayer of all manner of evil forces (figure 53). Created out of the body parts of the most powerful male gods

Durga achieves what they are not able to accomplish—slaying the demons that threaten the very order of existence in the universe. That she is able to do so solely with the help of female helpers (such as the fierce, blood-thirsty Kali whom she creates herself, out of herself) shows that in a dominant strand of Hindu belief the divine female is endowed with more power and potency than the male in vanquishing evil. Durga is in fact the paradigmatic Hindu goddess of "power, blood, and battle" (Kinsley 1987, 96). As such, she has to be appeased by periodic offerings of blood, the drinking of which restores her powers and potency.

As David Kinsley notes, "In many respects Durga violates the model of the Hindu woman. She is not submissive, she is not subordinated to a male deity, she does not fulfill household duties, and she excels at what is traditionally a male function, fighting in battle. As an independent warrior who can hold her own against any male in the battle field, she reverses the normal role for females and therefore stands outside normal society" (1987, 97). She would thus seem like a surprising prototype for what was after all fundamentally the bourgeois project of Indian nationalism dominated by men and meant to consolidate male privilege and powers. And yet she has been repeatedly invoked from the early days of Mother India's tenure as mother of the new nation, as in the foundational poem "Vande Mataram," by Bankim Chandra Chatterji (1838–1894) from around 1875: "Thou art Durga holding her ten weapons of war." Other examples include Subramania Bharati who wrote many verses in Tamil sprinkled with allusions to Bharat Mata as Bhawani, Vijaya, and Durga; as well as Bipin Chandra Pal (1858–1932) who in his *The Soul of India* observed that "hundreds of thousands of our people have commenced to hail their motherland today as Durga, Kalee, Jagaddhatree. These are no longer mere mythological conceptions or legendary persons or even poetic symbols. They are different manifestations of the Mother. This Mother is the Spirit of India" (1911, 187).

Durga's enduring influence on this novel goddess of territory is also apparent from the earliest surviving printed images of Bharat Mata, especially those that were produced and circulated among expatriate patriots—the work of artists who might not even have been nominally Hindu (figures 15 and 16). Indeed in many prints, if it were not for the outline map of India or the tricolor flag, Mother India would appear identical to Durga, especially in those pictures in which she is associated with the lion or holds a drawn sword.

Using Durga as a prototype was indeed enormously useful for many of Bharat Mata's votaries, for they were able to draw upon her association with battle and victory to empower their own new goddess as a warrior deity capable of going into war herself, if need be, and achieving success. Prior to penning his influential poem around 1875, Bankim had already established an analogy between the new goddess and her more well-established antecedent in another work in 1873–1874 in which its protagonist, in an opium-induced vision, breaks into a soliloquy: "Was this my Mother? Yes, it was she! I knew her for my mother, the land of my birth (*janmabhumi*), made of earth, in the form of clay, adorned with endless gems, now hidden in the womb of time. Her ten bejeweled arms—the ten points of the compass—stretched in these directions. They were adorned with various powers in the form of different weapons, the enemy crushed at her feet, the most valiant of lions taking refuge there, destroying the foe! I shan't behold this form now . . . But one day I shall—her arms the directions, wielding her various weapons, subduing the enemy, and roaming on a lordly lion's back . . . I saw in the midst of that stream of time this golden image of Bengal!"[55]

The verbal archive shows that Bharat Mata's devotees, especially in the colonial period, did not hesitate to present her to their fellow citizens as a mother under duress and a vulnerable woman who needed their care and attention. All the same, however, they had to ensure that this did not lead her to be perceived as weak and meek, especially at a time when the colonial state itself was trying to convince its subjects of their essential passivity, lack of courage, and incapacity for self-rule. Here as well, Durga's fierce and autonomous persona was useful, as her votaries sought to fashion Mother India into a woman of substance. And colonial officials were without a doubt roused to attention, notably in their concern over her fierce and combative persona as it was revealed to them during the swadeshi protests of the early years of the twentieth century or in expatriate activities and visual imagery. Indeed, their concern was such that many of them refused to acknowledge Mother India as a new goddess of national aspirations and insisted instead that she was none other than Kali, "the goddess of death and destruction"—

a "terrible goddess" whose worship appealed to "the grossest and the most cruel superstition of the masses."[56]

The "terrible goddess" Kali who made British administrators and writers like George Grierson, James Ker, and Valentine Chirol so anxious is a relative latecomer (at least in her full-blown form) to the diverse Hindu pantheon. In the foundational Sanskrit narrative the *Devi Mahatmya* (Glory of the goddess; circa sixth century CE), which is dedicated to praising the devi's creative and destructive powers, Kali "the black one" is a terrifying creature created from Durga's darkened brow in order to slay demons who threaten heaven itself. Over time as she grows in popularity within the Hindu-Indic tradition she becomes independent of her creator, and as she does she becomes even fiercer with a gaunt face, bloodshot eyes, pendulous breasts, and unbound hair. Often naked, she is adorned with a garland of skulls and a girdle of severed human arms. A lolling blood-red tongue hangs from her mouth as she roars into battle, slaying demons with her bare hands and drinking their blood. Her habits complement her appearance: she hangs out in cremation grounds and battlefields, and her favorite companion is often a ghost. As Kinsley notes, she is quintessentially the "goddess who threatens stability and order . . . She herself begins to destroy the world that she is supposed to protect . . . Even in the service of gods, she is ultimately dangerous and tends to get out of control. In association with other goddesses, she appears to represent their embodied wrath and fury, a frightening, dangerous dimension of the divine feminine that is released when these goddesses become enraged or are summoned to take part in war and killing" (1987, 120). She is indeed Durga run amuck in her thirst for blood, including that of humans.

Not surprisingly, from early in the colonial period the wild Kali became the morbid focus of British fascination, fear, and wrath, as is most strikingly exemplified by the state's attempts in the 1830s to rid the new colony of the infamous Thugees with their allegedly twin penchant for highway robbery and human sacrifice seemingly in devotion to her. But the colonial masters were never certain that this uncivil goddess had truly been banished from an India ostensibly embarked on the road to European-style civilization and modernity. And they were not really off their mark in such suspicions, for when the first poems and plays about the goddess who would eventually be identified as Mother India were composed in the 1860s and 1870s in Bengal it was the fierce Kali (who in the previous century had morphed into a merciful and compassionate mother in the Hindu imagination of that part of the subcontinent) who provided a model for her.[57] In Bankim Chandra's novel of 1881–1882 *Anandamath*, which chartered the proliferation of the mother/goddess in the next century, an explicit (albeit ambivalent) analogy is established between her and Kali, who is "covered by darkness, of a black color. She has been robbed of everything, that is why she is nude. Today, the whole country is a graveyard, that is why our Mother has a garland of bones, dead skulls. She is trampling her own welfare under her feet."[58]

In the beginning of the twentieth century when secret associations with violent anticolonial motivations and agendas mushroomed in many parts of India, the colonial state discovered that their members were indeed devotees of, in the words of H. L. Salked, "Kali-Adya Sakti, primordial energy—a manifestation of Durga, for the purpose of destroying the demons . . . The demons of oppression are, *of course*, the English, and naturally Kali is the favorite deity of the revolutionist who takes his vows before her image."[59] At least one patriotic worshipper of the goddess around 1906 confirmed this colonial suspicion: "The Mother asks for sacrificial offerings. What does the Mother want? The coconut? No . . . sheep or buffalo? No . . . She is thirsting after the blood of the Feringhees [Europeans] who have bled her . . . Slaying the Feringhee white goat . . . is not murder . . . for behold! Kali rises in the East."[60]

Predictably the colonial police were convinced that the ferocious blood-sucking goddess had switched her attention from some cosmic demon of the universe to white folks in India, so they turned to the bazaar where they seemingly found all manner of visual evidence to fuel their anxieties. The frontispiece to James Ker's widely read report from 1917 on the numerous anticolonial activities of the early nationalist century featured one such lithograph printed in Calcutta possibly around this time (figure 54).[61] The image shows a naked blue-grey Kali sticking out her bloodied tongue and wearing a garland of severed male heads. She holds a blood-stained scimitar in one hand, and a severed head in another, while she stands over the supine pale body of Siva laid out on a lotus. James Ker was a member of the influential Indian Civil Service and a personal assistant to the director of Criminal

KALI

Published by K. P. HAZRA.
92, Rajballav Saha Lane,
Howrah.

THE BENGAL ART GALLERY,
191, Maniktola Street, Calcutta.

FIGURE 54 Naren, *Kali*. Chromolithograph published by K. P. Hazra, Howrah, early twentieth century. (© British Library Board, T21493)

Intelligence from 1907 to 1913. His report is sprinkled with allusions to the wrath of Kali, whom he held directly responsible for inciting Indians to kill the British fueled by his belief that "the destruction of the demons is a regular metaphor in Indian revolutionary literature, the gods being the people of India and the demons the English" (1917, 50–51). So he insisted that "the Muzaffarpore bomb outrage," which claimed the lives of two Englishwomen on April 30, 1908, was "the first revolutionary sacrifice to the goddess Kali" (136) since it had been enacted on the night of a new moon, which was deemed by nationalists such as Bipin Chandra Pal to be the most auspicious time to appease the goddess.[62]

Given such views it is to be expected that Ker's report included not just Naren's *Kali* but also another image, titled *Rashtriya Jagruti* (National awakening), which was printed around 1909 by Sridhar Waman Nagarkar of the central Indian town of Nasik and subsequently proscribed. Ker was alarmed enough about the latter picture to include a detailed description of it based on a report prepared by Sir Charles Cleveland, who was charged with investigating seditious organizations in the Central Provinces. In this picture the goddess Devi, charged with killing the demon Mahisasura in Hindu mythology, is reincarnated as the multi-armed Rashtriya Jagruti. Ker interprets the picture for his colonial bosses in the following manner: "Her lion or tiger is labeled 'Bahiskar' (Boycott) and is attacking the bovine monster labeled 'Pardeshi Vyapar' (Foreign Trade), on whose back the goddess has placed her foot after, apparently, cutting off its head. The demon near the severed head of the monster is labeled 'Vilayati Mal' (English Goods) and is being bitten in the arm by a snake called 'Swabhiman' (Pride of Self), which is held in one of the hands of the heroine, while the same demon's head has been injured by the knife labeled 'Svavalamban' (Self-Independence). The demon being held by the hair [by the goddess] is labeled 'Desha Droha' (Disloyalty to Country) . . . the hand which holds his hair is labeled 'Desh Seva' (Service of Country)" (1917, 384).[63] Not surprisingly, such "seditious" pictures hastened the passage of the Press Act of 1910 that armed the colonial state with the power to proscribe such "mischievous" harbingers of the fall of the Raj.[64]

THE FAMILY ROMANCE OF INDIAN NATIONALISM

Powerful, independent-minded goddesses such as Durga and Kali with their demonstrable capacity to kill and destroy were not just a problem for the colonial state but also for a modernizing Hindu elite leadership for whom their more ferocious and uncontrollable proclivities were a potential embarrassment in a social climate increasingly governed by norms of bourgeois respectability and sexual propriety. Their autonomy was glaringly at odds with the normative expectation that females were to be always under the control of their male kin, and their husbandless status was a direct contradiction to the state of heterosexual matrimony to which women were unconditionally bound. Further, their penchant for battle, blood, and unruly behavior was a bad role model for the modest new woman who was the custodian of the Hindu-Indian home's morals and manners. And yet these goddesses were also shakti incarnate and thus venerable repositories of the power and potency that the patriot needed for his new goddess of territory who also had to be potent and powerful but not necessarily independent of the control of those who knew her best—her devoted sons. In trying to harness the potency embodied by these goddesses while at the same time containing their obvious capacity to cause havoc and death (which very much lingers on, as in a palimpsest) as they fashioned Mother India, these men were aided by the new ideology of bourgeois motherhood that was beginning to take shape in late colonial India. This ideology enabled the subordination of the fierce and bloodthirsty warrior female to the nurturing and compassionate mother.[65]

Over the course of the nineteenth century, as many scholars have demonstrated, the "woman question" loomed large in the consciousness of the newly westernizing and middle-class (Hindu) elite men. At first centered in the colonial metropolises of Calcutta, Bombay, and Madras they sought to counter the British censure of Indian culture and tradition by "reforming" and "improving" their women and transforming them into virtuous, educated companions. In the closing years of the nineteenth century, this reforming zeal yielded to a new patriarchy as the nation came to be valorized as a "home" and "family" whose well-being could be guaranteed by the figure of the educated mother who raised her children into productive citizens. The woman as wife or conjugal mate yielded to the woman as mother or nurturer and caregiver. In such imaginative labors, while the home is under the custodianship of the woman as mother, the nation as home is presided over by her archetype, Mother India. The Tamil poet and journalist Subramania Bharati captures the convergence of the woman in her guise as mother, and India as Bharat Mata, in an essay, "The Place of Woman," written in the opening years of the new century: "Nor is it without significance that the country of spiritual liberation, India, should, at this hour of her mighty awakening, have adopted as her most potent spell, the words 'Vande mataram,' i.e., 'I salute the Mother.' That means that the first work of a regenerated India will be to place the Mother, i.e., womankind, on the pedestal of spiritual superiority. Others speak of their Fatherland. To us, the Nation is represented by the word 'Mata' [mother]."[66]

Around the same time Bharati's sometime mentor, the fiery Bengali orator Bipin Chandra Pal, also cloaked national territory in the mantle of (bourgeois) maternality in a book called *Soul of India* published in 1911: "Is not the land we live in as much a symbol of the Divine Motherhood even as our own mothers or the mothers of our children are? We are born unto this land. It received us into its bosom even as our human mothers do. It supports our life with its own substance even as the nursing mother supports the growing life of her own baby. This land is literally the mother of our physical existence. It is indeed the physical body of the soul of our land and nation . . . In every way, we are nourished by, dependent upon, draw the strength and inspiration of our physical and mental life from, this complex Being, at once physical and spiritual, geographical and social, we call and tenderly worship as Mother in our motherland" (1911, 191–92). In the literary and folk traditions that Bharati and Pal inherited and were familiar with, mothers are nourishing as well as destructive, compassionate as well as malevolent, and benign as well as sexually threatening. Yet their Motherland is dominantly tender, pacific, and asexual. The virginal or autonomous mother/goddess frequently displays vengeful, punitive behaviors in the many accounts of such deities, both in scriptural Hinduism as well as in its many folk variants across the subcontinent. Although the palimpsestic figure of Mother India retains traces of the ferocious warrior and vengeful combatant, especially during the heady days of the swadeshi movement in the early years of the twentieth century, she is largely shaped, especially in her verbal accounts but also to some extent in her pictures, in the image of the "new" woman of the Indian home. As such she is a domestic paragon who is modest, chaste, virtuous, largely passive and content with arming her sons to do battle on her behalf rather than forging into the fray on her own, as is the wont of her divine prototypes Durga and Kali.

In the second decade of the new century one of India's foremost creative writers, Rabindranath Tagore (1861–1941), wrote a controversial novel in Bengali translated into English as *The Home and the World*. In the novel one of the protagonists—the very antithesis of Tagore in his political aspirations—declares passionately that "true patriotism will never be roused in our countrymen unless they can visualize the motherland [*desh*] . . . We must get one of the current images [*pratima*] accepted as representing the country [*swadesh*]—the worship [*puja*] of the people must flow towards it along the deep-cut grooves of custom" (2005, 120–21).[67] Two decades later Jawaharlal Nehru (1889–1964), a socialist by inclination who went on to become the independent nation's first prime minister, wondered as well about what Tagore referred to once as "the idolatry of geography": "It is curious how one cannot resist the tendency to give an anthropomorphic form to a country. Such is the force of habit and early associations. India becomes *Bharat Mata*, Mother India" (Nehru 1980, 431).[68] The force of such habits and associations meant that the scientific-geographic visualization of its territory as a measured geo-body laid out on a mathematically determined grid did not have easy passage into late colonial and postcolonial India, even as the consolidation of the new science put pressure on a prior imagination of land—itself also revamped for all the reasons discussed in this chapter—as sacred, female, and maternal. The result is the divinization and feminization of the mapped configuration of country, even as the mother/goddess herself gets carto-graphed. Bipin Chandra Pal put into words what many of the pictures that I have discussed in this book so far have already shown us: "The outsider knows her as India. The outsider sees only her outer and lifeless physical frame. The outsider sees her as a mere bit of earth, and looks upon her as only a geographical expression and entity. But we, her children, know her even today as our fathers and their fathers had done before, for countless generations, as a Being, as a Manifestation of Prakriti, as our Mother and the Mother of our Race. And we have always, and do still worship her as such" (1911, 188–89).

VANDE MATARAM

3

Toward the end of the nineteenth century Bharat Mata secured her own signature hymn. The title of the song, "Vande
Mataram" (I worship the mother), is based on the words of its
opening refrain.[1] As one of the new republic's unifying symbols the hymn was formally installed on January 26, 1950, as
independent India's national song.[2] Relative to the controversy
that would eventually surround it, the hymn had a rather innocuous beginning. Its first two key verses were possibly composed (in Sanskrit and Sanskritic Bengali) sometime around
1875, but apparently the material lay abandoned in the study
of its creator, Bankim Chandra Chatterji, because he did not
deem it suitable for public consumption.[3] In 1881–1882, supplemented by a few more verses that aligned it more closely
with hymns to goddesses such as Durga, Lakshmi, and Saraswati, it was incorporated as a poem into Chatterji's novel *Anandamath* (*The Abbey of Bliss*, in its first translation).[4] The novel
narrates the story of a band of selfless warrior-ascetics who appear in its pages as devotee-children (*santan*) of an unspeci-

fied motherland. The poem "Vande Mataram" serves as their battle hymn; its opening refrain is their salutation and rallying cry, their mantra. Its subsequent popularity was further assured when the poem was transformed into song, possibly around 1894, by none other than one of Bengal's (and India's) most revered figures, Rabindranath Tagore, whose own life intersects in fascinating ways both with the poem's complex life and with that of the country's future national anthem.[5] Tagore also sang it, possibly for the first time in a patriotic-public context, at the opening session of the Indian National Congress's annual meeting in Calcutta in 1896, and until the late 1930s that party's gatherings—and other nationalist conclaves—inevitably opened with the singing of the hymn.[6] "Vande Mataram" catapulted to national prominence with the announcement of the proposed territorial partitioning of Bengal in July 1905 when the colonial state's action was met with a fierce patriotic resistance that found solidarity in the singing of the hymn and in the invoking of its opening refrain. This is also possibly the first moment when the state directly confronted Bharat Mata, as the very invocation of the words "vande mataram," led to punitive action and arrests. It is worth noting that a territorial—and cartographic—act such as the partition of land received a populist response that was couched in the idiom of the anthropomorphic-sacred.

By this time the song had already moved out of Bengal into other regions of India in whose many languages it began to be translated from around 1897. One of the most notable of such efforts was Subramania Bharati's Tamil rendering in November 1905, and he subsequently went on to compose other poems featuring the words "vande mataram," as did other poets in other languages across the subcontinent. An early English rendering of the poem appeared in November 1909 when the fiery Bankim votary Aurobindo Ghose offered the following "translation in prose":

I bow to thee, Mother,
richly-watered, richly-fruited,
cool with the winds of the south,
dark with the crops of the harvests,
the Mother!
Her nights rejoicing in the glory of the moonlight,

her lands clothed beautifully with her trees in flowering bloom,
sweet of laughter, sweet of speech,
the Mother, giver of boons, giver of bliss!

Terrible with the clamorous shout of seventy million throats,
and the sharpness of swords raised in twice seventy million hands,
Who sayeth to thee, Mother, that thou art weak?
Holder of multitudinous strength,
I bow to her who saves,
to her who drives from her the armies of her foemen,
the Mother!

Thou art knowledge, thou art conduct,
thou our heart, thou our soul,
for thou art the life in our body,
In the arm though art might, O Mother,
in the heart, O Mother, thou art love and faith,
it is thy image we raise in every temple.

For thou art Durga holding her ten weapons of war,
Kamala at play in the lotuses
and Speech, the goddess, giver of all lore,
to thee I bow!
I bow to thee, goddess of wealth,
pure and peerless,
richly-watered, richly-fruited,
the Mother!
I bow to thee, Mother,
dark-hued, candid,
sweetly-smiling, jewelled and adorned,
the holder of wealth, the lady of plenty,
the Mother![7]

The mother's song also provided the martyr's slogan from the opening years of the twentieth century in the gathering storm unleashed by the swadeshi movement. Khudiram Bose (1889–1908), a young man who was hanged for attempting to assassinate a British magistrate (and instead killed two English women) in the eastern Indian town of Muzzafurpur, began his dying statement in Bengali with the words "vande mataram" (Samanta 1995, 5: 1384–87). Across the world in London, Madanlal Dhingra (b. 1887), an engineering student studying in the empire's capital, was hanged for the assassination of a British official in 1909; his last words reputedly were "vande mataram."[8] By this time "Vande Mataram" was also slowly gathering visibility, literally and otherwise, outside the territorial confines of British India. Its opening words were invoked in the activities, letters, and publications of expatriate nationalists settled abroad, including in the work of Bhikhaiji Cama, whom I discuss in chapter 6. Back in India, the words "vande mataram" had acquired such ferocious density—invoked by young students in schools and protest processions, by middle-class women flexing their patriotic muscles for the first time, and by aging nationalists increasingly taking an "extremist" turn in their anti-imperial agitations—that colonial authorities in East Bengal were compelled to ban its public invocation in Dacca in November 1905, an interdiction that only seemed to enhance its potency.[9] "Vande Mataram" might well be the leading candidate for a song that has been indubitably catalytic to a patriotic cause in the modern world. Indeed, it might not be an exaggeration to say that it literally brought a nation into being, such has been its reach to this day.

PICTURING THE MOTHER'S HYMN

Much has been written on the history and politics of "Vande Mataram." Few scholars, however, have attempted to relate it to the patriotic picture worlds of late colonial and postcolonial India, although it was in an illustration to accompany the poem in 1885 that Bharat Mata was possibly visualized in print for the first time in Bengal (see figure 10).[10] A pictorial history of the hymn provides some surprising yields that are not necessarily produced by routine textual analyses. For instance, consider a cinematic work by the prolific artist M. L. Sharma that was published sometime after 1947 (figure 55). It shows a youthful, muscular woman wearing an ornamental bodice that shows off her slim form. With her hair flying against the background of a large halo (or the rising sun) she rides a chariot pulled by two fierce lions. Within the circumference of the halo the newly authorized national flag flies above her. In turn, this entire ensemble is placed atop a purple half-globe

FIGURE 55

M. L. Sharma, *Bharat Mata Vande Mataram*. Printed by J.H.C., circa 1947–1952. (Courtesy of the Twin Studio Archive; © The Singh Twins, www .singhtwins.co.uk)

on which the Indian geo-body appears in a suggestive flourish. Across it the words "vande mataram" are inscribed in the Devanagari script. With the stroke of a pen and brush the mapped form of India, the mathematized outcome of scientific cartography, is adjoined to the realm of the anthropomorphic, the maternal, and possibly the worshipful. At the same time, the same strokes place the words in a cartographic context, although Bankim's "Vande Mataram" does not present land as geo-body. Pictures such as this remind us of the convergence of the scientific-geographic and the anthropomorphic-sacred—and their mutual supplementation—in the patriotic visual imagination of national territory in twentieth-century India.

The visual deployment of the refrain "vande mataram" discloses as well the undercurrent of Hindu sentiments and sensibilities, even Hindu nationalism, that has dogged the mother's hymn almost from the start. Pictures from early in the twentieth century such as Subramania Bharati's *Bharata*

Mata (figure 8), or more recent efforts such as that by Appu (figure 31), visibly show the yoking of the slogan to the Hindu form of Mother India, with verbal assurances by India's pluralistic nationalists to the contrary. In Appu's picture, for example, the twin words (in Devanagari script) are boldly painted across her body adorned in the colors of the official secular Indian flag, even as she adopts a guise and pose that an Indian viewer would inevitably associate with a Hindu goddess. Indeed, although the invocation "vande mataram" might hail a generic mother and one not necessarily associated with any particular religious community, as many apologists for the hymn insist, the field of associative meanings it has gathered over time consistently connects it with a Sanskritic Aryan Hindu life-world—associations that patriotic pictures only further visually consolidate in their presentation of Bharat Mata as a multi-armed and haloed mother/goddess.

Moving beyond the usual arguments about the song's idolatrous content and context that offends India's Muslim citizens, I intend to reflect here upon what the pictorial life of "Vande Mataram" tells us about the complex entanglement of the anthropomorphic-sacred and the scientific-geographic in the visual patriotism of late colonial and postcolonial India. To anticipate the principal argument of this chapter, I suggest that a pictorial history of "Vande Mataram" discloses the indispensability but inadequacy of the anthropomorphic-sacred form of Indian national territory as mother/goddess. Although the hymn is not cartographic in its celebration of mataram, as is apparent from even Aurobindo's rather stilted translation, a pictorial analysis of "Vande Mataram" discloses that the outline map of India is clearly desirable for her visualization, for, as I noted in chapter 2, the emergent nation cannot be just a mother/goddess but also is necessarily a geo-body defined by the calculations and contours of scientific cartography.

In turn this analysis might also help us understand why, as India moved toward independent statehood, a song celebrating the nation-space as fecund mother/goddess was subordinated—despite the Constitution's insistence on "equal status"—to a national anthem that celebrates the same space as a geo-body (albeit subtly anthropomorphized, as I will demonstrate). It is as if a sovereign polity needs to give precedence to the cartographic form of national territory as a stable geo-body whose borders are carefully and incontestably defined, governed, and defended. The fact, however, that the state felt compelled as well to install "Vande Mataram" as the national song in 1950 intimates that for the purposes of patriotic attachment and production of geo-piety the geographic delineation of the country, even while indispensable, is not in and of itself adequate.[11] The yoking together of the song and the anthem is a verbal affirmation of the necessary coexistence, even imbrication, of the anthropomorphic-sacred and the scientific-geographic imaginations of territory so visibly apparent in the carto-graphed pictures of Bharat Mata produced by patriotic visuality. Geo-piety in twentieth-century India needs the crutches of both the form and presence of the mother/goddess and the geo-body, each mutually reinforcing as well as simultaneously troubling the other.[12]

MAPPING "VANDE MATARAM"

The anchor image I use for my argument here is an oil painting called *Rastrabhakti Prema Ka Gaan Vande Mataram* ("Vande Mataram," the song of national devotion) (figure 13). Commissioned in 1999 to commemorate the putative 125th anniversary of the composition of the poem, the painting is centered on a seated woman clad in a modest white sari with a gold border, one of her hands resting on a male child. A large seated lion flanks her, its head dwarfing the citizen-child, and a demonic figure lies slain—presumably destroyed by her. This is the action in the bright foreground, but it is the fuzzy background that I am interested in here, for painted in the shadows are the multiple arms of the mother/goddess carrying symbols suggesting both her fecundity and her martial prowess; a faint crown also hints at her supramundane status as goddess and not just a mortal mother. Also visible is the shadowy silhouette of parts of the map of India—its northern, western, and eastern borders completely missing—with a partly visible lotus providing a cushion for the mother's feet at the tip of the Indian peninsula.

The painting is the inspiration of Milind Sabnis, an art instructor at a school in Pune—a hotbed of Hindu nationalism in western India for several decades but also a key site for at least a hundred years for the production of patriotic images.[13] The painting was placed in Sabnis's school, Dnyanada Pratisthan, and in December 2000 at the end of a year of celebrating the hymn one thousand students from sixty-five neighborhood schools formally gathered to sing the hymn in its entirety in the presence of the image. Convinced that the famous hymn had no accurate visual representation, Sabnis commissioned a local commercial artist, Sachin Joshi, to pictorialize Bankim's words. Joshi in turn read the hymn and studied a number of other paintings related to it, including that of Abanindranath Tagore (figure 6) and, in particular, that of J. B. Dixit (figure 33).[14] Dixit had painted Mother India in 1975 as a carto-graphed mother/goddess with four arms, one of which carries a club, and with her body occupying the lower half of the map of India and a halo around her head occluding the spectral formation of Kashmir. Sabnis himself worked closely with Joshi in the creation of the painting in order to visually capture Bankim's verbal imagination: the "richly-watered, richly-fruited" Mother, "dark with the crops of the harvest" and "her lands clothed beautifully with her trees in flowering blooms," finds a visual iteration in the flowers and the overflowing urns borne by the deity's many arms in Joshi's painting. In turn, Bankim's "Durga holding her ten weapons of war," reappears as a ten-armed Bharat Mata.

Crucially, however, as I have already noted, Bankim's poem is not cartographic because it is not readily apparent that it is the geo-body of "India" that is being saluted in this signature poem and song.[15] Even the geographic elements in the poem are limited to generic allusions to the fertility of the land and its "richly-watered, richly-fruited" terrain basking in the cool southern wind, clothed in the glory of the moonlight, and thronging with flowering trees. Yet Joshi and Sabnis felt compelled to incorporate the mapped image of India—partial and shadowy though it might—in the painting.[16]

This is not the only time that the hymn is rendered cartographically when translated into the visual realm. In fact, around the time of the centenary of its original composition in the 1870s numerous publications commemorating the hymn were published. Many of them invariably feature either a carto-graphed Bharat Mata or sometimes even just a map of India, its absence in Bankim's poem notwithstanding.[17] For example, a black-and-white reproduction of Dixit's painting of the carto-graphed Bharat Mata that so inspired Joshi and Sabnis (figure 33) serves as the frontispiece for a book from 1978, *Vande Mataram: The Song Perennial*, also published in Pune (Gadgil 1978). Similarly another book, *Vande Mataram*, published in 1977 in Madras, features a carto-graphed Mother India on its dust jacket; she carries not the Indian tricolor but a saffron pennant, and she occupies the roughly drawn outline map of India that includes Bangladesh as well as Burma (but not Pakistan). A black-and-white illustration on the inside (possibly the photograph of a painting called *Deshamatrika* [Mother of the land]) features a curvaceous Bharat Mata as a two-armed, doe-eyed young woman standing on a partial globe with her feet firmly planted on a partly visible map of India and one hand held in the abhaya gesture of blessing her viewer.[18]

Two other publications dispensed entirely with the mother's cartographed form and carried just the outline map of India to which homage is offered. In the cover illustration for Moni Bagchee's *Vande Mataram*, the Indian geo-body (with Bangladesh curiously a part of it) is filled with the bodies of Indian couples variously attired in the costumes of their respective regions, thereby showing the diversity of the body politic (figure 56). The chains of (colonial) servitude have been broken, as the map is transformed into an object to which homage is offered.[19] Similarly, in the Hindi play *Vande Mataram* by Gurudatta, published sometime in the early 1960s, Bankim's original poem is printed at the beginning, along with an illustration showing an outline map of independent India to which a woman in profile bows in homage. The image appears as well on the cover of the book in color (figure 57). Amarendra Gadgil's *Vande Mataram: The Song Perennial* (1978) even has a dramatic dust jacket of a map of India in flames with the refrain from the hymn inscribed (in English and Devanagari) across the geo-body whose northern, eastern, and western borders are nonexistent (figure 58). The illustration visually iterates the book's central lament about the displacement of Bankim's hymn as the national anthem by a rival.[20] The map *is* the mother in this instance (as in others), with the refrain "vande mataram" inscribed across its surface sealing the identification.

GRAPHIC POLITICS

Three-quarters of a century prior to these publications the Anti-Circular Society was created in Calcutta in November 1905 to defy the "circulars" that proposed repressive measures against students participating in politics and that banned the public invocation of the words "vande mataram." The society adopted as its emblem a rough outline map of India placed within a circle inscribed with the words "For God and Motherland" and "Fraternity, Liberty, and Equality" in English and "vande mataram" in Devanagari. Inside the

FIGURE 56 Cover illustration for *Vande Mataram* by Moni Bagchee. Bharatiya Vidya Bhavan, Bombay, 1977. (Reproduced with permission of Bharatiya Vidya Bhavan)

FIGURE 57 Illustration for *Vande Mataram* (*Naatak*) by Gurudatta. Bharatiya Sahitya Sadan, New Delhi, 196[?]. (Reproduced with permission of Hindi Sahitya Sadan)

FIGURE 58 *Cover illustration for Vande Mataram: The Song Perennial* by Amarendra Gadgil, Vande Mataram Centenary Special Publication. Gokul Masik Prakashan, Pune, 1978.

circle, on the map itself, appear the terms "United Bengal, 80,000,000" and "United India 300,000,000" (figure 59).[21] The Anti-Circular Society might have been set up to oppose the repressive measures that followed in the wake of the territorial partition of Bengal, but the map form alone appears inadequate for its project; indeed, it has been supplemented by the mother's presence, which is signified graphically by the words "vande mataram."[22] The mother's slogan, in turn, appears to need the geo-body to help visualize her dismemberment by the colonial partitioning decree.

The Anti-Circular Society's emblem serves as a reminder that the mother/goddess becomes visible to her citizen-devotee not just through pictures showing her anthropomorphic form but also through the *graphic* presence of the words "vande mataram." As W. J. T. Mitchell comments, "Writing, in its physical, graphic form, is an inseparable suturing of the visual and the verbal, the 'image-text' incarnate" (1994, 95). Picking up on this observation,

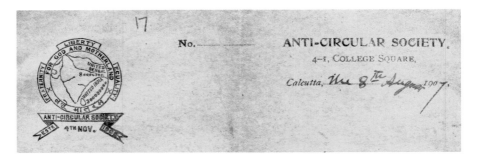

FIGURE 59 Logo of the Anti-Circular Society on letter from Krishnakumar Mitra to Aswinicoomar Banerji, August 8, 1907. (Individual List No. 89, Private Papers of Aswinicoomar Banerji [Correspondence with Krishnakumar Mitra], Nehru Memorial Museum and Library, New Delhi)

I consider the visual appearance of "vande mataram" as one such image-text incarnate. From the early years of the twentieth century, these words showed up visibly on house and street walls, on protest badges worn proudly by students and other protestors, on mastheads and cover pages of patriotic newspapers and nationalist publications, on personal letters, and even business correspondence.[23] It is also worth noting that the graphic inscription frequently resorts to Devanagari, the script most closely associated in the twentieth century with a Sanskritic-Hindu life-world—especially given the growing unease of Muslims with its deployment. The earliest "national" flag deployed by the Anti-Circular Society in August 1906 in Calcutta was emblazoned with the words "vande mataram" (in Devanagari), as was its immediate successor unfurled a year later in Stuttgart by Bhikhaiji Cama (figure 129).[24] Within a few years the latter flag boldly appeared on the masthead of a monthly journal called *The Bande Mataram: Monthly Organ of Indian Independence*, which was published by emigré patriots in Europe and banned in 1909 from circulating in British India (figure 15). A few years prior to this ban, students in the south Indian town of Rajahmundry marched in 1907 to the singing of Bankim's verse, "all wearing Vande Mataram badges, and carrying aloft beautiful banners glittering with bold letters of vande mataram and Allah-O-Akbar."[25]

Around the same time a patriotic firm in south India manufactured "Vande Mataram medals," which carried "on the obverse the figure of the goddess Lakshmi, and on the reverse 'the hands of the Indian nation praying for wealth and prosperity.'" The medal was meant to serve simultaneously "as an ornament, as a national badge, and as a charm-locket for success."[26] An irate district magistrate in the southern port city of Tuticorin found in early 1908 that the offensive refrain had been scrawled across the walls and fans of his very courtroom.[27] The *Andhra Kesari*, a Telugu paper published in the southern Indian town of Rajahmundry, carried a story on July 26, 1907, about a village school started by a local patriotic association that had chosen to affix the refrain to the school wall. A local British administrator, "terrified of the letters," commanded that the offensive piece of paper be taken down. In relating the story the paper went on to rhetorically ask, "Well, look at all this! It is true that the sheet has been torn off the wall. But there are walls, door-frames and *chattram*s [hostels] where the *vande mataram mantram* [slogan] is written or engraved. Have they been effaced? Has the expression *vande mataram* lost its influence, simply because the paper that was affixed to the [school] wall was taken away?"[28] In point of fact this new patriotic practice of writing or painting the two words "vande mataram" became so widespread across India that a confidential police report from Bengal in 1917 noted that "there is scarcely ever a revolutionary document that is not headed with Om Bandemataram [Hail Vande Mataram]."[29] This micropractice of graphically inscribing the phrase "vande mataram" on surfaces of all sorts ranging from street walls to banners and newspapers to personal letters is revelatory of the extent to which the anthropomorphic-sacred imagination of national territory had seeped into the everyday life of a growing number of patriotic Indians, both in the subcontinent and in its diaspora, and also finding visual expression as an image-text.

In addition to appearing graphically on patriotic surfaces of all sorts the refrain "vande mataram" was also depicted from early on with the faces of well-known patriots arranged within the contours of the words as they were printed or painted, typically in Devanagari. Obviously the colonial state worried about the converging power of words and images because they proscribed such pictures right away. Thus, we learn from government proscription records of a picture "containing portraits of Nana Fadnavis and others . . . notorious for acts or opinion of a violent and subversive character . . . arranged on the words Bande Mataram." This picture apparently circulated in the Bombay Presidency and other parts of western India.[30] Another such proscribed artifact was a picture, titled *Bande Mataram*, published sometime around 1907 in the central Indian town of Nasik. According to the government report, it had images of "well-known extremists and nationalists, with a leavening of allegorical pictures . . . inserted in the word Bande Mataram (in vernacular)."[31] Thus, the aural reach of the mother's hymn was visually complemented by deploying the refrain "vande mataram" as an image-text, as these words summoned into visibility Mother India's presence at a time when her pictorial persona was still in process.

As Bharat Mata's pictorial presence comes to be consolidated through the creative work of her visual votaries, the words "vande mataram" are inevitably incorporated into her developing iconography as well, and as such share honors with other signature markers like the map of India and the tricolor flag. For example, a *hundi* (promissory note) written in Gujarati by a possibly patriotic merchant based in Pune around 1924 carries as its printed header the logo of a carto-graphed Bharat Mata flanked by two prominent lion heads, with the phrase "vande mataram" inscribed in Devanagari below (figure 60).[32] In another example, a Tamil speaker's devotion to Bharat Mata is apparent from the image printed on a letter that he mailed from Colombo in 1940. At the head of the letter is an inscription with the words "vande mataram" in Tamil, which is flanked by a carto-graphed image of the mother/goddess as a four-armed figure carrying a flag in one hand and the Gandhian spinning wheel in another ("vande mataram" is also inscribed above and below the image in Devanagari and Telugu scripts) (figure 61).[33]

Examples like these, while episodic and elusive, also suggest that from at least 1905 the map of India accompanies the visual and graphic presence of "Vande Mataram" in the patriotic labors of the subcontinent, notwithstanding the absence of overt cartographic imagery in Bankim's poem regarding India as a geo-body. Thus Bharati's cartoons published in Madras and Pondicherry established a link between the carto-graphed form of the mother/goddess and the refrain "vande mataram" (figure 8), as did expatriate visual patriotism (figures 15 and 16). And in 1910 one of the earliest patriotic images proscribed by the colonial state, *National Heroes, Rushtra Purusha*, also visually connected the map of India and the refrain. Unfortunately, the picture has not survived, but an official description of its content reads as follows: "The National Hero holds in his left hand a miniature form of the map of India. 'Bande Mataram' is written on the wristlet worn and 'Eki' (union)

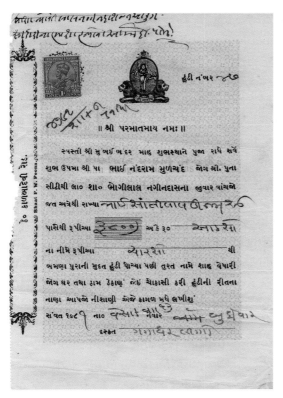

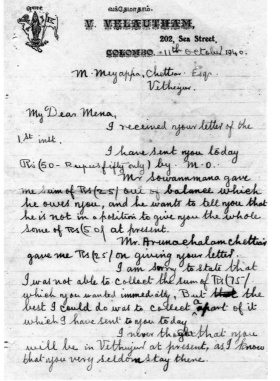

is written on the ring from which the map is suspended . . . Ceylon is represented as a bud of flower with 'mardani' (manliness) written on it." The hapless publisher of this "seditious" picture, Mohan Singh of Nasik in central India, was sentenced to three years of rigorous punishment for his crime.[34]

"BUT THIS IS MY COUNTRY; THIS IS NOT MY MOTHER!"

In the discursive domain as well, in the decades after Bankim's original creation, the song "Vande Mataram" is explicitly carto-graphed in ways that verbally echo what I have documented in the realm of the image. The most striking illustration of this process is found in a new English translation and adaptation of *Anandamath* published in 1941 in New York. In this work, "the Motherland" is presented explicitly to the reader in cartographic terms, and unambiguously identified as "Mother India." As such these identifications represent a significant departure from Bankim's novel. This is most apparent in the crucial scene where the protagonist Mahendra first encounters the Mother(land) in a partly underground temple in a remote forest, where, as he enters a dark room, "gradually a picture reveal[s] itself to him. It was a gigantic, imposing, resplendent, yes, *almost a living map* of India. 'This is our Mother India as she was before British conquest,'" he is told by his guide, Bhavananda. He proceeds to the next chamber where he sees "*a map of India in rags and tears*. The gloom over this map was beyond description. 'This is what our Mother India is today,'" Bhavananda reminds him. "'She is in the gloom of famine, disease, death, humiliation, and destruction.'" In the last room filled up with light that Mahendra enters, he observes that "the effulgence of the light was radiating from *the map of a golden India*—bright, beautiful, full of glory, and dignity. 'This is our Mother as she is destined to be.'" When he asks, "When shall we see our Mother India in this garb again—so radiant and cheerful?" Bhavananda intones, "Only when all the children of the Motherland shall call her Mother in all sincerity."[35]

In adapting and translating this work, Basanta Koomar Roy (an expatriate based in the United States who, interestingly, retitled *Anandamath* as *Dawn over India*), gives no explanation for why he introduced this explicit cartographic element into Bankim's Bengali narrative in which it was most certainly not a map of India that Mahendra encounters in Bhavananda's company but rather the enshrined images of the goddesses Jagaddhatri, Kali, and

Durga.[36] One may speculate that he did so because by 1941, when this translation was first published, the map of India had become such a diagnostic feature of Bharat Mata's iconography through the many efforts of barefoot cartographic practice that the one form could stand in for the other. In fact, as I discuss in the next chapter, the very first temple to Mother India, which was successfully completed and opened in 1936 in the north Indian city of Banaras, housed not an image of the mother/goddess but rather a made-to-scale relief map of India that reproduced in marble the numerous maps of the country made by the colonial surveys (see figure 64). The mother's anthropomorphic image is strikingly absent in this temple named after her, although the graphic inscription of the words "vande mataram" at both the entrance to the temple as well as on the inside walls signals her presence in another guise.

This interchangeability between the mother's form and the geo-body of the nation might have been useful to men like Basanta Koomar Roy (as indeed to those behind the creation of the Mother India temple) at a time and in the context of escalating Hindu-Muslim tensions from the 1920s leading up to the partition of British India. As the mother's obviously Hindu appearance was beginning to be more and more of a problem, not to mention an embarrassment for "secular" Indians (and possibly for expatriates like Roy living abroad), the outline map of the nation could step in, as it appeared less divisive, not obviously idolatrous, and more inclusive. If we follow this line of reasoning it also means, ironically, that the colonial state's geo-coded images of territory were more admissible than the anthropomorphic-sacred imagination of country and land that only alienated those who were not nominally Hindu because of the manner in which "the mother" and "the motherland" so readily became "mother/goddess."[37]

More likely though, I would argue that for men like Roy living in the United States, and even in the subcontinent where map-mindedness had only fitfully and incoherently disseminated outside a narrow circle of the educated by the 1940s, it would have been impossible to *not* imagine the form of the national territory in the hegemonic terms dictated by the protocols of scientific cartography. The nation appears to yearn for cartographic certitude. The map form, we have been told, assures the modernity of nation-states, underwritten as it is by the sciences of cartography and geography. As

Thongchai Winichakul notes, "A modern nation-state must be imaginable in mapped form . . . nationhood [is] literally formed by the demarcation of its body" (1996, 76). If it were not for the map the nation's territory—its geo-body—would remain an abstraction, thereby leaving its citizen-subjects without any material means to *see* the country, especially as an integral whole to which it is anticipated they are attached.

Yet, *seeing* the country in India is no straightforward, singular enterprise, for as I discussed in the previous chapter an alternate, even incommensurate, anthropomorphic-sacred imagination of land as female, maternal, and divine was also being revamped at the very start of the national movement to challenge the hegemony of scientific cartography's gridded lines and contours of the country. Indeed, the potential for dissonance between these two regimes of imagination is already apparent in *Anandamath* where in the scene preceding Mahendra's first introduction to the three successive manifestations of the Mother and Motherland, he hears "Vande Mataram" for the first time, as its first verse is sung by Bhavananda (who weeps as he sings). As the text tells it, "Mahendra was somewhat astonished by the song, could not understand it—this mother endowed with water, fruits, cooled by spring winds, verdant with crop, who is this mother? 'Who is Mother?' he asked." After Bhavananda sings the hymn's second verse in response, Mahendra insists, "'But this is my country; this is not my mother!' Bhavananda said, 'We do not recognize any mother besides her. One's mother and one's motherland are nobler than the heavens. We say, our motherland is the mother, we have no mother, father, brothers, friends, wives, sons, houses, families, we have only her who is endowed with water and fruits, cooled by the winds of the spring, green with corn.'"[38] As Sudipta Kaviraj observes regarding these lines, "To see the country as the mother is highly non-standard in Hindu mythology. It is a transposition, using traditional figures certainly, but to purposes that are highly innovative" (1995, 137). Sabyasachi Bhattacharya similarly underscores the novelty of poetically invoking "the motherland" at a time when the trope had not yet become a dead metaphor: "The poetic power of the personification of the country as the mother lay in its ability to enliven an abstract idea, *to animate the inanimate.*"[39]

Equally innovative and novel, however, was the cartographic practice of analytically seeing the country as lines and contours—as geo-body—that the colonial state and its institutions had sought to introduce to the natives, or at least the educated among them, from the closing years of the eighteenth century. It is against the potentially hegemonic influence of this novel science of cartography that Bankim is writing when he has Bhavananda insist that the country *is* Mother, indeed the *only* Mother who matters. Indeed, it is not just any land but the land that had given birth (*janmabhumi*) to the citizen. In this foundational text for the anthropomorphic-sacred imagination of India as Bharat Mata[40]—and for inaugurating a practice of transforming country into mother and deity to be worshipped—a subtle but palpable tension with a nonanthropomorphic modality for imagining the janmabhumi is already manifest in Mahendra's protest, "But this is my country; this is not my mother." Bankim was a highly educated writer and bureaucrat, and he would have been quite familiar with the mapped form of India (and of Bengal) that he would have been exposed to from his schooling as well as from his work. Yet he chose to resort to the language of sacred anthropomorphism rather than scientific cartography in describing land and country: the latter is striking by its absence. Nevertheless, through the interventions of barefoot cartography after his time, as we have seen in this chapter, the map form appears in its many pictorial productions as it is incorporated in various ways in the deployment of the refrain "vande mataram" by itself or in association with Bharat Mata's body.

THE IDOLATRY OF GEOGRAPHY?

Bankim is not alone, however, in privileging the anthropomorphic over the cartographic. Some of his influential peers as well appear ambivalent and skeptical of the capacity of an abstract diagrammatized image such as a map to adequately capture the sentimental, even worshipful, attachment to the country that is actually a mother/goddess. Thus Bipin Chandra Pal conceded in 1907 that love of India now means a loving regard for the "*very configuration* of this continent—a love for its rivers and mountains, for its paddy fields and its arid sandy plains."[41] Yet, all the same, India could never just be reduced to its configuration, for "the fact of the matter really is that as long as you look upon our country as 'India,' . . . you will get no closer and truer view of it than what the foreign officials and students have been able to do" (1911, 86–87). In his *The Soul of India*, first published in 1911 and addressed explicitly to the Indian patriot-in-the-making, Pal insisted, "This geographical habitat of ours is only the outer body of the Mother. The earth that we tread on is not a mere bit of geological structure. It is the physical embodiment of the Mother. Behind this physical and geographical body there is a Being, a Personality" (187).[42] Correspondingly, love for the country could never just amount to loving "an abstraction we called India,"[43] for the beloved country was far more than a "mere geographical expression." It is the living mother (1911, 80, 121).

Aurobindo Ghose, Pal's fellow Bengali comrade-in-arms, concurred with him. Sometime around 1905 when Aurobindo was employed as a college teacher in Baroda an interlocutor asked him for advice on how to become patriotic. It is claimed that in response he pointed to a wall map of India hanging in his classroom, and stated: "Do you see this map? It is not a map, but the portrait of *Bharat-mata* [Mother India]: its cities and mountains, rivers and jungles form her physical body. All her children are her nerves, large and small. . . . Concentrate on Bharat [India] as a living mother, worship her with the nine-fold *bhakti* [devotion]."[44] Around this same time, in a suggestive work called *Bhawani Mandir* (*Temple for Bhawani*), he described India as a "mighty Shakti" called Bhawani. It was most emphatically "not a piece of earth" (2002, 83).[45] Not least, in a revealing letter to his wife, penned in August 1905, Aurobindo even confessed to a third "madness" that reminds us as well that every so often love for one's country, even one imagined as one's mother, can take on an erotic charge: "My third madness is that while others look upon their country as an inert piece of matter—a few meadows and fields, forests and hills and rivers—I look upon my country as the Mother. I adore Her. I worship Her as the Mother. What would a son do if a demon sat on his mother's breast and started sucking her blood? Would he quietly sit down to his dinner, amuse himself with his wife and children, or would he rush out to deliver his mother?"[46]

Given the enormous influence of both Hindu and Hindu nationalist ideas on such musings about "the motherland" by Bankim, Pal, and Aurobindo it is perhaps not surprising that they subordinate the scientific-geographic to the anthropomorphic-sacred and privilege maternal-divine visions over mapped images of national territory. In the Hindu imagination it is because earth and land are deemed to be living presences (even the mother/goddess Prithvi) that attitudes toward territory have tended toward the anthropomorphic, the feminine, and the worshipful. Such archetypal notions that were in the colonial air—not least because they found renewed visibility through colonial knowledge practices—came to be useful for a nationalist project that under "revivalists" like Aurobindo or Pal consciously sought out autochthonous crutches against a full-blown British-style modernity.

What is surprising, though, is that even a figure like Rabindranath Tagore refused to cede India to the empire of science and geography, although ideologically after 1907 he vehemently opposed all manner of revivalist exhortations, including the call to worship the nation in the name of the all-powerful Mother. Meditating on the nature of modern pedagogy, Rabindranath complained, for instance, that the discipline of geography robbed "the child of his earth" and distanced him from "the dust" that he naturally loved.[47] Tagore's India was "not a geographical expression," and although he "loved" his country it was "not because I cultivate the idolatry of geography."[48] Nationalism, in turn, was "a *bhougalik apadevata*, a geographic demon" (Nandy 1994, 7). The Tagore family belonged to the reformist Brahmo movement, which from fairly early in the nineteenth century had defined itself against an idolatrous Hinduism. Yet Rabindranath composed in Bengali some of the most beloved patriotic poems and hymns on land as the living mother, especially around 1905 when Bengal was threatened with partition. One of these, "Amar Sonar Bangla" (My Bengal of gold) went on to be enshrined as the national anthem of the new nation-state of Bangladesh in 1972. Like Bankim's "Vande Mataram" it is saturated with the vocabulary of the anthropomorphic-sacred, with nary a place for the cartographic form of land and country:

> My golden Bengal, I love you.
> Your skies, your breezes, ever with my breath play the flute.
> O mother, in Phalgun [spring] the perfume of your mango groves drives
>   me mad.
> Ah,
> Mother, what honeyed smile have I seen in your laden fields in Agrahan
>   [autumn].

O what light, what shade, what boundless love, what changing bonds,
What sari's border have you spread round roots of banyan trees, on the
  bank of rivers.
O mother, the flow of words from your lips strikes my ear like a stream
  of nectar;
Ah,
Mother, when the skin of your face draws tight, O mother, I float in
  tears. . . .
O Mother, I offer at your feet this my lowered head;
Give me, O mother, the dust of your feet, to be the jewel upon my head.
O mother, whatever wealth this poor man has, I place upon your feet,
Ah, I die,
I shall no more buy in the houses of others, O mother, this so-called
  finery of yours, a noose around my neck.[49]

Or consider another revealing poem, replete once again with the somatic imagery of land as mother and the citizen as child:

O earth of this my country, I lay my head upon you.
In you is spread the border of the sari of the mother of the universe, of
  her with whom the universe is filled.
You have blended with my body,
One with my heart and mind;
. . . .
O mother, my birth was in your lap,
My death upon your breast,
My play on you, in sorrow and in joy.
You it was who raised the food to my lips,
And with water cooled my fever,
You who bear all, bear all, O mother of mother.
Much have I eaten of yours, much have I taken, O mother,
And what have I given in return?[50]

In 1909, when young Ullaskar Dutta was tried and sentenced to death for anti-British activities, he reportedly burst into a recitation of one of Tagore's poems (which, a contemporary newspaper report noted, even "hushed into perfect silence" the European sergeants in the courtroom waiting to take him away):

> Blessed is my birth—for I was born in this land.
> Blessed is my birth—for I have loved thee.
> . . . I do not know in what garden,
> Flowers enrapture so much with perfume;
> In what sky rises the moon, smiling such a smile.
> . . . O mother, opening my eyes, seeing thy light,
> My eyes are regaled;
> Keeping my eyes on that light
> I shall close my eyes in the end.[51]

And yet, Tagore increasingly became worried from around the middle of 1907 about the dangers of countering the "dust" of colonial geography by turning to the imagery of divinized anthropomorphism, for this seemed to only produce a Hinduism-inflected geo-piety that inevitably led to the alienation of Muslims and other non-Hindus. It was at this juncture that he apparently refused a request from Bipin Chandra Pal to compose a song that would celebrate the motherland as Durga,[52] and he even dared to mock the mother: "Infatuated by your seven crore children, O Mother, you have left them as Bengalis, but haven't brought them up as human beings."[53] In the words of Nikhil, one of his fictional heroes from 1915–1916 who refused "to accept the spirit of *Bande Mataram*" and who might well have been Tagore's own alter ego, "I am willing to serve my country; but my worship I reserve for Right which is far greater than my country. To worship my country as a god is to bring a curse upon it" (2005, 29).[54] In his prescient critique of nationalism published soon after in 1917 Tagore in fact tellingly wrote that "even though from childhood I have been taught that idolatry of the Nation is almost better than reverence for God and humanity, I believe I have outgrown that teaching" (1917, 127).

It was this complex man and poet who composed the hymn titled "Bharata-Vidhata" (Sustainer of India), a piece that eventually went on to be invested as independent India's "national anthem" in 1950.[55] In contrast to Bankim's "Vande Mataram" as well as countless other patriotic poems and songs in India's many languages, "Bharata-Vidhata" (more popularly known as "Jana

Gana Mana" from its opening words) does not begin by invoking the land as a fecund or powerful mother/goddess. This is apparent from Tagore's own translation (from 1919) of the first verse of the highly Sanskritized-Bengali poem that he sang in 1911:

> Thou art the ruler of the minds of all people,
> Thou Dispenser of India's destiny.
> Thy name rouses the hearts of the Punjab, Sind, Gujrat, and Maratha,
>   of Dravida, Orissa, and Bengal.
> It echoes in the hills of the Vindhyas and Himalayas,
> mingles in the music of Jumna and Ganges,
>   and is chanted by the waves of the Indian Sea.
> They pray for thy blessing and sing thy praise,
> Thou dispenser of India's destiny,
> Victory, Victory, Victory to thee![56]

Where Bankim's "Vande Mataram" leaves the subject of its poetic praise unnamed, Tagore explicitly names it as Bharata (in Bengali) and India (in English). While Bankim's "Vande Mataram" transforms the land itself into an object of worship—so necessary for geo-piety—in its very opening phrase, "I worship the Mother," Tagore's poem refuses this idolatrous gesture: to paraphrase him from a slightly later (fictional) context, he was willing to praise the country but not worship it as deity.

As important, however, for some of the arguments of my study, where Bankim's "Vande Mataram" explicitly personifies and anthropomorphizes land as mother, Tagore is much more ambiguous in this regard in his "Jana Gana Mana." The literary critic Rukmini Bhaya Nair insists that the poem emphasizes a "down-to-earth territoritality" (2001, 98).[57] Yet matters are not all that simple, which I believe reflects the dilemmas faced by men like Tagore in trying to praise land and country in a colonial and nationalist context where the scientific-geographic language of territory was indispensable but inadequate and where the language of gendered anthropomorphism while fulfilling to some was alienating to others. The penultimate verse of Tagore's poem—which is never invoked in the national anthem—alludes to the country as a female waiting to be awakened from her stupor and rescued from "dark evil dreams."[58] In the crucial opening stanza that is instituted as the Republic of India's national anthem, however, the country is presented qua country as constituted by its provinces, by its mountains and its rivers, and by the people who inhabit it, named Hindus, Buddhists, Sikhs, Jains, Parsis, Muslims, and Christians (as in good colonial sociology and geography). In a letter Tagore wrote years later in 1927 he offered the following explanation for why he felt compelled to memorialize India in this fashion:

> In the course of our history, India had once deeply realised her geographical entity; she established in her mind an image of her own physical self by meditating on her rivers and hills . . . In my song of the victory of Bharat-vidhata composed a few years ago, I have put together a number of Indian provinces; Vindhya-Himachala and Yamuna-Ganga have also been mentioned. I feel, however, that a song should be written in which all the provinces, rivers and hills of India are strung together in order to impress upon the minds of our people an idea of the geography of our country. We are nowadays profuse in the use of the term National Consciousness, but what kind of national consciousness can there be, devoid of actual geographical and ethnological realisation?[59]

Faced with the challenge of reciting India in a language that was not saturated with the anthropomorphic-sacred imagery of the mother/goddess in the wake of the intense patriotic mobilization around "Vande Mataram" during the swadeshi movement, Tagore (re)turned to geography and "strung together the names of provinces, rivers, and hills of India" so that Indians would develop a "national consciousness" about the geo-body they inhabit. But this (re)turn was not just to geography, for animating this first critical verse is the spirit of (implicitly masculinized) anthropomorphism as exemplified in the Sanskrit word *vidhata* and in the English words *thou* and *thy* of the English translation.[60] As such we see yet another illustration of the imbrication of the anthropomorphic and the geographic that is such a telltale feature of the imagination of territory in twentieth-century India.

Strikingly, for my argument, the ordering of the provinces in Tagore's imagination seems to follow the outline map of India (albeit only incompletely and somewhat idiosyncratically) almost as if the poet had just such a modern artifact in front of him as he burst into song and "strung together the names of provinces, rivers, and hills of India." It is not perhaps an exaggeration to see the modern cartographic imagination at work in the adoption of a north-south orientation, as the song begins with Punjab (but not Kashmir) and travels down the western coast of the geo-body to Dravida, when it takes a northeasterly turn to Orissa before ending in Bengal. Indian poet that he is, Tagore reprised terms from a precolonial (Sanskritic) lexicon that had been marginalized by colonial geography (Sindhu, Dravida, Utkala, Vanga, Himachala, Bharata), although his English translation resorted to their Anglicizations (the Punjab, Sindh, Orissa, Bengal, and most strikingly, India). And his geo-body is not merely lines and contours but throngs as well with people, albeit those who are primarily identified—in a standard colonial fashion—according to their religious affiliation: "Day and night, thy voice goes out from land to land, / Calling Hindus, Buddhists, Sikhs and Jains round thy throne / And Parsees, Mussalmans, and Christians."

SHIFTING CONTOURS OF GEO-PIETY

Tagore was not the first to draw upon the lessons of geography to poetically imagine the country. As Rosinka Chaudhuri has shown, more than half a century before Tagore another Bengali, Michael Madhusudan Dutt (1824–1873), attempted a similar formulation in a poem published in English in 1849–1850:

> Thus sang the bard from where the tide
> Of Indus rolls in sleepless pride. . . .
> Cashmera . . . land of found and rose,
> Sprung in wild haste from soft repose,
> Panchala . . . land of mighty streams . . .
> Husteena flung her banner high . . .
> Vyodhya fiercely twanged the bow . . .
> And from Bengala's sunny vale
> Came proud defiance on the gale . . .
> While in the countless-realmed Dekan
> Rose many a wild and warrior clan.[61]

In interpreting this poem Chaudhuri writes: "This definition of India as one land, bound together by a common history and heritage, was a rare thing in the indigenous poetry of India. In the local languages, poetry had been regional and feudal . . . The sort of concrete evocation we see in this section of Madhusudan's poem, however, sounds a note that belongs far more to modern India . . . bringing to mind Tagore's national anthem for India with its incantation of the names of its various regions . . . and is typical of the nationalism which came about in later Indian literary sensibilities."[62] In fact, Chaudhuri has drawn our attention to the hitherto ignored role of poetry in the imagination of the entity called "India." Poetry, she suggests, emerged prior to prose to provide "a language with which to speak of India." The idea of India, she notes, first found expression in verse (and in English verse at that), and such patriotic poetry is almost as old as the systematic establishment of British colonial rule in India, appearing from as early as the late 1820s to speak of "my country" and "my native land" (7).

Building upon Chaudhuri's research I would argue that it is not just the then-new disciplines of history and Oriental studies that were important for this evolving geo-pietic and poetic imagination but geography and cartography also put pressure on the manner in which land could be recited and invoked in patriotic song in colonial India. As in patriotic visuality, nationalist poetry transforms a carto-graphed terrain of mathematized calculation into an affect-laden homeland of longing and belonging. At the same time—and this is where a pictorial history is revealing—many collections of "patriotic poetry" and "national songs" that were published over the course of the first half of the twentieth century in the numerous languages of the subcontinent are frequently adorned on either their title covers or inside pages with a carto-graphed image of Bharat Mata, despite the fact that the verses themselves are not explicitly or even implicitly cartographic or geographic in their celebration of India. The map form, it seems, is necessary even while the land is being celebrated as maternal and divine. The sentiments of love and longing have to be supplemented by the mapped images of scientific cartography, and in that process the latter are moved as well out of the realms of science and state to inhabit an arena saturated with the spirit of the mother/goddess.

All the same, the fact that a large majority of patriotic poems regularly resort to the affect-laden worshipful language of the anthropomorphic-sacred suggests the indispensability of the mother/goddess for imagining national territory in poetry as indeed in pictures. In response, possibly even retaliation, to the imperial project of mapping "India" (that is, transforming it into geo-coded lines and contours), poets from at least the 1860s anthropomorphized the emergent nation as woman, mother, and goddess and named her, with neologisms assembled from indigenous words, AdiBharati, Hind Devi, and most consequentially Bharat Mata. In fact, Bankim was building on at least a decade of such patriotic poetry that had begun to invoke India/ Bharat as mother/goddess when he composed his "Vande Mataram" hymn in the 1870s. And as early as 1877 the young Rabindranath Tagore was even moved enough to passionately declare in one such verse: "To you, Mother, I dedicate myself, body and soul."[63]

DYING FOR A SONG

In concluding this chapter, I therefore insist that although the prosaic language of geography and the scientific protocols of cartography may very effectively bestow the certitude of mapped form, they never seem adequate enough to move patriots to love, longing, and ultimately, suffering and sacrifice. Indeed, they have to be inevitably supplemented by the sentimental language of poetry to generate geo-piety. And in (Hindu) India, the affective has tended, for the reasons that I have sketched out in the previous chapter, toward the anthropomorphic imagery of the divine and maternal in describing land and country. In fact, despite all of the associations of "Vande Mataram" with charges of idolatry and with fomenting riots between Hindus and Muslims, the framers of the Indian Constitution were persuaded, even compelled, to install the so-called "hymn of hate" as the national song because of its historic association with suffering and sacrifice.[64] In 1937 a committee of high-ranking members of the Congress charged with examining the hymn's troubled implication in the fostering of anti-Muslim consciousness was moved to note, in the future prime minister Nehru's words, that "during the past thirty years, innumerable instances of sacrifice and suffering . . . all over the country have been associated with 'Bande Mataram,' and men and women . . . have not hesitated to face death with that cry on their lips."[65] Years later, in defending the choice of "Vande Mataram" as "national song," Nehru once again associated it with "struggle" and "longing," and with "passion" and "poignancy."[66] Earlier in 1937, Rabindranath Tagore, waxed eloquently about "the spirit of tenderness and devotion" expressed in the first few verses of

Khudiram Bose

with "the stupendous sacrifices of the best

men who offered such a "stupendous sacri-
is martyrdom to country and mother in 1908
ment of the words "vande mataram" in the
g. His brave act also found graphic inscrip-
ti) that the colonial censors forfeited in 1910
because it contain____ ts to violence and words calculated to bring
into hatred and contempt His Majesty and the Government established by
law in British India, and to excite disaffection towards His Majesty . . ." Inscribed along the border of the five-yards-long dhoti was the following "in-
flammatory" poem in Bengali script titled "Farewell Mother":

> Mother, farewell
> I shall go to the gallows with a smile.
> The people of India will see this.
> One bomb can kill a man.
> There are a lakh of bombs in our homes.
> Mother, what can the English do? If I come back,
> Do not forget, Mother
> Your foolish child, Khudiram.
> See that I get your sacred feet at the end.
> When shall I call you again "Mother" with the ease of my mind?
> Mother, do not keep this sinner in another country.
> It is written that you have 36 crores of sons and daughters.
> Mother, Khudiram's name vanishes now.
> He is now turned to dust.
> If I have to rise again,
> See that, Mother, I sit on your lap again.
> In this kingdom of Bhisma, who else is there like you?
> You are unparalleled, Mother.
> When shall I depart from this world with a shout of Bande Mataram?[68]

This seditious dhoti—which today unfortunately is only a textual trace in
the colonial archive—is a material reminder of the convergence between the
mother's hymn and patriotic martyrdom from at least the time of a provin-

cial meeting of the Congress party in the small town of Barisal in Bengal in April 1906 when the colonial police lashed out at young men wearing badges inscribed with the refrain "vande mataram" as well as shouting the slogan (Sarkar 1973, 292–93). Numerous other examples that link "Vande Mataram" to a history of "suffering" and "sacrifice" exist as well, and some of these instances point to the power of the graphic use of the image-text "I worship the mother." In June 1907, a few months after the Barisal sacrifices, a British medical offer, Captain Kemp, beat a young schoolboy who had shouted the words "vande mataram" after him on the streets of the south Indian town of Kakinada. After the beating, when a crowd gathered demanding justice, he sought refuge in the local European Club. The government's tepid response precipitated one of the earliest graphic appearances of the mother's slogan in a cartoon in the Tamil newspaper *Intiya* on June 22, 1907, demanding justice for the student against the evil Kemp.[69] A few months before this incident, when some students of the nearby Rajahmundry Arts College started to show up for their classes wearing badges and lockets inscribed with the refrain "vande mataram," they invited the ire of the principal, Mark Hunter, who ordered the suspension of more than half the student body. The government in turn responded by expelling some students and barring others from taking their final examinations or even from being hired for a job in state educational institutions. The incident provoked prolific commentary in the local press, and several newspapers noted the suffering and indignities visited upon the students for rightfully displaying their patriotic feelings for country and mother. As one paper felt compelled to ask: "Do not Christians wear crosses, the votaries of the Theosophical Society hexagonal pendants, and the members of the Masonic lodges their badges? In the same manner Vande Mataram pendants are worn. What harm is there in doing so?"[70] Yet, as reports from all over the country showed, both the graphic inscription of these words in the public sphere and their oral invocation gave rise to consternation, anxiety, and even fear among the British. "Vande mataram" was not merely a string of innocent letters scrawled on a piece of paper, etched on a badge, or inscribed on the surface of a wall. Instead, the words graphically summoned into presence an otherwise absent Mother and an intangible world of sacrifice and self-effacing death (and a tangible one dedicated to the violent overthrow of British rule) with which she was increasingly coming to be associated, especially through the activities of various "secret societies" dedicated to her that the state was scrambling to bring into its net of surveillance.

One such secret society was the Bharata Mata Association, which was created sometime in late 1909 or early 1910 in the Tirunelveli district of Madras presidency and in the neighboring princely state of Travancore, possibly under the influence of similar organizations in Bengal as well as the patriotic writings of exiles like Subramania Bharati and Aurobindo based in Pondicherry. If it had not been for the fact that the group was implicated in the assassination of District Magistrate R. W. D. Ashe in June 1911, the Bharata Mata Association might have remained underground and therefore below the radar of the colonial state. In the aftermath of Ashe's assassination, however, the government gathered extensive information on this secret association and its activities based on the evidence given by two of its members who turned state witnesses. From their testimony it is clear that its sworn members greeted each other with the slogan "vande mataram," and they began their correspondence with each other by writing on their letterhead the name of Mother India—yet another instance of the materialization of the image-text. In addition to Mother India's lettered appearance in this fashion, the colonial police also recovered from the homes of the former members of the association all manner of "seditious" pamphlets and writings in which "India is personified and deified, and over and again . . . people are called upon to worship her and love her as a common mother. All this is done not only in powerful prose, but in verses of power and feeling." One such pamphlet contained a poem (which we now know was penned in Tamil by Bharati, although the report does not reveal this) with the lines, "When will subside this thirst for liberty? When will perish our love for servitude? Oh! When will snap our mother's manacles? And when will our troubles cease and become null?"[71]

Most dangerously from the colonial government's point of view, the rituals of incorporation of new members into the association were obviously aimed to create a brotherhood dedicated to living—and dying—for Bharat Mata. In the words of one of the witnesses as reported in the government records, "There was a picture of Kali there. There was red powder, sacred ashes, and flowers kept on the floor there. We five sat in a line, Nilakanta [the

head of the association] was a little aside and wrote on a paper. We put that red powder into water, and made a solution of it and each of us drank it separately saying that that was the white man's blood." As to what was contained in that paper, he remarked, "On the top, *vande mataram* was written. We should kill all white men. The affairs of this Society should not be revealed. We must sacrifice our personal property, and life for this Society."[72]

In point of fact, accumulating evidence (as described here) that placed Bharat Mata and the words "vande mataram" at the center of a proliferating web of sentiment that propelled patriots to suffering, sacrifice, and death convinced the colonial state in the early years of the twentieth century that Mother India was no harmless goddess or even hapless mother but rather an incendiary figure to be summarily dealt with. Not surprisingly, they increased their surveillance over her deployment in prose, poetry, and pictures by collecting and proscribing anything that confirmed their suspicion that she was the focus of a "seditious," "mischievous," and dangerous "cult" of extremism and violence. Thus pamphlets and letters that bore a seal in which the map of India appeared with the powerful words (in Devanagari) of "Mother and motherland are more glorious than heaven" were seized (figure 62), as were handbills inscribed with the refrain "bande mataram" coupled with incendiary calls issued in the course of commemorating Partition Day in Bengal in 1910: "Mere fruits and flowers will no longer be sufficient for the worship of the Mother; Mere empty words can no longer appease the hunger of the Mother. Blood is wanted; heads are wanted; workers are wanted; heroes are wanted. Accomplishments of objects, firm determination, and bands of devotees are wanted. Mere (?) fruits and flowers are no longer sufficient for the worship of the Mother."[73]

Later I will turn to how this insistence that "mere empty words" or "fruits and flowers" can no longer appease the Mother's "hunger" and "thirst" and that "blood is wanted" and that "heads are wanted" lead the visual votary to produce dramatic pictures of martyrdom for map and mother. But before I consider how love and longing can provoke beheadings and deaths for and on behalf of the country, I explore some further implications of such affect-laden and worshipful attitudes toward territory that become literally visible around the building of temples to Mother India across the nation.

ENSHRINING THE MAP OF INDIA

On October 25, 1936, an unusual shrine opened its doors to the public in Varanasi (Banaras), arguably Hindu India's holiest city (figure 63).[1] Named "Bharat Mata Mandir" in Hindi and "Mother India Temple" in English, it was in the words of one contemporary visitor, "a new kind of shrine which would call forth the devotion and service and sacrifice" of every Indian, "without distinction of caste or color or creed, race or sex." Its opening was attended by every major figure associated with the Indian National Congress, the leading political party spearheading the struggle against colonial rule. And no less a figure than Gandhi himself presided over the inauguration ceremony. Those who spoke at the opening noted that it was a shrine that summoned not "blind worship, but a dedication to an idea."[2] This new idea was nationalism, and it called for "a new kind of worship and a new kind of shrine."[3] In the words of one speaker, "It called forth all the children of the land to the worship of the Mother, forgetful of divisions and differences . . . The Father of us all had created us and given us the

FIGURE 63 "Bharat Mata Temple: Benares, Built by B. Shiva Prasad Gupta." Picture postcard, circa 1936. (Collection of P. and G. Bautze, Germany)

land to live on and food to eat. We, His children, often quarreled amongst ourselves, but the Mother called [us] together to forget [our] bickerings at her peace-giving feet." The temple was variously characterized in contemporary reports as "a new House of God," "a shrine of Love," "a place to forget communal differences," and in Gandhi's words, "a cosmopolitan platform for people of all religions, castes, and creeds" that would promote "religious unity, peace, and love in the country."[4]

But the most intriguing feature of the temple frequently noted by contemporaries was possibly not so much the idea of nationalism that it attempted to materialize in stone, novel enough as that was, but rather what it sought to enshrine within its walls as a diety. As Gandhi observed in his very opening words, "The temple contains no image of any god or goddess. It has *only* a relief map of India made of marble stone" (figure 64).[5] In the words of Mahadeo Desai, one of Gandhi's principal aides, "There is no image of an imaginary God or Goddess in the shrine, though Babu Shivprasad [the temple's founder] is a devout believer in India's Gods and Goddesses, inasmuch as he knows that there is the grand imagination of Indians behind those images. But he saw that the new times demanded a new kind of worship and a new

FIGURE 64 Interior of Bharat Mata Mandir, Banaras, showing view from first-floor gallery of relief map of India. Contemporary picture postcard. (Author's collection)

kind of shrine that would rally India's sons and daughters. A relief map of India in marble was what he conceived of."[6]

The story of what led the Banaras philanthropist Babu Shivprasad Gupta (1883–1944) to enshrine this cartographic form of India is inscribed, along with the details of the map itself, in the marble on the inside walls of the temple.[7] The idea of using the map of India to represent Bharat Mata dawned upon Gupta in 1913 when he visited a school established for young widows in the western Indian city of Poona by the Marathi social reformer D. K. Karve (1858–1962). He saw there a relief map of India fashioned out of mud and clay laid out on the ground. Subsequently on a visit to the British Museum in London he marveled at the many printed maps, big and small, on display.[8] Returning to Banaras he recruited in 1918 his friend Durga Prasad to design a relief map of India, made to scale and laid out on a grid.[9] The foundation stone for the temple was laid in April 1927, and work began on the temple with the help of thirty sculptors and twenty-seven masons (whose names are inscribed on one of the inside walls of the temple).[10] As described by Desai in an article in the *Hindustan Times*, these local sculptors, mostly natives of Banaras, had to be taught

> the new art of making mountains and plains, and rivers and lakes, of the right proportion, from slabs of marble. Seven hundred sixty-two square pieces (11″ × 11″) of marble (with smaller bits here and there) have gone to the making of this relief map, 31 feet and 2 inches long, and 30 feet and 2 inches broad. Every one of the physical features shown is to scale, a surface inch being equal to 6 miles and 704 yards, and an inch of height meaning 2,000 feet. Thus Mt. Everest has been cut out of one piece of marble 15 inches high. The height of all of India's plains and mountains from the sea level has been accurately shown and gradation of heights from 500 feet to 30,000 feet have been shown in figures to draw the spectator's attention to relative heights. Over 400 peaks of India's mountains have been shown, all her rivers with their relative length and breadth and depth have been shown, as all of India's principal lakes. All the latest geometrical knowledge has been utilized for making the relief map as accurate as possible, and all important cities and towns and villages have been shown. Twenty artisans were at work cutting, shaping and putting together these marble pieces, from day to day during five long years. The walls of the temple have maps in color showing the different periods of Indian History as also various features of physical geography.

So marveled Desai, and he concluded his ecstatic comments with the declaration that "the relief map is a poem in marble, and the whole shrine is a temple not only of art but of instruction and knowledge."[11]

What forces propelled the building of a temple with such a novel object of enshrinement, and why was it done so overtly in the name of Mother India? Even more intriguing, why was the figure of the mother/goddess so obviously *absent* in this very first temple successfully built in her name, and why was her anthropomorphic form replaced by the mapped configuration of the nation? Does this signal the trumping of the anthropomorphic-sacred by the scientific-geographic in the visualization of national territory at this particular shrine? If so, how successful a triumph has this been? Can the map form stand for, as well as stand in for, a *murti* (divine image)?[12] These are some questions that drive this chapter as I consider the Banaras Bharat Mata Mandir along with other temples attempted for and on behalf of Mother India before and since 1936.

DEIFYING INDIA

Although the Bharat Mata Mandir in Banaras was the first of its kind to be successfully completed, the idea of dedicating a temple to the motherland had been in the colonial air for at least half a century before 1936. One of Subramania Bharati's associates and admirers, Subramania Sivam (1884–1925), tried to build one in Madras province in the early 1920s. He acquired the land for the project near Dharmapuri in today's Salem district at a site that he named Bharatapuram (India Ville), worked ceaselessly to raise funds for its construction, and even tried to secure Gandhi's support for it on one of the Mahatma's early visits to the province in 1921. The foundation stone for the structure was eventually laid by another Congress nationalist, Chitta-ranjan Das, in 1923, and a ten-day festival in honor of the mother/goddess was conducted during which her image, adorned in garlands and jewels, was taken in procession around the little town. The temple itself was not completed, however, because of Sivam's untimely death in 1925. We have little knowledge of the manner in which Sivam envisioned Mother India's image, although given his association with Bharati it is possible that the image might well have been a carto-graphed mother/goddess (as in figure 9).[13]

A few years prior to Sivam's efforts the fiery teacher and revolutionary Aurobindo Ghose, recently returned from England, coauthored a short pamphlet in August 1905 titled *Bhawani Mandir* (*Bhawani's temple*) in which he called for the building of a temple "consecrated to Bhawani, the Mother, among the hills." The temple was to be built "in a place far from the contamination of modern cities and as yet little trodden by men, in a high and pure air steeped in calm and energy. This temple will be the centre from which Her worship is to flow over the whole country." It was intended as a site for the physical and spiritual training of young men who had dedicated themselves, life and limb, to the service of the motherland, imagined as the warrior goddess Bhawani.[14] Although the pamphlet attracted the attention of the colonial state, which worried over its potentially seditious message, and although Aurobindo's brother Barin sought unsuccessfully to bring the idea to fruition over the next few years, Bhawani Mandir never really became a reality. The pamphlet does not specify the form of the object that was to be enshrined in the Mother's temple, but as I noted in chapter 3, Aurobindo strongly resisted an exclusive reliance on the scientific-geographic imaginary for relating to national territory.

Given such views it is likely that if Bhawani Mandir had been successfully constructed the installed deity would have probably been an image of a Hindu goddess like the ones imagined in Bankim's *Anandamath* (1882), a novel that clearly exerted a great influence on Aurobindo (to the point that he partly translated it into English in 1909). In the pivotal scene in the novel, one of the protagonists, Mahendra, is led into a partly underground temple in a deserted forest where he encounters images of the Mother and Motherland enshrined in various connected chambers: as a goddess "more beautiful than Lakshmi and Sarasvati, with more grandeur then either," sitting on Vishnu's lap; as Jagaddhatri (Mother of the Universe, Bearer of the Earth), "rich in every limb, decorated with every possible ornament, . . . laughing, beautiful"; as a fiery Kali look-alike, "covered by darkness, of a black color . . . nude . . . [wearing] a garland of bones, dead skulls . . . trampling her own welfare under her feet, . . . a sword and scythe in her hands"; and finally as a dazzling "ten-armed golden idol in the middle of a marble temple, laughing in the light of the morning sun . . . [with her arms] spread in ten directions; in each a different weapon, a symbol of a different power, her enemy sprawled defeated at her feet, the lion she rides on mauling her adversary."[15] These successive images are iconic materializations of Bankim's anthropomorphic-sacred imagination of land and country that was so powerfully captured, as we saw, in his foundational "Vande Mataram" hymn. In Sudipta Kaviraj's reckoning, in Bankim's innovations, "space is invested with sacrality . . . It was not something which was fit to be geologically surveyed, but to be offered a political form of worship. From a neutral space, India becomes an evocative symbol, female, maternal, infinitely bounteous."[16]

Given such precedents Shivprasad Gupta's Bharat Mata Mandir, built in the Hindu heartland and yet enshrining no familiar-looking deity but a map of India as murti, was an unorthodox innovation in terms of customary modalities of icon worship as well as from the perspective of secular nationalism's invented rituals. As a monument to Bharat Mata the temple enshrines her land in a particular way, as extending from what we know today as Afghanistan in the northwest into and including Burma and part of the Malay Peninsula in the east, and from the Himalayas (and the plateau beyond) in the north to the ocean to the south, incorporating the island of Sri Lanka as well. In doing so it attempts to cartographically translate and fix the hitherto fluid notion of Bharatavarsha, the triangular or "bow-shaped" expanse of land that was imagined to have stretched from the Himalayas in the north to the oceans in the south, east, and west.[17] Under British rule the Sanskritic literary and Hindu ritual imagination about this landmass was partly transformed into geo-political fact by a modern empire seeking to extend itself to reach its "natural limits," with an early influential colonial survey even anticipating on paper what was eagerly sought after (albeit not with complete success) over the next century. In the words of Walter Hamilton, writing in 1820:

> According to the ancients, India, on its most enlarged scale, comprised an extent of forty degrees on each side, including a space almost as large as all Europe, being divided on the west from Persia by the Arachosian Mountains; limited on the east by the Chinese part of the peninsula beyond the Ganges; confined on the north by the wilds of Tartary; and stretching south as far as the Sunda Isles. These expanded limits comprehended the stupendous hills of Tibet, the romantic valley of Cashmere, and the domains of the old Indoscythians, the countries of Nepaul, Bootan, Camroop, and Assam, together with Siam, Ava, Arracan, and the bordering kingdoms as far as the China of the Hindoos, and the Sin[d] of the Arabian geographers, the whole western peninsula, and the island of Ceylon. (1)

Such an extended landscape also fueled fantasies among nationalist advocates of a "Greater India," although the colonial territorial reality (despite concerted British effort) was itself much more circumscribed. In attempting to capture in marble such an expansive vision, Gupta's map materializes a mythical reality that appears even more surreal after the end of empire, partition, and the creation of numerous independent nation-states in the region. In doing so this memorial to Bharat Mata also arrests a moment in time—ironically, under colonial rule—when much of this space was seemingly unitary and singular and operated under the sign of "India."[18] Like so many other artifacts of empire, this temple as well is a curious hybrid of ancient Sanskritic and modern British hopes, fantasies, and realities.

As such, the temple with its enshrined map becomes a site for the generation of visual piety for the nation's imagined territory.[19] Greater India is enshrined and presented to the viewer-patriot in much the same way that in the generic Hindu temple images of gods and goddesses are consecrated and displayed as murti, although the conventional form of the (anthropomorphized) deity gives way to the unconsecrated map laid out on the floor of the Bharat Mata Mandir. As Diana Eck notes, "The central act of Hindu worship, from the point of view of the lay person, is to stand in the presence of the deity and to behold the image with one's own eyes, to see and be seen by the deity."[20] Through such acts of seeing and being seen—as embodied in the practice of *darshan* (auspicious or reverential viewing)—regimes of allegiance and devotion, even intimacy, are constituted between the divine image and its worshipper. Thus much of Hindu worship is intensely ocular, predicated as it is on a series of visual interactions and exchanges between deity and devotee. Likewise, through the device of the map enshrined in the Bharat Mata Mandir, the nation's territory is presented to the patriot for visual contemplation and interaction. As such the map stands *for* as well as stands *in for* that which it represents. As Edward Casey, from whom I borrow this distinction, writes with regard to art objects such as a painting, "As standing *for*, it serves as a sign of its represented content or subject matter: in this regard, it is a semiological entity. As standing *in for*, it is a perceived object, a material object in its own right that has taken the place of something else material"(2002, 17). So what does the map in the Bharat Mata Mandir stand *for*, and stand *in for?* On the one hand it materializes—in marble, no less—the whole that is India that the patriot cannot otherwise see at one glance. It stands in for, and in the place of, an imagined whole called "India." On the other hand, as a representation of national territory the relief map of India is iconic (in the Peircian sense of the term), predicated as it is on an assumed formal correspondence or resemblance between sign (map) and referent (territory).[21] As a representation of Bharat Mata in this first temple built to memorialize her, however, the map is symbolic by replacing Mother India's anthropomorphic and divine form with a configuration convention-alized by the science of cartography.[22]

Even given the well-known iconoclasm of Gupta's particular religious leanings as they found exposition in the teachings of the reformist Arya Samaj movement (with its call to return to the pristine foundations of Hinduism sans image worship), it is surprising that he should have chosen to enshrine India by resorting to the (colonial) science of cartography. For the map of India in and by itself has had a limited purchase on the popular imagination outside the specialized realms of science and state. This was especially the case in the early years of the twentieth century when it more than ever seemed to need the anthropomorphic presence of Bharat Mata, as we have seen, to adequately represent the nation for patriotic purposes. Was the temple's effectiveness in generating worshipful reverence for the country therefore compromised from the start by having the map of India make a solo appearance without Mother India's assuring embodied form? I ask this question because the map of India was monumentalized at the Bharat Mata Mandir in order to generate what in chapter 3 I characterized as geo-piety. This is apparent from Gupta's own rendition of why he built the temple, as well as from the statements of those who were present at its inauguration. The temple with its enshrined map was a commemorative edifice that, unlike other sectarian shrines, sought to unify all inhabitants of a territory called India, regardless of their creed or calling. So in defending his effort from criticisms, Gupta announced on the eve of its inauguration that "the Mandir means *merely* a house in which a large relief map of India in marble is placed. The image is *merely* this map, and on the walls are painted astronomical and historical charts. The temple is open to all and every religion, creed, and caste."[23]

THE MYSTERY OF THE MISSING MOTHER

Despite Gupta's disavowals, the absent (Hindu) mother is seemingly present everywhere in the temple—in the very name of the temple, first, and in the inscription of her signature words "vande mataram" both on the portals as well as on inside walls. The inauguration ceremony in 1936 began with a hymn to Bharata Mata, and numerous speakers at the ceremony invoked her name. The famous Hindi poet Mythili Sharan Gupta composed and recited a poem in honor of the temple, which ended with reminding all those who had assembled in "Bharat Mata's courtyard" of the "fraternal bonds" that tied them together; the poet also recalled the Mother's "labor pains" in giving birth to her "sons." The ceremony closed with a recital of Bankim's "Vande Mataram" hymn, contentious though it had become by then.[24] Shivprasad Gupta himself repeatedly referred to the map of India enshrined in the temple as "matramurti" (mother's image); "mata ki murti" (mother's image); and even explicitly as "Bharata Mata ki murti," (Bharat Mata's image) (1983b, 389, 391). At the same time, as I noted earlier, visitors were quick to observe—*and* appreciate—that the murti of Bharata Mata was nowhere to be seen in the temple, and that *only* a map was to be found inside its walls. They were also keen to reiterate that no worship would be performed, and even today visitors are asked not to offer fruits or flowers to "the murti." In other words, despite being referred to as murti, the map has not been charged with the divine presence through rituals that routinely transform mundane image into sacred deity in a Hindu worshipful context.[25] The refusal—in fact failure—to create a set of secular rituals that would have increased the capacity of the monumentalized map to serve effectively as a patriotic object of veneration points in turn to the compromised character of the Bharat Mata Mandir, fatally suspended between the older familiar religion of Hinduism and the new religion of patriotism.

It is also important to underscore that all of those present at the inaugural ceremony were quick to point to the spirit of inclusivism that permeated the new temple. Such a claim carried special resonance in a decade punctuated by numerous temple-entry campaigns aimed at compelling high Hindu shrines to allow entry and right of worship to under castes. Newspapers reported that close to twenty-five thousand people from *all* of India's communities—Hindus, Muslims, Christians, Jains, Parsees, Buddhists, and the so-called Untouchables, Gandhi's Harijans—attended the inauguration of the Bharat Mata Mandir; prayers from all of India's religions were recited at the ceremony; and the temple was declared open to all regardless of sectarian affiliation. As one reporter present at the inaugural ceremony wrote, "The temple of Bharat Mata will be the first of its kind in India and has behind it a principle so very essential to the freedom of our country. The Muslims, the Christians, the Jews, the Parsis, and the Hindus need not now go to separate places of worship to realize the highest in them. Here is a temple dedicated to the most sacred goddess of Hindustan where all without distinction of caste and creed can offer worship and realize the highest moral and spiritual beatitude."[26]

The same spirit of inclusivism finds a place in a tourist guidebook published as recently as 2000 in which the Bharat Mata Mandir is introduced thus: "A unique temple dedicated to Mother India. The presiding 'deity' of this temple is a relief map of India, engraved on a marble slab. By avoiding the use of customary idols and images that go into the making of a Hindu shrine, this temple stresses the oneness of religion and seeks to foster unity among different communities of India" (Srinivasan 2000, 19). Yet, the undercurrent of Sanskritic Hinduism was apparent at the temple from its very conception, as it is in so many public places and events in colonial and postcolonial India: the foundation stone for the temple was laid in April 1927 with the recitation of hymns from Sanskrit scriptures and to the accompaniment of Hindu rituals of consecration; the inauguration ceremony took place on Vijaya Dashmi, one of the holiest days of the Hindu ritual calendar; contemporaries frequently referred to the map enshrined in the building as the murti; and the building that houses the map, although not resembling a conventional temple (figure 63), is after all referred to as *mandir*—the generic Hindi term for a Hindu house of worship.[27]

Most revealing, since at least the 1950s, the Bharat Mata Mandir has been incorporated into the popular pilgrimage maps of Hindu Banaras. Almost invariably the figure of Bharat Mata, sometimes occupying a map of India, marks the spot where the new goddess's temple stands on the pilgrimage route.[28] So in *Asli Bada Naksha Kashi Kshetra Ka: Map of Kashi* (Original large map of sacred Kashi), which has been available since at least the early 1950s, the temple appears in the upper-right quarter of the image, below a set of railway tracks on which a steam engine is shown pulling a set of green carriages (figure 65). But instead of a building marking the site identified (in English, Bengali, and Hindi) as "Bharat Mandir" (India temple), a female

FIGURE 65 *Asli Bada Nakshaa Kashi Kshetra Ka: Map of Kashi.* Printed pilgrimage map by Babu Madhoprasad Bookseller, Varanasi, circa 1950s. (Author's collection)

figure with a halo and the tricolor national flag has been painted in its place. In another map with a similar title (which circulates in a wide range of sizes today) the temple again appears in the same place on the upper-right-hand corner, just south of the railway line that snakes its way down the eastern edge of the picture (figure 66). In this print as opposed to the earlier one, a building has been inserted to mark the spot where the mandir stands on the map; laminated onto the front of the building is the figure of Bharat Mata (*sans* map) holding a trident in one hand, the other extended in a gesture of blessing. The Indian national flag (without the emblematic wheel) is also drawn on the building. The building is called Bharat Mandir in Hindi, and Bharat Temple in English. A car parked in front of it betrays, perhaps, the modernity of this particular site of pilgrimage.

Most strikingly, in a pilgrimage map of unknown provenance (with titles in English, Hindi, and Bengali) the temple is designated by a miniaturized carto-graphed form of Bharat Mata as a two-armed goddess holding a trident and occupying the map of India (figure 67). Shivprasad Gupta and his colleagues may have banished Bharat Mata's offensive, divisive, and embarrassing anthropomorphic form from the inner precincts of her temple, but

FIGURE 66 *Asli Bada Nakshaa Kashi Kshetra Ka: Map of Kashi.* Printed pilgrimage map by Puja Publications, Varanasi, circa 1990s. (Author's collection)

FIGURE 67 *Bada Naksha Asli Shrikashipuri Ka: Map of Kashipuri Asli* (detail). Printed pilgrimage map (with title in Hindi, English and Bengali), published in Varanasi, n.d. (Archives Varanasi Research Project, South Asia Institute, University of Heidelberg, Heidelberg)

still on all pilgrimage maps, even though it's not popular.

popular Hindu imagination appears to have reasserted itself and brought the mother/goddess back in (sometimes as a carto-graphed body, at other times without the map). In these bazaar pilgrimage maps, the anthropomorphic-sacred has triumphed over the scientific-geographic in the matter of repre-senting Indian national territory, or at least its enshrined form.

And yet Gupta intended the contrary, and the question remains why he turned to the map form to stand for—and stand in for—the country in the manner that he did. Product though it may be of colonial cartography, the re-lief map of India might have been useful for Gupta and his fellow nationalists for it shows the nation-space as a singular territory that is not divided and carved up into various pieces.[29] The physiographic map in relief also natural-izes India by presenting the country—in marble, no less, at the temple—as if it was a fact of nature like the very mountains, rivers, and valleys that appear on its surface. The visitor to the temple can take in at one glance the kind of terrain the nation possesses, for the relief map provides "a condensed image of the state's configured landscape" and brings into the beholder's vision "the drama of depth" (Casey 2002, 148, 150). Thus "India" is no figment of the patriotic imagination but rather is as tangible and substantial as the very land that constitutes it. Not least, the physiographic map with its emphasis on India's natural features also allows the nation's territory to be perceived as timeless as the mountains to the north and the rivers that make their way across its landscape, and as imperishable as the marble used to memorialize it within the walls of the Bharat Mata Mandir.

There is yet another reason that the scientific map form of India might have come in useful at this particular moment in history for men like Gupta, for as we saw in the previous chapter the new patriotic habit of imagining India as a mother/goddess had by the 1920s run aground on the reefs of Hindu idolatry. Mother India's very Hindu appearance, in other words, was increasingly a problem for all those nationalists who were interested—if only ostensibly—in visualizing India as a plural and diverse geo-body, especially one that its numerically most dominant minority would find hospitable as a homeland. In fact, the worship of images by Hindus had become by the early twentieth century a cultural and political embarrassment not just to those "secular" nationalists who came to believe that such a practice alienated non-idolatrous citizens of India, but even to many reformist Hindu men who at least since the early nineteenth century had responded to a scathing colonial and missionary critique of Hinduism by altogether rejecting the worship of images on various grounds. As Ashis Nandy notes, for these men "the country's main problem was its idolatry, and the rather poor personal quality of its gods and goddesses. These reformers wanted Indians to get rid of their superfluous deities and either live in a fully secularized, sanitized world in which rationality and scientific truth would prevail or, alternatively, set up a regular monotheistic God, as 'proper' Christians and Muslims had done" (2001, 131). Many such reformers, who by the closing decades of the nineteenth century began to participate in an emergent Hindu nationalism, even questioned the form of the temple itself as an institution that divided Hindu from Hindu. Thus in 1923 Dr. Balkrishna Moonje (1872–1948), a Hindu nationalist leader from the central Indian city of Nagpur, lamented "the absence of a common meeting place in the Hindu polity for the castes from the highest to the lowest [to meet] on perfectly equal terms, just as the Mohammedan has in his masjid [mosque] . . . Cannot our temples be made to serve the purpose which the masjid does for the Mohammedan?"[30] Almost as if in response to Moonje's rhetorical question, the Punjab-based Swami Shraddhanand (1856–1926)—a follower, like Gupta, of the reformist Arya Samaj movement—drew up an agenda for "saving" what he characterized as "the dying Hindu race." This agenda included as its very first step the building of

> one Hindu Rasthra Mandir [temple of the Hindu nation] in every city and important town, with a compound which could contain an audience of 25,000, and a hall in which *Katha* [prose selections] from [Hindu learned texts such as] Bhagavad Gita, the Upanishads, and the great epics Ramayan and Mahabharata could be daily recited. The Rashtra Mandir will be in charge of the local Hindu Sabha which will manage to have Akharas [places for physical exercise] for wrestling and *gatka*, etc. in the same compound. While the sectarian Hindu temples are dominated by their own individual deities, the Catholic Hindu Mandir would be devoted to the worship of three mother-spirits: the Gau mata [the cow-mother]; the Saraswati-mata [goddess of knowledge]; and the Bhumi-mata [Earth-Mother]. . . . *Let a lifelike map of Mother-Bharat [India] be constructed in*

a prominent place, giving all its characteristics in vivid colors so that every child of the Matri-bhumi [motherland] may daily bow before the Mother and renew his pledge to restore her to the ancient pinnacle of glory from which she had fallen.[31]

Even as Swami Shraddhanand was writing these words his fellow Arya Samajist Gupta was already attempting to materialize this vision in the Bharat Mata Mandir in Banaras. In Gupta's mandir, as we have seen, the marble relief map of India operates as a material stand-in for Bharat Mata by cartographically conjuring up for the benefit of the patriotic viewer "her" vast expanse, the beauty of "her" landscape, the majesty of "her" hills to the north, the fertility of "her" rivers, and so on.[32] The map of India, that proud product of secular science in all its physiographic glory, ironically becomes the murti in the new religion of patriotism that was sought to be generated in the Bharat Mata Mandir. In this new religion the embarrassment posed by the very Hindu form of Bharat Mata was countered by displacing the divine maternal form of the country with its putative map image, the anthropomorphic-sacred by the scientific-geographic. The work of barefoot cartography from the early decades of the twentieth century had helped create a dense relationship between Mother India's anthropomorphic form and the map form of India, as we have seen. This meant that when the deification of India's territory as an anthropomorphic Hindu mother/goddess became inopportune, as it increasingly did in the context of the nationalist mobilization of non-Hindus, the map could symbolically stand in for her idolatrous form as it did in the Bharat Mata Mandir.

But the question we are left with is whether the map form is actually able to accomplish this feat in its solo turn, especially given its association with the mother's anthropomorphic presence in its popular appearances. Soon after the temple was opened, the Bombay-based *Indian Social Reformer* expressed its doubt:

We view with some anxiety the prospect of the growth of new cults based not on religious but territorial idealism. The relief map of India, according to the *Guardian* of Madras, comprises the whole of India with its sister countries, like Afghanistan, Baluchistan, Tibet, Burma, part (why part?) of the Malaya Peninsula and Ceylon. All these are to be worshipped as Bharat

Mata which, according to the ancient Hindu geographers, was the land bounded by the Himalayas and the three seas. The temple, no doubt, will have its daily puja [worship] and hierophants to perform it. *The Indian has a passion for worship but we much doubt if his sentiments of reverence will be aroused by a map, even though it is done in Mekran marble.*[33]

The *Bombay Chronicle* was even more skeptical in its editorial titled "Cosmopolitan Temples." In commenting on Gandhi's approval of the temple, the paper stated:

We share [Gandhi's] hope, if only because India surely needs religious unity and peace. But we feel at the same time that a great deal more than building cosmopolitan prayer houses is necessary if that hope is to be fulfilled in any ample measure and in the near future. We do not see why all the existing temples, mosques, and churches should not be open to all persons seeking them. In any case religious unity is possible only to the extent that every religion is interpreted in a thoroughly rational manner and consistently with the dictates of humanity. In the absence of such an interpretation of religion, temples, mosques, and churches will be, as they have been in the past, a source of religious conflict rather than of religious unity. Bigotry glorified as religion has come to stink in the nostrils of all right-thinking men.[34]

Today the Bharat Mata Mandir wears an air of dismal abandon as it stands amid the hustle and bustle of Varanasi. The typical visitor to the temple nowadays is more likely to be a foreign tourist rather than an Indian patriot, although local schools occasionally bring young citizens to view the map and learn about the country.[35] The capacity of the temple to forge the new religion of patriotism was severely compromised not only because of the inadequacy of the map of India to serve by itself as a stand-in for Indian territory in a worshipful context, but also because of the failure to evolve effective nationalist rituals that would have transformed the newly fashioned map as murti into an effective deity of patriotic reverence (especially needed after its anthropomorphic crutch had been dispensed with). The temple does not even attract patrons of the older religion of Hinduism that the new patriotism around Bharat Mata sought to supplant. On the face of it, the fact that the temple was built in Varanasi was a historical accident because the man behind the enterprise was a wealthy native of the city. Nonetheless, it was a historical accident that could have been very productive given the city's reputation as the spiritual capital of Hindu India. One would have thought that the millions of devout Hindus who annually visit the city and its numerous temples would also take in the Bharat Mata Mandir, especially because it appears on maps in the company of the more well-known temples and it finds laudatory mention in various guidebooks. Distant though Gupta's edifice might be from the hallowed temples along the river Ganga, it still falls within the limits of the sacred geography of the holy city.[36] And yet it is largely ignored by Varanasi's faithful pilgrims.[37] In the opinion of its manager, Shyam Das Singh, with whom I spoke first in 1998 and who made much the same point to me when I saw him again in 2001, if only there had been a murti in the temple, not a mere map, then millions of Indians would come through its doors. And indeed a journalist who wrote about the temple a few years ago observed that "many pilgrims from rural areas who come to Varanasi, go to the Bharat Mata Mandir with flowers, Ganga water and other 'puja [worship] articles,' *only to find that there is no idol there.*"[38]

What we might facetiously characterize as the mystery of the missing mother in Varanasi's Bharat Mata Mandir offers a revealing lesson about the dilemmas of colonial and national modernity in India and about the incommensurable territorial imaginaries that have come to coexist over the course of the twentieth century. This is a modernity where many older practices of reverence have been rendered increasingly antiquated and even an embarrassment, but new ones wrought to replace these ancient ways have proven to be ineffectual. The map of India ought to have attracted millions of reverential citizens to this site of its grand enshrinement, but it fails to do so in a context where its purchase on the popular imagination, either as an iconic representation of Indian national territory or as a symbolic stand-in for Bharat Mata, is weak at best despite decades of barefoot cartographic activity and visual patriotism. At the beginning of the twentieth century, as we will see in the next chapter, a fictional protagonist in Tagore's *The Home and the World* had wondered whether the map of their country had the power to move Indians to die for their nation. A few decades later, when the *Indian Social Reformer* questioned whether "sentiments of reverence will be aroused by a map," it questioned the capacity of the map form to produce geo-piety for the territory it iconically represented. The flagging fate of the Bharat Mata Mandir in Hinduism's paradigmatic sacred city is yet another reminder that in the subcontinent the map form is an indispensable but nonetheless inadequate sign—neither having full purchase as iconic of the nation's territory nor succeeding as a symbol in standing in for the hallowed figure of the nation's embodiment as Bharat Mata.[39] In point of fact, as I entered the temple on my most recent visit in October 2004 the first thing I noticed at the entrance was a giant painting of a carto-graphed Bharat Mata. The painting was modeled on an image that has been widely used by various Hindu nationalist parties in their visual activities since the 1980s (figure 20), and it was done by a local painter "a few years ago," according to manager Singh who said he had commissioned it. With the introduction of this painting into the temple's precincts, the mother's idolatrous form clearly appears to have prevailed, notwithstanding Gupta's original intentions. The scientific-geographic had been supplemented by the anthropomorphic-sacred, so that the mother/goddess was no longer truly missing in this first temple completed in her honor in 1936.

"IT IS THY IMAGE WE RAISE IN EVERY TEMPLE"

Bharat Mata is emphatically not missing in yet another temple that five decades later was built to commemorate her in the Himalayan pilgrimage town of Haridwar, another Hindu favorite. The antecedents for this postcolonial multifloored temple, documented at some length by the anthropologist Lise McKean, are quite different from the colonial Banaras project. Inaugurated in 1983—by no less a figure than Prime Minister Indira Gandhi (1917–1984), despite her well-publicized, socialist-secular credentials and those of her party—the imperatives that led to its creation are most overtly Hindu nationalist rather than ostensibly pluralist like Gupta's. The force behind this temple was Swami Satyamitranand Giri, a key functionary in the Vishwa Hindu Parishad (World Hindu Council) founded in 1964, who appears to have learned from Gupta's cartographic blunder. For enshrined in the new temple on the entrance level are both a relief map of India (cast in color plaster) *and* a marble icon of Bharat Mata beaming down upon "her" territory from behind a glass enclosure. Inscribed on a marble plaque is the following announcement (in English and Hindi): "We are all sons of Bharat Mata: of one abode, society, humanity and culture. This land, from the Himalayas to the ocean, is one entity: from the dawn of creation, our genesis has been in her lap[;] many streams of ideas, ideals, cults, creeds, have blended like the many streams of Mother Ganga to create our own unique culture and nation-hood. This has grown in a span of many a millennia; thousands of us have conduced to this through sacrifice, dedication, deep research, austere penance[.] They have led us, above caste and class, to unity and supreme erudition. We are indeed a nation with a rich heritage: let us all proudly [vow] to preserve our sublime dignity."

The image of Bharat Mata has been sculpted in white marble in an iconographic style that has become generic for goddesses across northern India since the early years of the twentieth century. She has two arms, one holding a sheaf of grain and the other a milk urn "signifying the white and green revolution that India needs for progress and prosperity."[40] Despite the obvious combative thrust of Hindu nationalism that provides the inspiring force behind this temple and the many militant images of the mother/goddess that proliferate in the print literature of the movement, Mother India named as Bharat Mataram is presented in the temple as a figure of fertility rather than as a warrior deity. Although there are no proud claims here as in Banaras to the cartographic precision of the map enshrined in the temple, it too is cast in relief with the physiographic specificities of the country's mapped geo-body—its major mountains, plateaus, rivers, and river valleys—presented in color. The snowcapped Himalayas are as striking in the map as they are in the bazaar's printed patriotic images. The nation's important cities are highlighted, as they are in the relief map in the temple in Banaras, along with the major centers of Hindu pilgrimage, which a keypad installed next to the map allows the patriot-pilgrim to light up through the mediation of tiny electric bulbs embedded in the geo-body of the country. The sacred geography of Hindu India is reinscribed—and reinforced—using the rational science of modern cartography (not to mention electricity). Citizens of India who come to "see" their country as map and as mother at the temple learn about their nation not through its geography alone but also through history and religious mythology, for the other six floors of the temple are dedicated to various key figures from an evolving Hindu nationalist pantheon of gods and saints, warriors and martyrs.[41]

A century before this temple was created, Bankim proclaimed in his foundational 1874–1875 hymn to his mataram that "it is thy image we raise in every temple" across the land. In this country of proliferating deities and thronging temples, however, shrines to Mother India are ultimately few and far between.[42] Every now and then the image of Bharat Mata (sometimes carto-graphed, at other times sans map) may be found in temples interspersed among pictures and images of the more-established gods of the Hindu pantheon, as is the case in the disputed Krishnajanmabhoomi temple in the temple town of Mathura,[43] or in the Rani Sati temple in Jhunjhunu, Rajasthan (figure 68).[44] More contentiously, an icon of Bharat Mata as an eight-armed deity (without a map) was placed around 1948 in a small shrine within the precincts of the fourteenth-century Jami mosque (which, in some accounts, was itself built from parts of Hindu and Jaina temples) in the historic Daulatabad fort in south-central India (figure 69). Makeshift shrines housing carto-graphed images of the goddess occasionally have been set up in offices and schools associated with various Hindu nationalist parties (for example, figure 70).[45] A major developer announced in 2003 that housing complexes built across the country under its aegis would include a shrine for Mother India, the Bharat Maa Naman Sthal, where "the supreme religion of Bharatiyata [Indian-ness]" would be celebrated in the presence of "a huge statue of Bharat Maa" placed in an "expansive prayer space with extensive landscaping."[46] Despite the many secular and plural interests that have converged on and around the figure of Mother India over the course of the last century and more, she has found it difficult if not impossible to escape the vise of Hindu religiosity or of Hindu nationalism more generally. In fact, one could even argue that the very idea of building shrines and temples for the mother/goddess reveals the impossibility of pursuing a purely secular or non-religious project around the figure of Mother India, as pluralist intentions are constantly infiltrated by hegemonic Hindu ways of viewing and worship.

Two centuries and more of scientific cartography may have attempted to transform the land into a measured geo-body, a product of surveyed mathe-

FIGURE 68 Statue of Bharat Mata at the Rani Sati temple, Jhunjhunu, Rajasthan. Photograph by Rich Freeman, 2005. (Author's collection)

FIGURE 69 Bharat Mata shrine in Daulatabad, 2006. (Courtesy of Ram Narasinham)

FIGURE 70 School prayer time in Saraswati Shishu Vidya Mandir, Phulwarisharif, Patna, Photograph by Ranjan Rahi, circa 2007. (Courtesy of Ranjan Rahi)

matical mapped knowledge. The map of India, in turn, has been offered to the Indian viewer as an object of contemplation, learning, and identification in various public non-religious sites: government buildings, street billboards, and most systematically, of course, in textbooks, schoolrooms, and other educational contexts. But does the scientific-geographic imaginary *in and of itself* have the capacity to transform national territory into an object of geo-piety for which "sentiments of reverence will be aroused," to invoke again the *Indian Social Reformer*'s doubt from the 1930s? I close this chapter with two images—both drawn from Tamil schoolbooks—that suggest the beginnings of an answer.

In an illustration for a textbook lesson from 1955 a young boy is shown looking at an outline map of India hanging (presumably) on his school wall. Beneath the illustration, a poem printed in Tamil praises both the larger Indian geo-body as well as the Tamil country as beautiful and incomparable (figure 71). No emotions are manifest as the young boy looks, almost clinically, at the framed map on the wall showing the image of his country (*naadu*). In another textbook from two decades earlier, around 1933, a map of India illustrates an almost identical poem, titled "Engal Naadu" (Our Coun-

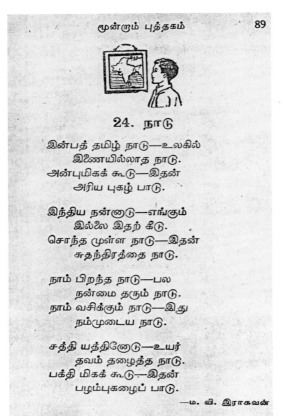

24. நாடு

இன்பத் தமிழ் நாடு—உலகில்
இணையில்லாத நாடு.
அன்புமிகக் கூடு—இதன்
அரிய புகழ் பாடு.

இந்திய நன்னுடு—எங்கும்
இல்லை இதற் கீடு.
சொந்த முள்ள நாடு—இதன்
சுதந்திரத்தை நாடு.

நாம் பிறந்த நாடு—பல
நன்மை தரும் நாடு.
நாம் வசிக்கும் நாடு—இது
நம்முடைய நாடு.

சத்தி யத்திணெடு—உயர்
தவம் தழைத்த நாடு.
பக்தி மிகக் கூடு—இதன்
பழம்புகழைப் பாடு.

—ம. வி. இராகவன்

FIGURE 71 Illustration for the poem "Naadu" (The country) in the Tamil schoolbook *Kovait Tamil Vaacakam* (Kovai Tamil reader) by S. Nagarajan. Standard Textbook Company, Erode, 1955.

try), similarly dedicated to the praise of the Indian geo-body as well as the Tamil country (figure 72). And yet there is one critical difference between the two images: in the illustration in figure 72, as the three young men look up intently at the map—their clothing identifying them as Muslim, Hindu, and Christian—they are moved to action. Their palms come together in homage as they visually take in (get darshan of) the map whose cartographic space is now occupied by Bharat Mata. The supplementation of the cartographic form of India by the anthropomorphic presence of Mother India appears to have elicited this reverential reaction from the citizen-viewer. The detached clinical gaze of figure 71 is countered by the worshipful attitude of figure 72.[47]

As historians of cartography have noted, the map form allows for the visual possession of the national territory to proceed. Thus the outline map of India has the capacity to deliver the national territory synoptically, as a

32. "எங்கள் நாடு"

1. உலகினிற் சிறந்ததும் எங்கள் நாடு—பல
உண்மைகள் தோன்றியதும் எங்கள் நாடு

2. தத்துவங்கள் நிறைந்ததும் எங்கள் நாடு
—பல
தவசிகள் வாழ்ந்ததும் எங்கள் நாடு.

3. செந்தமிழ் சிறப்பதும் எங்கள் நாடு—
வெகு
சிவஸ்தலம் ஓங்குவதும் எங்கள் நாடு.

4. வானவர் போற்றுவதும் எங்கள் நாடு—
திரு
வள்ளுவர் பிறந்ததும் எங்கள் நாடு.

FIGURE 72 Illustration for the poem "Engal Naadu" (Our country) in the Tamil schoolbook *Gokhale Irantaam Vaacakam* (Gokhale Second Reader) by P. T. Sreenivasa Aiyangar. V. S. Venkataraman, Kumbakonam, circa 1933.

whole, "at one glance." The citizen stands outside the nation, as he does in figure 71, taking stock of it as one singular entity. Yet how do such maps that picture the national territory as lines and contours on a printed page foster the sentiment of intimate belonging that is so crucial to the imagined community of the nation? How is it possible for the citizen who obviously stands removed from this territorial space, viewing it from a point outside, to come to see it as his "homeland," inside which he belongs? What is it that moves young boys (like the one who appears in figure 71) to develop passionate attachment to the territory that they live in and that leads them— as it has done again and again in the modern world—to kill others and to die themselves in order to acquire or hold on to a particular piece of earth, cartographically presented to them in the form of the impersonal map? As the feminist scholar Joan Landes reminds us, "The nation is a greedy institution—economically, physically, and emotionally. It is the object of a special kind of love—one whose demands are sometimes known to exceed all others, even to the point of death" (2001, 2). In other words, how can the young citizen featured in figure 71 feel moved to give up his life for this map? I propose that the supplementation of the inanimate geo-body of the nation by the anthropomorphic form of the mother/goddess pictorially converts the citizen-subject from being a detached observer of the carto-graphed image of India into its worshipful patriot, so that its territory is not just lines and contours on a map but a mother and motherland worth dying for. It is this argument that I develop in the next chapter by turning to Mother India's many devoted men, several of whom were moved enough by her not to just worship her and enshrine her image but to martyr themselves in her name and for her cause.

In goddess worship
only male animals
may be sacrificed
to the goddess--

BETWEEN MEN, MAP, AND MOTHER

5

The fictional exemplar of this chapter is Sandip, the anti-hero of the controversial novel *The Home and the World*. Written by Rabindranath Tagore, the novel offers a passionate denunciation of the swadeshi movement and discloses some risky outcomes of enshrining the country as mother/goddess.[1] As the very antithesis of the ideal man and citizen of the world to whom the poet-novelist Tagore himself aspired, Sandip typifies a new kind of Bharat Mata votary—one who is driven to arson, thievery, and even murder in her name. At a crucial moment in the narrative, Sandip addresses Bimala, the heroine of the story, and declares passionately: "Have I not told you that, in you, I visualize the *shakti* of our country? The Geography of a country is not the whole truth. No one can give up his life for a map!"[2]

Later in the novel, in a discussion with Bimala's husband Nikhilesh (a rationalist doubter of such passions and quite possibly the novelist's alter ego), Sandip insists, "True patriotism will never be roused in our countrymen unless they can visualize the motherland. We must make a goddess of her" (120). As the novel

critique of conceiving of the nation as a divine woman.... (misleading for men, destructive for women)...

unfolds, Sandip declares that Bimala is indeed the mother/goddess in flesh and blood: "When I see you before me, then only do I realize how lovely my country is" (73). Having declared that "no one can give up his life for a map," Sandip tells her that when he gives up his life fighting for the nation, "It shall not be on the dust of some map-made land, but on a lovingly spread skirt—do you know what kind of skirt?—like that of the earthen-red sari you wore the other day, with a broad blood-red border. Can I ever forget it? Such are the visions which give vigor to life, and joy to death!" (73).[3]

MEN IN THE AGE OF THE NATIONAL PICTURE

In taking inspiration from this fictional moment crafted by one of modern India's most creative thinkers, this chapter explores the complex triangulation of the geo-body of the nation with the mother's body and men's bodies in barefoot cartographic productions. In striking contrast to much popular and public art in India where women are hypervisible in incarnations ranging from the goddess to the vamp, it is men who are accorded prominence in patriotic pictures, thus visually endorsing a prevailing truth about nationalism as a masculinist project, fantasy, and hope.[4] In these pictures, to paraphrase John Berger (1972, 1), women appear but men act, so much so that even the few women who appear to act—with the exception of the singular figure of Mother India—are more often than not treated as honorary men, as I discuss in the next chapter. There are diverse models of male filial piety on display, as the prints analyzed in this chapter will reveal. Nonetheless the exemplary man is one who places life and limb at the service of map and mother.[5] In point of fact, these pictures appear to insist that the endgame for patriotic men is the crowning glory of martyrdom. The martyred male body—"the body in bits and pieces," bloodied, decapitated, or hanged—is the honorable prize of the pictorial transaction between men and maps in the name of the mother.[6]

In making these arguments I am encouraged by recent scholarship that develops masculinity as a *feminist* category of analysis. As Michael Kimmel observes in noting the coming to age of masculinity studies in the West as a scholarly field: "To engage masculinities through the prism of feminist theory or to write feminist theory using masculinities as an analytic dimension requires two temperamental postures. One must engage masculinity critically as ideology, as institutionally embedded within a field of power, as a set of practices engaged in by groups of men. And yet given the contradictory locations experienced by most men, men not privileged by class, race, ethnicity, sexuality, age, physical abilities, one must also consider a certain forgiveness for actual embodied men as they attempt to construct lives of some coherence and integrity in a world of clashing and contradictory filaments of power and privilege" (2002, x). I respond to Kimmel's call for "forgiveness for actual embodied men" by underscoring that nationalist ideology—masculinist though it is in conception and practice—burdens them with hardship and anxieties, along with bestowing privilege, power, and visibility. Men's martyrdom for map and mother, subsequently offered to other male citizens as worthy of emulation, is exemplary of this net of risk and death in which some get entangled. Images of male martyrdom, as indeed visual displays of male patriotism more generally, thus complicate the influential distinction that Laura Mulvey originally established between men as bearers of "the look" and women as its object, and thus compels us to attend to the male body as recipient of male acts of seeing and learning, of what we might call the patriotic gaze.[7]

The feminist scholar Eve Sedgwick in her *Between Men: English Literature and Male Homo-social Desire* developed the concept of male homo-sociality to analyze relationships between men that are routed through women who appear as exchange objects in transactions that dominantly enable and consolidate male interests of either competition or solidarity. As she writes, "Patriarchal heterosexuality can best be discussed in terms of one or another form of the traffic in women: it is the use of women as exchangeable, perhaps symbolic, property *for the primary purpose of cementing the bonds of men with men*."[8] In building on Sedgwick's project the art historian Abigail Solomon-Godeau observes in her marvelous work on images of masculinity in French neo-classicism that "in art and in life, homo-sociality does not necessarily depend on the outright elimination of femininity, but rather, on the more powerful bonds that unite men to one another and which collectively operate to secure the subordinate position of women" (1997, 86). In other words the woman, when she appears, serves as "the conduit through which collusions and collisions between . . . men are conducted" (Krishnaswamy 1998, 47), thereby enabling bonds of homo-sociality to evolve between men.

FIGURE 73 Prabhu Dayal, *Bharat Ke Bhagya Ka Nipataara: The Fate of Indian Sealed Up*. Printed by Shyam Sunder Lal, Cawnpur, circa 1930. (Courtesy of Urvashi Butalia, New Delhi)

Extending these insights I suggest that the barefoot mapmaker pictures the nation, especially in the late colonial period when it was still in the making, as a homo-social arena in which male citizens jostle for power and privilege but also work out their mutual fascinations, anxieties, and hostilities through and around the exceptional carto-graphed figure of Bharat Mata.

A striking revelation of this operation comes from the paintbrush of Prabhu Dayal who pictured the launch of the civil disobedience movement in January 1930 in a print called *Bharat Ke Bhagya Ka Nipataara: The Fate of Indian Sealed Up* (figure 73).[9] The print centers on a pair of scales whose pans are occupied by Lord Irwin, the viceroy of India, representing "Government," and by Gandhi representing "Congress" and hence the nationalist movement. Gandhi is pictured thrusting a sheet of paper at Irwin on which are written the words "11 conditions and the fate of India settled," and in his gesture the Englishman appears to be resisting these terms.[10] Lined up behind the two men are two groups of individuals, all men (with the exception of one sari-clad woman on the Congress side), one of whom carries a gun symbolizing the colonial state, the other a tricolor flag signifying the national movement. Hanging in balance between the two men on the pair of scales is the roughly drawn, partial geo-body of India occupied entirely by the face of a woman, undoubtedly Bharat Mata (although she is not named as such). Tears flow down her face as she gazes into the distance, appearing to have no say on the deal being worked out between the two men as her "fate" is "sealed up." The print visually interprets this critical moment in anticolonial nationalist politics as the homo-social negotiation conducted between two men—English and Indian—around the carto-graphed Mother India in tears.

PICTORIAL BIG MEN

Prints such as that by Prabhu Dayal and the many others included in this book reveal the barefoot mapmaker's preoccupation with male bodies, especially those of the "big men" of India's national movement.[11] Such men are typically the "Jewels of India," the "Gems of the Nation," and the "Leaders of the Country," to invoke the titles of some such prints from the late 1940s. For instance, a print by the Rao brothers published in Madras possibly sometime after independence shows Gandhi benevolently placing his arms around Prime Minister Nehru and Minister for Home Affairs Vallabh Bhai Patel (1875–1950), while a carto-graphed Bharat Mata, suspended above them in the dark firmament, blesses them (figure 74). The miniaturization of the mother/goddess who hitherto loomed so large in many patriotic pictures is a striking disclosure of the new politics of these pictorial big men. The print's English title is *Jai Hind* (Victory to India) but the subtitle is more revealing for my purposes: *Love-Service-Sacrifice*.[12] These are the values that yoke men to mother and map in the barefoot cartographic imaginary. When women appear in the company of the map of India, which is not all that frequently, they are generally shadowy or unnamed presences. They are typically not the focus of the barefoot mapmaker's adulation, nor are they critical to the love-service-sacrifice nexus in which the big men of India, the map of India, and Mother India are entangled.

The one woman who matters of course is Bharat Mata, and as the nationalist movement gathers momentum, especially in the critical years leading to independence, she frequently shares the cartographic space of India with

FIGURE 74 Rao brothers, *Jai Hind: Love-Service-Sacrifice*. Printed by Central Art Press, Madras, circa 1948. (Author's collection)

men, many of whom are identifiable (and named) figures from the dominant nationalist pantheon, most especially Mahatma Gandhi or "Bapu," "Pandit" Nehru, and "Netaji" Bose.[13] Together the extraordinary mother and her self-less, mostly Hindu, sons pictorially repossess what had hitherto appeared the domain of the British empire—colored pink or red—in colonial maps, atlases, and globes. Indian territory now passes under their joint custodianship as the (big) men of India inherit and rule the territory in the name of the mother. As Manu Goswami notes in her study of the new discourses on territory that emerged in late colonial north India, "The resolutely 'subject-centered' language of possession was transposed from individuals (upper-caste, Hindu, male) in relation to land to Bharat as a national territorial possession. Bharat Mata marks the historically significant reconstitution of colonial spatiality into national property" (2004, 203). Barefoot cartographic productions are exemplary of this significant reconstitution in that they draw upon the artifact of the map, through which all manner of claims to territorial possession have been imagined, anticipated, and made in modernity, and in that they deploy the figure of the mother—used for the transformation of India from a terrain of statist calculation into a nurturing homeland—to seal the deal in favor of the male citizenry.

In the company of her men Bharat Mata is invariably a stilled figure whose primary visual function appears to be to draw attention to the loyal sons who surround her and who have presumably selflessly devoted themselves to freeing her land and her map.[14] Thus in Brojen's *Shrinkhal Mukti* (Liberation from chains), which possibly was published by the Picture Publishing Company of Bombay to commemorate the imminence of independence, the mother/goddess (with the hint of a smile) occupies a roughly outlined map of India as Gandhi snaps the chains that shackle her hands (figure 75). Flanking them are other members of the Congress Party such as Nehru and Rajendra Prasad (1884–1963; the future first president of the Republic of India), along with Bose and soldiers from his expatriate Indian National Army, who share cartographic space with the two central protagonists. In return for their patriotic and filial love-service-sacrifice Bharat Mata blesses them, as also illustrated in a print titled *Naba-Bharat* (New India) (figure 76). In this image the carto-graphed mother/goddess occupies a map of undivided India (which is partly obscured by the halo around her head and the Indian flag), and she extends her blessings to Nehru and Gandhi while Bose, whose head is placed in a halo of its own, looks on. Such a gesture seems to signal her approval of their special, even exclusive, relationship to her territory and her map, even while it hallows those who are so blessed (see also figure 25).

In turn these men are generally pictured as figures of their times, with their poster countenances bearing remarkable similarity to their real-world or photographic appearance, whereas Mother India's face is invariably remote and other-worldly. Her body language, clothing, and jewelry mark her as a figure out of time placed on a pedestal (literally and figuratively) and protected from the vicissitudes of real-time politics with which only her sons can seemingly contend. This is especially the case in the postcolonial period when Nehru and other big men are frequently pictured against the background of the Red Fort, the Indian Parliament, or other symbols of the state and sites of real-world decision making (figures 77, 78, and 81). As

Shrinkhal Mukti

FIGURE 75 Brojen, *Shrinkhal Mukti* (Liberation from chains). Printed by Picture Publishing Company, Bombay, circa 1946. (Daniel Smith Poster Archive, Special Collections Research Center, Syracuse University, no. 2113)

Naba-Bharat 345

FIGURE 76 *Naba-Bharat* (New India). Chromolithograph published by Tower Half-Tone Co., Calcutta, circa 1947. (Courtesy of Christopher Pinney)

FIGURE 78 *Pandit Jawaharlal*. Printed by Hemchandra Bhargava, Delhi, circa 1950s. (Author's collection)

FIGURE 77 *Gandhi Jawahar*. Printed in Delhi, circa 1950s. (Courtesy of Erwin Neumayer and Christine Schelberger, Vienna)

Anne McClintock observes in her perceptive discussion of the gendering of "nation time" across the modern world, "women are represented as the atavistic and authentic body of national tradition (inert, backward-looking and natural), embodying nationalism's conservative principle of continuity. Men, by contrast, represent the progressive agent of national modernity (forward-thrusting, potent and historic), embodying nationalism's progressive, or revolutionary principle of discontinuity" (1995, 358–59). Kajri Jain, in the world of bazaar images that she analyzes, suggests that male leaders like Nehru function as embodied incarnations of the paternalistic state, with their images "imbued with its efficacy and its transcendental power" (2005, 327).

This state of embodied paternal incarnation is so much the case that in pictures that appear around the time of Indian independence and after, Bharat Mata is dispensed with altogether and the heads of her sons occupy the map of India in a gesture that Christopher Pinney has aptly characterized as the laminating of "physiognomy onto cartography" (figures 79 and 92).[15] In *Quit India* (figure 80) the outline map of India (more or less complete) is placed within a giant Q. Occupying the map are the towering bodies of Gandhi, Nehru, and Bose, which dwarf the trousered briefcase-carrying Englishmen on their way out of the country and on toward ships that will presumably return them to England.[16] A few years after the Quit India protests, when the All India Congress Committee met in Bombay in July 1946 (for a key convening when the party debated participating in an interim government as a prelude to independence) a large dramatic hoarding behind the dais showed a rough outline map of India, its center occupied by Gandhi's head placed in a roundel. The body of a male peasant, clad in a short dhoti with his ankles and wrists bound in chains, was stretched out across the map of India. The single word *ghulami* (slavery), in English orthography, snaked its way along the west coast of India. Photographs of the event show on the dais Gandhi, Nehru, and Patel, the future leaders of the land, who will presumably liberate the peasant from centuries of enslavement. Mother India, carto-graphed or otherwise, is nowhere in the picture.[17]

Similarly, in a print published some time after Gandhi's death in January 1948, three of independent India's leading men—Patel, C. Rajagopalachari (1878–1972), and Nehru—are shown next to a garlanded statue of

FIGURE 79 M. L. Sharma, *National Leaders*. Published in Calcutta, early 1950s[?] (Courtesy of Christopher Pinney)

FIGURE 80 *Quit India*. Artist and publication details not available, circa 1942. (Courtesy of Christopher Pinney)

FIGURE 81 D. D. Neroy, Garlanding of a statue of Gandhi by Sardar Patel, C. Rajagopalachari, and Nehru. Printed by Anant Shivaji Desai Topivala, circa 1948. (Courtesy of Priya Paul, New Delhi)

Gandhi (figure 81). The statue is placed on a pedestal on which an outline map of undivided India is etched, with the Mahatma's dates of birth and death inscribed above and below it.[18] Here as well the carto-graphed Mother India is visibly absent. It is as if with freedom from colonial rule the male citizenry's proprietary claim over Indian national territory is also secure, and after the mother had helped visually convert colonial territory into homeland then map and man can relate directly with each other without resorting to the mediating figure of the mother.[19]

Other than blessing her sons there is one other regard in which Bharat Mata does not appear as an impassive observer of things happening around and to her, and this is when she is moved to perform an action that only reaffirms the warrior masculinity of her more militarily inclined sons. Such warriors include men from the historic past such as the Rajput lord Rana Pratap and the Maratha ruler Shivaji (figure 82), and from the nationalist present such as Bose and soldiers of his expatriate Indian National Army. A

FIGURE 82 Aryan, *Rashter Ke Panch. Rattan* (The nation's five gems). Published by Kedar Nath Arya, Sialkot, date unknown. (Courtesy of Priya Paul, New Delhi)

revealing example of Bharat Mata's role as an instigator of male militancy is the print *Mata ka Bandhan Mochan* (Mother's liberation from enslavement) possibly published some time after 1950 by the Calcutta-based Rising Art Cottage (figure 32). Mother India appears within its frame as a four-armed goddess with a large halo around her. She stands on a globe almost entirely covered with a partial map of India. In one of her hands she holds a spinning wheel that she seems to be handing over to Gandhi (who stands, his palms together in obeisance, on a section of the map that partly outlines his native Gujarat). Nehru perches on the globe on her other side, his hands waiting to accept from her the Indian tricolor, a symbol of the new independent state. The center of this pictorial tableau is, however, occupied by Bose. Dressed in a soldier's uniform, he kneels down in front of the mother on the map of India, waiting to accept a sword that she holds out toward him. I will return later to Bharat Mata's *astra-daan* (granting of weapon) but for now note that

Pinney offers a nuanced reading of this image, which he writes symbolizes "the accession of non-violence to the power of violence" and "establishes a commensurablity between Gandhi's freedom through spinning, Nehru's freedom through conventional statist politics, and Netaji's liberation through the sword" (2004, 136).

Building on this reading, I suggest that *Mata Ka Bandhan Mochan* offers a retrospective vision of the three models of love-service-sacrifice for mother and map that had prevailed during the anticolonial struggle. In barefoot cartographic productions, and in patriotic pictures more generally, all three models are allowed to flourish and proliferate and no tidy resolutions are offered—in contrast to the evolving consensus of "real time" Indian political culture that by the mid-1940s increasingly favored the statist approach of Nehru over Gandhi's ascetic path and the militant ways of Bose. There is also a fourth model that, for a while, eclipses the other three, but before I address it I focus on these three big men and the manner in which their relationship to mother and map and to each other is worked out in barefoot cartographic productions.

MAPPING THE MAHATMA

In the pictorial transactions between men and the map in the name of the mother, Gandhi's special task is to secure the blessings of the gods themselves for the Indian national territory. He appears to connect the earthly India represented by its cartographic form with the celestial realm inhabited by the gods of the Hindu pantheon such as Shiva or Krishna (figure 83) and also, every now and then in the eclectic spirit of Gandhian nationalism, by the Sikh gurus, Buddha, and Jesus (figure 29, figure 84). With his apotheosis after his martyrdom in 1948, he leaves the earthly realm and enters the divine sphere from where he showers his blessings on India and the men (and the occasional women) who occupy it. India in turn is pictorially transformed from the disenchanted terrain of colonial calculation into the *punyabhumi* (hallowed land) of the (Hindu) nationalist imagination. In *Swargarohan* (Ascent to heaven), a print that possibly was published sometime after Gandhi's death, his garlanded figure rises to heaven seated in a gilded pavilion crowned by the Indian flag (figure 85). Waiting to welcome him are the three principal gods of the Hindu pantheon, Shiva, Vishnu, and Brahma,

ভারত মাতা   BHARAT MATA   भारत माता

FIGURE 83 *Bharat Mata.*
Chromolithograph published by Tower
Half-Tone Company, Calcutta, late 1940s.
(Courtesy of Erwin Neumayer and
Christine Schelberger, Vienna)

स्वर्ग में बापू

FIGURE 84 *Swarg mein Bapu* (Gandhi
in heaven). Printed by Indian School of
Photography, Delhi, circa 1948. (osian's
Archive, Research and Documentation
Centre, Mumbai)

FIGURE 85 *Swargarohan* (Ascent to heaven). Printed by Shree Vasudeo Picture Co., Bombay, circa 1948. (OSIAN's Archive, Research and Documentation Centre, Mumbai)

along with their wives. Instead of eagerly looking toward this heavenly welcome, however, Gandhi looks down at the world below from which he has departed, which is drawn as a globe occupied almost entirely by a topographic map of India—clearly appropriated from command cartography's productions. Gandhi's apotheosized gaze and blessing transforms India from any "map-made" land on the face of the earth into a special territory worth dying for, as he had demonstrated in and by deed.

And while Gandhi was alive he literally spun the very nation into life through his insistence that Indians should develop self-reliance, discipline, and sense of worth through the patient art of spinning. An anonymous poster (possibly from the early 1930s) features a rather youthful Gandhi (clearly modeled on a photograph from a time prior to the mid-1920s when he was still wearing a kurta and headdress), sans halo, sitting on a globe on which is drawn a partial map of India (with some of its internal administrative divisions as well as cities identified) (figure 86). Also perched on the map are a woman (possibly his wife Kasturba) and another man dressed in Gandhian

FIGURE 86 Mahatma Gandhi at the spinning wheel. Artist and publishing information unknown, circa early 1930[?]. (Courtesy of Erwin Neumayer and Christine Schelberger, Vienna)

garb. All three are at work carding cotton, spinning it into thread, and weaving it into cloth on a loom. The output of all their hard work is the stack of cloth piled on the map of India; a swathe from the pile reaches out across the terrain of the country. The entire mise-en-scène is blessed both by Mother India herself, who also holds in one of her hands the Congress Party flag of the 1920s with the Gandhian charka painted on it, and by Bal Gangadhar Tilak, the firebrand author of swadeshi from an earlier decade. For the unnamed artist who created this image, Gandhi's charka clearly enables the nation to reach the light of freedom—in which the map of India is bathed in this picture—by casting aside the darkness of economic slavery and poverty.

Many other artists appear to have followed this example when we consider their creations featuring Gandhi with the ubiquitous charka. An evocative sketch titled *Spinner of India's Fate* by the art-school educated and fellow Gujarati Kanu Desai (who did a series of lovely pen and ink portraits of

Spinner of India's Fate

FIGURE 87 Kanu Desai, *Spinner of India's Fate*. Pen, ink, and brush, circa 193[?]. (Courtesy of the National Gandhi Museum, New Delhi)

the Mahatma) shows Gandhi at his spinning wheel producing India itself, which is visualized looming above him as a rough outline map of the country occupied by the face of a woman, most likely Bharat Mata (figure 87).[20] Prior to Desai's sketch (and possibly even inspiring it), the Gandhi-led Congress Party published in 1922 a pamphlet on the virtues of homespun cloth in which a portrait of a youthful Gandhi clad in the fabric is placed above a spinning wheel. Both Gandhi and the charkha are blessed by Mother India who also holds a flag with the spinning wheel on it. Of critical importance here is the visual suggestion—as in Desai's sketch—that as the wheel turns it creates the nation, signified by the outline map of India and titled in Hindi as Bharat.[21]

So enduring and indelible is the connection between the map and the Mahatma that in a print showing Gandhi's cremation at Rajghat in New Delhi in February 1948, *Amar Bharat Atma* (Immortal soul of India), as the

अमर भारतात्मा

नैनं छिन्दन्ति शस्त्राणि नैनं दहति पावकः ॥
न चैनं क्लेदयन्त्यापो न शोषयति मारुतः ॥
—श्रीभगवान् कृष्ण

पावन तीर्थ "राजघाट" दिल्ली।
। मरा नहि वहि कि जो तिषा न आवके तिषे ।
मैं. गुप.

चित्रकार—के. आर. केतकर, ए. एस., केतकर आर्ट इन्स्टिट्यूट, गिरगाव रोड, मुंबई नं. ४. आणि आर्ट, ए. स., स. खुदिराम व्यायामंदिर, मुंबई नं. २४.

FIGURE 88 K. R. Ketkar, *Amar Bharat Atma* (Immortal soul of India). Printed by Ketkar's Art Institute, Mumbai, circa 1948. (Courtesy of Erwin Neumayer and Christine Schelberger, Vienna)

fumes from his funeral pyre vaporize into the skies above they are transformed into a cruciform map of India, out of which Gandhi's head emerges smiling cheerfully over his own cremation (figure 88).[22] The print seems to suggest that even in death Gandhi's body and the geo-body of the nation are inseparable: such is the strength of the bond between the map and the man who is seen as the "immortal soul of India."

Gandhi's love-service-sacrifice for map and country seems all the more precious to those who are drawn to picturing him, for after all he is *bapu*, the "father" of the nation, and thus one who is least expected to give it all up. Charmed by Gandhi's simplicity and austerity, the barefoot mapmaker unfailingly pictures him as a man of the people who lays claim to Indian territorial space, indeed the world, even while humbly clad in his dhoti and little else—his only other possessions being his spectacles, pocket watch, charka, and the Bhagavad Gita (possibly his favorite text). So in the print *Jay-Yatra*

(Victory walk) a bespectacled Gandhi strides across a partial map of India that appears as the only land that matters on the face of a gridded globe (figure 89). The chains that shackled the country to servitude have been cut, presumably under the stewardship of Gandhi as with staff in one hand and spinning wheel in the other, a watch hanging from his waistband, he walks across its geo-body inscribed with the words *svadheen Bharat*, "independent India." Gandhi, we know, traveled indefatigably all over the country almost until the time of his death, granting darshan to the eager follower, but even so, a large majority of Indians would not have had the opportunity to actually see him. In lieu of such personal visions, his fellow citizens would have gained glimpses of him through the circulation of such images, which only amplified the myth of the Mahatma that the man himself cultivated through words, deeds, and performances. He may have worried about being treated like a god, but in the eyes of the barefoot cartographer and patriotic artist, he was indeed one, as affirmed by the presence of the largo halo that glows around him in their work (especially after his assassination) (figure 90). The only other figure in patriotic art consistently adorned in a similar way, as we have seen, is Mother India herself.

Although in his prolific verbal discourse Gandhi did not invoke Bharat Mata as often as did some of his contemporaries, especially those who were overtly Hindu nationalist, he is thrown into the company of the mother's carto-graphed body in all manner of ways by the barefoot mapmaker. He is frequently shown at work at his charka, watched over by Mother India, as he produces the homespun khadi that would eventually clothe her body and the bodies of her children whom he urged to free themselves of dependence on foreign manufactures (figure 86). He breaks the chains that shackle both her and the map of the country (figures 56 and 89), and he connects her land to the world of gods by his saintly words and deeds (figures 83–85). In turn, she blesses him for his wondrous deeds, as is shown in H. L. Khatri's *Rastrapita Mahatma Gandhi aur Bharat Mata* (Father of the nation, and Mother India) (figure 90).[23] She also looks to him to save her, smiles upon him as he breaks the shackles that bind her (figure 75), sheds tears over his passing (figure 84), and gathers into her arms his bullet-punctured and bloodied body. Thus in a striking bilingual poster titled in English *Bapuji on Eternal Sleep*, she holds him in her arms as blood from the bullet wounds on his chest drips down to

FIGURE 89 *Jay-Yatra* (Victory walk).
Chromolithograph published by SNS,
Calcutta, circa 1947. (Courtesy of
Christopher Pinney)

FIGURE 90 H. L. Khatri, *Rastrapita
Mahatmaji Aur Bharatmata* (Father
of the nation and Mother India).
Chromolithograph published by Chimanlal
Chhotalal and Co., Ahmedabad, circa 1947.
(Author's collection)

চির নিদ্রায় বাপুজী   Bapuji on eternal sleep

FIGURE 91 *Bapuji on Eternal Sleep.* Printed by SNS, Calcutta, circa 1948. (Courtesy of Erwin Neumayer and Christine Schelberger, Vienna)

earth (figure 91). Although she is bedecked in a sari and the accoutrements of the Hindu goddess, and she is flanked by the recently installed national flag, in the image Bharat Mata is reminiscent of the Virgin Mary as she holds her dead son's body and gazes compassionately upon it in the manner of the famed Pietà.[24]

The dominant scholarly understanding of Gandhi is that he "feminized" Indian nationalism by basing his philosophy and practice of satyagraha and nonviolent resistance on his reading of the woman's capacity for self-suffering, patience, endurance, and toleration of intolerable difficulties and burdens; by surrounding himself in his daily life with Gandhian women who performed all manner of services for him including serving as his "walking sticks"; and by inducing women in large numbers to leave the sheltered spaces of their homes to join the public world of nationalist agitation. None of this, however, is readily or even remotely apparent in these pictures. Instead the barefoot mapmaker invariably presents Gandhi in a homo-social arena with other men—Nehru and Bose dominantly, but also others such as Rajendra Prasad, Sardar Patel, and Maulana Azad (but never Jinnah)—to whom he is shown handing over stewardship of the Indian geo-body and, as well, guardianship over Bharat Mata. As India moves toward freedom and beyond, it is the men who occupy the map of the country in these pictures that he blesses and bathes in the glow of his own beatitude (for example, figures 25, 74, and 76). It is these men who are pictured as his inheritors, not the many women who inspired him and were in turn inspired by him.[25]

THE WORLDLY SON

Foremost among these heirs in the picture world of Indian patriotism—as in the real world of Indian politics—is Jawaharlal Nehru, the leading Congress nationalist from the 1930s and independent India's first prime minister (from August 1947 until his death in May 1964) (figures 92 and 93). In a print that likely was published sometime after Gandhi's death just a few months after Nehru's formal ascension to the post of prime minister, we see a striking revelation of the homo-social transaction between these two men around the map, even as the mother is totally out of the picture (figure 77). In the print a smiling Gandhi (a halo around his head) beams down on a smiling Nehru whose upper body (adorned in his trademark jacket with the telltale rosebud pinned to the buttonhole) merges into the outer facade of a building recognizable as Parliament. Strikingly, Gandhi's lower body, swathed in white fabric, maps out the approximate cartographic shape of India. As with Ketkar's print discussed earlier (figure 88), we get another visual intimation of the impossibility of separating the map and this particular man: he *is* India, so completely and seamlessly is he one with it, or at least its cartographic manifestation. At the same time the picture's hierarchical arrangement also suggests a passing of the baton, so that the Mahatma phases himself out of the (patriotic) picture (literally and metaphorically). With Gandhi happy in the knowledge that the guardianship of Indian territory now rests with Nehru, whose smiling visage occupies the peninsular half of the map, there is little sense here (or in any other print) of the many tensions that dogged the relationship between the two men in the years leading up to independence.

Much more scholarship is needed on popular visual perceptions of Nehru

Pride of India

FIGURE 92 *Pride of India*. Print, circa 1950s. (Courtesy of Erwin Neumayer and Christine Schelberger, Vienna)

and his times, as Patricia Uberoi observes, and her own essay "'Unity in Diversity'? Dilemmas of Nationhood in Indian Calendar Art" (2003) makes an important beginning in this regard.[26] In the patriotic pictures of India's future prime minister that begin to appear from the 1930s, he is frequently shown as a pensive man—the smiling face in the print discussed above is a departure from his usual poster look (for example, figures 76 and 92). Indeed, a Brijbasi print titled in English *Pt. Jawaharlal Nehru (in Pensive Mood)* and signed by Chitrasala shows a preoccupied-looking man, in rather rumpled clothing, standing next to a table stacked with books and covered with a green cloth on which is drawn a partly visible map of India, its interior filled up with radiating lines (figure 93).[27] The print seems to suggest that Nehru's nation-building role had already begun in the 1930s, years before he had formally assumed the burdens of being independent India's first prime minister. In contrast to the otherworldly Gandhi who, I have noted, is shown in the com-

PT. JAWAHAR LAL NEHRU
(In pensive)

FIGURE 93 Chitrasala, *Pt. Jawaharlal Nehru (In Pensive Mood)*. Printed by S. S. Brijbasi and Sons, Mathura, circa 1930s[?]. (Courtesy of Erwin Neumayer and Christine Schelberger, Vienna)

pany of the gods and other celestial beings, Nehru is Bharat Mata's worldly son, with his worldliness suggested by his appearance with cartographic instruments as props as well as by his preoccupied demeanor (figures 94 and 95). As in Chitrasala's image that casts Nehru in a "pensive mood," in the print *Bharat Ki Chinta* (Worrying over India) the Kanpur-based publisher Shyam Sunder Lal (who printed several of the patriotic pictures analyzed in this book) shows a thoughtful Nehru seated at a table (draped in the Indian tricolor), his chin resting on his palm as he gazes off in the distance presumably in deep reflection on "India," whose cartographic outline is partly inscribed on the giant terrestrial globe in front of him as well as partially visible on the wall map behind him.

Bharat Ki Chinta in turn points to a work by K. S. Bhat, dated to 1937, in which the future prime minister, featured with a look that might be read

FIGURE 94 *Bharat Ki Chinta: P. Jawaharlal Nehru.* Printed by Bhargave Press for Shyam Sunder Lal, Allahabad/ Cawnpore, circa 1930s[?]. (Courtesy of Erwin Neumayer and Christine Schelberger, Vienna)

FIGURE 95

C. R. Krishnaswami, *Swarajya Sooryodhayam* (Birth of freedom). Printed by the artist, 1949. (Author's collection)

FIGURE 96 K. S. Bhat, *Pandit Jawaharlal Nehru, No. 67*. Printed by Maharaja Frame Works, Bangalore, 1937. (Courtesy of Centre for Indian Visual Culture, New Delhi, Collection of Jutta and Jyotindra Jain)

as pensive, clutches to his heart a Hindi book titled *Bharat Mata* whose cover illustration is a map of India painted red and occupied by the body of Bharat Mata carrying a trident in one hand and holding a tricolor flag in the other (figure 96). Years later, after Nehru had become prime minister, the well-known Delhi publishers Hemchandra Bhargava printed an image titled *Pandit Jawaharlal* that shows him standing in his office, his rumpled clothes replaced by the stylish "Nehru" coat (figure 78). The Parliament building, emblematic of a proud new democracy, is clearly visible through the large window, but also visible on the desk next to the prime minister is a miniature statue of a female figure holding the tricolor in her hands—it is possibly Bharat Mata, the symbol of the nation.

Such prints lead me to suggest that Nehru's task in the pictorial transaction between (big) men and the map in the name of the mother (albeit a mother who is increasingly miniaturized or entirely invisible) lies in securing

মহাযের ডাকিস   105   Call of time

FIGURE 97 Sudhir Chowdhury, *Call of Time*. Chromolithograph published by sns, Calcutta, circa 1950s[?] (Courtesy of Christopher Pinney)

and consolidating the hard-fought independence for which men like Gandhi and Bose had given up life and limb. The figure of the man is that of the nation-building moment, holding the reins of the chariot of the state, as is strikingly depicted in a print called *Free India*: *Svatantra Bharat*, published by the Simla-based Paul Pictures.[28] As crucially, the figure holds the fortunes of Bharat Mata in his hands, as well as the fate of the country (figures 78 and 96). As such, in a bilingual print by the Bengali artist Sudhir Chowdhury, the visage of Nehru is surrounded by bright orange flames of fire that also appear to threaten a gridded globe on which the outline map of India is partly visible (figure 97). Titled in English *Call of Time*, the print seems to suggest that both the Indian geo-body and Nehru are being tested by the fires of the nation-building moment, when the prime minister grappled with the fall-out from the partition of the national territory, the merger of autonomous princely states into independent India, the growing demand for linguistic

FIGURE 98 Mother India breaks her chains. Print circa 1947–48. (Courtesy of Christopher Pinney)

states, and the industrialization of a predominantly agricultural economy. The responsibilities of rule weigh heavily down on this man who in the 1950s is increasingly the object of the barefoot cartographer's attention, as Gandhi and Bose literally recede into the background.

Thus in *Pride of India* (figure 92) Nehru's pensive visage occupies the map of India (even as Gandhi and Bose look down upon him from the heavens), with the furrows on his face uncannily mirroring the creases on the high mountains on the map behind him, which his government was called upon several times to defend in the name of the nation. Indeed, in a picture from the late 1940s a rather-cinematic looking Bharat Mata herself stands carefree and joyous within the spectral outline of a map of India while Nehru stands straight and somber gazing up at her, his face wearing its customary pensive gaze (figure 98). In the visual imagination of the barefoot cartographer, it seems that power and privilege come at a cost that India's first prime minister wears not very lightly on his body, which is rumpled, creased, and aging.

a few years in the 1940s Gandhi and Nehru were rivaled in the bare-
t cartographic imaginary by the swashbuckling figure of Subhas Chandra Bose, or Netaji (leader) as he is frequently referred to by the artists who
picture him with a familiar affection that sets him apart from the reverential
awe with which Gandhi is visualized and from the remote respect accorded
to Nehru.[29] Although based in Delhi, the publisher Hemchandra Bhargava
presented the life of this Bengal-born patriot in its print *Life of Subash*. In it
vignettes from the life of Bose are laid out around the central image of him
as a uniform-clad and sword-bearing charismatic warrior who stands on
top of a terrestrial globe on which the map of India is partly occluded by the
presence of an aircraft (figure 99). This is a rare pictorial acknowledgment
of his accidental death in August 1945 in a plane crash, for, as we will see,
the barefoot mapmaker typically pictures Bose's martyrdom in a different
manner—one that borders on the macabre. His martyrdom was preceded
by his audacious attempt to launch an extraterritorial assault against British
rule in India with the help of the expatriate Indian National Army (INA,
founded in 1942 with recruits from Malaya, Singapore, and Burma). So taken
are patriotic artists with this feat that in their work, Bose frequently appears
as a carto-graphed personage occupying the map of the country all by himself (or with his followers), with the other big men of India literally pushed
to the margins from where they watch the show.

A striking illustration of Bose's hypervisibility may be seen in a print, possibly published sometime after 1943, with the words *Challo Dilli* (Onward
to Delhi) inscribed across the bottom (figure 100). Netaji—in his trademark
brown soldier's uniform—has taken confident possession of the map of India
on which he stands in his shiny high black boots and calls upon his fellow
citizens to give him their blood; he, in turn, will deliver to them their freedom
(tum hamko khoon do, mein tumko aazaadi doonga!). Gandhi and Nehru
merely look on in the face of this bold call that sought to shift the anticolonial strategy from the (mere) nonviolent opposition of British rule to the
politics of armed combat. Gandhi and Nehru are not even recognizable in
Netajika Swapna (Dream of Netaji), printed possibly around the same time
(figure 101).[30] In this image the lower part of Bose's body literally disappears

army of women

FIGURE 99 *Life of Subash*.
Printed by Hem Chander
Bhargava, Delhi, circa 1945.
(Courtesy of Erwin Neumayer
and Christine Schelberger,
Vienna)

into that of India—laid transversely across the print—while the sun rises
over the snow-covered Himalayas. In addition, soldiers of Bose's INA stride
across the map, rifles over their shoulders, saluting the carto-graphed Bose
who has become so indelibly associated with the topography of the country
that his bespectacled face is one of the peaks of the tall mountains stretched
out across its northern edge. A dark silhouetted figure (Gandhi?) has been
caricatured as a faceless outline, visible but not really recognizable.

Such prints remind us that Netaji's pictorial task is to yoke the nation's
warrior past to its present, and not surprisingly his poster image echoes and
recalls other (Hindu) militaristic figures—most typically the Rajput Rana
Pratap and especially the Maratha hero Shivaji, who are also lionized in the
male homo-social picture world of Indian patriotism (for example, figure 82).
Like them—and unlike any other man in the dominant nationalist pantheon,
and certainly unlike Gandhi and Nehru—he is invariably armed, although

FIGURE 100 *Challo Dilli: Tum Hame Khoon Do, Ham Tumhe Azadi Doonga* (Onward to Delhi: You give your blood, I will bring you freedom). Printed by Art Corner[?], 1940s. (Courtesy of Christopher Pinney)

FIGURE 101 *Netaji ka Swapna* (Dream of Netaji). Printed by Tower Half-Tone Co, Calcutta, circa 1940s. (Courtesy of Christopher Pinney)

not with a rifle but with a sword (figures 32 and 99). As Pinney notes insightfully, the sword might be a sign of "technological simplicity, but it was also a sign that linked the contemporary struggle to a mythic infra-structure that validated the freedom fighters' actions" and also recalls the "complex pan-Indian linkages between images of [the goddess] Bhawani's sword that crisscross from Maharashtra to Bengal and back again" (2004, 121). Thus in *Mata ka Bandhan Mochan*, discussed earlier (figure 32), the principal action of the print is the bestowal of the sword by Bharat Mata herself upon Netaji, very much in the manner of Bhawani granting a sword to Shivaji in bazaar prints.[31] Similarly in Sudhir Chowdhury's *Astra Dan* (Granting of weapon) an eight-armed Bharat Mata flanked by a ferocious lion and bearing not only a variety of weapons but also the tricolor (with the Gandhian spinning wheel drawn prominently on it) hands over a sword to a kneeling Netaji (figure 102).[32] This is the typical manner in which his artistic admirer responds to Bose's calls for an armed struggle to achieve freedom. Rather than being deemed antithetical to the nonviolent ethos of Indian nationalism as the dominant Gandhian-Nehruvian version would have it, his actions are blessed by Bharat Mata herself, who might have instigated them, and even possibly favored over the ways of Gandhi and Nehru. In turn such prints visually connect back to the early decades of the twentieth century and to a time before Gandhi's hegemonic influence when Bharat Mata is herself drawn as a sword-wielding female inciting Indians on to battle (for example, figures 14–16).

All the same, barefoot cartographic work is directed toward reconciling the alternate modalities of filial service to Mother India represented by Gandhi, Nehru, and Bose. In the real world of Congress politics and official nationalism Bose was cast out of the fold by the late 1930s, and he was ambivalently rejected by both Nehru and Gandhi who apparently told him, "We must sail in different boats."[33] One of the barefoot mapmaker's goal appears be to recuperate Bose and reintegrate him into the pantheon of patriots, to accord him a centrality that exceeded the importance granted to him by the Congress in the 1940s, and to visually propose that not only Bharat Mata herself but also her other two devoted men, Gandhi and Nehru, approved of his labors for map and mother. Not surprisingly, in numerous patriotic prints Bose appears happily in the company of the two men who had politically

अस्त्रदान   Astra Dan

FIGURE 102 Sudhir
Chowdhury, *Astra Dan*
(Granting of weapon). Print
by SNS, Calcutta, early 1940s.
(Courtesy of Erwin Neumayer
and Christine Schelberger,
Vienna)

isolated him, and he is even shown being blessed by them. A good example
of this is offered in *Jay Yatra Netaji* (Netaji's victorious journey) by Sudhir
Chowdhury, in which Netaji rises into the heavens above from the world
below (represented by a gridded globe with a partly visible outline map of
India) on a chariot drawn by many horses (figure 103). Bharat Mata waits
to greet him, one hand resting on Gandhi's shoulder, as if urging the latter
to embrace one of her most devoted sons as his own. Similarly, in a print
published by the Simla-based Paul Picture Publishers, produced after Independence and created by M. Singh, Nehru (now mimicking Bose in brown
soldier's uniform and high black boots) salutes a framed picture of his former
rival, and a garlanded globe with a physiographic map of undivided India
outlined on it is placed on a pedestal next to them (figure 104). For the barefoot mapmaker, regardless of the ideological differences between these three
men, they had all selflessly served the Indian geo-body and Bharat Mata each

FIGURE 103 Sudhir Chowdhury, *Jay Yatra Netaji* (Netaji's victorious journey). Print by SNS, Calcutta, circa 1948. (Courtesty of the Twin Studio Archive: © The Singh Twins, www.singhtwins.co.uk)

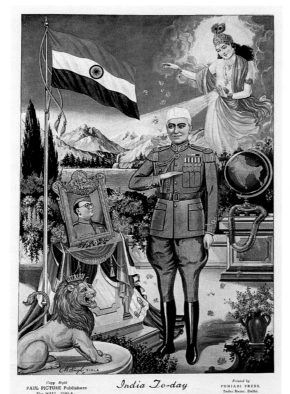

FIGURE 104 M. Singh. *India To-day*. Print by Paul Picture Publishers, Simla, circa 1947. (OSIAN's Archive, Research and Documentation Centre, Mumbai)

in their own way. Not surprisingly, the mapmaker strives for pictorial recon-
ciliation between them that is at odds with the verbal worlds in which they
come embedded to us.

The barefoot mapmaker might show his admiration for these big men in the
various ways I have described, but his productions also reveal his awareness
that love-service-sacrifice for map and mother came at a cost, including the
renunciation of worldly pleasures and joys of family life. For instance, these
men are rarely shown in the company of their wives who, even when they
put in a visual appearance, are reduced to marginal or miniature presences
 (for example, figure 95), while the "real" woman in their lives, Bharat Mata,
towers over them all (figure 28). Indeed, in prints such as Ramachandra Rao's
Vande Mataram (figure 28) or his *The Splendour that Is India* (figure 29), her
numerous sons are either tiny bodies huddled at her feet as she looms large
over them or are lost in the folds of her carto-graphed sari to the point of
being only partly visible themselves. In Brojen's *Shrinkhal Mukti* (figure 75),
even as Gandhi and her sons "liberate" her from her shackles Bharat Mata
dwarfs them while her form fills up most of the map of India that appears in
the print. Do such images betray an anxiety on the part of the barefoot mapmaker about the consequences of the love-service-sacrifice nexus in which
he imagines his heroes as entangled? Do they reveal as well some skepticism
about the real power of these seemingly masterful men who appear dependent on a woman (albeit one who is their goddess and mother) for working
out their homo-social compact with each other and with the mapped territory of India?

To explore these questions further I turn to some intriguing prints that
may have been first produced in the closing years of British rule. Sometime in
the mid-1940s Sudhir Chowdhury, who produced the larger-than-life poster
images of Netaji that we have already seen, created a work titled *Bharat
Santan* (India's child) (figure 105).[34] In this print an adult Bose (still clad in
his trademark soldier's uniform but without his sword) sits on Bharat Mata's
lap as she in turn perches on a gridded globe, her sari-covered legs possibly
mapping out the shape of India, holding a flag in which the Gandhian spinning wheel is partly visible. If it were not for her protective arm holding the

ভারত সন্তান   Bharat Santan

FIGURE 105 Sudhir Chowdhury, *Bharat Santan* (India's child). Chromolithograph published by SNS, Calcutta, mid 1940s[?]. (Courtesy of Christopher Pinney)

miniaturized (and pictorially infantilized) Netaji, he would very likely fall off the face of the earth in this visual rendering of his relationship to mother and map. A few years later, Brojen pictured Netaji (clad in white dhoti and shawl) sitting in a similar fashion on a carto-graphed Mother India's lap. As she sits on a globe holding the official flag of India in her hand, her feet rest on the peninsular part of the outline map of India that is partly occluded by the folds of her sari.[35] The artist Prabhu Dayal similarly presents "the father of the nation" in his *Bharatmata Ki Godh Mein Mahatma Gandhi* (Mahatma Gandhi in the lap of Mother India) (figure 106). An aging Gandhi, clad in his usual knee-length dhoti and carrying his spinning wheel (as if it were a toy), sits contemplatively on Bharat Mata's lap as they both occupy the Indian geo-body whose cartographic outline (in three-dimensional relief) merges in the north with the snow-clad peaks of the Himalayas. A Bengali variant on Prabhu Dayal's north Indian imagination is available in the Calcutta-based Tower Half-Tone Company's *Bharat Mata* in which Gandhi's visage bears a remarkable resemblance to his photographs as a middle-aged man, soon after his return to India (figure 83).

भारतमाता की गोद में महात्मा गांधी

MAHATMA GANDHI

महात्मा गांधी

FIGURE 106 Prabhu Dayal, *Bharatmata Ki Godh Mein Mahatma Gandhi* (Mahatma Gandhi in the lap of Mother India). Printed by Rashtriya Chitra Prakashak Karyalaya, Cawnpore, circa 1930s[?]. (Courtesy of Urvashi Butalia, New Delhi)

A Hindu-Indian viewer who chanced on such prints might have been able to relate them to similar images of the divine mother and child that she or he would have seen in bazaar pictures of Parvati holding the elephant-deity Ganesha, or Yashodha cuddling baby Krishna. These images in turn were undoubtedly also influenced by the Christian pictures of Mary and the baby Jesus in circulation in India—in various media—from at least the late sixteenth century.[36] Yet in striking contrast to these other images (which might have intervisually inspired the barefoot mapmaker), there is no attempt to portray India's new men as infants or young boys: instead it is as mature *adults* that they appear seated on the lap of the mother/goddess as she occupies the map of India. In chapter 1, I commented on the relative paucity in patriotic visual art of pictures of a carto-graphed Mother India engaged in obvious and overt acts of maternity—such as the benevolent nurture and suckle of her infants. Brojen, Prabhu Dayal, Sudhir Chowdhury, and other artists reveal, inadvertently perhaps, the risk in visually translating the verbal claim that we are all "children" of Mother India: the leading men of the nationalist fight against the mighty British empire are reduced to kids taking shelter on their mother's lap, thereby potentially undermining the patriarchal authority they surely needed to exercise in order to shore up their power and privilege.

This is not the only penalty these men seem to pay as they find themselves pictorially entangled in the love-service-sacrifice nexus. In contrast to the carto-graphed Bharat Mata who rarely appears aged, decrepit, or dead in any political picture—given that she is both the immortal goddess and the very embodiment of an ever-youthful nation, however ancient its origins—her sons are very mortal. Indeed, they are born, grow into young men, age into adults, and even die. A striking example of this is the well-known Nathdvara artist Lakshminarayan Khubhiram Sharma's creation from the late 1950s or even early 1960s, *Jawahar Jiwani* (Life of Jawahar), which offers a pictorial biography of India's first prime minister (figure 107).[37] Sharma places Nehru on a partly visible globe showing a partially outlined map of India (left unnamed). The nationalist salutations "jai hind" and "vande mataram" are inscribed in Hindi on neighboring territories, possibly to make room for Nehru's feet, which are planted on the Indian geo-body even as his own body reaches into the universe—thereby possibly suggesting that here is a man who has the world (and India) at his feet.[38] Any sign of enduring mastery, however, is undone by the fact that he looks quite old, with his customary pensive poster look deepened by unmistakable signs of aging. He may be a master of the globe and of India, but that he is still a mere mortal is underscored by the artist in the representation of various episodes from his life—ranging from birth to his development into youth and his maturation into adulthood with key moments in his political life—which are arranged as visual vignettes around him. A lifetime achieving mastery, the print appears to suggest, leads not to perennial immortality, but to old age and eventually death.

This view is even more strikingly apparent in another print by the same artist, *Bapuji ki Amar Kahani* (The eternal story of Gandhi), which must have been published after January 30, 1948, when Gandhi was assassinated (figure 108). Here the central image is of an aged Gandhi standing on a globe

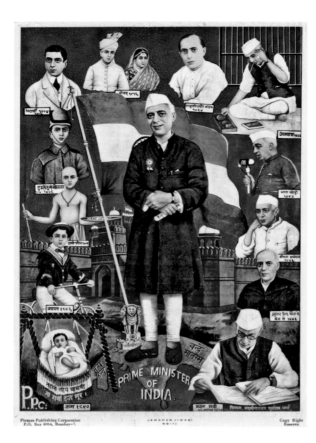

FIGURE 107 Lakshminarayan Khubiram Sharma, *Jawahar Jiwani* (Life of Jawahar). Print by Picture Publishing Company, Bombay, late 1950s[?]. (Author's collection)

with a halo around his head. In contrast to Nehru in *Jawahar Jiwani*, however, Gandhi is clearly dead: his corpse lies below the globe, draped in the national flag (inscribed with the last words he is reported to have uttered, "Hare Ram" [dear God]). It is the culminating episode in a life dedicated to the service of the nation, which unfolds in a series of visual cameos beginning with the Mahatma's appearance in the world as a patriotic baby in a cradle draped in the colors of the Indian flag. Sharma appears to have modeled these vignettes on readily available photographs of Gandhi at key moments in his eventful life: as a young London-bound student, as a stylish barrister in South Africa, as a satyagrahi who had cast off his Western ways, and then, from his later career as a nationalist leader back in India, launching and leading the historic Dandi march, behind bars at his spinning wheel, launching the Quit India movement, and so on. These vignettes are, in turn, arranged clockwise around what Sharma obviously saw as the central feature

FIGURE 108 Lakshminarayan
Khubiram Sharma, *Bapuji Ki Amar
Kahani* (The eternal story of
Gandhi). Print by Picture Publishing
Company, Bombay, after 1948.
(Author's collection)

of Gandhi's "eternal" life—his martyrdom for the nation and its map—an
image that does not exist in the photographic record but rather is his own
pictorial innovation. Occupying the center of the poster is the smiling, dhoti-
clad image of Gandhi holding a staff in one hand and carrying a red book
(possibly the Bhagavad Gita) in the other. Bright red blood from three carefully placed bullet wounds in his chest drips down to form a puddle on the
outline map of India drawn on the face of a terrestrial globe. Photographic
realism thus gives way to patriotic mythography. A revolver with small puffs
of white smoke curling up into the air is placed on the map, as the Mahatma
literally bleeds to death on the geo-body of his country.[39]

BLEEDING FOR MOTHER AND MAP

The adulation of Gandhi by barefoot cartography and its pictorial honoring
of his martyrdom is to be expected in that it visually reiterates official as well

as popular nationalism's reverence of the Mahatma, although his recasting as a carto-graphed body is a singular outcome of visual patriotism, as I suggest later. The most dramatic images of martyrdom for map and mother in the patriotic picture world are not so much of Gandhi, however, but rather of a young man who catapults to national visibility in the 1930s and remains prominent to this day in the pantheon of patriots who have given up life and limb for the nation. On March 23, 1931, Bhagat Singh (b. 1907)—a Punjabi Jat Sikh with avowedly socialist and atheist views on the nation and the world (and an inheritor of ideas from the earlier Ghadar revolutionary moment)— was hanged by the colonial state along with his "co-conspirators" Rajguru and Sukhdev for the assassination of a British police officer in Lahore in December 1928.[40] Almost immediately after the event, Bhagat Singh's execution become the subject of the visual imagination of patriotic artists nearly all over India but especially in Punjab, northern India, and Bengal, an official report even noting, "for a time, he [Bhagat] bade fair to oust Mr. Gandhi as the foremost political figure of the day. His photograph was to be met with in many houses, and his plaster busts found a large market" (Hale 1974, 64). Bhagat's life story remained popular for several decades thereafter, with much of the art converting his death by hanging into martyrdom by the sword for map and mother. With this dramatic passing a new category of male patriot emerges in the barefoot cartographic imaginary, which was frequently designated in its productions by a complex charged term—the *shaheed* (the martyr). The Arabic word *shaheed*, used in a Qur'anic context and in an Islamic universe for pious Muslims who died heroically bearing witness to God's truth, is resignified to refer to patriots who willingly—even eagerly— shed their blood for the ostensibly secular truth of the nation and its map.

Pinney, in his analysis of Indian chromolithographs, offers a skilful analysis of Bhagat's visual persona in popular prints (where he generally appears with a striking moustache and clad in Western clothes with a trilby on his head), which is interpreted as the bazaar's admiration for his "audacious mimicry" and ability "to pass" as the white British man. Pinney also insists that "official nationalism may have decried the activities of revolutionary terrorists, but popular visual culture asserted the nation's debt to those prepared to kill and be killed in the cause of freedom" (2004, 136).[41] In point of fact, it is with Bhagat's death that martyrdom for the nation becomes a sustained (and sustainable) visual subject that captures the imagination of India's barefoot cartographers as well as that of the colonial state's censorship apparatus.[42]

Soon after Bhagat's death by hanging, the Lahore-based Anarkali Publishers printed *Bandhan Mein Bharata Mata Ki Bhent: Lahore Conspiracy Case Decision—Sentenced to Death, No. 1403* (figure 21).[43] Proscribed by the colonial authorities, the print features Bharat Mata as a two-armed goddess, her hands bound in chains. Only the upper part of her body is visible; the lower half merges into a topographic map of India on which principal rivers and some mountain ranges are faintly visible. Standing in front of Bharat Mata are the decapitated bodies of several young men whom the print identifies (in English) as J. N. Dass, S. Bhagat Singh, Rajguru, and Sukhdev. Strikingly, each of these decapitated young male bodies is shown dispassionately offering his head to Bharat Mata, with Bhagat's standing out prominently— its trilby still proudly on, eyes prominently staring ahead.[44]

In this print, and in others published around the same time and subsequently, the severed heads of these youthful martyrs are frequently described in Hindi as *bhent* or *bali* (gift or offering) and additionally qualified in English as "first," "curious," and even "wonderful." In a print titled *Swatantra Ki Bhent* (Freedom's gift), published by the Kanpur-based Shyam Sunder Lal Picture Merchants (who issued several such "martyrdom" pictures), a female figure is shown in profile seated on a throne under a canopy placed in a theatrical setting (figure 109). Although she is not named Bharat Mata, that is her identity, as Nehru (no admirer of such expressions of fierce devotion) approaches her with a severed head on a plate, its eyes still open while drops of blood fall to the floor below. Bhagat (in his trilby and shorts) stands with folded hands, staring rather defiantly at the viewer. We know from the caption that the bleeding head belongs to the "immortal *shaheed* Yatindranath Das," an associate of Bhagat's who died in Lahore in a colonial prison in September 1929 after a hunger strike of more than sixty days. The print visually converts his death through starving into corporeal sacrifice for Mother India.[45] Its creator, Roopkishore Kapur, also painted *Sardar Bhagat Singh Ki Apoorba Bhent: Sardar Bhagat Singh's Wonderful Presentation* in which it is Bhagat's severed head that is handed over on a plate to Mother India while his "co-conspirators" Raj Guru and Sukhdev look on (figure 110).[46]

Similarly, in P. Shivshankar Tiwari's *Bhagat ki Vichitra Bhent: Bhagat's*

FIGURE 109 Roopkishore Kapur, *Swatantrata Ki Bhent: Amar Shaheed Yatindranath Das* (Freedom's gift: Eternal martyr Yatindranath Das). Print by Shyam Sunder Lal, Picture Merchant, Cawnpore, circa 1931. (Courtesy of Urvashi Butalia, New Delhi)

FIGURE 110 Roopkishore Kapur, *Sardar Bhagat Singh Ki Apoorba Bhent: Sardar Bhagat Singh's Wonderful Presentation.* Print by Shyam Sunder Lal Picture Merchant, Cawnpore, circa 1931. (© British Library Board [APAC: Proscribed Publications Collection], PP HIN F 66)

Curious Present, published by the Kanpur-based Ganganarain Beharilal, Bharat Mata sits on a rock with her hands reaching out (almost too eagerly) to accept Bhagat's bleeding head from which streams of blood pour down to the land below (figure 111). Below this mise-en-scène is inscribed (in English): "Mother! For thy freedom's sake I offer my life." The Hindi title glosses the scene with a telling difference, using terms that traffic in the vocabulary of the sacred, in contrast to the secular sentiments expressed in English: "Ma! Teri balivedi par pranon ki bhent chadatha hun" (Mother, on your sacrificial altar, I offer my life as offering). In Nandlal's *Dukhin Bharat ke Shaheed* (Martyrs of a grieving India), published by the Lahore-based Madan Half-Tone Co., a youthful Bharat Mata sits on a globe on which is drawn a rough outline of India, her hands in chains (figure 112). Bhagat Singh floats upward to heaven, holding the heads of Rajguru and Sukhdev in his hands. Although Bhagat may be dead his head remains in place in this print in which the martyrs who have preceded him shower him with flowers, presumably cheering on his ascent to their paradise. In the print *Heroes' Sacrifice*, published by the Lahore-based Krishna Picture House, an old Sikh gentleman and two elderly women clad in Punjabi suits walk up the stairs toward a "national" shrine in which Bharat Mata stands (figure 113). The three elders—possibly the martyrs' parents?—hand over on platters the severed heads of Bhagat, Rajguru, and Sukhdev in return for which gift Bharat Mata blesses them. Prabhu Dayal's *Dukhi Mata* (Grieving mother), published in the early 1930s by the Allahabad-based Bhargava Press, pictures the severed heads of Bhagat and his fellow martyrs as moths caught in the flames of freedom while Mother India stands in grief, her hands manacled in chains (figure 114).

In these pictures, the recipient of this bloody sacrifice of the severed head on the platter is generally the carto-graphed Bharat Mata who sometimes receives the bloody offering impassively, at other times with tears flowing down her face and her arms and hands in chains, and still at other times by reaching out to receive the gory gift all too eagerly. Even when the map of India is not present in the print, "India" is evoked in the form of snow-capped mountains, green fields, gushing streams, and silhouettes of temples. The lush life-affirming plenitude of the background serves only to reinforce even more dramatically the act of life-effacing martyrdom to map and mother being performed in the foreground.

FIGURE III P. Shivshankar Tiwari,
*Bhagata ki Vichitra Bhenta: Bhagat's
Curious Present.* Print by Ganganarain
Beharilal, Cawnpore, circa 1931.
(© British Library Board [APAC:
Proscribed Publications Collection],
PP HIN F 69)

FIGURE II2 Nandlal, *Dukhin Bharat
Ke Shaheed* (Martyrs of a grieving
India). Photograph of print by Madan
Half-tone Co., Lahore, circa 1930s[?]
(Sardar Kulbir Singh Collection,
Nehru Memorial Museum and Library
Photo Archive, 03.2 BS, 36517)

"HEROES SACRIFICE"

Printed at The Janki Printing Press, old mewa mandi, Lahore.   Published by Krishna Picture House Lohari Gate, LAHORE.

FIGURE 113 *Heroes Sacrifice*. Print by Krishna Picture House, Lahore, circa 1931. (© British Library Board [APAC: Proscribed Publications Collection], PP HIN F 72)

DUKHI MATA

दुखी माता

Copyright No. 68.   Bhargava Press, Allahabad.

प्रकाशक :—
श्यामसुन्दर लाल
पिक्चर मर्चेंट, चौक, कानपुर.

Published by :—
Shyam Sunder Lal,
Picture Merchant,
Chowk, CAWNPORE.

FIGURE 114 Prabhu Dayal, *Dukhi Mata* (Grieving mother). Print by Shyam Sunder Lal, Picture Merchant, Cawnpore, circa 1930s. (Courtesy of Urvashi Butalia, New Delhi)

Most strikingly, in many prints the blood from Bhagat's severed head and decapitated torso gushes out to form a puddle on the map of India. Thus in *Shaheed Bhagat Singh*, which possibly was published sometime after 1950 by the Calcutta-based Rising Art Cottage, Bhagat kneels before a two-armed Bharat Mata (whose eyes are surprisingly closed or downcast) standing on a terrestrial globe and holding the newly authorized national flag (figure 115). Bhagat hands over to her his bloodied head, presumably severed by the sword that lies next to him, while blood from his decapitated body flows onto the globe and over some roughly marked territories that appear to be parts of India and the adjacent country of Burma. In return, Mother India blesses him for his act of corporeal sacrifice.[47] When the photographer and journalist Richard Lannoy traveled in India in 1958, he photographed a similar print posted in a goldsmith's stall in a Banaras bazaar of Bhagat kneeling on a globe (on which a partial map of India, colored yellow, is visible). The blood from his decapitated body flows down to form red rivers on the map below him, while the blood from his severed head that he offers on a platter to Mother India gathers in a puddle at her feet (figure 116).[48] A few years later in a dramatic poster from the mid-1960s titled *Ma ki Pukar* (Mother's call), Bharat Mata occupies a map of India, with the halo around her head occluding the contested territory of Kashmir (figure 117). Dressed in white shorts and shirt, Bhagat obligingly kneels in front of her and dispassionately hands over his severed head (still wearing the trilby, but this time with his eyes closed). Blood gushes from the torn head to Bharat Mata's feet and onto the map of India, and bright red blood also spurts out of the decapitated torso.[49]

As others have shown, the severed male head has a long pedigree in the Indo-Islamic world of sacrifice. Some of the earliest documented visual expressions of decapitations and auto-beheadings are known to us from monumental sculptures in southern India created in the later first millennium CE.[50] Acts of (real and symbolic) heroic self-mutilation by men were generally directed toward warrior goddesses like Durga, Kali, or Korravai for the sake of victory in battle. Louis Fenech persuasively suggests that later Muslim and Sikh popular veneration of decapitated and dismembered martyr-saints in their belief worlds drew succor, especially in Punjab and northern India, from the widespread Hindu worship of blood-thirsty goddesses like those I described in chapter 2.[51] Barefoot mapmakers appear to have mobilized this

শহীদ ভগত সিংহ
J. P. Co./R. 106

ভারত মাতার মুক্তি সাধনায়
শহীদ ভগৎ সিংহ

Shaheed Bhagat Singh

FIGURE 115 *Shaheed Bhagat Singh*. Print published by Rising Art Cottage, Calcutta, circa 1950. (Courtesy of Christopher Pinney)

FIGURE 116 A goldsmith's shop in Banaras bazaar. Photograph by Richard Lannoy, 1958. (Reproduced with permission of Richard Lannoy)

मां को पुकार

FIGURE 117 *Ma ki Pukar* (Mother's call). Recruitment poster published by Anil Calendar Company, Delhi, acquired circa 1966. (Courtesy of J. P. S. and Patricia Uberoi, Delhi)

long-standing macabre (and pluralist) expression of "fierce" devotion and re-directed it toward the new patron mother/goddess Bharat Mata and the map of India. So although Bhagat was killed by hanging and not by decapitation, his martyrdom for mother and map is shown as such, for it allows the patriotic artist to connect his death at the hands of the cold, calculating apparatus of the colonial state to the desired and desirable death of other exemplars of self-effacing devotion, such as the mid-eighteenth-century Sikh martyr Baba Deep Singh whose passing is depicted in a similar manner in many bazaar prints.[52]

And what of Bharat Mata's role in this visual pedagogy mounted around the wounded or decapitated body of the martyr?[53] A densely packed print from the early 1930s published by the Kanpur-based Shyam Sunder Lal Picture Merchants might be helpful here (figure 118). One of Prabhu Dayal's creations, it is titled *Svatantrata Ki Vedi par Biron Ka Balidan: Bharat Ke*

FIGURE 118 Prabhu Dayal, *Svatantrata Ki Vedi par Biron Ka Balidan: Bharat Ke Amar Shaheed* (India's immortal martyrs: Sacrificial offerings on the altar of freedom by [our] heroes). Printed by Shyam Sunder Lal, Picture Merchant, Cawnpore, circa 1931. (Courtesy of Urvashi Butalia)

Amar Shaheed (India's immortal martyrs: Sacrificial offerings on the altar of freedom by [our] heroes). It shows a female figure standing in the foreground with a bloodied axe in one hand and a severed head in another, while other heads and decapitated bodies lie strewn around. The print identifies these decapitated martyrs as Ashfaq, Rajendralahiri, Ramprasad Bismil, Lala Lajpat Rai, and Yatindradanath Das.[54] Two young men—one of them clearly Bhagat Singh in his trademark trilby—wait before the altar with their heads ready to be axed by the goddess, while identifiable luminaries from the national movement including Gandhi and Nehru queue up behind them. In this print Prabhu Dayal pictures the unnamed goddess (most likely Mother India) as directly exacting from her sons the bloody price (*balidan*) of their devotion. This is a rare picturization of maternal filicide, for in a majority of other cases the most that Bharat Mata does is arm her warriors with the sword of battle with which they presumably kill others, or possibly behead themselves in order to feed her "hunger" and quench her "thirst." As the national movement picks up in fervor and as Gandhian nonviolence appears to yield few concrete results, the print suggests that the mother might no longer be content with waiting around, and thus was capable of turning into an executioner herself to satisfy her cravings.

Indeed, the corporeal fragment of the severed bloodied head as the "gift" (*bhent*) or "sacrificial offering" (*bali*) to map and mother becomes such an overdetermined signifier of (youthful) male martyrdom in patriotic visual labors that even the premature but mysterious death of Subhas Bose—who was not executed by the colonial state—is inserted into this familiar template. Thus in a striking print possibly from the 1940s published by the same firm that earlier issued similar pictures of Bhagat Singh, a decapitated Bose is shown standing with his (smiling) head in hand, from which the blood gushes onto a framed outline map of India on which is inscribed *Jai Hind* (Victory to India)—a phrase he had elevated to the status of national salutation (figure 119). Here the martyr's blood appears to pictorially nourish and rejuvenate the nation's geo-body, presumably also fed by bloodied bodies attached to the other severed heads shown in the picture. Like prints of Bhagat's decapitation from a decade earlier, this one as well is titled *Subhaschandra Bose Ki Apoorva Bhent* (Subhaschandra Bose's extraordinary gift).

Similarly, in posters like *Subhas Balidan* (Subhas's sacrifice) (figure 120), a headless Subhas is shown kneeling before the figure of Bharat Mata, a resplendent two-armed goddess, flanked by the ubiquitous lion, with her hand held out in a gesture of blessing. He holds out to her a plate on which rests his bodiless head with its trademark army cap and glasses still intact. Blood from his head as well as his decapitated body pours out profusely to join what looks like a river of blood in which are floating the bodiless heads of other well-known (male) patriots, including that of Bhagat. In *Shaheed Smrity* (Memory of martyrs), Sudhir Chowdhury places Bharat Mata in a patriotic pastoral landscape with the sun rising on the horizon of freedom (figure 121). Nehru stands in front of her gesturing to a number of platters that have been placed before her as ritual offerings akin to those presented in puja ceremonies by devout Hindus to their enshrined gods. Patriotic worship turns carnivorous and even cannibalistic, however, in contrast to the

FIGURE 119 *Subhaschandra Bose Ki Apoorva Bhent* (Subhashchandra Bose's Extraordinary Gift). Print by Shyam Sunder Lal, Cawnpore, circa 1945. (Courtesy of Erwin Neumayer and Christine Schelberger, Vienna)

vegetarian offerings that customarily accompany puja, for on each platter is laid out the severed head of a young man identified by name: Bhagat Singh, Khudiram Bose, Surya Sen, Debvrata, Rameshwar, and Kanailal Dutt. These men were either hanged or shot to death for various anticolonial activities, but their deaths are here visually presented as ritual decapitation in a manner akin to the illustrations that accompany, for instance, published medieval stories of the "self-slaughter" performed by Shiva's "fanatical" devotees in southern India (Hudson 1989) or that echo Nanak's injunction to his Sikh followers, "If you want to play the game of love, approach me with your head on the palm of your hand. Place your feet on this path and give your head without regard to the opinion of others."[55]

Indeed, there is a new "game of love" at play in the barefoot cartographic imaginary, and its object is the nation—and the mother and the map. This love finds expression in a novel aesthetic that presents the nation's anthro-

सुभाष बलिदान

Copy-Right
PAUL PICTURE Publishers
The MALL, SIMLA

Printed by
Deyal's Press Delhi

FIGURE 120 *Subhash Balidan*
(Subhash's sacrifice). Print by Paul
Picture Publishers, Simla, circa 1945.
(Courtesy of Erwin Neumayer and
Christine Schelberger, Vienna)

FIGURE 121 Sudhir Chowdhury,
Shaheed Smrity (Memory of martyrs).
Print by SNS, Calcutta, circa 1947.
(Courtesy of Erwin Neumayer and
Christine Schelberger, Vienna)

pomorphized geo-body as the impassive recipient of the sacrifice of the wounded or dismembered youthful male body with its severed head, decapitated torso, bullet-scarred chest, and gushing life-blood. This, the barefoot mapmaker seems to suggest, is the ultimate fate of masculine patriotism in twentieth-century India—and one that has the blessings even of the apostle of nonviolence, who in several prints showers his blessings on such violent expressions of devotion to Bharat Mata.[56] In turn, Mother India herself expresses her satisfaction with the outcome by taking up residence, literally, in the chests (visualized as torn asunder) of such martyrs, as shown in a vivid print by Hasan Raza Raja that intervisually engages on the one hand with Christian pictures of Christ's sacred heart and on the other with Hanuman's devotion to his beloved Rama and Sita (figure 122).[57] Without exception, the martyred male body, even when in bits and pieces, invariably appears in a state of perfect composure, devoid of pain or suffering and even taking pleasure in sacrificing itself to the whole that is the nation. It is indeed an exceptional body prepared to go to bits and pieces in order that the body politic does not. At the same time these pictures disavow the empirical fact of death, as the brave patriot is shown transcending death by identifying with the greater life of the nation that lives on—indeed is renewed by—the shedding of his blood.[58]

MARTYRDOM IN THE AGE OF THE NATIONAL PICTURE

If this be the fate of men then what about the mother and the map, the other participants in the love-service-sacrifice nexus of visual patriotism? On August 14, 1947, on the eve of Indian independence and the day of the birth of the new state of Pakistan, the Hindu nationalist weekly *Organiser* (whose masthead was dominated by a large and bold outline map of undivided India), published a cartoon to visually mark the momentous twin births (figure 123). Entitled "The Wise Pandit," the cartoon shows a carto-graphed Bharat Mata, her face contorted in pain and a far cry from her usual glorious "poster" self, laid out transversely across a map of pre-partition India. (Pandit) Nehru, seated on a cushion outside the nation's geo-body, hacks away at one of her arms (stretched out over the land that had been declared Pakistan on that day) with a sword in one hand. His other hand seems to pull at her hair (laid out over the disputed territory of Kashmir), while a disembodied

FIGURE 122 H. R. Raja, Bhagat Singh with Bharat Mata in his heart, acquired in Delhi in 1988. (Courtesy of J. P. S. and Patricia Uberoi, Delhi)

THE WISE PANDIT

सर्वनाशे समुत्पन्ने अर्धं त्यजति पण्डितः

FIGURE 123 Prani, "The Wise Pandit." Cartoon in *Organiser*, New Delhi, August 14, 1947. (Courtesy of *Organiser Weekly*, New Delhi)

Jinnah snarls at him. The menace implicit in this illustration is heightened by the brevity of the caption in (garbled) Sanskrit: "Total destruction caused by the evil Pandit [Nehru]."[59]

Three years later on the eve of the declaration of India as a secular republic on January 26, 1950, a cartoon titled "State of Nation" was published in the *Organiser*. The image shows an anthropomorphized Indian geo-body in tears as it is stabbed on either side by the "dagger" of Pakistan, with drops of blood spilling out from the severed parts (figure 124). Ideologically the *Organiser* was at the other end of the spectrum from Gandhi, but it is worth recalling that the apostle of nonviolence frequently used the trope of vivisection (the cutting up of the body of a living organism) to refer to the territorial partitioning of India. These cartoons represent some rare but striking images of vivisection of mother and map.[60] They are rare because although the verbal archive is filled with allusions to Mother India being assaulted, in pain, disrobed, and even raped, these do not find ready expression in the visual practices of barefoot cartography (for example, figures 125 and 126).[61] The outer limits of visual patriotism are reached in picturing a bloodied or wounded Bharat Mata and female martyrdom more generally.

In the next chapter I further explore how the limits of visual patriotism are reached when confronted by the figure of the female martyr, but I conclude here with a final observation on the carto-graphed body of the male patriot-martyr. This body is a product of the contingent intersection of the pictorial politics of corporeality and cartography. As such, its revelation is the outcome of a scholarly exercise in pictorial history, for it is only this manner of historical investigation that brings it to visibility. As W. J. T. Mitchell notes, "An imbrication of the sayable and the seeable, telling and showing, the articulable and the visible occurs at every level of verbal expression, from speech to writing to description, figuration, and formal/semantic structure" (1995a, 542–43). Correspondingly, rarely do images circulate in public spaces without some connection to the verbal and the textual: there are few pure images untouched by the verbal, the discursive, and the linguistic. Pictorial history challenges us to dwell dialectically in the overlapping zone between the sayable and the seeable so as to shuttle back and forth between the two. It exhorts us to explore those aspects of the human experience that are unsayable and nonverbalizable, but also correspondingly to come to terms with

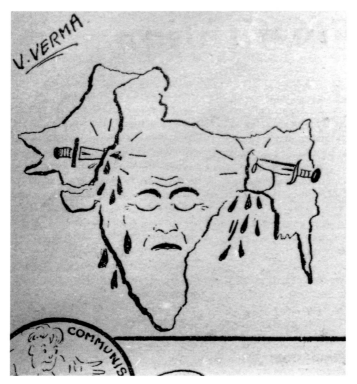

FIGURE 124 V. Verma, "State of Nation." Cartoon in *Organiser*, New Delhi, January 23, 1950. (Courtesy of *Organiser Weekly*, New Delhi)

FIGURE 125 *Heart Rendering Effect of Hindu Muslim Riot at Cawnpore.* Printed card published by Babulal Bhargava, Kanpur, circa 1930s. (Courtesy of Priya Paul, New Delhi)

|| वंदेमातरम् ||

अमरावती जिल्ह्यांतील

सत्याग्रहाचा

त्रोटक-इतिहास
(१९३०)

पीडित मातृभूमी

किंमत ५ आणे.

FIGURE 126 *Peedit Matrabhoomi* (Tormented motherland). Cover illustration of the Marathi book *Amaravati Jilhyaanteela Satyaagrahaaca Trotaka-itihasa* (Concise history of the Satyagraha in Amaravati District), T. G. Josi, Amravati, 1931. (© British Library Board [APAC: Proscribed Publications Collection], PIB 6/20)

those that are unpicturable, even unseeable. Such an epistemology also compels us to pay attention to phenomena that cannot readily or immediately be translated into language, that are unsayable and *only* seeable. The figure of the carto-graphed patriot-martyr, then, is one such only seeable image. It is the sedimentation of an ineffable surplus that can only be excavated by the practices of a new pictorial history that takes seriously Mitchell's argument that pictures "want equal rights with language, not to be turned into language" (2005, 47). Poetry and prose on the patriots and martyrs whom I have considered in this chapter abound in the official and subaltern verbal archives of the subcontinent, yet these will not yield the figure of the carto-graphed martyr because it is exclusively a product of the pictorial archive. Such images recall for me the title of James Elkins's fascinating book *On Pictures and Words That Failed Them* (1998).

In the visual economy of popular messianic nationalism, to invoke Pinney (2004), Bhagat's death and the death of other martyrs made sense when seen as acts of selfless sacrifice for the mother and motherland. Ironically, the only way to see that motherland as an integral whole is to resort to the indispensable modern science of cartography, inadequate though it might be in capturing the affective intensity with which the patriot relates to the geo-body of the emergent nation. And this is because the form of the map *alone* makes India visible as an integral whole and identifiable as a particular piece of delimited territory on the face of the earth. Barefoot cartographic work transforms that which is indispensable but inadequate by supplementing the mapped form of the nation with the anthropomorphic presence of Mother India, producing in the process a cartography of affect and patriotic efficacy to counter the impersonal lines of power of command cartography. Its productions synoptically enframe the map of India, the mother/goddess, and the martyr's body to pictorially show what is unutterable and verbally inexpressible. The carto-graphed body of the smiling martyr with its livid blood dripping down on the map of the nation is the ineffable surplus made visible by the practice of pictorial history. In the words of Tagore's Sandip, "Such are the visions which give vigor to life, and joy to death!" (2005, 73).

DAUGHTERS OF INDIA

6

"No one can give up his life for a map! When I see you before me, then only do I realize how lovely my country is." So declared Sandip to his muse in Rabindranath Tagore's *The Home and the World*. On hearing these words, Bimala, the heroine of the novel and the focus of his adulation, tells the readers of this courageous attack on nationalism's gendered penchants: "Sandip's eyes took fire as he went on, but whether it was the fire of worship, or of passion, I could not tell . . . When, in Sandip's appeals, his worship of the country gets to be subtly interwoven with his worship of me, then does my blood dance, indeed . . . I felt that my resplendent womanhood made me indeed a goddess."[1]

Energized by being transformed into the recipient of such (passionate) worship, Bimala insists that "in this great day the men of the country should realize its goddess in its womanhood" (32). And yet she is also driven to wonder: "Would Sandip Babu find the *Shakti* of the Motherland manifest in me? Or would he simply take me to be an ordinary, domestic woman?"

(32–33). The novel's tragic outcomes provide one answer to Bimala's rhetorical question by reminding its readers, especially perhaps its female ones, of the risk of seeing the feminized country in its women. The emergent nation might be imagined and visualized—and sung and praised—as the exceptional Mother India, but make no mistake the novel appears to warn them: the women of India cannot and should not let their "blood dance," even if it is for the sake of their beloved mother and motherland. They cannot and should not mistakenly come to believe that they *are* indeed "India."

The women of the emergent nation in fact occupy an unenviable place in the brave new world of patriotism created around Bharat Mata and her sons. On the one hand, as I noted in chapter 2, Mother India was partly modeled on the "new" mother presiding over the reformed urban middle-class household hesitantly emerging in different parts of colonial India, itself imitative of Victorian domesticity but yet not sacrificing the essential "tradition" and "spirituality" of an authentic (Hindu) past. This in turn meant, more so than ever as nationalism gathered strength, that the representative Indian woman's dominant function was the production and reproduction of the nation itself, with her primary identity that of motherhood. It also meant that the nation's women had to remain essentially, authentically, and *visibly* "Indian," even Hindu.

On the other hand, the new valorization of motherhood and of the nation's anthropomorphic appearance as female did not mean that women's public powers and privileges were correspondingly enhanced without qualification or control. Their primary place remained the home and the hearth, and any kind of public prominence was only possible *after* tending to their domestic and spiritual responsibilities and their duties to their male kin. They were to complement rather than compete with men for public resources and responsibilities. Bimala's voiced fears are indeed well founded in this regard.

In fact, as I briefly noted earlier, a pictorial history of Indian nationalism demonstrates a consequential *invisibilizing* of women in the political imagery of late colonial and early postcolonial India. Feminist scholarship has painstakingly demonstrated the many complex ways in which Indian women's lives became entangled with the national movement, notwithstanding the strictures placed on them, and the prominence that some women increasingly reached in the struggle against British rule, especially with the putatively feminine turn taken with and by Gandhi. Yet few productions of barefoot cartography reveal this. It is as if the male homo-social patriotic compact between the mother, her men, and her map necessitated the absenting of women from the picture(s). This absenting is especially striking given the hypervisibility of the female body across the spectrum—"from goddess to pin-up"—in public art and places throughout the twentieth century.[2] Do women indeed own and inhabit a country in the same way that men do?[3]

"INDIA BELONGS ONLY TO ME"

This chapter seeks answers to this question by undertaking a feminist pictorial history that explores whether the love-service-sacrifice nexus that I sketched out in chapter 5 looks different when we consider the entanglement of the women of India in efforts to map the Indian geo-body and to picture Bharat Mata. What indeed happens when the woman (artist) looks back?[4] And there is possibly no better place to start such an intervention than with a painting in oil called *Mother India* dated to 1935 (figure 127). Rather than encountering the usual resplendent and carto-graphed mother/goddess decked in fine jewelry and wearing her pale "poster look" of complacent beatitude, we meet an unexpected other: dark-complexioned, completely unadorned, and with her sari covering her head, she holds a young boy in her arms while her daughter—a younger echo of the adult woman—flanks her. Nothing in the dominant pictorial history of Mother India that I have focused upon so far in this book prepares us—or the Indian viewers of its time—for such a vision created in the idiom of an emergent Indian modernism. In fact, if it were not for the naming of the painting as such I would probably not include *Mother India* in a visual history of Bharat Mata.

Yet its creator—the talented young part-Sikh, part-Hungarian Amrita Sher-Gil (1913–1941)—deliberately named it as such, although she gives us few clues about why she was moved to do so.[5] Painted soon after her return to her native India (where she says lay her "destiny as a painter") after a long stint in Europe where she studied modern art in Paris, and at a time when she was convinced that she alone could visually represent India ("India belongs only to me"), it is possible that *Mother India* captured Amrita's dominant impression of her rediscovered homeland: "Desolate—yet strangely

the "real"
mother India

FIGURE 127 Amrita
Sher-Gil, *Mother India*. Oil
on canvas, 1935. (National
Gallery of Modern Art,
New Delhi, Acc. No. 1134)

beautiful—. . . endless tracks of luminous yellow-grey land . . . dark-bodied,
sad-faced, incredibly thin men and women who move silently looking almost like silhouettes and over which an indefinable melancholy reigns . . .
so different from the India, voluptuous, colorful, sunny, and superficial, the
India so false to the tempting travel posters that I had expected to see."[6] In
painting melancholically against such a "tempting" poster look, and possibly
also in response to the then-influential artists of Bengal who were attempting
a "national mystical spiritual art of India,"[7] the young Amrita took on as her
particular artistic goal the task of interpreting "the life of Indians and particularly the poor Indians pictorially; to paint those silent images of infinite
submission and patience, to depict their angular brown bodies, strangely
beautiful in their ugliness; to reproduce on canvas the impression their sad
eyes created on me."[8] *Mother India* is exemplary of this artistic agenda, which
in one interpretation, is the work of someone who pictured India from "the
point of view of the outsider, who wanted to become an insider" (Anand

1989, 23). I prefer Geeta Kapur's characterization of Amrita's work as acting out "the paradox of the oriental subject in the body of a woman designated as Eurasian" (2000, 7).

Mother India was largely ignored by critics at the time (and since), but Amrita herself seems to have thought well enough of her own effort at first; in a letter to her sister she described it as "an excellent picture of a beggar woman and her brats," and she offered it as a gift to a close friend. That she chose to represent Mother India in the body of "a beggar woman" with "great soulful eyes in a melancholy face" seems sacrilegious in the face of the dominant patriotic understanding of her namesake as a goddess of promise and plenitude, albeit one who is sometimes pictured in tears or in chains.[9] How do we account for this sacrilege? Given the avant-garde literary and artistic circles in which Amrita had recently moved in Europe, it is possible to regard *Mother India* as a modernist expression of the dominant Western understanding in the 1920s and 1930s of the Indian woman as essentially abject, abused, and victimized—a view that was so notoriously captured in the American author Katherine Mayo's pungent text, also titled *Mother India*, which created such a stir across three different continents when first published in 1927.[10] As others have noted, Mayo had cleverly appropriated Mother India's name and substituted "a pathologized mother for the glorified Mother of nationalist discourse" (Shetty 1995, 51). A few years after the publication of her *Mother India*, and in the aftermath of the storm it created in India, Mayo defended her choice of the title in another publication titled *The Face of Mother India* (1935): "By the title of an earlier book some of you have been offended. Mother India, you say, is to you and yours a sacred figure—the embodiment of your Hindu race-loyalty . . . That title was chosen with an object. Its purpose was to awaken your intelligent patriotism and the consciousness of your men, *by making inescapable the contrast between, on the one hand, florid talk of devotion and 'sacrifice' poured out before an abstract figure, and, on the other hand, the consideration actually accorded to the living women*, mother of the race."[11]

There is no empirical evidence that Amrita had read Mayo's *Mother India*, but it is hard to believe that she was unaware of the controversies surrounding the book given the circles in which she moved as well as her own wide-ranging reading habits. Under the circumstances her naming her picture

Mother India in the wake of the controversy is not perhaps accidental, and possibly it was even an attempt to reenvision the terms of the discourse about the nation's mother(s)—although not necessarily in the direction of either official narrative *or* of the dominant visualizations of patriotic art and barefoot cartography. Amrita's *Mother India*, like Mayo's incendiary commentary, implicitly draws attention to the contrast between the glorified figure of nationalist devotion and the reality of subaltern female life in colonial India. The abject woman of India ought to matter, the painting seems to tell us, objectified and orientalized though she might appear in the work. In contrast to many of her fellow artists, both populist and at the high end, Amrita's incipient feminism—vividly apparent in many of her other, more well-known works—led her not toward celebrating a feminized India but to a lament on its piteous state. There is little sense we get from her letters and diaries—or from the accounts others have left of her elite life as a minor celebrity—that she was overtly concerned with India's colonial condition or that she actively espoused the patriotic cause. Nonetheless, *Mother India* is a striking political visual statement. By locating the essence of India not in the hallowed glow of a glorious goddess but in the humble subaltern body and a melancholic female one at that, Amrita's painting attempts to shift the terms in which the country was being imaged in the patriotic art of her time. The exceptional female body is replaced by the quotidian, the glorious by the ungainly.

Strikingly, Amrita's singular visualization of Mother India in 1935 found a textual echo in her good friend Jawaharlal Nehru's memoir *Towards Freedom*, published just a year later in 1936. Like Amrita, but contrary to many of his fellow patriotic citizens, the future prime minister of independent India did not rush to picture Bharat Mata as "a beautiful lady, very old but ever youthful in appearance . . . And yet India is in the main the peasant and the worker, not beautiful to look at, for poverty is not beautiful. Does the beautiful lady of our imaginations represent the bare-bodied and bent workers in the fields and factories? Or the small group of those who have from ages past crushed the masses and exploited them, imposed cruel customs on them and made many of them even untouchable? We seek to cover truth by the creatures of our imaginations and endeavor to escape from reality to a world of dreams" (1980, 431). I have seen no documented evidence that Nehru saw

Amrita's *Mother India*, although the artist herself in a letter acknowledging his gift to her of a copy of his autobiography remarks, "I don't think you were interested in my painting really, you looked at my pictures without seeing them."[12] Whether he "looked" without "seeing," his Bharat Mata has an uncanny resonance to her *Mother India*, in itself a refusal "to escape from reality to a world of dreams."

Three decades after Amrita's painting, another visual production by the same title made its appearance in what is perhaps Bombay cinema's most emblematic film. It too resolutely refused to escape from reality to a world of dreams in narrating "a story of our soil and its children."[13] In using the figure of the long-suffering peasant female body to stand in for the feminized nation, Mehboob Khan's memorable *Mother India* (1957) appears to pick up the challenge posed to the nation by Amrita's painting.[14] In dramatic contrast to Bankim's "richly-watered, richly-fruited" terrain, or the lush pastoral plenitude of patriotic art, the Mother's land featured in the film is inhospitable and unyielding; there is no easy living there as the peasant toils under the blazing sun, patiently (and fearfully) waits for the rains that threaten to never come, and then surrenders most of her meager harvest to the rapacious moneylender. The publicity brochure for *Mother India* proudly invokes the much-quoted words of the famous German orientalist Max Muller: "If I were to look over the whole world to find out the country most richly endowed with all the wealth, power, and beauty that nature can below—I should point to India."[15] Yet no amount of cinematic manipulation, or panoramic shots of glorious dawns and beautiful sunsets, can distract the film's viewers from the grim reality of the (Indian) land on which the peasant (woman) labors almost to the point of death.

Strikingly, the glorious goddess of the Indian nationalist imagination makes absolutely no appearance at all in the film; she has been completely displaced and replaced by Radha, the tender but resolute and embattled but courageous peasant bride-woman-mother (who, importantly, remains a married woman throughout the film).[16] The missing husband-father is notable by his absence for a good part of the narrative, as the mother and her two sons struggle to make a living out of the intractable land that is India. In a pivotal scene, after the villagers have succeeded in combating a ravaging flood and in reaping a good harvest out of this difficult land, they break out into song

FIGURE 128 Film still from Mehboob Khan's *Mother India*. Released in Bombay, October 1957.

as they thresh their crop. As they do so their produce and bodies form into an outline map of undivided India (with the independent island country of Sri Lanka as well claimed for the Indian nation) (figure 128). Ten years after Indian independence, not only is the fact of partition denied (and in a film directed by a Muslim man), but undivided India is resolutely claimed by and for the peasantry as it is cartographically condensed in the bodies of the dancing villagers. The scene strikingly resonates with Nehru's developmental vision, which in turn reflects the emergent social realism of a new generation of "progressive" writers and artists: "And yet India is in the main the peasant and the worker, not beautiful to look at, for poverty is not beautiful."

This is not the only critical reversal that *Mother India* effects, for the title role of Radha is played by Nargis, who was one of the most well-known movie stars of her times (as well as a Muslim).[17] As one contemporary critic noted, "Remove Nargis and there is no Mother India."[18] In an arresting moment from earlier in the film, Nargis-Radha–Mother India breaks out in a song exhorting her fellow villagers who are set to flee from their ravaged land: "O you, departing ones! Do not leave your homes. Your Mother is call-

ing out with folded hands . . . Where would you go, leaving all this behind—
these cities, roads, tenements? Maybe this land is spoilt just now; but you
can never be happy anywhere in the world, if you break mother's heart."[19]
No viewer of the film can miss the many times that Nargis's body appears
onscreen clothed in the very mud that makes up the terrain of India. The
film's opening shot in fact is of Radha-Nargis clawing at the wet earth and
holding up a fistful; as the camera zooms in on her mud-caked wrinkled face,
a chorus chimes in: "All our life Mother-Earth [*dharti-mata*], we will sing
in your praise. And each time we are born, we will be born into your lap."[20]
That the Muslim female body could so convincingly incarnate and instanti-
ate Mother India / Mother Earth is as effective a poetic revenge as one can
imagine on Bankim, and on the very-Hindu pictures of so much patriotic
art.[21] So powerfully did Nargis come to embody Mother India for generations of Indians that in 1975 when M. F. Husain set out to paint Prime Minister Indira Gandhi as Mother India in a controversial triptych, he reportedly
had the actress in mind (Chatterjee 2002, 76). And Nargis herself willingly
ceased to act after *Mother India*, almost as if in having become so indelibly
the nation it was impossible to be anything else.[22] Indeed from then on she
dedicated herself to social and public causes that might be broadly conceived
as nation building.

Yet beyond the elite circles in which Amrita Sher-Gil displayed her work,
and outside the cinema halls in which Mehboob's *Mother India* played (in
some accounts, for decades after its original release in October 1957), such
reinscriptions had little impact on barefoot cartographic labors, which continued to be resolutely focused on the exceptional—and very Hindu—Bharat
Mata and her famous sons, with the mother's daughters hardly visible at
all. In Allah Bukhsh's oil painting from the 1920s (figure 12), or in the occasional postcolonial lithograph (figure 36), anonymous women dressed in the
clothing of diverse communities appear in acts of offering worship to Bharat
Mata and visually reaffirm their foundational role as bearers of the spiritual
essence of the nation. They also appear as wives, thereby lending support to
their husbands' labors on behalf of mother and map (see, for example, figures
28, 84, and 95). However, any other form of work autonomously performed
by the woman for the map of India or the carto-graphed mother/goddess is
rarely pictured.

Yet that they were involved in such patriotic labors, frequently independently of male kin, is obvious from at least the opening years of the twentieth century, and a pictorial and cartographic focus enables us not just to bring (back) to visibility some women who are otherwise on the margins of the dominant and official (male) narratives of the nation, but also compels me to examine the question I posed earlier: Do women inhabit and dwell in the mother's territory differently from men? One answer to this question is provided by the patriotic performances of Sarala Devi Chaudhurani née Ghosal (1872–1945), a highly educated cousin of Abandindranath—the artist who so prominently figures in any history (pictorial or otherwise) of Bharat Mata. By all accounts, especially her own, Sarala had already started favoring a brand of nationalism that was more activist, even favorable to violent action, than those espoused by the male members of the influential Tagore family to which she was related through her mother, the writer Swarnakumari (1856–1932). The intersection of Sarala's life with Bharat Mata's story can be traced to the 1890s: a recent biography by the historian Bharati Ray credits her for having set to music in 1896—along with her famous uncle Rabindranath—the mother's signature hymn "Vande Mataram."[23] Later in 1905, at the height of the protests against the partitioning of Bengal, she was invited to sing the song in Banaras at the annual convening of the Congress. On this occasion she changed, in the course of her rendering, Bankim's allusion to the mother's seventy million children to three hundred million; in so doing, this verbal and numerical change effectively transformed Bankim's Mother Bengal into Mother India.[24] It may have been Sarala's version of the "Vande Mataram" song that Gandhi arguably first read across the ocean as a lawyer in South Africa. "The song, it is said, has proved to be so popular that it has come to be our National Anthem . . . Just as we worship our mother, so is this song a passionate prayer to India," he wrote in his *Indian Opinion*.[25] By this time, Sarala had already been involved in the various secret societies that mushroomed across Bengal in the early years of the new century, with several of them such as the Anusilan Samiti and the Suhrid Samiti coming under state surveillance for their anticolonial activities. The Suhrid Samiti is believed to have first popularized the use in April 1905 of the "vande mata-ram" refrain as a patriotic slogan for the emergent national movement. The Samiti also staged *Anandamath*, perhaps for the first time, in 1905.[26]

Prior to her involvement with the mother's song, Sarala had started a gymnasium in her father's house for training young men in swordplay, fenc-ing, boxing, and even the use of firearms, and in 1902 she proclaimed her intention of moving on "from speech to writing, and writing to deeds."[27] Her biographers note that Sarala required members of her gymnasium—all young men—to take a pledge in front of a map of India that they would serve their country with their bodies and minds (Chakravarti 1990, 62–65; Ray 2002, 9). Although no material trace of the map she used for this pur-pose appears to have survived, this might be the first time that the nation's cartographic form is drawn into patriotic agitprop activities in this man-ner, even possibly predating its adoption by the Anti-Circular Society as its logo in late 1905 (figure 59). Her biographers also note that Sarala modeled herself on warrior goddesses like Durga, and on militant heroines like Devi Chaudhurani of Bankim's Bengali novel of that title (Ray 2002, 105–6). In a poem that she published in 1896 in the Bengali journal *Bharati*, edited by her mother, the nation is imagined as a goddess with a sword in her hand and a bleeding head in another, modeled possibly on Kali but also eerily an-ticipating Prabhu Dayal's print from the 1930s discussed in chapter 5 (figure 118) (Banerjee 2002, 206). Despite her later affinity with the Mahatma, the Bharat Mata of Sarala's youthful imagination was clearly not Gandhian in her partiality for armed violence for a just cause. Indeed, Sarala frequently appeared in public mimicking Durga's visual appearance, invoking her name in her speeches and writings, and calling on her to bless the emergent nation: "Please, Mother, we beg you, give us your milk mixed with blood to feed our valor. We need to grow up as a healthy, strong, well-developed nation."[28] In an essay that she published in *Bharati*, she called on the "women of India" to "wake up!" "Let the world know you for your true identity, in the image of Durga, wielder of power and authority. Find yourself! Know yourself!"[29] In her lived life, therefore, Sarala appears to have been a model for the fictional Bimala that her uncle Rabindranath later re-created in the pages of his *Ghare Bhaire*, a woman who was aware that "my resplendent womanhood made me indeed a goddess," a woman who appeared to literally perform the emergent sense that the nation's women are flesh-and-blood, living-and-breathing, surrogates of the mother of them all, Bharat Mata.

Around the same time, another woman's life intersects with Bharat Mata's pictorial entanglements with swadeshi mobilizations during the partition of Bengal. The woman's name is Margaret Noble, although she is more familiar to Indians as Sister Nivedita (the Dedicated). Born in 1867 in Dungannon in northern Ireland, Margaret was a schoolteacher with fairly radical socialist leanings in London in 1895 when her life took a turn for the unexpected after she met the global Hindu missionary Swami Vivekananda (1863–1902) who brought to England (and to the rest of the West) "news from a far land."[30] That "far land" turned out to be India, to whose cause (and that of her new-found mentor) she dedicated her life from then on. Finally convinced that Margaret had "a great future in the work for India," Vivekananda encouraged her desire to relocate to Calcutta, where she arrived in 1898 and largely lived until her early death there from dysentery in October 1911. In an older critical scholarship on this remarkable female exemplar of the strategic exchanges and affinity between Ireland and India in the colonial period, some have dismissed her as an insignificant bit player in the grand drama of Indian nationalism, with fine historians like Sumit Sarkar questioning hagiographic attempts to pass Nivedita off as an Indian Joan of Arc.[31] Yet some new work demonstrates that for a history of the development of the imagination of Mother India, it is instructive for at least two reasons to consider this Irish-turned-Indian woman's not-uncontroversial presence.[32]

First, Nivedita's work gives us an intimation of the role played, however tangentially, by those who by birth were neither "Indian" nor "Hindu" in the fashioning of a "national" icon for an emergent India. As she has reportedly claimed at one point, "I have identified myself with the Idea of Mother India, I have become the idea itself."[33] This was so much the case that in *Aggressive Hinduism* (1905)—in a voice akin to that adopted by Bharat Mata herself in various contemporary poems and texts—she called on Indians with the words, "Sons of the Indian past, do ye fear to sleep at nightfall on your shields? . . . On, on, soldiers of the Indian Motherland, seize ye the battlements and penetrate to the citadel! Place garrison and watch within the hard-won towers, or fall, that others may climb on your dead bodies, to the height ye strove to win" (33).[34]

Second, Nivedita's engagements reminds us of an early moment in the evolution of the Bharat Mata figure when the presence of goddesses like Kali and Durga, or overt Hindu symbols and markers in the imagination of this new embodiment of nation and country, is unembarrassed, even aggressive. A year after her arrival in India, and inspired by the musings on the subject by her spiritual mentor, Nivedita delivered in February 1899 a lecture in Albert Hall in Calcutta titled "Kali and her Worship." This remarkable lecture began with the Irish woman declaring that she had "the right of an Englishwoman to express public regret for the part which countrymen and women of my own have played in vilifying a religious idea." And this is the idea of the God as Mother: "For India, there is one relationship that makes the home—that makes sanctity—that enters into every fibre of the being, and it is not Fatherhood. What wonder that in India, God's tenderest name is that of Mother?"[35]

In this lecture that her biographers note created a "sensation," Nivedita stopped short of suggesting that the country itself was Mother, although she must have been aware that some Bengali men (and women like Sarala) were already beginning to do this. Soon after, in the course of an invited lecture that she delivered in the less secular space of the Kali temple at the (in)famous Kalighat in Calcutta, when she countered some objections that had been raised by reform-minded Hindus to her praise of the blood-soaked worship of the goddess, Nivedita provocatively accused her Indian critics of seeing Kali through "European eyes." Seen thus, "the most prominent feature about her is her horridness. She is naked and dances on the bosom of her husband. She has a garland of decapitated heads around her neck and her tongue is outstretched to drink the warm blood of her victims. Weapons and terrible agents of Death adorn and surround her . . . She is all terror" (2: 440). Yet her modern Hindu "brothers and sisters" were confusing appearances for inner reality, and "the Indian people ought to take their eyes off the West and cease to compare." If they do so, and put "more and more idealism in their own way into the portrayal of the Mother," they would succeed in producing something "national and great" (2: 445–46).[36]

A few years later at least one Indian artist did take "his eyes off the West" in order to paint "the Mother" in an idealistic and national way. Nivedita went into raptures about this "first picture of India the Mother that an Indian man makes for his people": "How can a man be a painter of nationality? Can an abstract idea be given form and clothed with flesh, and painted? Undoubtedly it can. Indeed if we had questioned this, Mr. A. N. Tagore's exquisite picture of 'Bharat Mata' would have proved its possibility" (1967, 3: 14).[37] Abanindranath's *Bharat Mata* (figure 6) was, in her opinion, a true "Indian painting," for it appealed "to the Indian heart in an Indian way":

> This is the first masterpiece in which an Indian artist has actually succeeded in disengaging, as it were, the spirit of the motherland,—giver of Faith and Learning, of Clothing and Food,—and portraying Her, as she appears to the eyes of Her children. What he sees in Her is here made clear to all of us. Spirit of the motherland, giver of all good, yet eternally virgin, eternally raft from human sense in prayer and gift. The misty lotuses and the white light set Her apart from the common world, as much as the four arms, and Her infinite love. And yet in every detail, of "Shankha" bracelet, and close-veiling garment, of bare feet and open, sincere expression, is she not after all, our very own, heart of our heart, at once mother and daughter of the Indian land[?] (3: 58)[38]

And she directly contrasted such an ideal image of the Indian mother with the "picture of a fat woman lying full length on the floor and writing a letter on a lotus leaf!" which hung on the walls of every Indian home that she had seen (3: 15).[39] Instead, if it were up to her she would take Abanindranath's *Bharat Mata* and "reprint it, if I could, by tens of thousands, and scatter it broadcast over the land, till there was not a peasant's cottage, or a craftsman's hut, between Kedar Nath and Cape Comorin, that had not this presentment of Bharat-Mata somewhere on its walls" (3: 61). The geo-body of the nation, it seems, was incomplete with the mother's anthropomorphic form.

Given Nivedita's fervent (but mostly covert) patronage of some secret societies (such as the Anushilan Samiti) that advocated violent action against the colonial state as well as embraced Kali as a ferocious bloodthirsty mother/ goddess, her praise for Abanindranath's *Bharat Mata* seems both excessive and inconsistent. Contrary to her expectations though, the barefoot map-

maker largely ignored Abandindranath's idealized Bharat Mata in favor of modeling Mother India on the typical goddess and female figure of the bazaar art that the Irishwoman-turned-Indian disparaged. But her ecstatic reviews of Abanindranath's *Bharat Mata*, and attempts to draw upon it to theorize about "the function of art in shaping nationality," are important to register for both a feminist pictorial history of Indian patriotism and for an early moment in the development of art criticism by women in the subcontinent.

Nivedita's place in a visual and gendered history of Indian patriotism can also be reckoned through her efforts to design a flag for the emergent national movement. In early 1905 students in her school in Calcutta stitched "a national flag" under her direction, which she mentions in a letter to a friend: "We have chosen a design for a National Flag—the thunderbolt—and have already made one. Unfortunately I took the Chinese war-flag as my ideal and made it black on red. This does not appeal to India, so the next is to be yellow on scarlet."[40] Her official biographer Pravrajika Atmaprana notes that Nivedita's students went on to create such a flag in scarlet and yellow, and that it was displayed at a meeting organized by the Congress party in 1906. In her biography of Nivedita, Pravrajika Atmaprana reproduces a facsimile of the flag, which is square in shape with a bright yellow thunderbolt, interpreted as the symbol of "the Selfless Man." The words "vande mataram" are also printed in Bengali script on either side of the thunderbolt symbol.[41] Despite its incorporation of the popular slogan "vande mataram," Nivedita's flag was not adopted for wide-scale use by nationalists of the time. It vied for attention with another flag, the so-called Calcutta flag, which was designed by two Bengali men, Sachindra Prasad Bose and Sukumar Mitra, and was a green, ochre or yellow, and red banner with the words "vande mataram" inscribed in Devanagari across the central panel. (In a later lithograph, this flag is shown under the numbers 1906 [figure 26; see also figure 121].) Srirupa Roy notes that "Nivedita's self-conscious location as an outsider may well have pushed her to adopt an overtly Orientalist version of what the authentic inner core of India looked like—oil lamps, renunciatory shades of yellow and scarlet, and holy thunderbolts as the visible signs of Hindu spiritualism" (Roy 2006, 499). I would also suggest that it is not surprising that Nivedita should have chosen the phrase "vande mataram" to adorn the banner she created

FIGURE 129 Bhikhaiji Cama with the national flag. Photograph of postcard. (Nehru Memorial Museum and Library Photo Archive, Album # 812, No. 8038)

for the nation, given the mother-centered view of religion and politics that she espoused.

These early flags emblazoned with the mother's slogan left their visible mark as well on another banner that was unfurled in the name of India and displayed in Stuttgart, Germany, in August 1907 at the Second International's annual gathering (figure 129). Like the 1906 flag, this banner was tricolored. The sun and crescent moon putatively signifying the Hindu and Muslim communities of India were retained, as was the by-now de rigueur invocation of "vande mataram." In terms of my concern with documenting the entanglement of cartographic and anthropomorphic forms in Indian patriotic visuality, it is worth noting that both the 1906 and 1907 flags used eight lotuses to signify the eight provinces of British India. When Bose and Mitra, the designers of the 1906 Calcutta flag, presented it to nationalist elders,

<u>Bhikaji Cama</u> unfurling
a flag of Indian Independence
designed by Hemachandra Das
Kanugo (close associate of
Aurobindo) before an int'l
audience of socialists in
~~Bhikaji~~ Stuttgart (1907) &
London (1908 — after Muzaffarpur bomb)
— One of the foremost
    pro-Independence voices
    outside India.

— Parsi by birth, upbringing
  and marriage... but freely
  invokes the image of
  Mother India (and depicts her
  as a 2-armed Durga).

held at the Imperial Institute
of the Univ. of London

— 1911 — First Universal Races
  Congress (London) meets
  W.E.B. DuBois (who is inspired
        to write Dark Princess)

some of them apparently "suggested that the eight lotuses, representing the then eight provinces of the country be placed *according to their respective location on the map of India*, instead of showing all the eight in a row on the top green band of the flag."[42] However, this attempt to bring the constituent parts of the mother's land in line with the command cartographic vision of the country was rejected both in Calcutta and overseas when the 1906 flag was used as a template for the banner unfurled in Stuttgart.

The Stuttgart flag is important for the feminist narrative I sketch in this chapter because it emerged to visibility through the "seditious performance" of an Indian woman who lived abroad and was by all accounts transformed there into a votary of Mother India (Roy 2006, 500).[43] Her name was Bhikhaiji Cama and as a Zoroastrian by birth, upbringing, and marriage she also reminds us that every now and then Bharat Mata also captured the attention of Indians who are not nominally Hindu. Born possibly around 1861, Bhikhaiji was the daughter of affluent Parsis in Bombay, and she was married for a while to a wealthy lawyer from whom she was estranged when in 1902 she moved to England, ostensibly for medical treatment. Although she had been exposed to the activities of the Congress in the late 1890s when she lived in Bombay, it was when she moved abroad (where she led a semi-peripatetic life between Germany, France, Switzerland, Britain, even the United States) that she was radicalized. The first audible sign of her transformation came in a startling speech on August 22, 1907, in Stuttgart at the annual meeting of socialists in the Second International on behalf of the "dumb millions of Hindustan who are undergoing terrible tyranny under the English Capitalists and the British Government."[44] Unlike many of the gentlemanly moderates of the Congress at home, and akin to the firebrand expatriates at London's India House (founded in 1905) with whom she chose to willingly associate, Bhikhaiji categorically called for an end to British rule in India on the grounds that "no people should be subject to any despotic or tyrannical form of government." At the end of her fiery speech she famously unfurled her flag—the first time an Indian banner had been displayed outside the territorial confines of the emergent nation in the name of that nation—and reportedly declaimed: "This flag is of Indian Independence. Behold, it is born. It is already sanctioned by the blood of martyred Indian youths. I call upon you gentlemen, to rise and salute this flag of Indian Independence. In the name of this flag, I appeal to lovers of freedom all over the world to cooperate with this flag in freeing one-fifth of the human race."[45]

Although several hagiographic accounts of Bhikhaiji Cama's life and deeds claim that she was the creator of this flag, it was possibly a joint production in which her India House associates Vinayak Damodar Savarkar and Shyamji Krishna Varma might have been involved. The flag itself was made, and possibly designed, by the young Bengali anarchist Hemchandra Das Kanungo, as Bhikhaiji herself alluded to in December 1908 as she once again triumphantly displayed the flag, this time in London: "The lives of four young men who are done to death, are burnt away just like incense on the altar of Motherland. Bande Mataram. On the altar of truth, justice, and liberty, these noble lives are sacrificed. This flag of Bande Mataram which I wave before you, was made for me by a noble selfless young patriot who is standing at the bar of the so-called court of justice in our country. What a mockery to talk of justice and jury!!"[46]

It is clear from the "history sheet" produced on her by an alarmed colonial state in 1913 that "Madame Cama" unabashedly displayed the *Bande Mataram* flag" on several occasions, for "she was in the habit of speaking under that flag." On one occasion in London in November 1908 she is also reported to have "displayed a national flag woven in silk and gold with the inscription, 'In memory of the martyrs of 1908.'"[47] Although Bhikhaiji's banner itself has not survived, a visual trace of it might be found in a grainy picture postcard featuring a woman identified by a colonial censor as "Mme B. S. Cama." In the postcard, she proudly displays the flag with the words "vande mataram" emblazoned across it in Devanagari script (figure 129).[48]

Bhikhaiji's seditious performances in the name of mother and India (and their martyrs) were not limited to such public displays of the flag, or even to reputedly wearing saris with the words "vande mataram" inscribed along their border. Equally alarming from the perspective of an embattled colonial state was her leading role, starting in September 1909, in the publication of the expatriate revolutionary newspaper *The Bande Mataram: Monthly Organ of Indian Independence*. Funded partly with her resources (which she was only able to proffer through "self-denial"), the paper appeared until 1913 from Geneva. Its radical message and revolutionary content led the colonial state to ban its circulation in British India as early as December 1909.[49] Echoing an earlier "seditious" newspaper by the same name that had appeared between 1906 and 1908 in Bengal before being shut down by colonial censors, Bhikhaiji's *The Bande Mataram* is nonetheless innovative from my perspective for its visual inscriptions.[50] The masthead of the newspaper was adorned with the Bande Mataram flag that Bhikhaiji had unfurled proudly in Stuttgart in 1907 (figure 15). As important, in its March 1913 issue the front page carried (albeit incongruously next to a "Chinese patriotic song") an illustration of a carto-graphed woman, indeed one of the earliest surviving images to bring the mapped form of the emergent nation into association with its female form. Inscribed across the banner held aloft over the mother's head by the two cherubs are the words "vande mataram" in Devanagari, and a verse from the Hindu sacred text Bhagavad Gita is inscribed below the central image: "[This war has offered itself to you as your duty] / If you refuse to fight this righteous war, sacrificing both the law of your life and renown, / you will incur sin" (figure 15).

As I note in my discussion of this illustration in chapter 1, Parsi though Bhikhaiji might be by birth her Mother India is quite Durga-like in her visual persona. Sword in hand, lion by her side, she is all primed to do battle as she faces West, and the weapons arranged around her only reaffirm her latent militancy. All the same, she is a two-armed rather than a four-armed figure, and her visual persona humanizes her in a manner that makes her more akin to the Bhikhaijis of the mortal world (however uncommon, certainly in her own time) rather than a hallowed divinity. Soon after, this carto-graphed Bharat Mata migrated from the pages of *The Bande Mataram* in Europe to appear on the roughly printed pamphlet covers of the Punjabi, Hindi, and Urdu publications of the California-based Hindustan Ghadar Party (see, for example, figure 16). It is possible that the inspiration for the shared image was one of Bhikhaiji's associates and fellow travelers in expatriate revolutionary circles in Europe, Har Dayal (1884–1939), an editor for a few months of *The Bande Mataram* and a key instigator of the Ghadar movement in the United States. Nonetheless, the Bharat Mata of Bhikhaiji's *The Bande Mataram* echoes in its visual persona her own real-life politics: her refusal to abjure the use of violence as an anticolonial strategy just because of the expectation that as a (middle-class) woman, she was essentially passive and nonviolent;

and a belief that it was time to pay the price to secure liberty from foreign rule even if that meant the sacrifice of lives on "the altar of the Motherland." Not surprisingly, one of the official confidential reports on her noted that she was "regarded by the Hindus as an incarnation of some deity, presumably Kali."[51] Whether this regard is founded in historical reality is beside the point for the larger truth it points to that like Sarala, Bhikhaiji appears to have interpreted the charge of being Bharat Mata's flesh-and-blood surrogate to establish a frankly public and interventionist relationship to the project of Indian nationalism that was fiercely at odds with the prevailing expectations regarding the daughters of Mother India. That she self-consciously asserted her claim to the motherland only after literally leaving its shores is perhaps revelatory of the burden posed on many a woman saddled with the charge of being confined to the home as protector and producer of that intimate domestic space.

Yet it would be a mistake to assume from these startling examples of Sarala, Nivedita, and Bhikhaiji that women's participation in the evolving love-service-sacrifice nexus around Mother India always tended toward the radical and the revolutionary. A contrary model is the Women's Indian Association (WIA), which was founded in Madras in 1917. The WIA had mixed origins in Irish and Indian women's activism, and its early officeholders included Annie Besant, Margaret Cousins, and Dorothy Jinarajadasa. They aimed to improve the lot of the Indian woman through investment in four areas: adult literacy and education, female franchise, nonsectarian religious activity, and housing for widows and the indigent (Forbes 1996, 72–75). The logo used by WIA —the earliest nationalist organization I know of that incorporates such an image—shows a sari-clad woman occupying a map of India, with its outline roughly conforming to the cartographic shape for the country that the British had envisaged, albeit with the presence of the island of Sri Lanka (figure 130). The words "Women's Indian Association" are inscribed in a circle around this central figure. The WIA offered the following explanation for its choice of the logo:

> The work has begun in the Madras Presidency (the place of the woman's feet), but its life-force springs from religion (her heart is in the region of Benares), and its intellect must be as clear and cool as the Himalayan re-

FIGURE 130 Logo of the Women's Indian Association, *The Fourth Report*, 1926–1927. (Courtesy of Mrinalini Sinha)

gions into which rises her head. Serene and self-reliant must stand each member, with hands outstretched to sisters and brothers, both in the East and the West, to give them from her active right hand Beauty and Prosperity represented by the lotus, the flower that bears within itself male and female qualities equally, and from the lamp in her left hand to extend the steady flame of inspiration which will light the fire of the united life of man and woman, the fire of devotion to our Sacred Religion and of love for humanity, the fire of patriotism, the fire of zeal for reform. Thus she represents Religion, Knowledge, Organization, Service, Beauty, Prosperity, Inspiration, and Co-operation, all offered freely to Mother India by each of her daughters.[52]

This explanation is especially remarkable because it envisages the contribution by women to nation building in explicitly territorial and cartographic terms by drawing upon the outline map form of India, familiarized by then not only by colonial state apparatuses but also, to a more limited extent, by mass media productions. In the process, the Indian woman herself is overtly carto-graphed, with the body literally mapped on to the geo-body of the emergent nation: her feet are Madras, her heart is Benaras, her head, the "clear and cool" Himalayas, and her outstretched arms the country's eastern and western reaches. The WIA was by no means a radical organization—its rather paternalistic, upper-caste, and neo-Hindu ideology only hesitantly challenged the revamped patriarchy of an inherited majoritarian tradition. It nonetheless created a sociopolitical environment for woman qua woman at a time when Indian nationalism was largely dominated by men. The logo, in the WIA's words, represented "the ideal influence of women" in "every part of India." The figure of the sari-clad woman occupying the length and breadth of the map of India was meant to image this key sentiment. The logo appears to visually declare that if India is indeed Mother India, her daughter—or at least her influence—is everywhere, in "every part of India." The women of the WIA too, like Sarala and Bhikhaiji before them, deployed the symbolism of female surrogacy to establish a possessive relationship to a feminized India. The Indian woman did not just "have" a country, she *was* the country and dwelt in every part of it, the logo appears to announce.

But in this deployment we can look in vain for the swords and guns of Sarala and Bhikhaiji's imagination from just a few years earlier. Instead the WIA women opted for the lotus and the lamp—signifying beauty and inspiration rather than militancy and martial leadership. The WIA essentially adopted a safe, tempered, and domesticated relationship to the project of India, one in which women reproduced the nation-space by not abandoning their essential qualities of a spiritualized femaleness and maternal self-sacrifice. Correspondingly, the Bharat Mata of their imagination was the "serene" and "self-reliant" mother who presided over the Indian "home," rather than the warrior-deity who strapped on weapons to lead her devotees into war against the colonial state. Nonetheless, given that Mother India herself was just beginning to be visible in a carto-graphed form and moving in to occupy the map of India in the pictorial labors of barefoot mapmakers, this was a singular moment in the special claim on the mother and her land made by some women of India (and their foreign partners).

THE MOTHER'S LIONESSES

The WIA is also important for this analysis because one of its key members became visible in patriotic art in a manner not readily accorded to other

भारत की सिंहनी का धरसाना के नमक करखाने पर धावा ।   Srimati Sarojini Naidu at Dharsana Salt Depot

श्रीमती सरोजिनी नाइडू

Published by—
SHYAM SUNDAR LAL,
Picture Merchants,
Chowk,CAWNPORE.

प्रकाशक:—
श्यामसुन्दर लाल,
पिक्चर मर्चेन्ट्स,
चौक, कानपुर ।

FIGURE 131 *Bharat Ki Sinhani Ka Dharsana Ke Namak Karkhane Par Dhaba: Srimati Sarojini Naidu at Dharsana Salt Depot,* Print by Shyam Sunder Lal Picture Merchants, Cawnpore, circa 1930. (Courtesy of Erwin Neumayer and Christine Schelberger, Vienna)

women. This woman, Sarojini Naidu (1879–1949), was hailed by Gandhi as the "Nightingale of India" on the strength of the many verses and poems she composed (in English) in the first few decades of the twentieth century on the sights, sounds, and smells of India, and especially about its (timeless and self-sacrificing) women.[53] Sometime in 1930 Shyam Sunder Lal Picture Merchants, based in the north Indian city of Kanpur and a prolific publisher of many of the pictures that I have considered in this book, released a black-and-white print centered on a sari-clad Sarojini holding a banner in her hand. In the image she is leading a group of khadi-clad Congress workers heading for a very obvious face-off with a gun-bearing British officer backed by other colonial troops (figure 131). In the distance is a building with the words "Dharsana Salt Factory" inscribed in English on its facade. The English caption to the picture, "Srimati Sarojini Naidu at Dharsana Salt Depot," is unexceptional, but the words in the Hindi title reveal the artist's possible fascination with the protagonist of the picture, for they identify the represented image as "the assault of the Dharasana salt factory by the lioness of Bharat." The "lioness" (*sinhani*) is none other than Sarojini, and this title might have been the publisher's interpretation of her declaration in May 1930 as she led her crowd of over two thousand Congress workers to the state-owned Dharasana salt works about 150 miles north of Bombay: "I am here not as a woman but as a General."[54]

The larger context for this print is the event that shot Gandhi to global fame and has been memorialized in so many pictures, photographs, and paintings: the famous march to the sea near Dandi from March 12 to April 6 1930 that the staff-carrying Mahatma led against the British government's unpopular salt tax. While Gandhi was reportedly at first reluctant to let women participate in his symbolic march, circumstances soon overtook him in the form of female followers eager to join in. Sarojini was nominated after his arrest (and that of Abbas Tyabji who took over from him) to continue on with the insurgency, and this she did first on May 15, when she was arrested for a day, and then on May 21 when she received a nine-month prison term for her action—and secured the admiration of patriotic artists as exemplified by this print. The work itself is a relatively rare instance in the late colonial period of a political picture centered on a woman in action, especially on a woman leading men against armed troops.

The woman so lionized, literally, had started her public career by writing verse that was highly sentimentalized and in some regards deliberately archaizing. Some of these works were in celebration of Mother India, such as the poem "Ode to India" (recited in English in 1904 at a meeting of the Congress), which asks the mother/goddess to wake up from her gloom-filled slumber and "beget new glories from thine ageless womb!" A few years later, in a poem called "Awake" (recited at another Congress gathering in 1915 and, interestingly enough, dedicated to Muhammad Ali Jinnah whom she admired as "the ambassador of Hindu-Muslim unity"), Sarojini once again implored the Mother to wake up and respond to the pleas of her various children: her Hindu children crown her with "the flowers of our worship"; her Parsi and Christian progeny wait upon her respectively with "the flame" of their hope and "the song" of their faith; and her Muslim offspring declare that it was "with the sword of our love" that they would "defend thee." Inclusive though "Awake" might be in its incorporation of Muslims into Mother India's love-service-sacrifice nexus, they are predictably cast in stereotypical terms as demonstrating their "love" for mother and nation with their sword.[55]

By the time Sarojini penned such verses, other poets—and women like Sarala—had already composed many poems on Bharat Mata and had called upon her to awaken from her centuries-long stupor so that her children too would awaken. Thus these verses are not unusual, although Meena Alexander (1985, 69) notes that the choice of words in Sarojini's verse suggests that the mother's daughters—in the process of crying out to her to wake up—are also attempting to cast off their own bondage. What is important, however, is that the poetess who produced these words went on to be elected the first Indian woman president of the Congress in 1925 at a time when that organization was still overwhelmingly male. She was quick to stake out a particular relationship to Bharat Mata as "a loyal daughter" in her first message as president-elect: "Mine, as becomes a woman, is a most modest domestic programme: merely to restore to India her true position as the supreme mistress in her own home, the sole guardian of her own vast resources, and the sole dispenser of her own hospitality. As a loyal daughter of Bharat Mata, therefore, it will be my lovely though difficult task, through the coming year, to set my mother's house in order, to reconcile the tragic quarrels that threaten the integrity of her old joint family of diverse communities and creeds, and to find an adequate place and purpose and recognition alike for the lowliest and mightiest of her children and foster-children, the guests and strangers within her gates."[56] The familial and domestic idiom of this speech verbally echoes Sarojini's insistence from a few years before when she had campaigned vigorously on behalf of the WIA for extending the franchise to women and when she had noted that such an act would not threaten the "separate" spheres of responsibility accorded to man and woman: "Men and women have their separate goals, separate destinies and that just as man can never fulfill the responsibility or the destiny of a woman, a woman cannot fulfill the responsibility of man . . . We ask for the vote, not that we might interfere with you in your official functions, your civic duties, your public place and power, but

MAHATMAJI MEETING THE KING-EMPEROR IN BUCKINGHAM PALACE

FIGURE 132 *Mahatmaji Meeting the King Emperor in Buckingham Palace,* circa 1931. (Courtesy of Erwin Neumayer and Christine Schelberger, Vienna)

rather that we might lay the foundation of national character in the souls of the children that we hold upon our laps, and instill into them the ideals of national life."[57]

Thus verbally at least Sarojini, like so many others in her time, considered the country as the mother's home, and the women's task in that home and homeland as essentially that of motherhood and compassionate nurture. But her actions exceeded her words in her relationship to the emergent Indian nation-space as she fiercely campaigned, between 1917 and 1919 and then again in 1931, to extend the franchise to women so that they might inhabit the mother's land as equal rather than subordinate political citizens. The patriotic artist once again took pictorial note: an anonymous colored print from the 1930s recalls the Mahatma's famous "half-naked" encounter with the king-emperor in London when Gandhi attended the second Round Table Conference in late 1931 (figure 132). Sarojini accompanied Gandhi to London as the representative for the women's organizations in India, and she is shown seated confidently in the picture while the monarch and the Mahatma have their discussion. Drawing upon the verbal record on India's "nightin-gale," Parama Roy argues that Sarojini was largely accorded a ceremonial and symbolic place in official Congress politics, "even kept at arm's length or rendered trifling" (1998, 150). Yet in the mass-produced picture world of Indian patriotism in the late colonial period, she stands out as the only one of Mother India's daughters whose gendered performances appear to warrant images in which she is the central (sometimes even the sole) protagonist.

Even so, India's artists are able to accommodate Sarojini, Kasturba, Kamaladevi, and a few other Gandhian women like them in their creations because they remain within the prescribed limits of feminine patriotism safely anchored in married domesticity while they assume a public political role, with the most important visual marker of their accepted femininity their modestly sari-clad body. Indeed, a visual documentation of the Indian national movement as provided by valuable narratives like Radha Kumar's *The History of Doing: An Illustrated Account for Women Rights and Feminism in India, 1800–1900* (1993) or Geraldine Forbes's *Women in Modern India* (1996) reveal through the power of the black-and-white photograph the increasing visibility of the sari-clad Indian woman in the public spaces of political India, especially after Gandhi himself becomes visible in that domain. An unusual photograph from the early 1930s, for instance, shows a group of sari-clad women belonging to the Poona-based Women's Home-spun Committee marching down the street holding a banner with a carto-graphed "Hind-Devi," Mother India (figure 133).[58] The photograph is another revealing visual trace of the point I have been making throughout this chapter of the selective deployment by women in colonial India of the symbolism of surrogacy: women have a special claim on (a sari-clad) Mother India by virtue of being (sari-clad) females themselves.

What is unexpected, though, is the appearance of another sort of woman in the pictorial productions of the 1940s in the wake of Subhas Chandra Bose's assumption of the leadership of the Indian National Army (INA) in 1943. As news reached India of the war that this army waged against the British in the jungles of southeast Asia, populist admiration spilled beyond Bose and his brave men to the thousand-odd women, mostly Tamil speaking, who constituted the Rani of Jhansi Regiment. This group of female soldiers was named after the much-lauded queen-mother of a central Indian king-

FIGURE 133 Members of the "Women's Homespun Committee" in a Poona procession, circa 1931[?]. (*Times of India* Collection, Nehru Memorial Museum and Library Photo Archives, No. 2177)

dom who almost a century earlier had bravely faced off against the colonial state and died (figure 134).[59] The regiment trained under the charge of Captain Lakshmi (Sahgal neé Swaminathan), who makes her appearance in the occasional patriotic picture alongside Bose clad, like him, in a military uniform, carrying a rifle (for example, figure 135).[60] In Brij Lal's celebratory *March to Independence*, Lakshmi strides next to the prancing lions that pull the victorious chariot carrying Bharat Mata toward freedom; in contrast to the sari-clad Mother India and her other female attendant, she is in khakis and carries a rifle as she marches smartly forward (figure 38). In other pictures that celebrate Bose and the INA's commitment to map and mother, the female soldier of the expatriate army that so caught the imagination of the colonial public puts in an anonymous appearance, rifle in hand and body clad in military uniform (figures 75, 99, 100). Thus in *Challo Dilli*, Netaji stands in uniform on a pale purple map of India, printed below which is the exhortation, "You give me your blood, we will deliver you freedom." While Nehru and Gandhi look benevolently down on Bose's carto-graphed body, the Indians who appear to respond to this command are the (androgynous) women of

जय जननी

FIGURE 134 Aryan, *Jaya Janani* (Victory to mother). Date and publication information not known. (Courtesy of Erwin Neumayer and Christine Schelberger, Vienna)

FIGURE 135 Subhashchandra Bose and Lakshmi Sahgal on Horseback, as Bharat Mata looks on. Hand-painted collage, Jodhpur, early 1940s[?]. (OSIAN's Archive, Research and Documentation Centre, Mumbai)

the INA (figure 100). Several decades later the (androgynous) female soldier presumably ready to give up her life for map and mother appears again in *Ma ki Pukar* (Mother's call), where inspired by the examples of the decapitated Bhagat and the saluting Bose she too takes up a rifle and stands shoulder to shoulder with the male citizen to defend the snow-covered Indian territory under attack by enemy forces (figure 117).

In the barefoot mapmaker's representation of these women in combat, I am struck by their indeterminate gender, so that it is only a visually cued and alert eye that can pick up the faint traces of womanliness that are allowed to mark the visage, such as the length of the hair peeking out from beneath their caps or the suggestive curve beneath the uniform. *I.N.A. Officer with Netaji* is an exception in this regard in its portrayal of Lakshmi as a sari-clad woman, but she is stripped of her rank as captain—indeed, she is the only one among the INA officers in the poster who is not in a soldier's uniform (figure 136).[61] In masculinizing these women thus, the barefoot mapmaker was possibly only visually—and realistically—reiterating the reality of the lives of the INA's female combatants: though there had been some discussion of clothing the Ranis in saris, it was soon concluded that like their male compatriots they too should wear the standard uniform of trousers, shirts, and caps. Most of the Ranis also had had their hair cut short, and they were issued rifles as they underwent combat training. These sartorial transformations (instituted by Bose and Lakshmi in order to make the point that women, like men, were capable of serving their nation by taking up arms), were useful for the barefoot cartographer whose own vision of love-service-sacrifice could seemingly only accommodate the male body as the armed defender of map and mother.

Prepared and primed though they were, the women soldiers of the Rani of Jhansi Regiment did not engage the enemy in battle directly. But other women in India before them had taken up arms, helped smuggle guns and explosives and make bombs, and had actually killed sundry British men and women in various acts of insurgency. By the 1920s in Bengal, as Tanika Sarkar writes, "the woman terrorist was no longer the mother or sister sheltering the fugitive but a full-fledged comrade-in-arms, revolutionizing all precedents and norms for political action."[62] Feminist scholars have recently begun to recover the story of such female "revolutionaries," including that of the teen-

I.N.A. Officer with Netaji.

FIGURE 136 Sudhir Chowdhury, *I.N.A. Officer with Netaji*. Print by SNS, Calcutta, 1940s[?]. (Courtesy of Erwin Neumayer and Christine Schelberger, Vienna)

agers Shanti Ghoshe and Suniti Chowdury who assassinated a colonial judge in 1931.[63] Another young woman, Bina Das (b. 1911), was arrested in February 1932 after a failed attempt to assassinate the Bengal governor. In court she insisted that as "a daughter of India I felt I would go mad if I could not find relief in death. I only sought the way to death by offering myself at the feet of the country and invite the attention of all by my death to the situation created by the measures of the government."[64] The paternalist colonial government was not willing to oblige Bina and the other young women like her, including the "rebellious" Kalpana Datta. Thus they were not executed but instead were sent off to prison, a move that stood in stark contrast to the readiness with which male insurgents were disposed of at the gallows. Not surprisingly, one such young woman—Pritilata Waddedar (b. 1911), a school teacher in Chittagong who led a raid in September 1932 against the European Club in the city, killing an elderly European woman in the process—consumed poison and "martyred" herself. She left behind a testament that asked rhetorically, "I wonder why there should be any distinction between males and females in a fight for the cause of the country's freedom? If our brothers can join a fight for the cause of the motherland why can't the sisters?"[65] Regardless of the specific differences between such acts and that of Bhagat, the violent deaths of these women do not appear in barefoot cartographic productions in a comparable manner as sacrifice for map and mother.[66] Indeed, in this regard, *pace* Pinney's recent argument about popular visual culture in India offering an alternative take on the official narrative sketched out by a dominant nationalism, barefoot cartography is rather evasive in visualizing the death of the female patriot for the mother and her map. To do this might possibly expose Mother India herself to pictorial death and herald the end of the patriotic artist's project: the symbolic politics of female surrogacy acted out by her flesh-and-blood representatives dwelling in Indian national-space thus reached its limit in the figure of the female citizen-martyr. In other words, the violent death of Bharat Mata's daughter for mother and map appears to be largely un-representable and perhaps even pictorially inconceivable.[67]

"EVERY DROP OF MY BLOOD WILL INVIGORATE INDIA"

So what happens when the barefoot mapmaker is confronted with the violent death of Mother India's most powerful daughter and is not able pictorially to dodge such a cataclysmic event? This came to pass after October 31, 1984, when Prime Minister Indira Gandhi was gunned down by two of her bodyguards, Beant Singh and Satwant Singh, on the grounds of her own official home in New Delhi.[68] In comparison with the men I discussed in the previous chapter, and especially unlike the man with whom she shared her famous surname and unlike her equally famous father Jawaharlal Nehru, Indira did not start out as a particular favorite of the barefoot mapmaker. Indeed, she rarely appeared in the early days of her political ascendancy in the company of the map of India. A standard image from around 1966, most likely based on an official photograph of the newly installed prime minister, is B. G. Sharma's *Indira Gandhi*, a portrait of a rather grim woman, possibly only a hint of a smile on her deeply lined face. The pale sari she wears, and the absence of the usual signs of female auspiciousness, visually underscore her widow status (figure 137).[69] Such printed portraits—displayed in Indira's lifetime in government offices, schools, and other public spaces—deploy the aesthetic of photorealism but nevertheless also suppress recognizable markers of detracting femininity. This is so much the case that in one post-humous picture she is presented as one of the "sons" of Mother India in a laminated collage print that cobbles together recycled images from earlier generations of patriotic art, with newer photographic shots of soldiers at war (figure 138) (Pinney 2004, 207). *The Sons of Bharat Mata* was possibly pub-lished sometime in 2000, more than a decade after Indira's death but soon after the Indian state turned formally nuclear (a process that had been ini-tiated during her premiership in the 1970s), and this hybrid print celebrates the nation's military might as dedicated to the (rather cinematic-looking) mother and the map, both cast in the hues of the national flag. A smiling Indira is one among the many "sons" whose heads are scattered across the Indian geo-body centered on Mother India. No other woman is visible in this print that reprises the male homo-social love-service-sacrifice nexus of the late colonial and early postcolonial moment.

It could be argued that when Indira was on the road to political ascen-dancy in the 1960s the genre of political art that produced pictorial repre-sentations of national leaders was itself on the wane, as disenchantment set in after the heady days of the freedom struggle and before the resurgence of Hindu nationalism in the 1980s.[70] But was the relative lack of pictorial imagination in this regard a product as well of the representational dilemma facing the barefoot mapmaker when it came to the matter of displaying the autonomous flesh-and-blood woman as a symbol of supreme authority and sovereign power taking sole possession of the map of India? Was the lone female leader—not obviously anchored in married domesticity and playing solicitous "help-meet" to male partners or patrons, and a widow to top it all—an unvisualizable anomaly, especially at a time when there were few ex-amples in the received templates of love-service-sacrifice for mother and her map into which she could be readily accommodated? Interestingly in this regard I have not seen Indira cast in the familiar mold of the young, widowed Rani of Jhansi, who is much admired by patriotic Indians as the heroic queen

FIGURE 137 B. G. Sharma, *Indira Gandhi*.
Print by Sharma Picture Publications,
Bombay, circa 1966. (Courtesy of Erwin
Neumayer and Christine Schelberger,
Vienna)

FIGURE 138 *The Sons of Bharat Mata*.
Laminated print, circa 2000. (Courtesy
of Christopher Pinney)

FIGURE 139 H. R. Raja, Indira Gandhi and Durga. Acquired in Delhi in 1974. (Courtesy of J. P. S. and Patricia Uberoi, Delhi)

who had taken on the British on behalf of her young son's royal privileges during the so-called first war of Independence in 1857–1858 (for example, see figure 134).[71]

By 1971 history conspired to help the barefoot mapmaker out of his dilemma over how to picture the most powerful Indian who also happened to be a living-and-breathing woman. And the goddess Durga helped as well in this conspiracy. Indira's successful stewardship of India through yet one more war with its long-time enemy Pakistan and the role that she played in the creation of the new nation of Bangladesh fueled a populist identification of Indira as Durga—an identification that she herself did nothing to deter, her secular and socialist political inclinations notwithstanding.[72] Thus the Meerut-based H. R. Raja—mentioned earlier as the creator of some striking images of male martyrs to the nation—painted Indira and Durga within the same frame with the two female faces bearing a remarkable resemblance, although the widowed prime minister's does not carry the critical marks of auspiciousness (figure 139). Durga's lions are in the process of clawing to death two of India's mortal enemies, presumably Pakistani soldiers. Also in the background are various enemy weapons of mass destruction in the process of being annihilated, and an unarmed Indira backed by the power of her alter ego, a multiply-armed Durga (wielding all manner of archaic weapons such as a sword, a club, a discus, a bow, and a trident), is apparently single-handedly responsible for the obvious destruction of the enemy's modern military technology.[73] The Puranic once again comes to the rescue of the patriotic, as its plethora of autonomous and invincible but still sensuously feminine divinities provides a model for yet another mother/goddess of India.

But it is not just local calendar artists like Raja who took to analogizing Indira with Durga. M. F. Husain, a global reputed artist by the 1970s, also was drawn into doing so. Between June 12, 1975, when a court judgment voiding Indira's recent election to Parliament was issued, and June 26 when she suspended all civil and political liberties and declared an unprecedented state of national emergency, Husain painted three large canvases, each measuring eight feet by four feet, that pictorially presented Indira as India in Danger and Indira as the Savior-of-the-Nation. The art historian Yasodhara Dalmia describes the triptych in the following manner: "The first, made on 12 June, has a headless body with accusing fingers emerging from four arms thrust in a menacing fashion towards a pale, victimized Sita. The second, painted on 24 June and titled *Uthal Puthal*, has a nude female body outstretched in the shape of the map of India. The configurations of the hair form the Himalayas, while the feet stretch toward the Bay of Bengal. The painting shows Mother India in distress as the national flag is shred to rags. In the painting made on 26 June, Mother India emerges in the form of Durga riding a roaring tiger. She is crowned with triple heads and in her ferocious aspect is determined to eliminate all evil" (2001, 115).

Ila Pal, a close friend of the artist (and a painter herself), interprets the accusing hands of the first canvas as signifying the opposition parties ganging up on an embattled Indira to the point of daring to take her to court. The second canvas—painted on the same day that one of Indira's principal opponents, Jayprakash Narayan, called upon the army to disobey the unjust orders issued by the embattled prime minister—signified Indira under attack, as her (nude) body roughly outlines the shape of India while the national tricolor lies sullied.[74] And in the last canvas, the embattled Indira, in her new incarnation as the three-headed goddess Durga riding a roaring tiger readies herself for battle—and eventual triumph. Tellingly, the triptych, which was unveiled in one of the capital's most celebrated art venues and inaugurated by none other than the president of India, was accompanied by a brochure that the artist had titled "The Triumph of Good over Evil."[75]

Much can be said about the *India June '75* triptych, which cost the famous Husain quite a bit of his reputation (although not irreparably),[76] but for the purposes of my argument the single point I want to emphasize is that these canvases, possibly widely viewed in their time, at least by India's political and cultural elite, helped consolidate an image of Indira as India, *and* India as Indira, that had especially gained currency during the Emergency years (mid-1975 to early 1977). In associating Indira with India and the map of India Husain was not alone, as we know from verbal rhetoric as well as from other contemporary images (for example, figure 140). Indira moves in now to occupy the map much in the same manner that the other "big men" of India had done prior to her, as we saw in chapter 5. But as a woman she could pass for Mother India in a manner that they obviously could not, hence the potency of her occupation of Indian cartographic space. We see this deployed—very effectively and to great political end—in an election campaign poster from Bombay in 1985, which shows her occupying a map of India with a bold caption in English, "Mother India Needs You" (figure 141). The politician who used this poster—Sunil Dutt (who also happened to be the husband of the movie star Nargis who, as noted earlier, played the title role of *Mother India* on the big screen)—won a resounding victory at the polls.[77]

It is just such a woman and icon whose violent assassination in October 1984 confronted artists of modern India, and they contended with the horror of it all in numerous ways that are revealing of the gendered politics of representation—and representability. On the one hand, Husain himself painted a series of fascinating modernist images of the event showing Indira's faceless horizontal body falling to the ground.[78] At the other end of the art spectrum, the assassination became the subject for the folk artists of Bengal who absorbed it into their performative tradition of narrative scroll painting (*pata-chitra*). One such painting by Ajit Chitrakar of Theakuachak village in Midnapore district (dating to 1986), which narrates the life of the prime minister up to her ascent to heaven after her assassination, begins with a

FIGURE 140 Indira Gandhi in map of India. Photograph of street poster, 197[?]. (Photo Archives, Album No. 834, No. 13326, Nehru Memorial Museum and Library, New Delhi)

FIGURE 141 "Mother India Needs You," election hoarding in Bombay. Photograph by Behroze Gandhy, 1985. (Courtesy of Behroze Gandhy)

Sunil Dutt (Birju in Mother India)
running for Congress
after I. Gandhi's assassination

carto-graphed Indira (anachronistically) holding aloft the national flag with the Gandhian spinning wheel (figure 142). Although one of the frames of the scroll shows her being gunned down by her bodyguards, the artist does not paint her bleeding for the map of India (that she so effectively embodies) in the manner of Bhagat, Bose, or Gandhi.[79]

Bazaar artists responded in inconsistent ways to the horror of the assassination. On the one hand, N. L. Sharma's *Prime Minister of India* (figure 143) appears to be in total denial, as it provides a visual biography of Indira that is much like the visual biographies of the big men of India discussed in chapter 5 but without the critical incorporation of the mapped form of India (figures 99, 107, and 108). The central image is that of a beaming Indira while arranged all around it are various key episodes from her life culminating in her death, shown here by her body lying in state draped in the Indian flag. The fact that she was assassinated goes unacknowledged as her body lies

FIGURE 143 N. L. Sharma, *Prime Minister of India*, circa 1985. (Courtesy of Erwin Neumayer and Christine Schelberger, Vienna)

peacefully at rest. The innocuous printed words *mrtyu* and *death* (in Hindi and English), followed by the date of the event, wipe out the horror of the manner of her passing.

In another example a hint that perhaps all is not well is provided in H. R. Raja's visualization of the event (figure 144). Inscribed across the front of this print are the following words in Hindi: "Mere Khoon Ka Har Katara Desh Ko Mazbut Karega." Painted after the assassination, the poster shows a smiling, sari-clad Indira who does not appear to be dead. Yet all those who can read Hindi and look at the picture of the smiling Indira looking back directly at her viewer will be drawn to the words inscribed on the front of the picture: "Every drop of my blood will strengthen the nation." These words were uttered by Indira on October 30 during her last election speech (in the eastern Indian city of Bhubhaneshwar) the day before her assassination, and today they are immortalized in the Indira Gandhi Memorial Museum in

FIGURE 144 H. R. Raja, *Mere Khoon Ka Har Katara Desh Ko Mazbut Karega* (Every drop of my blood will strengthen the nation). Printed by Mahasankari Offset Printers, Sivakasi, circa 1984. (Courtesy of Christopher Pinney)

the nation's capital: "I do not care if I live or die. I have lived a long life. I am proud that I spent the whole of my life in the service of my people. I am only proud of this and nothing else. I shall continue to serve until my last breath and when I die, I can say, that every drop of my blood will invigorate India and strengthen it."

Viewers of Raja's painting will also be drawn to the red streaks and blobs on the left side of the picture, which in the version I have shown here serves incongruously as an advertisement for the Ragam Brand and Indian Lion cardboard matchboxes produced by several southern Indian manufacturers. As Christopher Pinney notes, Raja pictorializes Indira's last publicly uttered words with a "visual trace" of her blood: "In Raja's portrait the only space that matters is that between Indira and the viewer, the space determined by her gaze meeting one's own and in which the viewer can reach out and touch the blood on the surface of the image" (2004, 179–80). Raja was heir to the bazaar tradition of producing political pictures that did not hesitate to show, in the most graphic manner, the martyrdom of men like Bhagat, Bose, and Gandhi as bleeding for the mother or her map. And yet he refuses to show a dismembered or even wounded Indira, although the very manner of her death as well as the martyred status she had attained by virtue of such a death lends itself to such representation.

Indira's own party, the Congress (I), did not hesitate or refuse to turn graphic and macabre in this regard, however. Soon after the assassination a number of street hoardings were put up in public spaces in the city of Hyderabad and elsewhere in the south Indian state of Andhra Pradesh during the elections of that year, which carried her party and son Rajiv to power. These images have been remarkably captured on camera by Raghu Rai, one of India's most celebrated photographers and an acute visual chronicler of the life and times of his country's first female prime minister. In one such street hoarding Indira stands occupying an outline map of India, much in the manner of the carto-graphed Bharat Mata yet with one critical difference (figure 145). In contrast to Bharat Mata who is rarely shown injured or wounded, Indira is obviously in a dire state as blood from her wounded belly that she clutches desperately drips down the gridded pattern of her sari. Also inscribed on the hoarding is the party's election symbol—a palm facing out—along with a version of Indira's last public words (written in the local language Telugu): "When my life is gone, every drop of my blood will strengthen the country."[80] Three women look up at Mother Indira (or is it Mother India herself?) as one of them (on the far left) has her palms together in the conventional gesture of reverence. All three are obviously engaged in a conversation about what they are seeing before their eyes.[81] Much in the manner of the textbook illustration with which I ended chapter 4 (figure 72), here too the presence of an exceptional being occupying the map of India elicits the homage of the beholder.

In another remarkable photograph Raghu Rai has managed to convey to us a sense of what the cityscape looked like with the deployment of such macabre images on street hoardings during the campaign by Indira's party (figure 146).[82] The front of the photograph has a rather prosaic cutout image of Rajiv, Indira's elder son and political heir. Placed behind him, however, are

FIGURE 145 A Bleeding Indira Gandhi, With Three Women Who Look On, election poster in Hyderabad. Photograph by Raghu Rai, December 1984. (Courtesy of Raghu Rai)

two stunning large hoardings of his slain mother. The first of these, mounted on a vehicle, shows a purple-colored map of India occupied by the head of the dead prime minister in profile. A garland hangs around the carto-graphed image, as the bloody red color that outlines the map of India itself bleeds out into the yellow canvas. Placed above and to the right of this dra-matic hoarding is an even more striking one that shows a highly anthropo-morphized map of India (colored black) holding the slain body of Indira in its "arms." Blood from Indira's slain body drips down to the map of India, its red color standing out against the white background of Indira's checked sari and the black map. Tears flow down the map's "face." Inscribed once again in Telugu across the hoarding is a version of Indira's putative last words: "When my life is gone, every drop of my blood will strengthen the nation."[83]

In contrast to the carto-graphed male martyrs discussed in chapter 5 who

FIGURE 146 "Every Drop of My Blood Will Strengthen the Nation," election hoardings from Hyderabad. Photograph by Raghu Rai, December 1984. (Courtesy of Raghu Rai)

wear an air of serene composure and even nonchalance, Indira's face in this hoarding—as indeed in all the others I have considered here—is distorted and grotesque, not unlike the contorted face of Mother India herself in the few rare images that show her under assault (figures 123, 125–126). This is certainly a body in pain, to draw upon Elaine Scarry's formulation, and not one that seemingly enjoys or transcends it. There is no attempt in these images to flinch from visually imagining "the female subject in her apprehension of pain" (Sunder Rajan 1993, 33). In turn, the death of Mother Indira has also transformed the map of India. Painted a demonic black it is simultaneously a geo-body that has been reduced to tears as it clutches her wounded bleeding body. The risks of visualizing the carto-graphed body of any female martyr, but especially one like Indira, are on full display here. Assimilated as she had been into the figure of Mother India so that "India is Indira" and "Indira is India," the death of Indira means the potential destruction and demise of Bharat Mata and thus also of the mapped form of India and the territorial totality that it iconizes. The limits of patriotism's barefoot cartographic imagination have been reached in this hoarding that runs the risk of pointing to the death of the very mother and map for which many of its martyrs had given up their life in its visual economy.

Epilogue **PICTORIAL HISTORY IN
THE AGE OF THE WORLD PICTURE**

Mahasweta Devi (b. 1926), one of contemporary India's most powerful activist-writers, in her poignant story from the 1980s "Douloti the Bountiful" narrates the life of the daughter of a bonded laborer who is forced to turn to prostitution to pay off family debts. Toward the end, her body racked with venereal disease, Douloti lies down to die on the bare earth. Her body is discovered next morning, laid out on an outline map of India that earlier had been drawn in chalk by Mohan (a local schoolmaster) to celebrate India's Independence Day. Mahasweta concludes her story thus: "Filling the entire Indian peninsula from the oceans to the Himalayas, here lies *bonded* labor spread-eagled, kamiya-whore Douloti Nagesia's tormented corpse, putrefied with venereal disease, having vomited up all the blood in its desiccated lungs. Today, on the fifteenth of *August*, Douloti has left no room at all in the India of people like Mohan for planting the standard of the Independence flag. What will Mohan do now? Douloti is all over India" (1995, 93).[1]

Gayatri Spivak, who translated this story into English from Bengali, notes that Mahasweta's conclusion demonstrates the reinscription of "the official map of the nation by the zoograph of the un-accommodated female body restored to the economy of nature" (1992, 112). I want to suggest also that in Douloti's dying gesture Mahasweta's story mocks a century of barefoot cartographic practice in which the exceptional female form of the mother/goddess has been deployed to supplement the cartographic configuration of the nation and re-present it to its devoted patriots, especially male citizens, as a mother and motherland worth dying for. By literally dying on the anniversary of Independence Day on the geo-body of the nation—"the dust of some map-made land"—Douloti's disease-ridden body compels us to reflect on the inadequacies of the plenteous form of Mother India so proudly displayed by India's barefoot mapmakers to compensate for the inadequacies of statist cartography. In its dying gesture, Douloti's body points as much to the sham of the somatic supplement as to the unhomeliness of the map-made land that is India.

Although rarer, earlier visual intimations of Douloti's dying carto-graphed body in the barefoot cartographic imaginary do exist, especially from the 1920s and 1930s when "the peasant question" became central to nationalist mobilizations. Thus, an illustration on the front page of the Hindi weekly magazine *Abhyudaya*, published in the north Indian city of Allahabad in 1931, shows the emaciated (and dead or dying) body of a peasant—the everyman. He is crucified onto the cross of *lagaan* (land revenue) that occupies the outline map of India, and blood from his wounds drips onto the nation's geo-body (figure 147). He pathetically holds onto a small sickle in one hand and a sheaf of grain in the other, while birds representing plague, drought, deluge, poverty, and influenza peck away at him. At the base of the cross huddles his grieving pathetic family.

The emaciated skeletal peasant body also occupies the geo-body of India in Devnarayan Varma's stark illustration "Bharatki Loot" (The plunder of India), printed possibly in 1931 as part of a series of patriotic illustrations (figure 148). Framed by statements in English (with translations in Hindi) that draw attention to the systematic plunder and exploitation of India under colonial rule, the illustration shows John Bull occupying "England" while reaching out to grab the paltry food on the carto-graphed peasant's plate.

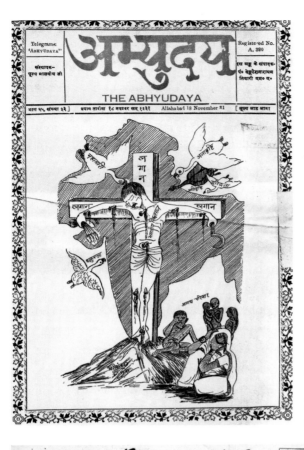

In response the poor man recoils in fear, with his wife and children at his side. Despite the mother's salutation of "vande mataram" inscribed above the illustration, the bare mapped terrain of "Bharatvarsh" that the peasant occupies indicts the pastoral plenitude of many of the bazaar pictures shown in this book. The barely clothed peasant's body also offers a striking counterpoint to the sumptuously adorned Bharat Mata whom I have focused upon in these pages. In another example, an illustration published around the same time in the Tamil magazine *Cutantira Canku* (which was dedicated to the ideals of a Gandhian Congress Party), the skeletal body of the peasant bearing the enormous burdens of taxes (and the new expenses produced by the much-publicized international Round Table Conferences in London), is placed within the Indian geo-body. The caption to the illustration reveals how the peasant feels, "I cannot bear [this]."[2] A little over a decade later, at the meeting of the All India Congress Committee in Bombay in 1946, a giant hoarding displayed the carto-graphed peasant body, with his barely clothed torso stretched to partly fit the outline map of India and his limbs in shackles. The Hindi word *ghulami* (slavery), inscribed in English across the hoarding, signals the real relationship of the everyman of India to the map of his country, as the nation's big men engage in deep conversation over its imminent independence.[3]

In 1947, soon after Indian independence, the widely read Tamil magazine *Ananda Vikatan* published on its cover a luminous color illustration titled *Gramarajyam* (Village rule) (figure 149).[4] The peasant's skeletal body has been replaced by the muscled body of the well-nourished farmer who plows his fertile fields with well-fed oxen, and he is accompanied by his buxom wife holding a healthy child in her arms. That a new dawn had arrived for the poor peasant with the coming of independence is also possibly suggested by the rosy hue that tinges the background of the painting. The farmer apparently now "rules" in this new and rosy India, as authorized by Mother India herself who is about to place a gold crown on his head. She is not so much relinquishing her own crown as she is investing with a replica the farmer at his plough, acknowledging possibly that it is his unacknowledged labors that sustain the country of which she is designated mother/goddess.

Just a few years before this picture appeared, Nehru had openly worried that his fellow citizens repeatedly sought to escape the truth of the ugliness of

FIGURE 149 Ketai,
Gramarajyam (Village rule).
Printed in *Ananda Vikatan*,
Madras, 1947. (Roja Muthiah
Research Library, Chennai)

poverty and exploitation by turning "to a world of dreams" centered on that "beautiful lady of our imaginations" (1980, 431). He attributed this escapism to an ancient habit, which Indians apparently found hard to break, of giving "an anthropomorphic form to the country" in the guise of Bharat Mata. I have argued that this ancient habit was seriously updated and transformed in late colonial modernity as the apparent deep Indian predilection for anthropomorphism contends with a new penchant for another form introduced into the subcontinent by the science of cartography. In this book I have explored this charged "formal" encounter between the map of India and the figure of Mother India in order to understand two principal questions: Why does the modern nation yearn for form, and where does the yearning take it in late colonial and postcolonial India?

The answer I have offered over these many pages to the second of these questions is that such a longing simultaneously takes the nation down at least the two paths that I have characterized as scientific-geographic, and the anthropomorphic-sacred. In 1931 the "rationalist" Tamil poet Bharatidasan asked: "In the days when we did not know the shape of India, it might have been a woman . . . Have not, however, the British taught us about the geographical shape of India as early as the fourth grade? Even this has not driven out the blind faith and old-fashioned superstitions of [these patriots]. How can a country constituted by stone and soil, rivers and forests, mountains and gorges be thought to be a woman?"[5]

Contrary to Bharatidasan's rationalist hope and expectation, the colonial and modernist project did not entirely succeed in establishing the rule of "the geographical shape of India," although it did become a force to contend with, backed as it was by the power and reach of state and science. From the pictorial evidence provided by barefoot cartography, I have suggested that from at least the early years of the twentieth century when Indians were being mobilized against the colonial state, the map form of the nation is thrown into the company of the anthropomorphic presence of the mother/goddess in order to generate love-service-sacrifice for the country in which they found themselves emplaced by the science of cartography. For her part, Mother India seeks out the map form to create for herself a distinctive persona, so that she does not get (too readily) confused and conflated with the many other goddesses who are such a palpable presence in the life-worlds of the devout in (Hindu) India. As the cartographic form of the country and the anthropomorphic form of the nation feed off each other, the map of India stands anthropomorphized, and Mother India is carto-graphed in the many diverse productions of patriotic art that I have explored here. Throughout this work I have insisted that it is only a pictorial history that places visual representations and practices at the center of analysis (even while shuttling back and forth to and from the world of words), that reveals this complicated entanglement between the scientific-geographic and the anthropomorphic-sacred imaginations of national territory. In the patriotic-pictorial realm the two are mutually imbricated and implicated.

Regarding the first question—Why does the nation long for form?—I have sought answers in the visual realm as well. Recent scholarship on colonial history and knowledge production suggests that the British learned to rule India by knowing the country, and such knowing proceeded by taking measure, literally, of the new lands that came, frequently haphazardly, under their command.[6] From the 1770s, under men such as James Rennell and Colin McKenzie, and George Lambton and George Everest, the British "surveyed" India, eventually coming to cover it with a masterful grid through which the state sought to pin down the land, its resources, and its people (for example, see figure 5). The result of the scopic activities of the Survey of India (not innocent of the involvement of Indians, as Kapil Raj has shown persuasively) was the consolidation of the mapped image of India as an entity that stretched between certain mathematically determined coordinates on the face of the earth, "dots on paper sheets" (Anderson 1991, 170–71). The map is the principal visual vehicle for the official objectification of India as a geo-body, and it is through its mediation that Britain's Indian subjects began to relearn and see the land they inhabited *differently*. This relearning and seeing—mediated through various state agencies such as the school and the bureaucracy, as well as mass-produced print culture—progressively resulted in the consolidation of the mapped image of India as the dominant official picture of national territory: delimited, self-contained, and available at one glance, guaranteed by the science of cartography that underwrote its initial production.

The philosopher of science Bruno Latour has deftly studied the processes by which lived realities have been transformed into "in-formation" and transported "with the minimum of deformation" over space and time to result in what he refers to as "immutable mobiles" (1998, 424–28). As Elizabeth Bolt writes in her analysis of Latour's argument, "The printing process enabled cheap, mass produced re-presentation of inscriptive processes (words, drawings, maps, etc.), which could then be widely distributed amongst the populace. As a result of this mobility, data became moveable even as it became immutable. Thus scientific empiricism and its vehicles, immutable mobiles, facilitated a fundamental shift in the way humans came to understand their world. . . . Reality is fixed and set before human subjects as an object of investigation" (Bolt 2004, 24–25).[7] If we follow this argument, the printed map comes to stand in for an absent world and the lived human relations on them, thereby offering "a reduced, manageable and readable model of it" (1988, 22).[8] It is a contrivance that has "the properties of being mobile but also immutable, presentable, readable and combinable with one another" (1986, 7). It makes "present absent things," enabling "translation without corruption," through "the same homogeneous language (latitude, longitude, geometry) that allows you to change scale, to make them presentable, and to combine them at will" (1990, 27). Latour suggests as well that in the process of the circulation of scientific knowledge, "information is never simply transferred, it is always radically transformed from one medium to the next . . . it pays for its transport through a heavy price in transformation" (1998, 425).[9] As such, "inscriptions allow *conscription!*" (1990, 50).

We may locate one such "conscription" by agents operating outside (or on the margins of) the centers of calculation of science and state cartography in what Benedict Anderson has identified as the logo-map. As the map of the country is conscripted and displaced from the centers of scientific empiricism for other tasks, all manner of complex and painstaking (even painful) calculating processes of measurement, triangulation, and mathematization that go into its making are masked or erased, even while some semblance of the original form is retained: "In its final form [as map as logo], all explanatory glosses could be summarily removed: lines of longitude and latitude, place names, signs for rivers, seas, and mountains, neighbors. Pure sign, no longer compass to the world. In this shape, the map entered an infinitely reproducible series, available for transfer to posters, official seals, letterheads, magazine and textbook covers, tablecloths, and hotel walls. Instantly recognizable, everywhere visible, the logo-map penetrated deep into the popular imagination, to form a powerful emblem for the anti-colonial nationalisms being born" (1991, 175).

We have encountered the logo-map again and again in this pictorial study, in precisely those mass media that Anderson identifies: posters, letterheads, magazine and textbook covers, tablecloths, even the movies. I have, however, also sought to demonstrate that there is no easy dispersal of the map form of the country—either as immutable mobile or as simplified logo—from the realms of science and state into popular-patriotic Indian consciousness through the mediation of what I have styled barefoot cartography. Matthew Edney in his pioneering work *Mapping an Empire* notes that both the colonial state and Indian nationalists came to hold "India to be a single, coherent, self-referential geographical entity coincident with the bounds of the South Asian subcontinent and the extent of British power but which nonetheless predated British hegemony" (1997, 15). This is indeed the power of the geo-body at work, that it managed to persuade so many on both sides of the colonial aisle with its capacity to make the country visually available *at one glance*. My study, however, troubles Edney's corresponding insistence that the colonial "geographical conception of India was *adopted without question . . .* by Indian nationalists" (16; emphasis mine). While this is indeed more or less true of official nationalism, the pictures I have presented in this book are a striking reminder of at least one tangible difference between (colonial and postcolonial) statist and scientific inscriptions of India's territory on the one hand and those of the barefoot mapmaker on the other. In the latter's productions the scientific-geographic is repeatedly confronted, disrupted, and "deformed" by the anthropomorphic-sacred, primarily in the shape and presence of Mother India but also, as we have seen, by some of her sons and, to a less visible extent, by a few of her daughters.

What I hope is convincing in this pictorial history is that there is no cata-strophic erasure by the natives of "precolonial" or "indigenous" conceptions of land with the arrival of new modalities of visualizing territory ushered in by the colonial state through the mediation of the modern science of cartog-raphy. Neither is there some outright rejection of the latter's hegemony. In-stead, in taking my cue from recent studies of colonialism and the postcolo-nial condition I see the "formal" encounter between the cartographic and the anthropomorphic as a much more confused and messy process marked by both disavowal and desire for the West and its (apparently) magical gifts and artifacts. I have tried to understand this complicated state of simultaneously disavowing while desiring—and desiring while disavowing—by adapting from Jacques Derrida's discussion of the logic of the supplement and from Dipesh Chakrabarty's theorizing about the (post)colonial condition as one that concedes the indispensability of the West even while disclosing its in-adequacies. Even as the map of the nation is desirable and indispensable for all manner of reasons—including and especially the fact that it bestows coherent cartographic form—it also appears to influential voices and in the many pictures that I have included here as insufficient for patriotic mobi-lization. These have convinced me that at least for some Indians who took to drawing such pictures and producing them in such large numbers over such a long period of time, mere lines on a piece of a paper could never be adequate enough for cultivating worshipful reverence or for persuading men to die in their defense—for "love-service-sacrifice."[10] The map form had to be supplemented by something else in order to do the deadly work of patriotism—and one of the enduring ways of supplementing it takes recourse, again and again, to the anthropomorphic form of the glorious plenteous mother/goddess. Rather than inhabit disparate realms of "science" and "religion," or "rationality" and "superstitious blind faith," these then come to coexist, and even help each other out, through a supplementary relationship in the many patriotic pictorial works of barefoot cartography. Because the mathematized geo-body is historically antecedent, bureaucratically hegemonic, and pedagogically normative, I see the anthropomorphic form of Mother India as supplemental in the many complex ways I disaggregated in chapter 1: occupying and filling up empty cartographic space; merging partially with it; perched, seated, or standing on it; vacating it in order to relegate it to a shadowy silhouette; and most destabilizing of all, dispensing with it entirely and standing instead for the geo-body of India. I have argued that for many barefoot mapmakers who drew such carto-graphed images of Mother India, the secular-scientific map of the nation is after all what it is—namely, contours and lines drawn between various mathematically determined coordinates on the earth's surface. What and where is the divinity and maternity of the land depicted between such lines? How could mere lines chart out *punyabhumi* (sacred land) and mother and motherland? Once brought into proximity with the map form of the nation, the plenteous, sensuous, and divine female form disclosed what was wanting—missing, absent—in one of the Enlightenment's and colonial science's proudest innovations.

At the same time, *pace* Bharatidasan or Nehru, I have also intended this work to demonstrate that the anthropomorphic form of Bharat Mata is not a primeval residue or archaic survivor that somehow lingers on into the modern, and is then excavated by India's patriots as they hit their nationalist moment to supplement the mathematical inscriptions of the colonial state. On the contrary, the imagination of Mother India from the very start in the 1860s and 1870s assumes as a given the new geographical common sense of India as a carto-graphed form, a geo-body. This is possibly not surprising since the founding figures who powerfully propelled this imagination in the beginning were educated elites who had been to colonial schools and were products of a Western (geographic) education. All the same, it is only a visual history that in considering pictures as constitutive reveals the essential modernity of Mother India, a figure who relies on the colonially wrought cartographic form of her dominion to distinguish her from the other goddesses of the Indic life-world, and to guarantee her singular status as embodiment, sign, and symbol of national territory. Undoubtedly, as I show in chapter 2, she is a figure who is modeled on goddesses who have a long prior history in the subcontinent and who leave palpable traces on the new deity's persona. Indeed, it is because she retains such prior and other divine presences that Bharat Mata has been able to so capture the imagination and attention of the devoted (Hindu) patriot. Nonetheless, in her visual appearance, despite the aura of primeval antiquity she wears, she is very much a product of a paradigm shift in representational practices that I have learned to associate with the modern moment from the German philosopher Martin Heidegger who evocatively wrote that "the fundamental event of the modern age is the conquest of the world as picture." "The word 'picture' now means the structured image that is the creature of man's producing which represents and sets before. In such producing, man contends for the position in which he be that particular being who gives the measure and draws up the guidelines for everything that is" (1997, 134).

Consequently, "the age of the world picture" does not mean a picture of the world in the sense of being its copy, "but the world conceived and grasped as a picture" so that it appears as an "enframed" image. For Heidegger, enframing is revelatory of the emergence of the modern subject who stands abstracted from a world that he can observe, manipulate, and have at his "disposal": "The fact that the world becomes picture at all is what distinguishes the essence of the modern age . . . There begins that way of being human that mans the realm of human quality as a domain given over to measuring and executing, for the purpose of gaining mastery over that which is as a whole" (1977, 129, 130–32).[11]

If we follow Heidegger in this regard, we could argue that through the mediation of the scientific map the country becomes a "standing reserve," an object of calculation and mastery, re-presented through lines and grids. Can such a carto-graphed place serve as mother and motherland, a field of care in which the patriot may dwell with a sense of belonging and longing?[12]

Chess . . . ?

To ask again a question I posed earlier with regard to figure 71 in which a schoolboy looks, almost clinically, at a map of India hanging in his school room, what persuades the citizen to develop passionate attachment to the country that he inhabits and that leads him—as it has repeatedly done in the modern world—to kill others and to die himself in order to acquire or hold on to a particular piece of earth, cartographically presented to them in and through the map form? I have suggested that in the productions of the barefoot mapmaker the carto-graphed Bharat Mata is dispersed to convert the citizen from a detached observer of the mapped form of the nation into its devoted patriot, so that the country is not "just" lines connecting some mathematically determined coordinates but rather a mother and motherland worth dying for—"picture" though India might still be and remain.

The recourse to Mother India to supplement the map of India in order to render it homely and not merely the "dust" of geography has other costs that a pictorial history such as this also seeks to reveal. For "the mother" is not merely an unmarked female with a broad cross-religious appeal, especially in the guise of a suffering matron. Almost invariably, as we have seen, her pictorial presence endows her with all manner of telltale signs that no Indian viewer would fail to identify with the majoritarian religion of the nation. On the one hand, there is an impulse that many pictures show to operate with an inclusivistic definition of (modern) Hinduism, so that signs associated with religions such as Buddhism, Jainism, or Sikhism are incorporated into the body of the mother/goddess either in the form of the heads or torsos of their founders or of their principal sites of worship (for example, figure 29). Rarely, however, are Islam or Christianity accorded this honor despite their long histories on the subcontinent, their figural traces often on the margins of the geo-body and sometimes even outside it (for example, figure 36). Mother India's body thus functions as a microcosm of the nation's plural religious history, even while it is used to signal what can—and cannot—be included within its ample fold. Her carto-graphed form is pictured to suggest that members of India's diverse religious communities are co-dwellers of the Indian geo-body, but some more intimately than others.

On the other hand, the mapped form of India is rendered Hindu through its association with Bharat Mata's obviously (reformed modern) Hindu form. The putatively secular science of cartography is used to consolidate an essentially religious and (modern) Hindu view of the nation's geo-body. In the early years of the twentieth century, Subhas Chandra Bose—the militant patriot described in chapter 5 whose adult nationalist imagination was not inflected by Hindu revivalism—wrote as a teenager a letter to his mother Prabhabati on the occasion of the annual Durga *puja* (festival): "India is God's beloved land. He has been born in this great land in every age in the form of the Saviour for the enlightenment of the people, to rid this earth of sin and to establish righteousness and truth in every Indian heart. He has come into being in many other countries in human form but not so many times in any other country—that is why I say, India, our motherland [*janmabhumi*], is God's beloved land" (1912–1913, 20).[13]

The popular print industry of the bazaars, the streets, and studios of the emergent nation—which mass-produces countless numbers of god posters showing Hinduism's many "old" divinities and the new deity of territory, Bharat Mata, as tangible and meaningful presences in the lives of modern Indians—has brought to visual reality this implicit belief that India is indeed the beloved land of the Hindu gods, the place to be on the map of the world. In the verbal discourses of nationalism, especially on the secular left, it was and remains commonplace to insist that Bharat Mata is the mother of us all, and that all of India's citizens—be they Sikh, Christian, Muslim, or Hindu, to name the numerically most numerous communities—are equal in her eyes. In the course of picturing Mother India, however, the barefoot mapmaker seems to be unable to escape the vise of Hinduism. When we literally "see" her in the many pictures that circulate across the length and breadth of the country in the many media that I have considered here, it is impossible to deny the undertow of (a modernized) Hinduism that has propelled the imagination of India as Mother India.

From being denigrated and dismissed for over a century for their vulgarity, garishness, crassness, repetitiveness, and lack of originality, the humble but ubiquitous "god posters," "framing pictures," and "calendar art" of modern India's vibrant public spaces and private places alike are now increasingly being rescued by visual-minded scholars from obscurity and invisibility in the grand telling of Indian history to occupy center stage in new narratives where such "bazaar" images now complicate our understanding of everything from the postcolonial condition to vernacular subalternity to the very creation of India's first Hindu nationalist political regime. What had hitherto been seen through the contrary lenses of lack and inadequacy on the one hand, and of excess and kitsch on the other, now reemerges in the new visual history in all its lush plenitude as well as delicious subversions to clear the way for new interpretive possibilities. But the new pictorial history is not just content with complicating old certitudes and with delivering new interpretations based on the premise that visual artifacts and images are world making rather than merely world mirroring; instead, it seeks to do more conceptually and methodologically. As Kajri Jain in her masterful work *Gods in the Bazaar* asks, "What happens when ungraspable numbers of lurid, pungent, frequently tatty, often undatable, questionably authored, haphazardly archived, indeterminably representative, hitherto undisciplined Indian bazaar pictures come crowding into the chandeliered baroque halls and immaculate modernist spaces of art history?" (2007, 17). The answer, the visual-minded scholar would say, does not just lie in filling in the gaps left out by a text-based historiography written in the shadow of the hegemony of the word, or even in using images to complicate verbal histories, for these would merely amount to an unwillingness to treat the visual domain on its own terms and would result in a history written by other means, as Christopher Pinney (2004, 8) has noted. Instead, following James Elkins, we need to make pictures more difficult to think and write about than they have been: "It appears as if pictures themselves present no problems: everyone knows how to apply theories to them, how to describe them, how to pose and solve problems about what they mean" (1998: xi). Yet parts of pictures—and the picture-worlds that produced them—are disorderly, unpredictable, and incoherent, and unless we are willing to deal with them in all their glorious unruliness, we may miss seeing what is truly innovative and inventive about them. We need to work with pictures in all their denseness and resistant otherness, and fight the urge to immediately translate them into recognizable certitudes of a (textual) history we already know from elsewhere.

We also need to work with such pictures to rethink the very terms on which we look at them, understand them, and evaluate them. As Kajri Jain has persuasively argued, as a result of the growing power of a post-Enlightenment system of aesthetic value that dispersed from the nineteenth century in places like India, a bourgeois-liberal ethos has consolidated its hold on both scholars and the Western-educated public. This ethos is "predicated on the privatization or domestication of religion, the secularization of spectacles of power, and the temporal supersession of cult by art." In such a situation, as she notes, the open celebration of the sacred and the cultic by calendar and bazaar art, itself brazenly appropriating many of the protocols of "fine art" even while refusing to abide by many of its terms, constitutes the "real scandal." Their lush hybridity behooves us as scholars studying such "scandalous" images to not completely limit ourselves to "working entirely within *or entirely without* the terms of post-Enlightenment bourgeois aesthetics, or the modernist heuristic frame of 'art' versus 'kitsch'" (2007, 176). Like these images, our theories too need to embrace an ethic of the eclectic, the heterogeneous, even the inconsistent and the scandalous.

Finally, with critical theorist W. J. T. Mitchell, we need to be willing to ask, What do pictures like these want? In his intriguing *What Do Pictures Want? The Lives and Loves of Images*, Mitchell challenges us to imagine pictures as "animated beings with desires, needs, appetites, demands, and drives of their own." The question to ask of pictures "is not just what they mean or do but what they *want*—what claim they make upon us, and how we are to respond. Obviously this question also requires us to ask what it is that we want from pictures." This line of reasoning leads Mitchell to insist that "What pictures want from us, what we have failed to give them, is an idea of visuality adequate to their ontology . . . Pictures want equal rights with language, not to be turned into language." Strange as it sounds, he tells us, the visual-minded scholar cannot avoid asking what pictures want. "This is a question we are not used to asking, and it makes us uncomfortable because it seems to be just the sort of question that an idolater would ask" (2005, 47, 25–26). Seemingly undeterred by this discomfort, Mitchell calls upon us to adopt a position of "critical idolatry" as an antidote to that reflexive critical iconoclasm that governs intellectual discourse today.[14]

Challenged by Mitchell's question, I have sought to adopt a position akin to critical idolatry (despite the scandalous history of that term in modern India) to argue that the pictures that I have analyzed in these pages "want" the devotion and worshipful reverence of the Indian citizen. They want action and sacrifice, to invoke Nehru again, on behalf of nation and country; they want martyrs for map and mother. To recall Tagore's Sandip: "True patriotism will never be roused in our countrymen unless they can visual-ize the Motherland. We must make a goddess of her. . . . *We want to per-form the impossible.* So our country needs must be made into a god" (2005, 120, 122; emphasis mine). The performance of the impossible by the bare-foot mapmaker has mutually implicated the scientific-geographic and the anthropomorphic-sacred. As a consequence the geo-body is feminized and divinized, and Bharat Mata is carto-graphed in the hybrid pictorial products that are circulated to produce love-service-sacrifice to the point of death for mother and map. This is the provisional verbal verdict to which I am led by my idolatrous foray into the colorful and scandalous picture worlds of late colonial and postcolonial India.

A pictorial history, though, demands a pictorial finish: I leave you to con-sider a recent Hindu nationalist greeting card printed in New Delhi that visu-ally summarizes what has taken me so many words to explain: the mapped form of India is anthropomorphized in a bold, even reckless, throwback to the heady days of imperial cartography when the country stretched from Afghanistan to Burma and beyond (figure 150). The mother/goddess stands carto-graphed, there but strangely not quite there, present only in her two hands, her crown, and her lotus pedestal. She has morphed yet again into another form—perhaps offering a new trajectory for another century. But that is another story, one that will have to possibly await its telling by some-one else.[15]

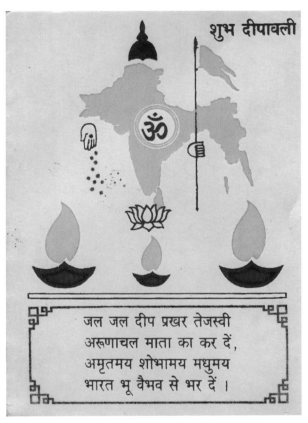

FIGURE 150 *Shubh Deepavali* (Diwali wishes). Greeting card printed in Delhi, circa 1990. (Courtesy of Christiane Brosius, Heidelberg)

PROLOGUE: YEARNING FOR FORM

1. The Sanskrit word *Bharata* (which combines with *mata*, a generic Indo-Aryan term for mother, to form the compound *Bharat Mata*) has a long and complicated history that can be traced to at least the first millennium BCE as the name used to designate the territorial space that we now refer to as India, the people who lived in a part of this land, and the ideal king who ruled over them. For an important discussion of how this term was recuperated in late colonial India, see Goswami 2004, esp. chapter 6. The Constitution of India (which went into effect on January 26, 1950) specifically identifies the country as Bharat, thereby disclosing the Sanskritic, Aryan, and Hindu moorings of this democratic republic that in 1976 after a critical amendment also declared itself to be "secular" and "socialist." See also my discussion in chapter 4, n. 17.

2. In contrast to the term *Muslim*, the word *Hindu* (and the religion associated with it, Hinduism, an appellation largely of nineteenth-century provenance) is notoriously difficult to define. Given the territorial focus of my work, it is worth noting that the term *Hindu* is the ancient Persian variant of the Sanskrit name Sindhu, which refers to the Indus River and is in turn the inspiration for the Greek name India. From the sixth century BCE the plural form of *Hindu* identifies the people of the region ("the Indus people"). Importantly, with the arrival of Islam in the subcontinent the term *Hindu* came to be used first as an ethnic designation for non-Muslim people in Persian sources from the late first millennium CE, regardless of their differing belief systems. From the eleventh century, but especially after a series of Mongol invasions in the thirteenth century, the term *Hindu* comes to take on an explicit religious connotation in distinction from *Muslim* in Arabic and Persian narratives of the region. Although no single tenet or practice is universally shared across the subcontinent by those who call themselves Hindu, the recognition of the authority of the Vedas, a conviction about reincarnation and the doctrine of karma, and a social system rooted in caste-based distinctions are diagnostic elements. More pertinently for this work, the wide acceptance of a multiplicity

of deities, a recognition that virtually anyone or anything has divine potential, a proclivity toward bestowing form (particularly anthropomorphic form) on the divine, and the establishment of ritual programs to worship such embodied forms distinguish the Hindu from the Muslim in theological as well as social terms over the course of the twentieth century.

3. There is a vast and rich literature on the idea of modernity, which when addressed in a note, runs the risk of caricature. My normative understanding follows from what Jürgen Habermas (1983) called the Enlightenment project of modernity with its emphasis on the accumulation of knowledge for the purpose of human emancipation and the enrichment of daily life; the scientific domination of nature; the autonomy of art; and the development of rational forms of social and political organization, and of rational modes of thought that seek to liberate the individual from myth, religion, and superstition. Much of the past two decades of postcolonial scholarship on Europe's colonies, India included, have been dedicated to debating the extent to which such processes devolved in places and societies far away from the metropole, and to foregrounding the violence wrought in the name of modernization by Europe over the rest of the world (see, in this regard, Bhabha 1994; Chakrabarty 2000; Cohn 1996; and Nandy 2001). Also important for my argument are the insights of Martin Heidegger (1977, 134) who draws attention to novel forms of representation ushered in by modernity that result in "the conquest of the world as picture" so that the world appears to us as framed or frameable. The scientific map form is a critical example of such processes, and I address this issue further in the epilogue.

4. I am adapting here from Brennan (1990) who considers how the novel bestows form on the nation, and from Biggs (1999) who demonstrates how cartography bestowed geographical form on the territorial state in early modern Europe.

5. I have been influenced by my reading of scholars like James Elkins, Martin Jay, W. J. T. Mitchell, and especially Barbara Stafford (1995) who offers a powerful set of arguments against the "degradation of images" and "entrenched antivisualism" in post-Enlightenment thought.

6. In asking such questions I am adapting from many recent works that have contributed to the new visual or pictorial turn in cultural history (in particular Landes 2001 and Pinney 2004). My larger understanding of colonial Indian visual history has also been informed by the exemplary analyses found in Freitag 2001; Guha-Thakurta 1992, 2004; Jain 2007; and Mitter 1994.

7. *Times of India* (Bombay), special supplement, August 15, 1997. Ganesha, widely revered across India by devout Hindus as the remover of obstacles, is one of this Muslim artist's favorites as well.

8. This was the standard phrase that was used numerous times both in print and on the Internet. See, for instance, "MF Husain Disrobes Even Our Beloved Bharat Mata," March 2006, Vivekayayoti, vivekajyoti.blogspot.com; see also Dhavan 2007,

31–32. It is interesting to note that most of the anger was directed against the putative nudity of the mother/goddess rather than the use of the map of India in the painting (in fact, many do not even comment on its presence) (Ramaswamy 2010b).

9. "Husain Seeks Transfer of Case to SC," *Hindustan Times*, March 23, 2006. I am very grateful to Sharan Apparao of Apparao Galleries in Chennai for discussing with me in August 2006 the chain of events that precipitated this crisis. Apparao noted that Husain left the painting unnamed, and that she herself decided to name it *Bharat Mata* on the eve of the auction. For a discussion of the legal, political, and social consequences of the many controversies that have troubled the artist since 1996, and especially recently, see Ramaswamy 2010a.

10. "Red Alert on Husain," *Hindustan Times*, May 5, 2006. Subsequently, on May 8, 2008, the Delhi High Court dismissed the numerous cases filed against the artist across India. The Supreme Court of India also quashed all cases filed against his nude paintings on September 8, 2008. As of July 2009, the artist, now ninety-three years old, has chosen to remain in self-imposed exile outside India. See Ramaswamy 2010a.

11. Born in Pandharpur in western India and raised partly in the central Indian city of Indore in a devout working-class Suleimani Muslim family, Husain is largely a self-taught artist who began his professional life in the late 1930s painting street hoardings for cinema studios in Bombay. His artistic career took a major turn in 1947 when he joined the Progressive Artists Group, which was founded to encourage Indian modernists to pursue their individualistic vision, free from the strictures of academic art. He received the first of many national awards from the Indian state in 1955, and in 1971 he was a special invitee along with Picasso at the Sao Paolo Art Biennale. Today he is possibly India's highest-selling painter in the international art market. Since the mid-1990s he has also emerged as one of the most controversial of living artists, with his paintings and films drawing criticism from both Hindu and Muslim dogmatists in the subcontinent. Scholarship on this brilliant multidimensional artist is scattered, but some of the best insights appear in the work of Geeta Kapur who notes that his paintings "mark the conjunction between the mythic and the secular, and then between secular and aesthetic space" (2000, 366). In an earlier assessment Kapur noted that Husain "is the one artist who has had the energy to spin out a vision of India and scatter it everywhere, at home and abroad" (1978, 125). See also Bagchee 1998; Guha-Thakurta 2004, chapter 8; Juneja 1997; and Zitzewitz 2003 for nuanced discussions of Husain's artistic engagement with the nude bodies of Hindu goddesses, of his modernism, and of his eclectic deployment of the archaic, the mythic, and the folk. Bartholomew and Kapur (1972) have some perceptive observations about Husain's enduring preoccupation with the female form: "The central concern of Husain's art, and its dominant motif, is woman" (46). For the proceedings of a recent interdisciplinary conference on the

artist and the complex cultural politics of the reception of his work in the last decade, see Ramaswamy 2010a.

12. In spite or perhaps because of the many controversies in which the artist is embroiled, including the recent one surrounding his nude Bharat Mata, his admirers, among them the country's leading artists and writers, launched a campaign in 2006 to persuade the Government of India to bestow upon him the nation's highest civilian honor, the Bharat Ratna. In the words of the nominating petition, Husain's "life and work are beginning to serve as an allegory for the changing modalities of the secular in modern India—and the challenges that the narrative of the nation holds for many of us." "Letter to the President of India," in *Maqbool Fida Husain* 2008, 122.

13. Following from an understanding of cartography as a set of practices and techniques through which spatial knowledge is produced through the visual technology of the map (Biggs 1999), I use the neologism "carto-graphed" to draw attention to the yoking together of the human or divine body and cartographic products like maps and globes to produce a particular kind of spatial knowledge. In this study a carto-graphed body is one that is inscribed in the form of a map, or drawn to accommodate, outline, or be attached to the map form of a country.

14. Throughout this study I subscribe to a revisionist understanding of maps as "graphic representations that facilitate a spatial understanding of things, concepts, conditions, processes or events in the modern world . . . Maps are artifacts that store, communicate, and promote spatial understanding" (Harley and Woodward 1987, xvi). My understanding of scientific or cartographic maps as mathematizing the world is also informed by J. Brian Harley's brilliant work in *The New Nature of Maps* (2001), by the writings of several postmodern historians of cartography and geography (see Cosgrove 2001, 2005; Pickles 2004), and by Bruno Latour's many meditations on mediation (see Latour 1986, 1988, 1990, 1998).

15. Husain quoted in Dalmia 2001, 105.

16. Thongchai Winichakul introduces this term to refer to the novel representation of territory as an objectified bounded whole created by the sciences of geography and cartography. As he states: "Geographically speaking, the geo-body of a nation occupies a certain portion of the earth's surface which can be objectively identified. It seems to be concrete to the eyes and having a long history as if it were natural . . . The geo-body of a nation is merely the effect of modern geographical knowledge and its technology of representation, a map" (1996, 70).

17. Edney 1997 presents a comprehensive scholarly study of the British mapping of India, but see also Raj 2006 for a sustained argument about Indian participation in what is presented in the official colonial archive as a "British" achievement. For some attempts to chart "map mindedness" among colonial and postcolonial Indians, see also Gole 1983; Goswami 2004; Schwartzberg 1992; and Ramaswamy 2001; 2003; 2004, 182–222; 2006a, 2007b; 2010b.

18. John Pickles defines a geo-coded world as one "where boundary objects have been inscribed, literally written on the surface of the earth and coded by layer upon layer of lines drawn on paper" (2004, 5).

19. Casey 2002, xv. For the phrase "lines of power," which is drawn from the Swedish geographer Gunnar Olsson's critique of cartographic reason, see Pickles 2004, 3–6. Olsson's work explores the "rich geopolitics of lines, boundaries and limits in which the geographical imagination is pushed to . . . the dematerialized point of abstractness" (3).

20. Here I am adapting from Dipesh Chakrabarty's well-known call to "provincialize" European thought, which he argues is simultaneously "indispensable" but "inadequate" for other parts of the world (2000, esp. 6). See also his observation that scientific realism "could never answer all the needs of vision that modern nationalisms create" (149).

1. FORMAL CONCERNS

1. There is no scholarly monograph on Mother India despite her salience, but see Bagchi 1990; Banerjee 2002; Bose 1997; Brosius 2005; Chowdhury 1998; Goswami 2004; Gupta 2002; Kaur 2003; McKean 1996; Sarkar 2001, 2006; and Sen 2002 for important discussions about her emergence in Bengal in the late 1860s, her growing popularity as a nationalist symbol by the early years of the twentieth century, the escalating anxieties among some over her role in alienating Muslim citizens, and her recent resurgence in the cultural politics of Hindu nationalism. Her visualization is discussed in Guha-Thakurta 1992; Jha 2004; Mitter 1994; Sen 2002; Uberoi 1990, 2003; Sinha 2006; and especially Neumayer and Schelberger 2008. Virtually no one has elaborated on the critical role played by the map of India in Mother India's iconography, but for some important beginnings in this direction, see the work of the anthropologist Christiane Brosius (1997; 2005, ch. 4; 2006) and the art historian Geeti Sen (2002). My scholarship in these pages and in other essays builds on this body of work (see Ramaswamy 2001, 2002, 2003).

2. Some scholars have suggested that the famous south Indian painter Raja Ravi Varma (1848–1906), renowned for his pictorial attempts to capture in oil the numerous deities of the Hindu pantheon as well as epic heroes and heroines of the Sanskritic past, painted in the 1890s a Durga-like goddess who has been interpreted as Mother India (Neumayer and Schelberger 2008, 44). Another of his works, *Padmini*, is particularly interesting because the woman's sari is arranged in a manner that has been read as reproducing parts of the outline map of India (Del Bonta 1989, 454). Although the artist's patriotic proclivities are quite apparent from his large body of work, Ravi Varma himself did not name either of these figures as Bharat Mata or Mother India.

3. Abanindranath Tagore, a scion of one of the most famous and wealthy of the upper-

caste *bhadralok* families in Bengal, is widely regarded as the leading protagonist in the driving imperative from the early years of the twentieth century to found a new "national art" that sought to wean away India's artists from their indebtedness to the Western "academic" style taught in the colonial art academies. Quoting from Abanindranath's memoirs his statement "The Motherland in the image of four-armed deity emerged out of the world of artistic contemplation and took shape in a picture," Tapati Guha-Thakurta observes that the painter "was conscious of creating, for the first time, an artistic icon for the Indian nation" (1995, 26). The best studies of Abanindranath's art can be found in Guha-Thakurta 1992 and in Mitter 1994. His *Bharat Mata* has been discussed by many scholars, including Guha-Thakurta 1992, 255–60; Mitter 1994, 294–99; and Sen 2002, 17–60.

4. As a wide-ranging set of protests and militant activities that began in Bengal around 1905 but soon spread to other parts of colonial India, the swadeshi movement had a number of political, economic, and cultural goals that aimed to unshackle the colonized from their dependence on the West, especially industrial Britain, and return them to native Indian sources of inspiration and work. The classic study of the movement's complex history in Bengal remains Sarkar 1973, but see also Goswami 2004.

5. Nivedita 3: 60–61. Nivedita's article, titled "India the Mother," was published in the August edition of the *Indian World*. In the last sentence of this quote, *shiksha* refers to education, *diksha* to spiritual initiation, *anna* to food, and *bastra* to clothing.

6. Guha-Thakurta 1992, 255. For scattered observations in English on Banga Mata, see Bagchi 1990; Bose 1997; and Chowdhury 1998. Mother Bengal was portrayed in illustrations that appeared in *Indian Charivari* (1874), *Hindi Punch* (1891, 1906), *Intiya* (1909), and other publications. On the occasion of the 1905 partition, the Bengali newsmagazine *Sanjivini* published a cartoon in which "a European with a smiling face is represented as sawing vertically a Bengali woman dressed like a Hindu widow, her life-blood flowing out in a torrent from the edge of the saw. With her fist clenched and lips pressed together in great agony, she is shown as calmly resigning herself to her fate. Another European is represented as standing near by and laughing heartily at the sight, whilst some Indians look as if greatly agitated and incensed by the scene. The letterpress is "The Partition of Mother Bengal," *Report on Native Papers in Bengal for the Week ending the 29th July, 1905, No. 30 of 1905*, 721 (available at the National Archives of India, New Delhi).

7. Soon after, one of Abanindranath's more prominent students, Asit Kumar Haldar (1890–1964), painted a watercolor in 1906 (when he was barely sixteen) called *Mother India Awakened*. Like his mentor's *Bharat Mata*, Haldar's Mother India is a four-armed goddess with a halo radiating around her head, and she is clad in a sari in a similar style. However, the resemblance ends there. Haldar's Mother India is most determinedly an armed goddess, as she looks directly at her viewer while

holding a trident in one hand and a fierce scimitar in the other, even while one other hand carries a sheaf of grain and the other is held in a gesture of blessing. See Mittra 1961, plate 1, for a reproduction of this painting; see also Mitter 1994, 296; and Sen 2002, 29.

8. Samanta 1995, 2: 146. The police also found on the premises pictures of recent "martyrs" who had been executed by the colonial state and of several nationalist leaders, as well as several pictures of the goddess Kali (about whom I write in greater detail in the next chapter). Nagendranath Sen Gupta, a young admirer of the Samiti, writes in his memoirs that to his fellow Bengalis, "partition meant the mutilation of the embodied Mother, and where was the son who could stand by and silently witness the sundered body of the Mother?" (Sen Gupta 1974, 23).

9. For Bharati's complex place in the evolving history of Indian nationalism and his investment in the figure of Bharat Mata, see Ramaswamy 1997. For a discussion of his visual patriotism (albeit not couched as such), see Venkatachalapathy 2006, 42–58.

10. This last refrain, which I consciously translate as "I worship the Mother," had become Mother India's signature slogan by 1907, as I discuss at greater length in chapter 3.

11. On the cow as a "proto-nation," see Pinney 2004, 106–12; and Uberoi 2003, 206–13.

12. These images have, valuably, been reproduced in Venkatachalapathy 1995 and in Viswanathan 1998. For Bharati's fulsome praise of a painting called *Bharati Mata*, completed possibly in 1907 by T. A. Gopinatha Rao and printed by the Vivekachintamani Publishing Committee in Madras, see the magazine *Bala Bharata*, January 1908, 66–67. Unfortunately, I have not been able to locate this painting or print, but Bharati's long description of it suggests that it quite possibly might have featured a carto-graphed Mother India.

13. For an elaboration of this argument, see Ramaswamy 2010b. The advertisement appeared in *Intiya* several other times in 1909. For a few months when *Vijaya* started publication in September 1909 in Pondicherry this image was not featured on its cover (although I have not come across any discussion on why it was decided against doing so). Nuanced feminist scholarship on the representability of the female breast in nationalist art in Europe can be found in Gutwirth 1992, 341–68; Landes 2001; and Warner 1985, 267–93. For important discussions of how the female body's nudity in Indian art becomes a modern "problem," see especially Guha-Thakurta 2004 and Juneja 1997.

14. I am grateful to Taymiya Zaman for this insight.

15. See Das 1984, 215. On the artist Harishchandra Haldar, a graduate of the art school in Calcutta and an acolyte of the influential Tagore family, and a critical evaluation of this early patriotic effort, see Guha-Thakurta 1992, 89–91.

16. I thank Milind Sabnis and Asha Kirloskar for discussing Satwalekar's work with me. Satwalekar was one of the early graduates of the J. J. School of Arts. Although an artist by training and profession, he went on to immerse himself in Sanskrit and Vedic studies, and he received numerous honors for his achievements in the literary field including a coveted Padma Bhusan from the Government of India. See also Sabnis 2000, 15–16.

17. Neville Tuli attributes this work to Allah Bukhsh (2002, plate 62). For a discussion of this artist's body of work, which included several images drawn from Hindu mythology, see Naqvi 1998, 98–133. Naqvi does not mention this painting. I thank Salima Hashmi for discussing Allah Bukhsh's life and work with me.

18. Illustration copy from *Om Arya Kailendar*, published by Somadeva Sharma, Faizabad, 1919.

19. On the final page of the calendar appear the following words: "You must have seen the portraits, you must have read the words in the margins. Now compare in your mind the past condition of Bharat Mata with her present state. You will realise to what extent the mother has suffered through the foreigners, and how your condition is growing worse. And still if you wish to see the times of old you must protect Bharat the land of your birth, asking for your birth right, Swaraj, from today. Be ready with body, mind, wealth and strength to obtain your birth right." All English translations are from the three-page summary attached to the proscribed calendar (British Library [APAC]: Proscribed Publications Collection, PP HIN F. 10). It is quite likely that the publisher of this calendar was associated with the proto-Hindu nationalist organization, the Arya Samaj (Society of Aryans). This group was founded in 1875 by Swami Dayananda (1824–1883), whose portrait appears on the page for January and whose influence at this time was widespread in western and northern India, especially Punjab.

20. This is verse 2.33 in the critical Sanskrit text the Bhagavad Gita, which through the activities of nationalists like Tilak had recently achieved the status of a (Hindu) national "scripture" (although the inscription gets some of the words wrong). I am grateful to Rich Freeman for identifying the verse and providing the translation. The same image recurs (with some minor modifications) over the next few years in publications of another expatriate organization, the Ghadar Party, dominated though it was by Sikhs (see, for example, figure 16).

21. See especially Boehmer 2002; Lahiri 2000; and Visram 2002, esp. 123–68. That the colonial state in India worried about such incendiary expatriates based in London, Paris, and other places is clear from the long discussion in Ker 1917, 170–316.

22. The map titled "The United States of India" is available in the British Library ([APAC], London, Mss. Eur. C.228). Miniature replicas also appeared on the party's banner printed in various publications of the Hindustan Ghadar Party; see, for example, British Library (APAC): Proscribed Publications Collection, PP PANJ D

27 and EPP 1/20. For a visual history of the Ghadar Party, see "Echoes of Freedom: South Asian Pioneers in California, 1899–1965," Doe Library, University of California, Berkley, http://www.lib.berkeley.edu.

23. Two revealing official documents explicitly notice the carto-graphed Ghadar image of Bharat Mata, although they do not identify her by name. Thus the governor of Fiji in a letter dated June 20, 1914, brought to the attention of his colleagues in India some pamphlets published in Punjabi in the Gurmukhi script that his government had seized: "The title page exhibits a form of the map of India filled with the figure of a woman, in garb which may be Indian, drawing or sheathing a sword. The region of India where, in the map, Bombay should lie is filled by a head (without a body). The island of Ceylon is not represented. Beneath is a tracing to me that is unintelligible. *The map, however, is suggestive in the highest degree and would of course be nothing if not indicative of the character of the contents or substance of the pamphlet*" (National Archives of India, Government of India, Home, Political [Confidential], October 1914, No. 59 [Deposit]; emphasis mine). Similarly, another document remarks on the prohibition in 1915 of "a revolutionary pamphlet in Urdu and Gurmukhi by Lala Hardayal entitled 'The New Era,' published by the Ghadr Press, San Francisco," and notes further that "the title page is decorated with the picture of a woman with disheveled hair standing over the map of India with a half-drawn sword in her hand. The letter-press runs: The sword of Mutiny is in the hand of India . . . The whole pamphlet is in metrical form and is highly seditious" (National Archives of India, Government of India, Home, Political [Confidential], March 1915, Nos. 407–412 [Part A].

24. It is a reminder as well of the limited capacity of such "image texts" to be readily available to an audience beyond the verbally literate (I borrow the concept of "image text" from W. J. T. Mitchell who develops it to draw our attention to the fact "that 'pure' visual representations routinely incorporate textuality in a quite literal way, insofar as writing and other arbitrary marks enter into the field of visual representation" [1994, 95]). In commenting on the routine reliance upon words in many putatively visual media in India, Kajri Jain astutely observes that it is almost as if "the image is potentially treacherous, that it cannot be trusted to do the job on its own" (2007, 10).

25. Valuable introductions to colonial proscribed materials can be found in Barrier 1974 and Shaw and Lloyd 1985. Neither works, however, highlight the pictorial dimensions of this archive of sedition that Christopher Pinney (2004) has discussed with such effectiveness.

26. See also Uberoi 2006, 49–51, for an excellent restatement of the ubiquity of the visual aesthetic of calendar art in religious, patriotic, filmic, and decorative productions of modern India's "culture industry."

27. See Freitag 2001; see also Freitag 2007 for a more recent analysis of the consumption-driven imperatives that steer bazaar production.

28. She identifies four aspects of the bazaar ethos that are important for any under-standing of this art form: "(1) its mediation between formal and informal econo-mies; (2) its maintenance of an extensive network of personalized, reciprocal re-lationships through a gift economy; (3) its explicitly religious or communitarian affiliations . . .; and (4) its ability to work both with and across communitarian, re-gional and linguistic differences to inscribe an extensive web of circulation" (2007, 69).

29. See Pinney 2004. By corpothetic, Pinney means the sensory embrace of and bodily engagement with images that is so characteristic of the modern visual regimes of the subcontinent, especially at the popular and devotional level across numerous religious, regional, and ethnic divides.

30. I write this in spite of the fact that recent scholarship has effectively shown the extensive reliance by the British on native subordinates (bare feet and all) in the work of the colonial surveys and mapping of the subcontinent (Raj 2006). My use of this conceptual category draws on the everyday reality of the average Indian's privileging of bare feet in numerous contexts ranging from the sacred to the mun-dane. The analytic is meant to capture a metaphorical sense of "barefoot-ness" as a condition of being that facilitates a more earthbound and fleshly relationship to soil, land, and territory than is arguably possible when following the rarified protocols of scientific cartography. The analytic also capitalizes on the appear-ance of Bharat Mata—*always* with bare feet resting on the map of India. For some suggestive reflections on the artist M. F. Husain's habit of walking and working in bare feet, see Bagchee 1998. Husain follows in the footsteps of other artists who are routinely shown in many images at work in their bare feet. For the colonial period, Bernard Cohn writes of British attempts to make Indians adhere to their "custom" of baring their feet instead of donning shoes and quotes a colonial judge, F. J. Shore: "Nations have different customs; ours is to uncover the head—yours to uncover the feet, as a token of respect" (1996, 133). See also Patricia Uberoi's provocative discussion of "podo-eroticism" in Bollywood films, which draws attention to the (eroticized) semiotics of exposed feet (2006, 114–37).

31. The text of the poem is in Kuppusamy Das 1948, 20.

32. See Ramaswamy 1997. In fact, Tamil devotion generated its own alternate carto-graphic imaginary centered on the figure of Mother Tamil (Tamilannai or Tamilt-taay) that contested the national patriotic habit. In the most ambitious of such images, Mother Tamil cartographically lays claim to the entire subcontinent as she occupies the map of India, thereby challenging Mother India's sole proprietorship of the land. Occasionally she also appears in the company of the terrestrial globe clearly centered on India. In such visualizations Mother Tamil is transformed from a goddess of language and learning into a mistress of territory and polity. (See Ramaswamy 2001, esp. 108–9, and my image essay, "When a Language Becomes

a Mother/Goddess," Tasveer Ghar: Digital Archive of South Asian Popular Visual Culture, www.tasveerghar.net).

33. I am indebted to Patricia Uberoi for reminding me of this. For the pictorial deployment of Bharat Mata in the visual activities of recent Hindu nationalism, see Brosius 2005. Brosius discusses the appearance of this particular image in the company of two recent Hindutva "martyrs," the Kothari brothers (268–69).

34. This image is reproduced and discussed in Jha 2004, 34–35.

35. I have not been able to learn anything about this artist, although he used maps and globes in his pictures not just of Mother India but also when he painted the more time-honored deities of the Hindu pantheon (see, for example, Ramaswamy 2007b, figure 12).

36. To underscore a point I make at several other junctures in this study, in most popular patriotic pictures featuring Mother India, it is largely her nominally Hindu "sons" who are visible, as in this poster where she is flanked on the globe by (from left to right) Vallabh Bhai Patel, C. Rajagopalachari, Jawaharlal Nehru, and Rajendra Prasad. Interestingly, these men do not stand on the geo-body of India but on those of neighboring countries. Note also that bust images of Subhas Bose and Vivekananda are suspended between the celestial and terrestrial realms.

37. On Dravidian nationalism's alternate cartographic visualizations of the territorial space of India, see Ramaswamy 2001, 108–9. On Ramaswami Naicker, see Ramaswamy 1997.

38. On the artists Vishnu Sapar, his brother Bharath, and his son Venkatesh, see Jain 2007, 171–72.

39. I borrow this felicitous idea from Helgerson 1986, 51.

40. Derrida's complete statement is as follows: "It intervenes or insinuates itself in-the-place-of; if it fills, it is as if one fills a void. If it represents and makes an image, it is by the anterior default of a presence. Compensating . . . and vicarious, the supplement is an adjunct, a subaltern insistence which takes-(the)-place" (1976, 145).

41. As Cleo Kearns remarks, the very existence of the supplement in Derrida's reading "testifies to a lack in or absence of that to which it is supplementary and puts its supposed fullness in doubt" (2001, 321). I am also reminded here of Dipesh Chakrabarty's observation that scientific realism can "never answer all the needs of vision that modern nationalisms create. . . . What if the real, the natural, and the historically accurate did not generate the feeling of devotion or adoration?" (2000, 149).

42. Lalita asana is one of the most common sitting modes preferred by and for deities. In addition, Banerjea notes that "deities who are profusely endowed with ornaments are often depicted in this pose" (1956, 272).

43. Here I follow Kajri Jain in her discussion of the "*ongoing* negotiation between naturalism and iconicity" that characterizes bazaar images (2007, 119). For other helpful

discussions of this negotiation, see Guha-Thakurta 1992; Mitter 1994; and Pinney 2004, esp. ch. 1. See G. Kapur 1993 for a critical discussion of "frontality"—that is, the imperative to represent images, especially divine ones, as directly facing the viewer as worshipper in order to promote a reciprocal exchange of auspicious looking (*darshan*).

44. The civil disobedience movement (1930–1933) was launched in the wake of the resolution by the Indian National Congress to demand complete independence, *purna swaraj*, from British rule. Under the leadership of Gandhi, it sparked off a wide range of oppositional activities including the famous Dandi Salt march to protest the levying of a salt tax by the colonial state. It is also important to note here, following Christopher Pinney's important observations on the profound recursivity of popular printed images in colonial and postcolonial India, that although a specific print might have been generated in response to a particular political event or happening, its themes or motifs might be resurrected years later in another context and deployed for fresh purposes, so we have to be cautious about reading images "in an overly 'epidemiological' manner as specific symptoms of time-sensitive conditions" (Pinney 2005, 266).

45. For perceptive comments on the Aryanized complexion and facial features of poster women, see Jacob 1997, 148–49. See also Uberoi 2006, 57–58.

46. See also Babb 1981 for a similar formulation.

47. As I write this I am mindful of Anuradha Kapur's comment that "to show deities battling would be to drop them into everyday time, and to therefore make them less divine, almost human" (1993, 89). For a rare example from the 1960s in which an armed Bharat Mata, sword drawn, gets ready to take on the Chinese dragon, see Neumayer and Schelberger 2008, plate 324.

48. See Srinivasan 1997 for a useful analysis of an enduring iconographic penchant in Hindu religious art from a very early period for bestowing multiple limbs, heads, and eyes on divinities, as well as a discussion of the theology behind this "multiplicity convention."

49. On the visual deployment of Bharat Mata to spread Gandhi's call to Indians to wear homespun cloth (*khadi*), to spin everyday, and to reject objects made in the West, see Trivedi 2003.

50. On the life and work of the award-winning Sikh artist Sardar Sobha Singh, see his Web site, http://www.sobhasinghartist.com, and Kaur 1987. Sobha Singh had one year of formal education, at the industrial school at Amritsar, before he joined the Indian army in 1919 where he began his career as a draughtsman. On his return to India after serving in the Middle East, he became a professional artist and set up studios in Amritsar, Lahore, and Delhi in turn before retiring to the Kangra Valley. His fame rests on his paintings of the Sikh gurus, romantic themes drawn from Punjabi literature, and national heroes. His portrait of Kartar Singh Sarabha shows

the martyr posing in front of a map of India. Sobha Singh's painting of Bharat Mata (figure 37) is not mentioned in the published writings on him or on the Web site dedicated to his work, although the print clearly bears his signature.

51. On the visual politics of clothing the female body in Victorian-Indian modernity, see Guha-Thakurta 2004, 238–67. Emma Tarlo's insightful study *Clothing Matters* (1996) is also indispensable for any understanding of the politics of cloth and dress in colonial and postcolonial India.

52. On this reform see Banerjee and Miller 2003, esp. 5, 254 n.6.

53. On the history of the evolution of the Indian national flag, see Roy 2006; Singh 1991; and, especially, Virmani 2008.

54. Casey 2002, 26–27; see also 39, 55. I am indebted also to Christopher Pinney's nuanced discussion of "pastoral realism" in popular prints of the bazaar (2004, 79–104).

55. See Svetlana Alper's "The Mapping Impulse in Dutch Art" (1983) for a wonderful discussion of Vermeer's painting and mapping of the Dutch landscape. (The quote in the text is from page 158 of Alper's volume.)

56. This absence is even more striking given the ubiquity in modern India's popular art of infants of all sorts ranging from "god" babies to "commodity" babies (Uberoi 2006, 85–113).

57. Notwithstanding the colonial, especially missionary, disparagement of Hindu idolatry and modern Hindu reformist apologetics over the prevalence of "image worship," there has been a strong tendency toward *nirguna* ("quality-less") or *nirakara* ("formless") devotion that has disavowed representing the divine as a seeable entity. Nonetheless, nirguna Hinduism has a powerful competitor in the saguna habits of the religion in which deities have been imagined as "with form," especially anthropomorphic and quasi-anthropomorphic form. Ever since the emergence of practices of worshipping consecrated images in temples from the early centuries of the first millennium CE, saguna Hinduism has offered a wide array of visible deities in all their glorious multiplicity and plurality (Davis 1997, 26–50; Eck 1981; and Srinivasan 1997).

2. OTHER WOMEN, OTHER MOTHERS

1. The putative antiquity of this phrase, much quoted in twentieth-century nationalist discourse, remains under question. At least one (Hindu) nationalist conceded, "I cannot tell you whether the expression janma-bhumi or motherland is a modern or ancient usage in Sanskrit. The text I have quoted, however, is very modern" (Pal 1911, 144). The phrase famously occurs in a key (Hindu) nationalist text from the early 1880s, *Anandamath*, and Julius Lipner (2005, 242) notes its presence as an inscription in a Kali temple on the outskirts of Calcutta that was completed around 1855. On its possible nineteenth-century roots, see Pradip Bhattacharya, "The Prob-

lem of Janani Janmabhumischa in Anand Math," 2006, Boloji.com, http://www.bo-loji.com; but see also Lipner 2005, 241–42, for some premodern precedents. I thank Madhav Deshpande and Julius Lipner for discussing this matter with me.

2. Hunt 1992, xiii–xiv, modifies Freud's term "family romance" to capture "the collective, unconscious images of the familial order," and "the familial grid" that operates at both the conscious and unconscious level in French revolutionary politics.

3. For a key discussion of the category of "new woman" (albeit limited to evidence from colonial Bengal), see Chatterjee 1989. Chatterjee argues that nationalism in India is based neither on a total rejection of the West nor a complete embrace of it but rather by a critical division of symbolic labor in which the "new woman" is associated with the (imagined) inner, spiritual, and autonomous space of the home, which is also the site where the authentic nation would be nurtured in a colonial context of subjugation. The "new man" was in turn burdened with the task of taking on the external, outer world of science and materialism, confident that even while he was tainted by the West, the inner authentic self of the nation was being cared for by the modern-yet-Indian woman.

4. Appadurai 1996, 179, 180–81. Here I borrow his words to discuss the nation.

5. I have been influenced here by a number of scholars, especially Landes 1988 and Chatterjee 1989.

6. John Ruskin quoted in Helmreich 2003, 18.

7. See Sinha 2004, 194–95; see also Banerji, Mojab, and Whitehead 2001.

8. Its richness and suggestiveness notwithstanding, there are not many sustained scholarly analyses either of this painting or of the artist (a native of Corfu who had just recently moved to London and secured this commission through some influential contacts), but see brief discussions in Allen 1990, 27; Davis 1997, 168–70; and in Groseclose 1995, 51–52. The painting is now housed in the Foreign and Commonwealth Office, London.

9. For a digital reproduction of this work, see British Library, http://www.bl.uk/cata-logues (Shelfmark F8); for a reproduction in print, see Groseclose 1995, 49. The sculpture is now housed in the Foreign and Commonwealth Office, London.

10. This phrase is Anne McClintock's. See McClintock 1995, 25–26, for her useful discussion of Jan van der Straet's *America* (ca. 1575), a print in which the newly "discovered" continent is shown as "a naked and erotically inviting woman" who is seemingly eager for her (sexual) encounter with Europe, signified by Amerigo Vespucci. See also Montrose 1992.

11. A cartoon titled "The Indian Andromeda," showing a bare-breasted India shackled to "oppression," "over-taxation," "robbery" and the like, appeared in November 1872 in the comic magazine (published in Calcutta by expatriate Britons) called the *Indian Charivari*. In an oleograph dated to the 1890s commemorating the businessman turned nationalist Dadabhai Naoroji's election to the House of Commons in 1892, "India" shows up as a bare-breasted woman seated on an elephant

(Neumayer and Schelberger 2008, plate 18). But with the consolidation of Indian nationalism such images are relatively rare by the later years of the nineteenth century.

12. These images are reproduced in Groseclose 1995, 48–76.

13. There is as yet no comprehensive scholarly analysis of such imagery, and my comments here are based on a general overview of published sources (Groseclose 1995, Helmreich 2003) and on some archival research.

14. For historians of cartography, the significance of this map lies in the fact that it was the first to frame the area that we today call India (Edney 2003, 68). On the complex publication history of this map (made of two large sheets) and the accompanying *Memoir* (1783) with which it generally circulated, see Edney 1997, 99–100. Interestingly, in 1788 Rennell reissued the map, with substantive changes, under the new title *A Map of Hindoostan*, but the striking cartouche does not appear in it or in other reprints published in 1792 and 1793. The cartouche was drawn and engraved by E. Edwards and J. Hall, according to an inscription affixed to it. There is as yet no scholarly study of the circulation history in the subcontinent of the *Memoir* and its map. Matthew Edney writes that "of the fifty copies of the map purchased by the company, only twenty were allocated for the use of senior British officials in South Asia, whereas thirty were distributed among the company's directors in London, most of whom had never been to India (2003, 67).

15. See also Edney 1997, 13–15, and Ludden 1993. For a recent argument that considers the important place played by Indian knowledges as well as labor in the creation of Rennell's map, see Raj 2006, 60–94. Raj notes that only some of the data that went into Rennell's famed map was based on actual survey activity.

16. Pinney 2004, 27. Partha Mitter (1994, 178) identifies the lithograph as "Begging India back from England." In her study of the influential Hindi poet-nationalist Bharatendu Harishchandra, Vasudha Dalmia (1997, 287–88) discusses a poem with the title "Bharat Bhiksha" (Alms for Bharat), published around 1875 to commemorate the visit of the Prince of Wales to India. Based on a Bengali poem with the same title attributed to Hemchandra Bannerji, Bharatendu's "Bharat Bhiksha" casts India (named Bharat Janani) as a destitute who laments the sad state of her country and her people, and pleads with the prince and his imperial mother to take charge. I thank Sadan Jha for alerting me to this reference. On the impact on bazaar visual culture of the Calcutta Art Studio, established around 1878, see Guha-Thakurta 1992.

17. Quoted in Chowdhury 1998, 96.

18. Quoted in Chowdhury 1998, 99.

19. Ibid. In the play, "the Motherland speaks and weeps." As a figure of "absolute abjection" she is at the mercy of white men who appear on the stage to torment her (Sarkar 2006, 3965). For a recasting of this play in 1901, see Chowdhury 1998, 155, 166n.

20. Quoted in Chowdhury 1998, 105.

21. From a play dated to 1894, as quoted in Chowdhury 1998, 109.

22. Quoted in Chowdhury 1998, 25–26. The Hindu Mela was co-instituted by Mitra for the support of swadeshi arts and literature.

23. For *Indian Charivari*, see, for example, "Intra-Provincial Arts Exhibition" (March 21, 1873); "Britannia Hoodwinked" (April 3, 1874); "Well Met Stranger" (November 13, 1874); and "The Spirit of India recognizes Her Prince" (January 7, 1876). For *Mookerji's Magazine*, see D. D. Dhur's "India Presenting a Coronal to Lord Northbrook on the Abolition of the Income Tax," vol. 2 (1873). For the *Oudh Punch*, see Ganga Sahai's "The Coming King," June 15, 1880. *Hindi Punch* (earlier published as *Parsi Punch*) was a bilingual illustrated weekly published in English and Gujarati from 1888 for about twenty-six years. Its publisher and editor Barjorjee Nowrosjee belonged to the flourishing Parsi community of Bombay that, despite its well-known Anglophilia, also produced men and women who were prominent among India's first social reformers and nationalists. Although generally supportive of the "moderate" liberal nationalism espoused by the Congress Party in the 1880s and 1890s, many of *Hindi Punch*'s cartoons from the 1890s that featured Hind or the Congress Party poked gentle fun at their submissiveness to Britannia (Mitter 1997 and Sarkar 1969–70).

24. On January 12, 1889, *Hindi Punch* published a cartoon captioned "Makar Sankranti," which shows "United India" as a multiarmed "fierce goddess" riding a buffalo and carrying arms of every sort—a spear, a scimitar, a cannon, a rifle, and a revolver—which she is shown using against "Russia." But such a precocious image is rare in its pages.

25. Although published writings on Sardar Sobha Singh and his Web site (http://www.sobhasinghartist.com) do not mention his *Bharat Mata*, his biographers proudly detail his patriotic inclinations, and his paintings of nationalist figures like Gandhi, Nehru, and Bhagat Singh. Indeed his painting of Shaheed Bhagat Singh bears elements (the toppled crown, the snarling lion) that may be seen in his *Bharat Mata*.

26. See also Honour 1975 and Le Corbellier 1961.

27. For a comprehensive study of the significance of this production, declared to have been the most expensive and best-selling book in the later half of the sixteenth century in Europe, see van den Broecke, van der Krogt, and Meurer 1998.

28. Botero quoted in Honour 1975, 92.

29. See the thoughtful review of this process in Biggs 1999.

30. This is not the first time, though, that "Europe" comes to be anthropomorphized (although scholars differ on the gender of the body). For discussions of Opicinus de Canastris's *Europa Regina*, dated to the 1330s, see Gandelman 1991, 84–85, and Lewes 2000, 133–34.

31. Elsewhere I have used the term *bodyscape* to draw attention to the use of the human body to represent mapped territory, especially national territory (see Ramaswamy 2001).

32. Cited in Montrose 1992, 138. See also Kolodny 1975.

33. Until the Ordinance Survey of 1794, Saxton's cartographic work (brought together in an atlas in 1579, and transferred to a wall map in 1583) was the source of all printed maps of England and Wales for the subsequent few centuries. This geographical image was also circulated on playing cards and woven into tapestries hung in fine English homes (Biggs 1999, 391). Such was their enduring influence that his mapped image of England outlasted Elizabeth, thereby opening up "a conceptual gap between the land and its ruler" (Helgerson 1986, 56).

34. For a black-and-white reproduction of this frontispiece attributed to Hogenberg, see Strong 1987, figure 82.

35. These are discussed in some detail in Strong 1987.

36. On this, see Higham 1990 and Kolodny 1975.

37. For a reproduction of this image, see Helgerson 1986, figure 8.

38. In a frontispiece dated to 1684, Britannia similarly appears "draped with what looks like a cloak limn'd with the map of England" (Dresser 1989, 32–34).

39. Dresser 1989, 40. See also Warner 1985, 38–60.

40. For a recent discussion of this map that explains the subtle critique of empire it offers, see Biltcliffe 2005.

41. For a helpful note contextualizing this image, see the Wellcome Library, http:// catalogue.wellcome.ac.uk (record=b1179000). On the nexus between the commercial and the patriotic in which iconic figures like Britannia get entangled, see McClintock 1995.

42. See Brading's volume *Mexican Phoenix* (2001) for his work on Guadalupe. For Agulhon's work on Marianne, see his *Marianne into Battle* (1980).

43. For the Gaelic League poster, see Loftus 1990, figure 73. In her analysis of this poster Loftus does not, however, mention the map that Eire occupies.

44. See Nandy 1980, 1–46, esp. 8–9; Bagchi 1990; and T. Sarkar 2006, 3966. For a religious history of Bengal in the eighteenth and nineteenth centuries, see McDermott 2001.

45. For more on Prithvi and Varaha, see Ramaswamy 2007b.

46. The image is reproduced in Venkatachalapathy 1995, 85.

47. "Innovations in the Ramlila processions," National Archives of India, Government of India, Home, Political (Confidential), December 1911, No. 14 (Deposit), p. 3 (my emphasis). The report notes that in many places across the United Provinces citizenry were using "the Ramlila . . . a crude form of religious drama representing the life history of Rama," to deliberately "foster seditious and disloyal feelings by the display of figures or pictures representing the Rani of Jhansi, Bharat Mata, Tilak,

Lajpat Rai and Aurobindo Ghose." So in 1909 and 1910, for instance, the Ramlila processions in the city of Allahabad included tableaux of Bharat Mata, accompanied by shouts of "Bande Mataram and Bharat Mata ki jai [Long live Bharat Mata]." The report gives us an unusual wealth of details about the producers of such images. One of them, for example, was made by Lachmi Narayan Khatri, a petty railway clerk; another was made by Mahadeo Prasad who worked as an assistant to a Allahabad-based lawyer and had shown other signs of involvement in nationalist politics. Unfortunately, the report does not give details about the figure of Bharat Mata or whether her iconography included the map of India (*contra* Goswami 2004, 260).

48. The inscription is quoted in Kinsley 1987, 181.

49. For an ethnographically grounded analysis that also suggests that the patriotic imagination that has yielded Bharat Mata has drawn upon local "goddesses of land" of whom Prithvi is the prototype, see Falk 2002.

50. In the patriotic visual landscape, the one other context in which I have seen Prithvi or Bhumi Devi is in the "Gau Mata" pictures in which she is shown—in a throwback to her appearance over the course of two millennia—as a highly miniaturized figure sitting inside the belly of the sacred cow.

51. See also Sircar 1973, 6–7. There is no consensus regarding the number of pithas, the names of the goddesses worshipped there, or their association with particular parts of Sati's body, but Sircar's study shows the continuing influence of the legend over many centuries.

52. For a similar argument regarding "India" as a land constituted by the devis and their shrines, which are ritually reconnected by devotees through pilgrimage circuits, see Eck 1999, 34.

53. As quoted in Raychaudhuri 1988, 39 (emphasis mine). I thank Abhijit Bhattacharya and Mandira Bhaduri for confirming the use of the Bangla word for motherland, *matribhumi*, in the original.

54. I thank Susan Bean of the Peabody Essex Museum for alerting me to this image and for providing me with some background details. The museum's cataloguing notes on the painting are as follows: "Signed, lower right. 'Husain, Parvati,' inscribed on the back of the stretcher in another hand" (Peabody Museum, e-mail message to the author, February 7, 2008). See also Ramaswamy 2010b.

55. Quoted in Lipner 2005, 87. Here as in many of Bankim's other writings the images of Durga, Mother Bengal, and Mother India shade into each other, as scholars have noted (see Lipner 2005, 88–89). For a slightly different translation of this passage, see Kaviraj 1995, 134. For an analysis of this work as the "secret autobiography" of its author, see Kaviraj 1995, 27–71.

56. Quoted in Bhattacharya 2003, 65. See also Ker 1917, 43–48.

57. See Chowdhury 1998, 96–97; and Kopf 1989, 119–20. For a detailed study of the

eighteenth- and nineteenth-century transformations of Kali in the Bengali imagination, see McDermott 2001. Hugh Urban insists that "nationalists seized upon
the bloody, destructive figure of Kali as a symbol of Mother India *precisely because*
she represented threat and terror to the colonial imagination" (2003, 171).

58. Quoted in Kaviraj 1995, 138.

59. H. L. Salked quoted in Bhattacharya 2004, 66 (emphasis mine). Salked was the
magistrate on special duty assigned to investigate the militant secret society Anushilan Samiti in Dhaka in 1908. He was alarmed to discover pictures of Kali on its
premises, and in response to the discovery he writes, "In this picture of Kali, Siva
upon whom she is dancing, the severed heads which form her garland and the various limbs and heads lying above and receiving the attention of crows and jackals,
are white. *I am told this is a recent change in the setting of pictures of Kali*" (quoted
in Samanta 1995, 2: 146, [emphasis mine]).

60. Quoted in Kopf 1989, 120. For other similar exhortations, see Chirol 1910, 18–19,
341–42.

61. Interestingly, a later Indian reprint in 1973 of this influential publication does not
include this print.

62. The bomb was actually intended for Magistrate Kingsford, but instead it led to the
death of Mrs. and Miss Kennedy. For an analysis of later prints from the 1930s commemorating the martyrdom of Khudiram Bose, the young man who was hanged
for this crime, see Pinney 2004, 118–19.

63. This print is reproduced in Ker 1917, facing p. 382. Another British critic was drawn
to "a very popular picture of the goddess" showing her "holding in her hand her
head, which has been severed from her body, whilst the blood gushing from her
trunk flows into her open mouth . . . The great goddess as seen therein symbolizes 'the Motherland,' decapitated by the English, but nevertheless preserving her
vitality unimpaired by drinking her own blood" (Chirol 1910, 102–3). I have been
unable to locate this picture, but Chirol's description is suggestive of the fierce
Chinnamasta, a goddess who is *not* a popular model for Bharat Mata. (For a late
nineteenth-century print of Chinnamasta, see Pinney 2004, figure 20.)

64. See Pinney 2004, 120–21. Despite the Press Act such images continued to be
printed. In 1924, "a crude picture of the Hindu goddess Kali, 'the Destroyer,' slaying a European," caused colonial worries, especially as it was found affixed to a
"vile document" issued by a group that called itself Red Bengal. The document,
which had been circulating in all manner of public places, called for the "ruthless"
assassination of British police officers (British Library, IOR/L/PJ/6/1884). Unfortunately, there is no material trace of this "crude picture" in the colonial files on this
subject.

65. See Kopf 1989 for an excellent discussion of the dilemma that fierce goddesses like
Kali posed to Bengali modernists over the course of the nineteenth century.

66. Quoted in Ramaswamy 1997, 124.

67. Here, as elsewhere in this novel, the English translation (done by his nephew with considerable involvement on the part of Rabindranath himself) departs in some interesting regards from the Bengali original. I thank Mandira Bhaduri for help with understanding this. See also chapter 5, n.1.

68. For Tagore's use of the phrase "idolatry of geography," see chapter 3.

3. VANDE MATARAM

1. The Sanskrit word *vande* is conjugated in the first person singular from the root *vand*: to praise, celebrate, do honor, adore, venerate, and worship. I consciously translate it as "I worship the Mother" to draw attention to its vulnerability to charges of idolatry. I thank Rich Freeman for help in understanding the semantic range of this phrase. See also Lipner 2005, 244.

2. As it was implicitly assumed to be the "national anthem" from the early years of the twentieth century (even Gandhi in distant South Africa referred to it thus), many nationalists, especially those partial to Hindu revivalist ideas, called for the adoption of the song as such during the 1930s as India moved towards independence. Many Muslims (although not all) challenged such a call by drawing attention to the hymn's idolatrous content and divisive context of origin. The matter was discussed by the Constituent Assembly of India in the late 1940s, which finally—and without an open debate on the subject—resolved on January 24, 1950, that "the composition consisting of the words and music known as Jana Gana Mana is the National Anthem of India . . . and the song Bande Mataram, which has played a historic part in the struggle for Indian freedom, shall be honoured equally with Jana Gana Mana and shall have equal status with it (Applause)" (quoted in Lipner 2005, 81). From the 1930s to this day, the Indian public has debated making its singing mandatory.

3. Bankim's original poem used the words "vande mataram" in Sanskrit, but following Bengali linguistic convention *vande* was soon replaced by *bande* in Bengal. A bureaucrat in the colonial administration, Bankim was one of the most influential polymaths of modern Bengal and India, albeit one whose work helped foster an emergent Hindu nationalism by the 1890s. Despite the range of his work, he is perhaps best remembered in India today for his authorship of this song that one influential commentator has dismissed as "a purposeless creation of a poet musing and singing to himself" (Bhattacharya 2003, 74). For my understanding of the history of the song and its creator, I have relied on Bhattacharya 2003; Das 1984; Kaviraj 1995; Lipner 2005, 3–124; and Sarkar 2001. Tanika Sarkar (2006) offers an adroit reading of the continuing significance of the song to the installation of the nation as "a new divine project" and for today's politics.

4. Asish Nandy describes *Anandamath* as "arguably the most important political

novel ever written in India" (2001, 25). First serialized in the literary journal *Banga-darshan* over the course of 1881–1882, the novel was published in its entirety in 1882 in Bengali and subsequently was published in several editions (some with changes) over the course of the next few years. It was translated into other Indian languages from 1897, and its first English translation appeared in 1906 at the height of the swadeshi movement. For a new translation of the novel with a critical intro-duction that questions several existing assumptions and interpretations, see Lipner 2005. Lipner translates the novel's title as "The Sacred Brotherhood."

5. It is impossible to summarize in a footnote the life and influence of this iconic figure of modern Bengali and Indian intellectual life, but for the purposes of this book the most important aspect to underscore about this complex man of letters and art is his growing ambivalence toward the ideology of nationalism. He reached a breaking point sometime during the swadeshi movement, in which he had par-ticipated with some degree of passion in its opening months. Among the many scholarly works on Tagore those most useful for this project include Datta 2003; Chakrabarty 2000; Dutta and Robinon 1995; Nandy 1994; and Sen 2005.

6. For other claims for the transformation of poem into song and its public invoca-tions, see Lipner 2005, 74–75.

7. Ghose 1999, 467–68. As Aurobindo noted, "It is difficult to translate the National Anthem of Bengal into verse in another language owing to its unique union of sweetness, simple directness and high poetic force" (467). For his attempt to trans-late it into verse, see 465–66. A recent scholarly translation can be found in Lipner 2005 84–85.

8. According to official records, the statement found in Dhingra's pocket (possibly authored not by him but by a key figure among expatriate nationalists in London, V. D. Savarkar [1883–1966]) concluded: "It is my fervent prayer, may I be reborn of the same mother and may I redie in the same sacred cause, till my mission is done and she stands free for the good of humanity and to the glory of God" (quoted in Ker 1917, 180). See also Visram 2002, 156–60; and Lahiri 2000, 89.

9. The ban was instituted by the so-called Lyon or "Bande Mataram" Circular. A later government report notes that the song itself was never banned across India (National Archives of India, Government of India, Home, Political, 1937, 71/37). See also Sarkar 2006, 3963.

10. See Guha-Thakurta 1992, 89–90, and Lipner 2005, 104–5, for a discussion of this illustration in relation to the poem.

11. Yi Fu Tuan suggests that "geo-piety covers a broad range of emotional bonds be-tween man and his terrestrial home," and leads us "to see how human territoriality, in the sense of attachment to place, differs in important ways from the territori-ality of animals unburdened by symbolic thought" (1976, 11–13). Significantly, Tuan singles out patriotism as a form of geo-piety, although he does not limit what he calls "a compassion for the vulnerability of one's native soil" to modernity. In his

critical identification of patriotism as geo-piety, Tuan also highlights the role of the sentiments of love and attachment to "one's native land, the place of one's birth, the hearth in which one was nurtured, the domicile of the deified souls of departed ancestors (manes) and of the gods" (23–24).

12. For another reading of the yoking of the song and anthem that sees it as an attempt at "conciliation, on the one hand, and history, on the other," see Lipner 2005, 80–81.

13. On the subversive anticolonial politics of the so-called Poona pictures, see Pinney 2004, 45–58.

14. The description here is based on my interviews with Milind Sabnis and Sachin Joshi in Pune, December 2001 and February 2008. Joshi studied Abanindranath's painting in printed reproductions. Dixit's canvas was available to view at the Raja Dinkar Kelkar Museum in Pune. Joshi's mother posed for him, but he also studied the map of India to "get the proper shape for Bharat Mata."

15. Many scholars have drawn attention to the fact that the lines, "Terrible with the clamorous shout of seventy million throats, and the sharpness of swords raised in twice seventy million hands," indicate that Bankim was thinking of Bengal when he composed his poem in the 1870s. Seventy million was roughly the population of this part of British India around 1871 (Muslims included)—a figure that was unknown before the first colonial census of that year (Bhattacharya 2003, 69). The subsequent translations, versions, and renderings of this poem change this figure, as the Mother of Bengal becomes Mother India (80–81).

16. The painting appears as well on the cover of Sabnis's privately published book, *Vande Mataram: Down the Memory Lane* (2000), and was mass-produced on posters, bookmarks, and other objects.

17. The 1952 Hindi motion picture *Anandmath* (directed by Hemen Gupta for Filmistan) indeed opens with a relief map of India, and the words inscribed across it declare that the Bankim's *santan*s were involved in the first war for independence. I was told by research officers at the National Film Archives (Pune) that a 1939 Telugu film titled *Vande Mataram* (which has a social reformist and patriotic agenda) includes a song featured with the map of India, but unfortunately I was not able to see this movie. I was also not able to see a 1926 silent film titled *Vande Mataram Ashram* (The vande mataram hermitage).

18. Accompanying this illustration is the following explanation: "When one realises that the Motherland is a living entity—his Eternal and Divine Mother—the manifestation of Maha Shakti, and develops the spirit of intense passion and devotion to her and ultimately identifies oneself with her, it is called Desatmabodh—the consciousness of the unity of one's own soul with that of the soul of the nation" (Rangarajan 1977, 47).

19. The volume was published by Bharatiya Vidya Bhavan, an educational trust founded

in 1938 in Bombay but now with a worldwide presence. The publication of this volume by the Bhavan is not surprising given its Hindu revivalist and Hindu nationalist leanings. On its founder K. M. Munshi and his Hindu nationalist predilections, see Davis 1997, 210–21.

20. I thank Lee Schlesinger for bringing this publication to my attention.

21. The numbers refer to the populations of Bengal and India respectively.

22. Sumit Sarkar has commented on the society's "uncompromising opposition to any form of Hindu revivalism," and on the various activities undertaken by its members to promote Hindu-Muslim unity (1973, 365–66). Nevertheless the appearance of the words "vande mataram" on the society's logo as well as on the "national flag" that was designed under its patronage in August 1906 (see chapter 6) troubles such assertions.

23. Although Gandhi was generally restrained in his invocation of Mother India, he wrote that he was, in his younger days, "gripped" and "enthralled" by the mother's hymn, and closed his letters to friends—at least into the 1920s—with the words "Vande mataram from Mohandas" (Lipner 2005, 81–82).

24. See Sarkar 1973, 307. As I discuss in chapter 6, a flag believed to have been designed by Sister Nivedita in 1905 as well had the words "vande mataram" inscribed (in Bengali script) across its front. Importantly, the words are dropped from the various flags of the nation that were adopted by the Indian National Congress from the 1920s, and the current national flag of the Republic of India is conspicuous by its absence (for a visual reminder of this, see figures 26 and 121). In addition to its inscription on early national flags, "vande mataram" was frequently emblazoned on banners that were displayed during nationalist processions and marches in the first few decades of the twentieth century.

25. Quoted in Bhattacharya 2003, 55. It is worth recalling the *Vijaya* image from 1909 that also brings together the words "vande mataram" and "Allahu akbar" (figure 8).

26. National Archives of India, Government of India, Home, Political (Confidential), January 1908, No. 8 (Deposit). Unfortunately, because the medal has not survived in the official archives (the fate of many such ephemera) we do not know how "the Indian nation" was visualized on it. The language of the government report, however, hints at its anthropomorphization.

27. National Archives of India, Government of India, Home, Political (Confidential), November 1908, Nos. 45–52 (Part A).

28. *Native Newspaper Reports* (Madras), No. 31 of 1907, 329–330, Tamilnadu State Archives, Chennai.

29. Quoted in Samanta 1995, 2: 336. The report went on to note that "the words 'Bande Mataram'—Hail Motherland—acquire a very special sacredness to the Hindu when conjoined with the greatest and holiest of all mantras, the 'Word of Power,' AUM,

or OM, which is the word-symbol of Brahman the Absolute, and in its esoteric significance sums up all creation and eternity as conceived in the Vedanta" (ibid.). A decade earlier, the south Indian newspaper *Deshabhimani* published a letter from a correspondent in which he proudly declared, "In every (private) letter and in every (public) notice the first thing that meets our eye is Vande Mataram" (Tamilnadu State Archives, *Native Newspaper Reports* (Madras), No. 29 of 1907, 169–70).

30. Quoted in Samanta 1995, 2: 5.

31. Ibid. 4: 46. See also National Archives of India, Government of India, Home, Political (Confidential), October 1908, No. 29 (Deposit), and April 1912, No.1 (Deposit). Unfortunately, these examples have not survived in the official archives of the state. For comparable use of the Devanagari script to similarly picture another nationalist slogan, *Jai Hind* (Victory to India), in the 1940s, see Pinney 1997, 851–53. Interpreted in figural terms, Pinney suggests that such charged phrases assume "the same representational power as images."

32. I thank Robert Del Bonta for sharing this letter and Jyotindra Jain for translating it.

33. I thank Mala and G. Sundar at the Roja Muthiah Research Library, Chennai, for bringing this letter to my attention.

34. Quoted in Samanta 1995, 4: 46.

35. Chatterji 1941, 62–63, emphasis mine. As the novel unfolds, the guide Bhavananda again reminds Mahendra of "the oath before the golden map of Mother India" (192). I first discussed this edition of the volume, translated by Basanta Koomar Roy (1941; reprinted in 1992), in Ramaswamy 2003. See Lipner 2005, 120–24, for a subsequent discussion in which he rightly alerts us to Roy's "translation" as misleading good scholars by making invisible the presence of Muslims in Bankim's original text. See also Sen 2002, 55.

36. In the 1920s, Roy, a writer and biographer of Tagore, was a lecturer at the University of Wisconsin, in which capacity he was also associated with Ghadar Party activities in San Francisco (see "Echoes of Freedom: South Asian Pioneers in California, 1899–1965," Doe Library, University of California, Berkley, http://www.lib.berkeley.edu).

37. Interestingly, the 1952 film *Anandmath* shows images of the mother/goddess rather than the map form as the song is sung, reverting to Bankim's original imagination.

38. Translation by Kaviraj 1995, 137. For a slightly different translation, see Lipner 2005, 144–45. The phrase "janani janmabhumischa svargadapi gariyasi" occurs in this exchange, and it is translated here as "one's mother and one's motherland are nobler than the heavens."

39. Bhattacharya 2003, 77, emphasis mine. Bhattacharya also directs our attention to the inherent contradiction between Bankim's refutation of idolatry as "anti-

science" in 1874 on the one hand, and the deification of land as goddess in his hymn around the same time (81–82).

40. It is important to note though, as Julius Lipner (2005, 100) has reminded us, that Bankim does not name the Mother as Bharat Mata in his novel.

41. Quoted in Goswami 2004, 241. As a native of Bengal and educated in colonial schools and colleges as well as at Oxford, Pal was described in an influential British essay as "a man almost at home in London as in Calcutta" (Chirol 1910, 9). He joined the Indian National Congress in 1886 soon after it was formed, and by the early years of the twentieth century he was one of its leading men. In this role he triggered the party's "extremist" turn away from liberal constitutional politics toward the ideology of swadeshi as well as the deployment of Hindu symbols and imagery. As a fiery orator, journalist, and founder of the revolutionary newspaper *Bande Mataram*, Pal left for England in 1907 to escape colonial repression, returning only in 1911. Pal's religious views changed over his lifetime. In his youth, like the Tagores, he espoused the reformist views of the Brahmo Samaj, but in the 1890s, he became a more mainstream Vaishnava Hindu (and from 1911, even wrote on Bengali Vaishnavism). During the swadeshi movement, his activities and discourse were heavily influenced by Shakta ideology with its divinization of feminine energies. With the rise of Gandhi to prominence by 1920, Pal's influence faded. For analyses of his political views, see Goswami 2004; and Heehs 1998, 98–118.

42. For Pal, however, the soul of India is not Mother India but Lord Krishna, "the Principle and Personality in and through whom, as in the past so also in the present and in the future, the great Indian synthesis was, is being, and will be worked" (1911, ii).

43. Quoted in Goswami 2004, 241. Nagendranath, a young admirer of Pal, similarly wrote later in his reminiscences recalling the heady swadeshi days when he was a school student, "Mother India did not consist only of fields and rivers and mountains; she was a mother in flesh and blood outwardly somewhat weary and tear-stained as a result of centuries of foreign rule, but potentially always radiant and powerful and able to inspire and succor her children" (Sen Gupta 1974, 26–27).

44. Quoted in Dave et al. 1962, 38. I thank Richard Davis for this reference. Born in Calcutta in 1872, and educated in England from 1879 to 1890, Aurobindo returned to India in 1893 when he took up employment in the princely state of Baroda for a few years. In the first nine years of the new century he was one of the fiery leaders of a powerful subcontinent-wide movement committed to return the nation to its Hindu roots. His interpretation of such a "return" included the espousal of violence (in journals such as *Yugantar* and especially in *Bande Mataram*) for which he was imprisoned by the colonial state in 1908. Acquitted in 1909 in what is known as the "Alipore Bomb Conspiracy," but still under British surveillance, he exiled himself to the French colony of Pondicherry in February 1910 where soon after he

renounced politics and lived the rest of his life as the globally influential mystic "Sri Aurobindo" (Heehs 1993). I am also persuaded by Elleke Boehmer's argument (2002, 79–124) of his preoccupation with Hindu revivalism and the Mother India figure as attempts to "re-authenticate" himself after years of living abroad.

45. Aurobindo also insisted in a speech that he gave in 1907 that "Nationalism is not a mere political programme; Nationalism is a religion that came from God. Nationalism is a creed which shall have to live" (quoted in Heehs 1998, 100–1).

46. Quoted in Purani 1958, 82. I am grateful to Peter Heehs for directing me to this source.

47. Quoted in Chakravarty 1961, 219.

48. Ibid., 196. I thank Lee Schlesinger for alerting me to this reference.

49. As translated in Dimock 1971, 1. I thank Mandira Bhaduri for help with the Bengali original.

50. Ibid., 5.

51. Quoted in Dutta and Robinson 1995, 153–54. For other such poems, see Chowdhury 1998, 110, 154–55. To recall, Tagore's upbringing in a Brahmo household would have made him suspicious of idolatry, but as Dipesh Chakrabarty reminds us in a nuanced analysis of poems such as these, "one does not have to be a believer to have *darshan*. . . . *Darshan* belongs here to the history of practice and habitus" (2000, 175).

52. See Chowdhury 1998, 162–63, for a description of Tagore's later recollection of this moment.

53. Quoted in Banerjee 2002, 216. A *crore* is 10 million, and here it refers to the population of Bengal around 1875 when Bankim's original hymn was composed.

54. The connotation of the Bengali original is slightly different.

55. The Sanskrit word *vidhata* (usually an epithet for the Hindu god Brahma) is an agentive noun meaning one who distributes, disposes, arranges, or accomplishes, or who is a maker, an author, or a creator. I thank Rich Freeman for help with understanding the range of its meaning. Surprisingly, there is very little critical scholarship on the song, but for a useful collection of the primary sources and debates surrounding the selection of Tagore's composition as India's official anthem, see Sen 1972 and also Pradip Kumar Datta, "India's National Anthem: Are We Still Singing for the Empire?," South Asia Citizens Web, www.sacw.net, September 8, 2004. For Prime Minister Nehru, "Jana Gana Mana" lent itself to the status of anthem because it was deemed "adaptable to orchestral and band music, and for being played abroad . . . *Bande Mataram* does not yield itself to good orchestration or military playing." Even more revealing, he noted that "a National Anthem is something different from a song which represents the struggle and the longing which *Bande Mataram* so powerfully represents. A national anthem should be something of victory and fulfillment, not of past struggle" (quoted in Nair 1987, 55–56).

56. Quoted in Sen 1972, 4.

57. This smartly theorized essay, however, recirculates the erroneous charge (produced under very specific historical circumstances of growing communalism) that Tagore composed the song in praise of the King-Emperor George V on the occasion of his coronation at the so-called Delhi Durbar of 1911. (For Tagore's spirited defense against this allegation against him in the 1930s, see Sen 1972, 6–7.)

58. See Sen 1972, 5, for a reproduction of this verse.

59. Quoted in Sen 1972, 22–23.

60. I thank Lee Schlesinger for alerting me to this.

61. Quoted in Chaudhuri 2002, 116–17.

62. Chaudhuri 2000, 117. Unfortunately, she completes this fine argument with the erroneous assertion, "Tagore's poem was originally written for the arrival in India of the King of England."

63. Quoted in Bhattacharya 2003, 78. For the poetry prior to Bankim on India as woman and India as goddess, see Chowdhury 1998, chapter 1.

64. The characterization of the song as "the hymn of hate" was made by a British administrator in 1937 in a letter to Lord Baden-Powell in which he drew attention to the fact that "an objectional poem entitled Vande Mataram" had been included in "Scouting for Boys in India." As such, he gently requested its author, the esteemed Lord, to expunge it from the next edition of the book (which was accomplished). The relevant archival file on this matter contains a valuable "note" on the song (National Archives of India, Government of India, Home, Political, 1937, 71/37. For other colonial associations of the song with death and destruction, see Das 1984, 222–24).

65. "The Bande Mataram song," Nehru Memorial Museum and Library, New Delhi, AICC Papers, Reel No. 63, file # 34 of 1937.

66. Quoted in Nair 1987, 43, 56.

67. Quoted in Bhattacharya 2003, 33.

68. National Archives of India, Government of India, Home, Political (Secret), April 1910, Nos. 36–39 (Part A). The seditious dhoti was manufactured in the Bengali town of Midnapur, and although the ban was restricted to Bengal, other presidencies and provinces were warned of similar artifacts circulating. For a discussion on the potential creators of this seditious dhoti, see *Report on Native Papers in Bengal for the Week ending the 16th July 1910*, No. 29 of 1910, National Archives of Indian, New Delhi. See also Pinney 2004, 116.

69. The cartoon is reproduced in Venkatachalapathy 1995, 56–57.

70. *Native Newspaper Reports* (Madras), No. 19 of 1907, 191, Tamilnadu State Archives, Chennai.

71. Government Order # 474–75 (Judicial), dated March 23, 1912, Tamilnadu State Archives, Chennai.

72. Ibid.

73. National Archives of India, Government of India, Home, Political (Confidential), December 1910, Nos. 47–53 (Part B). For a different version of the same poem published in the "seditious" monthly magazine *Suprabhat* in 1907, see Ker 1917, 88–89.

4. ENSHRINING THE MAP OF INDIA

For an earlier version of this chapter, which is conceptualized somewhat differently, see Ramaswamy 2006. Since the time I wrote that essay Charu Gupta has also discussed the Bharat Mata Mandir in Banaras in her *Sexuality, Obscenity, Community* (2002, 198–203).

1. On the enduring importance over more than two millennia of Varanasi (also called Kasi) and its imagination as a microcosm of all of Hindu India, see Diana Eck's classic work *Banaras: City of Light* (1982).

2. These quotes are drawn from the *Hindustan Times* (Delhi), October 26, 1936.

3. *Indian Social Reformer* 47 (10) (November 7, 1936): 154.

4. The quotes are from the *Hindustan Times* (Delhi), October 26, 1936; and Gandhi 1958, 388.

5. Gandhi 1958, 388 (emphasis mine).

6. *Hindustan Times* (Delhi), October 26, 1936.

7. There are few critical studies of this fascinating figure, although I have benefited from the discussion in C. Gupta 2002, 198–203, and from an unpublished essay titled "Babu Shiva Prasad Gupta and Benoy Kumar Sarkar" by Giuseppe Flora (I thank Sharda Shankar Dwivedi for sharing this with me). Babu Shivprasad Gupta hailed from a family of wealthy Banaras landed magnates and British loyalists. In his reminiscences, he writes of the fact that as a young adult he was exposed to the reformist Arya Samaj movement with its trenchant critique of orthodox Hindu rituals and idolatry. Under its influence, his traditional religious views underwent a radical transformation, and his "mind moved away from idol worship" (Gupta 1983a, 88). Soon after, he also began to support the activities of Bengali nationalists. Around 1914 Gupta set out on a world tour that took him first to Egypt and then to London where he met the fiery Arya Samaj leader Lajpat Rai, with whom he subsequently linked up again in New York. In October 1915, when he was homeward bound via Japan and Singapore, Gupta was arrested on the charge of consorting with seditious conspirators against the British Raj, but he was released soon after on the intervention of his uncle Raja Sri Moti Chand, a loyalist. A government report from 1916 characterizes him as "an active nationalist and Arya," and it noted his penchant for the company of "known revolutionaries." On his return to Banaras in early 1916 after his travels he started in 1920 the Hindi daily *Aaj* (which continues to be published to this day), and in 1921 he donated one million rupees toward the establishment of the Kashi Vidyapith, a center for national education in

accordance with Gandhian principles. On June 28, 1988, the Government of India issued a postage stamp in commemoration of his contributions to the national movement. Regarding Gupta's motivations, in his essay "Shri Bharatmata Mandir" (Auspicious Mother India Temple) in *Kashi Vidyapith Heerak Jayanthi: Abhinandan Granth* (Kashi Vidyapith Diamond Jubilee: Commemoration volume) (1983b), he describes in detail his reasons for building the temple, the sources of his inspiration, and his hopes for the memorial.

8. By the time Gupta visited the British Museum in London, relief maps of India (on paper as well as models) had been on display in the empire's capital from at least since the 1870s. J. Forbes Watson's prospectus for the India Museum, for example, proposes that such a map was essential for introducing the subcontinent to visitors. The many International Exhibitions held in Victorian London invariably had such a map on display. In India, the Calcutta International Exhibition of 1883–1884 also displayed a relief map, as did the Madras Educational Exhibition of 1907.

9. Although Durga Prasad (1875–1952) was identified by some contemporaries as a "professor of science," he appears to have been a local antiquarian and numismatist as well as an amateur geographer (Singh and Rana 2001, 159). He taught at the Kashi Vidyapith and was a member as well of the Executive Committee of the Banaras Hindu University. It appears that Prasad made extensive use of the detailed relief maps of the subcontinent produced by the colonial Survey of India (Gupta 1983b, 391).

10. For details of the *shilanyas* (foundation stone) ceremony presided over by the eminent scholar of Sanskrit and educationist Bhagwan Das, see Dwivedi and Singh, forthcoming.

11. *Hindustan Times* (Delhi), October 26, 1936. For further details regarding the construction of the map, see also Gupta 1983b.

12. In Sanskrit and many other Indian languages the term *murti* refers to "'anything which has definite shape and limits,' 'a form, body, figure,' 'an embodiment, incarnation, manifestation.' Thus the *murti* is more than a likeness; it is the deity itself taken 'form'" (Eck 1981, 38).

13. Photographs published in Srinivasavaradhan 1947 seem to suggest this as well. In many respects Sivam was emulating the model proposed in Bankim's *Anandamath*; he too created a celibate order for young men called Bharat Ashram whose goal was to propagate the new religion of Bharatiya ("Indian-ness") centered on the worship of Bharat Mata (Padmanabhan 1984, 62–72).

14. The text of the pamphlet is given in *Bande Mataram: Political Writings and Speeches, 1890–1908.* Vols. 6 and 7 of *The Complete Works of Sri Aurobindo* (2002). Bhawani, a Durga-like goddess, had been the tutelary deity of the seventeenth-century Maratha ruler Shivaji, whose sword was divinely blessed by her. At the time of the writing of this pamphlet, Aurobindo was based in western India in the princely state of Baroda, which was of Maratha origins. That he chose to name his

temple after Bhawani rather than Durga, her more well-known Bengali equivalent, is a reflection of the many subterranean networks that connected anti-colonial "extremist" factions across the subcontinent, especially in Bombay and Bengal (Ker 1917).

15. Translations are from Kaviraj 1995, 138–39. For a slightly different gloss, see Lipner 2005, 149–51.

16. Kaviraj 1995, 114. Although I agree with Kaviraj's point about the sacralization of space, I disagree with his characterization of "geologically surveyed" space as "neutral." Instead I interpret the opposition in Bankim's statement as between the scientific-geographic and the anthropomorphic-sacred imaginaries, neither of them "neutral," both ideologically motivated in their own way.

17. Over the millennia, the geographical specificities of Bharatavarsha have been un-stable, although the term has endured as a toponym for a land that is implicitly Aryan, Sanskritic, and Hindu. By the early centuries of the Common Era it covered what we recognize today as the Indian subcontinent including the island of Sri Lanka, but in the later half of the first millennium CE, it also incorporated terri-tories that we today identify as Burma, Thailand, and the Malay Peninsula (Sircar 1967). In the early years of the twentieth century, Bipin Chandra Pal insisted to his fellow Indians that while the stranger and foreigner called their land "India, thereby emphasizing only her strange physical features," her own children have "known and loved her by another name," and that name is Bharatavarsha (1911, 87–88).

18. Despite the fact that many imperial maps, especially from the later half of the nineteenth century into the first few decades of the twentieth century, showed the entire region from Afghanistan into Burma as a single undivided region named the Indian Empire, colored pink or red, about two-fifths of this area was under the nominal control of Indian princes (the so-called native states in British adminis-trative parlance).

19. David Morgan suggests that visual piety is "the visual formation and practice of religious belief" (1997, 1). He writes that "the act of looking itself contributes to religious formation," and he rightly observes that prints, pictures, and drawings can visually summon up the ontological presence of someone or something sacred (3–9).

20. Eck 1981, 3. See also Babb 1981 for a variety of ways in which the exchange of glances and of making eye contact with the deity works across different regimes of contemporary Hinduism. For reflections on darshan as an "unconscious habit" that erupts beyond the realm of the overtly sacred and religious, see Chakrabarty 2000, 172–79.

21. In his well-known semiotic theory of signs, Charles S. Peirce defines the sign as a thing that stands for something to somebody in some respect or capacity. He dis-tinguishes three types of signs: an index, a symbol, and an icon (although a single

sign may simultaneously be all three). An icon is a sign that stands for something by similarity or likeness with it (like a portrait or photo of its subject); an index is a sign that assumes an existential contextual connection or contiguity with the object (such as a weathervane as a sign of the wind direction); and a symbol is a sign that is based on convention or by virtue of associations (such as the White House and the U.S. presidency).

22. Geeti Sen reminds us that in India "there had always existed the predilection to worship through sign/symbol in place of iconic representation. Recall some of these: the Bodhi tree, the *dharma chakra*, and the *stupa* to represent the Buddha; calligraphy as the noblest medium to invoke the name of Allah; the *Guru Granth Sahib* to invoke the Sikh Gurus; the *tulsi* plant for Vishnu, the *linga* as the purest of the 'signs' to represent Shiva, and the *Shri Yantra* to invoke the Devi. And in certain senses. . . . was the map [in the Bharat Mata Mandir] not a *yantra* [a ritual diagram] to invoke and represent the Motherland [Bharat Mata]?" (2002–2003, 167–68). See also Eck 1981 for a discussion of the widespread worship of "aniconic" images in Hindu India.

23. *Hindustan Times* (Delhi), October 25, 1936; emphases mine.

24. *Leader* (Allahabad), October 28, 1936.

25. For prescriptions and rituals regarding the creation and consecration of images, see Eck 1981, esp. 51–55, and Davis 1997, 33–38.

26. *Leader* (Allahabad), October 26, 1936.

27. Note also the following comment in an inexpensive guidebook, *Banaras*, published by Oriental Publishers in 1957: "We call this building a temple and we Indians pay our deep regard and respect to it in the same devotional way which we do to other temples in general. But why? It is enjoined in our Vedas . . . that the MOTHER AND THE MOTHERLAND ARE GREATER THAN HEAVEN ITSELF. . . . And it is in the same way that our early Indian thought deified our MOTHER-INDIA and elevated patriotism into a religion. And accordingly since the earlier days of our Indian culture every Indian meditates BHARAT-MATA (Mother India) as a physical and visible form in her various aspects. This deity of secular democracy, the deity of the Cosmic Mind, the deity of the common, collective, and the national mind, which claims and commands universal homage and worship from each and every Indian was enshrined in this building."

28. I am grateful to Jeorg Gengnagel who urged me to consider these examples and then shared many of them with me. In a four-inch Banaras guide map published by the colonial Survey of India in 1933 the site for the Bharat Mata Mandir is clearly labeled but no pictorial depiction is given (British Library Maps 53345 [7]). By contrast—and very tellingly—a recent tourist guide map of the city uses the same symbol to designate the site as it does to mark all Hindu temples (Srinivasan 2000).

29. Interestingly, though, Indian national territory is shown broken up into numerous colored patches (signifying the constituting states) on the map of India painted on the signboard outside the temple announcing the Bharat Mata Mandir. The signboard is obviously a much later addition to the premises.

30. Quoted in Jaffrelot 1996, 22.

31. Ibid., 22 (emphasis mine). Jaffrelot quotes here from Shraddhanand's *Hindu Sangathan—Savior of the Dying Race*, published around 1926, but in this context incorrectly glosses Bhumi-mata as "motherland," and Matri-bhumi as "earth mother." Shraddhanand and Gupta were close friends and might have mutually influenced each other in their visions of building a shrine for Bharat Mata (C. Gupta 2002, 336–37).

32. See the following comment in the guidebook *Banaras* from 1957: "The Himalayan range with its high pointed peaks, the plateau of Tibet, commonly known as the roof of this world behind them, the rivers with their rise and falls, the seas and oceans with their islands, the variations of the heights of the different parts of the country from the sea-level, the famous KHAIBER-PASS and the BULAN-PASS— through which invaders entered the country—are all vividly displayed in this extraordinarily beautiful and most natural relief map of the vast land" (31). And a more recent response to the enshrined map states as follows: "Every mountain range has been shown with its individual features. The valleys, ravines, and passes through the range have been shown true to their depth. Four hundred odd peaks of the Himalayan range recreated in such a magnificent way that their height can be visualized merely by looking at them. For a visitor, following the range of Kailash mountain ranges with all their magnificent peaks and glaciers on the map will be an experience" (Bharathi Bhattacharya, "Once Deified," *The Hindu*, March 5, 1993).

33. *Indian Social Reformer* 47 (9) (October 31, 1936): 131 (emphasis mine).

34. *Bombay Chronicle*, October 27, 1936.

35. Nita Kumar, personal communication with the author, December 2001; and interviews with students of the South Point School, Nagwa, Varanasi, December 2001. Interestingly, the students also told me that one of the principal reasons that schoolchildren visit the temple is to buy printed maps of India for their school geography lessons from the shop on its premises. Members of the paramilitary Hindu nationalist RSS (Rastriya Swayamsevak Sangh) are known to frequent the temple and salute the map (Ramu Pandit, personal communication with the author, December 2001). On one of my many visits to the temple in October 2004, I talked to a group of young Bihari men who had taken a break from their work to visit the temple. Only one of the men had been to school, where he learned how to draw a map of India. Another observed that it was good to see the whole country as a *murti*.

36. I am thankful to Jeorg Gengnagel for urging me to stress this. Charu Gupta notes

that one of the poems recited at the inauguration of the temple in 1936 stated that after a ritual bath in the Ganga and a visit to the mighty Viswanath temple, "a glimpse of the mother [India] made the day complete" (2002, 201).

37. In contrast, Diana Eck writes of the Bharat Mata Mandir, "It is a popular temple with today's pilgrims, who circumambulate the whole map and then climb to the second-floor balcony for the *darshana* of the whole. Looking down at this map, they can see at a glance the great distances many of their ancestors traveled on foot" (1982, 39).

38. Bharathi Bhattacharya, "Once Deified," *The Hindu*, March 5, 1993 (emphasis mine). Of course, such a comment is countered by the numerous examples across Hindu India of the worship of aniconic images (Eck 1981, 32–36).

39. My conclusion obviously differs from that of historians of Hinduism such as Diana Eck and David Kinsley who seem to suggest that the map functions adequately as murti (see, for example, Eck 1999, 34–35; and Kinsley 1987, 183–84). See also Geeti Sen's recent observation that "to this day homage continues to be paid by the ritual of circumambulation (*parikrama*) of a vast map of the country, laid on the ground with its rich undulating topography of mountains, rivers, seas" (2002, 36).

40. Quoted in McKean 1996, 269. Soon after the opening of the temple, the image of Bharat Mata was also taken in procession through the country in a "unity sacrifice" (*ekatmata yajna*).

41. For details of these figures, see McKean 1996. See also Eck 1999.

42. A Congress activist, Ponnapati Eswara Reddy, was the inspiring force behind the so-called Trigandhi temple in Andhra Pradesh's Guntur District, which was built sometime in the 1990s. The temple enshrines the busts of the three Gandhis—the Mahatma, Indira, and her son Rajiv—and a large image of a carto-graphed Bharat Mata as a two-armed goddess flanked by a roaring lion. The western, northern, and eastern borders of India are dissolved, and a large halo around the mother's head occludes Kashmir (*India Today*, April 12, 1999). A new temple to Bharat Mata has been recently opened in a small village in the south Indian state of Karnataka. The image of Mother India housed in the temple is a two-armed goddess holding the Indian tricolor. She is five feet tall and made of black rock. The Indian map is not part of the iconography (*Star of Mysore*, August 14, 2006). I thank Shalini R. Urs for drawing this to my attention. Gayatri Sinha (2006, 62) refers to a temple to Bharat Mata constructed in the last few years by the industrial group Sahara in the north Indian city of Lucknow.

43. Since photography is strictly prohibited in this disputed temple, I can only provide a verbal description of this painting that shows Bharat Mata (identified as such) as a four-armed goddess holding a book, a sheaf of plants, a small length of cloth, and a string of beads. The first two verses from Bankim's hymn are inscribed below the painting.

44. I thank Ian Barrow for alerting me to the existence of this image that shows Mother India standing on a globe. Construction of this temple began in 1917 and was completed in 1936 under Marwari patronage, the same year as the Banaras Bharat Mata Mandir. For a discussion of how the temple and its ritual practices fit into an evolving Hindu nationalism in the 1990s, see Hardgrove 1999.

45. On these shrines, see Sarkar 1995, 196–98. The photograph in figure 70 shows a schoolroom in the north Indian city of Patna in 2007 in which young students watch while their teacher offers worship (*puja*) to several framed images, including that of a carto-graphed Bharat Mata in the guise seen in figure 20. In a recent ethnographic study of contemporary schooling in the western Indian town of Kolhapur in the late 1990s, the anthropologist Veronique Benei has extensively documented the widespread invocation of Bharat Mata in the poems, writings, drawings, and performances of middle- and lower-class children (2008). She concludes, "Even the most secular-minded teachers—whether neo-Buddhist, Muslim, Maratha or Brahmin—did not clearly object to some of these distinctly Hindu songs and prayers being sung in the space of the school" (263). No shrines to Mother India (with or without the map), however, appear in her analysis.

46. *The Hindu*, October 29, 2003.

47. It could be argued that figures 56 and 57 (discussed in chapter 3) provide counter-examples to my suggestion here that the map of India in and of itself does not elicit a worshipful attitude. I would propose that those images appear in the context of illustrating the "Vande Mataram" hymn, and the mother's presence is implicitly assumed (see also Hansen 1999, 109–10).

5. BETWEEN MEN, MAP, AND MOTHER

1. *The Home and the World*'s earlier Bengali incarnation was first serialized between May 1915 and February 1916 in an avant-garde magazine and subsequently was published as *Ghare Bhaire* (with some cuts) in 1916. A new edition (with the cuts restored) was published in 1920. An English "translation" was serialized (as *At Home and Outside*) in 1918–1919 and then published in book form in 1919, with considerable supervision by the author himself. In his introduction to the latest Penguin edition of *The Home and the World*, William Radice observes that a systematic analysis of the various versions of the novel is needed, as is an exploration of why Tagore cut parts of it (possibly in response to readers' criticisms, it is speculated). Although I take seriously Radice's contention that *The Home and the World* "is in many ways a different book from *Ghare Bhaire*," I also consider that the English version reflects Tagore's own intentions by his own admission, "A large part of it I have done myself and it has been carefully revised" (quoted in Radice 2005, vii-viii). I therefore treat *The Home and the World* as an autonomous text, although with Mandira Bhaduri's assistance I have compared it with *Ghare Bhaire* for criti-

cal statements. For an important collection of essays that offer fresh insights into the novel and its charged context of production, see Datta 2003.

2. Tagore 2005, 73. Interestingly, Tagore retains the English word *map* in *Ghare Bhaire*. As I noted in chapter 1, in most languages of the subcontinent the word *shakti* can serve as the proper name for a goddess as well as refer to power, energy, and life force.

3. For the evocative phrase, "dust of some map-made land," Tagore uses the Bengali words "bhugol biboroner maati" (earth described in geography).

4. See Enloe 1989, 44. For scholarly discussions of representations of the female body in calendar art, see especially Uberoi 1990 and 2000.

5. The anthropologist Lisa McKean has coined the term *matriot* to refer to those patriots who present themselves as "Bharat Mata's devoted and dutiful children . . . The nation is figured as a loving Mother and her devoted children; the secular state and Muslims (as heirs of Muslim invaders) figure as the tyrannical Father" (1996, 252). McKean, however, does not necessarily single out the special place of men among Mother India's "matriots." For a useful comparative discussion of "matriotic" discourse in modern Iranian nationalism, see Najmabadi 2005.

6. The quotation is from Axel 2001, 149. For a discussion of the deployment of the trope of "men with a capital M" in later twentieth-century Hindu nationalist practices, see Brosius 2005, 233–77.

7. See Mulvey 1989, 19. For a useful evaluation of Mulvey's reading for "gendered spectatorship" in India, see Uberoi 2006, 13–16.

8. Sedgwick 1985, 29; my emphasis. Abigail Solomon-Godeau rightly reminds us that for Sedgwick "the rivalries that foster powerful bonds between men need not have anything to do with sexual desire" (1997, 48–50).

9. Prabhu Dayal, who appears to have been based in the north Indian city of Kanpur in the 1930s, also painted the proscribed *Bharat Uddhar*, which is much discussed in recent scholarship (Pinney 2004, 114). He also produced several other images of Gandhi's interactions with Viceroy Irwin (see Neumayer and Schelberger 2008, 122–23).

10. Gandhi's "eleven points demand," as articulated in his letter to Irwin and pictured here, was a heterogeneous set of grievances ("the substance of Independence") reflecting various class and business interests. Of these only two were typically "Gandhian" concerns: a fifty percent reduction in the tax burden on the peasant, and the abolition of the salt tax and the British monopoly on salt production. When the viceroy declined his demands, Gandhi focused on one of the eleven points articulated in this letter, and he launched the Salt March in March 1930 that catapulted him to global visibility.

11. I adapt the term "big men" from the anthropologists Mattison Mines and Vijayalakshmi Gourishankar, who use it to develop a model of leadership and status building through "the redistribution of benefits, [the leader's] generosity as a bro-

ker, and [the leader's] prestige" (1990, 763). Some women can also be "big men." See also figure 95, in which the artist C. R. Krishnaswami shows the "big men" of India looming large over the people of India miniaturized at their feet, as well as over their wives (Kasturba Gandhi and Kamala Nehru), who are reduced to heads placed within mini-roundels.

12. The print must have been published sometime after Gandhi's death on January 30, 1948, for it includes a suggestive halo around his head and inscribes the following words from one of his last speeches: "'There is no difference of outlook between Sardar, Panditji, and myself'"—Mahatmaji's Prayer Speech of 20–1–1948").

13. Most noticeably Muhammad Ali Jinnah (1876–1948), one of the most important leading men of Indian politics from the early years of the twentieth century, does not appear in the company of the carto-graphed Mother India (for some examples of how he appears in postcolonial popular and patriotic art in Pakistan and India, see Dadi 2007 and Neumayer and Schelberger 2008, 129–31). Indeed, other than the anonymous Muslim body represented invariably by a fez-capped head (Amin 2000), Muslim men who generally appear in patriotic pictures in association with Bharat Mata are "loyalists" associated with Gandhi and the Congress such as Maulana Abul Kalam Azad (1888–1958) and Khan Abdul Ghaffar Khan (1890–1988) (see, for example, figures 28, 38, and 79), and an associate of Bhagat Singh's called Ashfaqullah (figure 118). For a recent analysis of how Muslim identity has been forged and circulated in popular South Asian visual culture, see Freitag 2007. The absence of Bharat Mata or even the map of India in the imagery she considers is worth noting.

14. As I have already noted, earlier in the century and especially prior to the rise of Gandhian nationalism, Bharat Mata is pictured as an activist figure, poised for battle in her own right (see, for example, figures 14–16).

15. Pinney 1997, 847. The rather androgynous-looking female figure in figure 79 is most likely Vijayalakshmi Pandit (1900–1990), Nehru's younger sister and India's envoy to the United Nations soon after independence. I thank Kavita Singh for this identification.

16. Also inscribed across the poster are slogans associated with Bose, "Jai Hind" (Victory to India) and "Challo Dilli" (Onward to Delhi). In spite of these phrases and in spite of the presence of Bose in this picture, he did not participate in the Quit India movement to demand immediate independence (which was launched in August 1942 under the leadership of Gandhi), although he did endorse it in a speech from Europe.

17. These pictures are reproduced in Baros 1949 (no. 214) and in Sen 2002, 39. Geeti Sen unfortunately misreads this photograph as representing a shackled Bharat Mata whose "gaunt feet appear near the southern tip of the peninsula."

18. Inscribed in Devanagari at the bottom of the pedestal are the words of one of

Gandhi's favorite hymns in praise of Lord Rama. Curiously, the critical territory of Kashmir is flattened almost beyond recognition on the map.

19. Such pictures also remind me of Derrida's insistence that "unlike the complement . . . the supplement is an 'exterior addition'" (1976, 145). As such, it is vulnerable to being dispensed with.

20. These sketches might have been inspired by Desai's participation in Gandhi's Salt March to Dandi. Desai (1907–1980) was influenced by the famous Bengali artist Nandlal Bose with whom he studied and worked for a while after his apprenticeship under the Gujarati artist Ravi Shankar Rawal. Later in his life, Desai provided art decoration and set design for over sixty Hindi commercial films, working with some famous producers and directors (Jyotindra Jain, personal communication with the author, July 20, 2008).

21. This has been reprinted in Trivedi 2003, figure 1. In a cartoon titled "Spinning a Web" Gandhi is shown sitting at a loom; as he weaves, the pattern of the outline map of India (with Sri Lanka thrown in as well) becomes manifest. (The cartoon is reprinted in Durga Das 1970, 99; I have not been able to ascertain its date or source.) See also Ramaswamy 2008.

22. For a more detailed analysis of how the Mahatma's death is visually likened to Jesus's martyrdom, see Ramaswamy 2008.

23. The title of this print suggests a verbal pairing of Bharat Mata and Gandhi as a parental unit of the nation, although clearly this is no routine family given the reversal of gender dominance suggested by the fact that it is "the mother" who blesses "the father."

24. For a deeper discussion of the context of this particular imaging, see Ramaswamy 2008.

25. For a complication of this argument, see chapter 6.

26. See also Neumayer and Schelberger 2008, 151–78, for another discussion of popular visual interest in the age of Nehru.

27. For a photograph from the 1930s that shows this print on display in the Karachi office of Brijbasi, see Pinney 2004, 98.

28. A copy of this print is in the personal collection of Urvashi Butalia, New Delhi.

29. For a detailed historical biography of this important figure, see Gordon 1990. This exemplary study does not, however, analyze the popular pictorial productions around this fascinating figure (although it alludes to them in passing on several occasions). Bose rose to prominence in Indian nationalist politics after his return from Cambridge, England, in 1921. Known for his radical socialist politics, he was elected president of the Congress in 1938, and then abortively in 1939. A growing ideological disagreement with Gandhi, however, led to his alienation from the Congress, and in 1941 he left India to pursue alliances with Britain's Axis enemies (note the appearance of Hitler with Bose in *Life of Subash* [figure 99]). He died in

a plane crash off Taiwan in August 1945, although the denial of his death is part of his continuing mystique.

30. The publisher put out two versions of the same poster, one with the title in English and the other in Hindi.

31. See, for example, Pinney 2004, plate 31.

32. In Brojen's *Abhayer Dan* (Grant of fearlessness) which bears the date of 1946, the artist features a four-armed Bharat Mata, halo around her head and holding the Gandhian flag, handing over a sword (painted in the three colors of the national banner) to Bose who kneels before her (in uniform and shiny black boots); two Hindu deities look on from the heavens above (Larson, Pal, and Smith 1997, plate 48).

33. For Gandhi's use of this phrase and an analysis of the complex ideological and personal tensions between these three big men, see Gordon 1990, 374–440.

34. The resonance of the word *santan* with Bankim Chandra's use of it for the dispassionate devotee of the mother and motherland in his *Anandamath* would not have been lost on at least the educated Bengali viewer of this print. For a discussion of this term, see Lipner 2005, 32–33.

35. This print can be found at the Smith Poster Archive at Syracuse University (No. 2114).

36. As the Irish-born Sister Nivedita, a contemporary observer of the Indian art scene, wrote in the early years of the twentieth century: "One can hardly go down the Chitpore Road [in Calcutta] without catching sight of one of these [pictures of the Madonna and Child]. Now it is clear that in this case it is the intimate humanity of the motive, with the bright and simple colour, that appeals to the humble owner. A barrier to his sympathy lies in the foreignness of the subject. He knows the names of the two characters, it is true, but very little about them. He cannot imagine their daily life together. He knows no stories of *that* Divine Childhood! Yet, it is after all a mother and her child, and the whole world understands. A thousand incidents of every day are common to these and their like everywhere. So the human in the great work redeems the local. But let us suppose an equally great masterpiece, equally simple and direct and full of the mingling of stateliness and tender intimacy, to have for its subject an *Indian* mother and her babe. Will it be more loved, or less by its devotee?" (1967, 3: 6).

37. See Pinney 2004, 156–58, for a discussion of this artist's lineage and work.

38. In the Indian context, the earliest known examples of historically known men standing in a similar fashion on a terrestrial globe are from the seventeenth-century Mughal atelier (see Ramaswamy 2007a).

39. See Pinney 2004, 142–44, for a discussion of a similar chromolithograph by Dinanath Walli called *Evolution of Gandhiji*, in which he compares such prints to bazaar images of Vishnu surrounded by his cycle of divine incarnations (*avatar*).

In *Gandhi Jivani* (Life of Gandhi) published by Hemchandra Bhargava, blood from the Mahatma's bullet-marked chest drips down to the land below, which is not inscribed on a globe but rather rendered as a verdant green patch. Interestingly, in a recent incarnation of this same format used as a school chart, Gandhi stands on a globe with a halo around his head and the palms of his hands folded in a gesture of obeisance. He is clearly dead—his memorial occupies one of the vignettes arranged around the central image of him on the globe—but the manner of his violent death goes unremarked (Rao, Geetha, and Wolf 2001, 94). For a rare print by the Kanpur-based Shyam Sunder Lal that shows Gandhi's assassin Nathuram Godse performing the act, see Neumayer and Schelberger 2008, plate 253.

40. Given the importance of this event in its own time, and especially subsequently, the scholarship on Bhagat Singh is surprisingly rather poor and mostly hagiographical, but see Noorani 2001; Habib 2007; and Singh 2007. Bhagat was born in a Punjabi village in a family that had already demonstrated its patriotic allegiances; one of his uncles apparently started a secret organization called the Bharat Mata Society in the early years of the twentieth century, and several kinsmen, including his father, had been imprisoned at various times for political activities. In Bhagat's own public utterances and private musings, Bharat Mata is rarely invoked (although see a letter attributed to him when he was a teenager in which he declares that he is willing "to sacrifice everything for [Bharat Mata's] sake" (quoted in Noorani 2001, 11). In 1919, soon after the massacre in Amritsar's Jallianwala Bagh that proved to be a turning point for Gandhi's loyalism, Bhagat reportedly kissed "the earth sanctified by the martyrs' blood and brought back home a little of the [blood] soaked soil" (10; see also McLain 2009, 181–82). Bhagat was a key member of the radical Hindustan Republic Association (founded in 1923, and renamed in 1928 as the Hindustan Republican Socialist Army); its manifesto declared, "The food on which the tender plant of liberty thrives is the blood of the martyr" (quoted in Hale 1974, 218). Bhagat was an admirer of Rousseau, Marx, and Lenin rather than a devotee of Mother India, despite patriotic art's attempts to visualize him as one of her own. Rather than the slogans "vande mataram" or "Bharat Mata ki jai," the slogan with which he is most associated is "Inquilab zindabad!" (Long live revolution!).

41. See also the useful discussion in Pinney 2004, 128–33, 168–80, of the work of artists such as the Kanpur-based Roopkishore Kapur (1893–1978), and Yogendra Rastogi and Hasan Raza Raja (b. 1937), both of Meerut, who specialized in such images and who inspired others to produce such prints as well.

42. The earliest known image of martyrdom for Bharat Mata is possibly a painting from 1906 by a Bengali academic artist, Avinash Chandra Chattopadhyay, called *Nirjatite Ashirvad* (Blessings amidst torture), in which a young man Chittaranjan Guha stoically bears the beatings of the colonial police: "The hero stood firm and unmoving, showered with heavenly blessings by the motherland, who appears

as goddess Durga" (Guha-Thakurta 1992 196). Pictures of "martyrs" like Prafulla Chaki and Khudiram Bose began circulating from 1908 soon after their deaths and were frequently proscribed (Samanta 1995, 2: 146–48).

43. The first part of the title in Hindi may be translated as "Offering of the Shackled Mother India." The (second) Lahore Conspiracy Case of 1929–1930 was mounted by the colonial state against those implicated in the assassination of a British police official named J. P. Sanders in Lahore on December 17, 1928. One of the most contentious political events of the late colonial period, the judgment delivered by a Special Tribunal in October 1930 sentenced three men (Bhagat Singh, SukhDev, and Rajguru) to death. Seven others were transported for life, and two men were given shorter terms of imprisonment (Noorani 2001). With astonishing specificity, all these men are identified by name in the print.

44. See also Brosius 2005, 258–61, 322–23, for an interesting discussion of "images of headless 'extreme nationalism.'"

45. A Lucknow-based publisher, Bharat Bhusan Press, issued a similar print in which Yatindranath Das's sacrifice is identified (by the title) as *Azadi ki peheli bhent* (Freedom's first offering).

46. For more about Rajguru and Sukhdev and their role in the so-called Lahore conspiracy case, see Noorani 2001.

47. The print is possibly modeled on a painting done in the 1930s by Roopkishore Kapur that might have been printed as a chromolithograph. We learn from Kapur's grandson that "the day Bhagat Singh was hanged, [Kapur] painted in a day [a picture] of Bhagat Singh beheaded, giving his head on a plate to Bharat Mata. Bharat Mata is weeping. He painted it and [displayed it in Sambal] and shouted Bande Mataram [Homage to mother] and he was taken by the police and was imprisoned for one or two years" (quoted in Pinney 2004, 128).

48. For an earlier version of this image, titled in English *Bhagat Singh Martyr*, see Neumayer and Schelberger 2008, plate 229.

49. This may well have been used as a recruitment poster by the paramilitary organization National Cadet Corps (Uberoi 2006 66). The acronym NCC appears on the bottom left of the print.

50. Jean Philippe Vogel includes detailed discussions as well as plates of such imagery, and he argues as well that by the early second millennium CE "the sacrifice of one's own head was a well-known motif. The deity to whom this supreme sacrifice is made is always a goddess" (1931, 543). See also Harle 1963. For a discussion of medieval Tamil accounts of "fierce" self-sacrifice by male devotees of Lord Shiva, see Hudson 1989. For a detailed textual and ethnographic analysis of decapitation and self-mutilation rites in the Tamil cult of the goddess Draupadi, see Hiltebeitel 1988.

51. See Fenech 2000, 157–77; see also Brosius 2005, 322–23.

52. See McLeod 1991, figures 53 and 38–40; Fenech 2000, 95–99; and Axel 2001, 139–40.

53. I borrow the notion of "visual pedagogy" from Antoine de Baecque's work on late-eighteenth-century France in which he argues that images of the wounded body of the martyrs of the revolution are repeatedly deployed in paintings and prints in order to "to make compassion arise," to "open the path of political awareness" in the community, and to produce a ritualized call to political action (1997, 281–307).

54. The venerable Lajpat Rai's presence among these young martyrs is anomalous, but it was his death in 1928 at the hands of the colonial police that sparked off the chain of events that eventually led to Bhagat's execution. For brief discussions of the other men named in this print and their role in a clandestine economy of bomb making, transporting explosives, plotting to assassinate key colonial officials, and so forth, see Noorani 2001.

55. Quoted in the epigraph to Fenech 2000.

56. See Pinney 2004, figure 102. I have yet to see Gandhi's sacrifice represented in this picture-world as decapitation.

57. For a further discussion of the mobilization of this imagery, especially in recent Hindu nationalist visual practices, see Brosius 2005, 256–58. On Raja's patriotic visual oeuvre, see Pinney 2004, 174–80; and Singh and Singh 2003, 122.

58. Here I am paraphrasing from Lloyd 1993, 73.

59. I thank Urvashi Butalia for drawing this image to my attention. *Organiser* published similar images of the map of India under attack over the next few years (in its issues of August 21, 1947; January 21, 1952; and March 26, 1962). Notwithstanding these images, I concur with Christopher Pinney's observation that "the trauma of Partition was never visually represented by the commercial picture production industry" (2004, 146). Indeed, as I have repeatedly noted, many of the productions of barefoot cartography are in denial over this historic event.

60. For another example from 1947 from the Marathi press of a cartoon showing the map of India under attack, see Kaur 2003, 241. In recent years under the force and pressure of a resurgent Hindu nationalism, many more such pictures of the map under direct attack have started to appear in print (example, Kaur 2003, 240). An incendiary image disseminated on the Web sometime in the 1990s by the Hindu nationalist publisher Arvind Ghosh shows Bharat Mata stabbed in the chest by four men representing Islam, Christianity, Marxism, and the English language. From her stabbed wounds blood spurts across her white sari, and her face is contorted with pain (and possibly anger?). I thank David Smith for alerting me to this image (see also Smith 2003, 184–86).

61. See also Pinney 2004, figure 141.

1. Tagore 2005, 73–74. For the context of this quote, see chapter 5.

2. I borrow this phrase from Uberoi 2000.

3. This formulation is based on my reading of Menon and Bhasin 1998. In this oral history of the horrific memories regarding the partition of the subcontinent retained by women who had lived through that catastrophic territorial event, the authors write, "Each time we asked the women we were speaking to whether they would die for their country, we got an elliptical response" (230). A Sikh woman named Taran even lamented, "As a woman, if I cannot call a home my own, if my home is not mine, how can a country be mine?" (248). Taran's lament echoes an earlier formulation by Virgina Woolf in her anti-fascist and pacifist book-length essay *Three Guineas* (1938): "As a woman, I have no country. As a woman I want no country. As a woman my country is the whole world" (Woolf 1998, 313).

4. See Landes 2001, 16. I also take my cue from Griselda Pollock (1983) who writes that a feminist analysis cannot be additive or compensatory but has to undertake a thorough-going critique of art history.

5. For the most perceptive feminist analysis of Sher-Gil's life and work, see Kapur 2000, especially pp. 3–17. Kapur draws our attention to Amrita's "intelligent masquerade as the oriental/modern/native woman" (302). See also Dalmia 2006; Mitter 2007, 45–65; and Sundaram et al. 1972.

6. These quotes are drawn from Amrita's autobiographical musings (see Sher-Gil 1942, 1971a, 1971b).

7. Quoted in Anand 1989, 1.

8. Quoted in Sher-Gil 1942, 93. As Baldoon Dhingra, a family friend of Amrita's, observed, "She felt like Tagore that India was 'where the tiller is tilling the hard ground and where the path-maker is breaking stones. He is with them in sun and in shower, and his garment is covered with dust.' But much more than that she wanted, again with Tagore, to have people, 'put off the holy mantle to come down on the dusty soil'" (1965, iii).

9. Sundaram et al. 1972, 95, 132. The painting was included in an exhibition of Amrita's work that was shown in the imperial summer capital of Simla in September 1936. It was also part of a traveling exhibition of her work that toured different cities in India around that time (Vivan Sundaram, personal communication with the author, August 2006). Later her modernist sensibilities appear to have been embarrassed by the pathos implicit in her portrayal of Mother India (Mitter 2007, 63).

10. The definitive analysis of the global reception of Mayo's work and the controversies it sparked off in India, especially between mid-1927 and the end of 1929, is given in Sinha 2006. Sinha does not discuss Amrita's painting in this connection.

11. Quoted in Shetty 1995, 61 (emphasis mine).

12. The letter is dated April 6, 1937 (Nehru Memorial Museum and Library, New Delhi, Nehru Papers, Vol. 94: 5502).

13. These words were used by Mehboob Khan in a letter introducing his film to the president of the India (quoted in Chatterjee 2002, 74).

14. There is nothing in the documented evidence that I have seen that suggests that Mehboob Khan was aware of Amrita's work. However, he clearly thought of his film as a "challenge" to Mayo's notorious *Mother India* (Chatterjee 2002, 20; Sinha 2006, 248–50). Sinha observes that with the film's phenomenal success, "the ghost of Katherine Mayo was eventually exorcised from the most famous nationalist catch-phrase" (248). For a detailed analysis of the making of the film and for biographical details about its Gujarati Muslim producer-director, see Chatterjee 2002. Although no single work details the appearance of Bharat Mata in Indian cinema prior to and after Mehboob's *Mother India*, for some suggestive leads see Baskaran 1981; and Dwyer and Patel 2002. In the course of a brief analysis of films housed in the National Film Archives in Pune in 2001, I was able to track the appearance of the carto-graphed mother/goddess in hit films such as *Tyagabhoomi* (Tamil, 1939); *Kismet* (Hindi, 1943), *Shaheed* (Hindi, 1966), and *Hindustan Ki Kasam* (Hindi, 1997).

15. Quoted in Chatterjee 2002, 31.

16. It is tempting to argue that Mehboob Khan's Muslimness might have something to do with this displacement, but I hesitate to do this considering that some other artists who I have considered here—Ustad Allah Bukhsh, H. R. Raja, and Maqbool Fida Husain—are also devout Muslims who have not hesitated to picture Bharat Mata as a goddess. It is more likely that Mehboob's nonconformist, realist, and possibly leftist filmic inclinations account for this refiguring of Mother India for the new nation-building secular project of industrialization and development (Shetty 1995, 59–60).

17. See Roy 1999 for a compelling analysis of the emergence of Nargis as a "national icon," precisely on the basis of playing the title role in *Mother India*, and her complex negotiation of her Muslim identity in postcolonial India.

18. Quoted in Roy 1999, 160.

19. Quoted in Chattejee 2002, 58.

20. Quoted in Chatterjee 2002, 22–23.

21. I have benefited here from Parama Roy's sharp examination of the question, "How does the Other become the icon that represents nationness?" (1999, 154). Indeed, the very naming of the title character as Radha (rather than Durga, Bhawani, or Vijaya) moves "Mother India" into a very different realm of subversive possibilities, for Radha is widely known across India from numerous myths and legends as the childless, adulterous woman who yearns for union with the libertine lord Krishna. She is possibly Hindu India's frankest erotic and sensuous (divine) heroine and in

this regard, the very opposite of the de-sexualized Mother India of patriotic nationalist imagination, verbal and visual. I thank Sadan Jha for sharing his thoughts on this aspect of the film with me.

22. A decade after *Mother India*, Nargis acted in one more film in order to help out her brothers at a time of financial crisis (Roy 1999, 58–59).

23. See Ray 2002, 9. Much of Ray's work is based on Sarala's Bengali memoir *Jibaner Jharapata* (Fallen leaves from the tree of life) which is "often jumbled, confuse[s] certain dates, and occasionally [gives] the impression of being somewhat exaggerated" (ix). I have not seen this claim of co-creation mentioned by other scholarly authorities on "Vande Mataram," and Sisir Kumar Das even categorically states that the song's text "belongs to Bankim and its music to Tagore" (1984, 215).

24. See Bhattacharya 2003, 23–24, on the basis of Sarala's claim in her autobiography to have done this.

25. Quoted in Bhattacharya 2003, 24.

26. See Sarkar 1973, 304–5, 397, for a discussion of Sarala's leadership in these activities. In his influential official report on the "politico-criminal activities" that plagued the colonial state from 1907 to 1917, James Campbell Ker remarked that it was under Sarala's influence that the Suhrid Samiti turned from a nonpolitical body into "a dangerous center" in the east Bengal town of Mymensingh, and had to be banned in January 1909 (1917, 7). See also National Archives of India, Government of India, Home, Political (Secret), May 1909, Nos. 135–147 (Part A).

27. Quoted in Sarkar 1973, 470–71.

28. Quoted in Ray 2002, 11. The *Bangabasi* was carried away enough on one such occasion to ask, "Has goddess Durga appeared among us?" (quoted in Ray 2002, 102).

29. Quoted in Ray 2002, 79.

30. For a chromolithograph circa 1910 titled *The Light of Asia, Swami Vivekananda*, which shows him against the background of a world map, see Neumayer and Schelberger 2008, plate 13).

31. Sarkar 1973, 475–76. Note also Dipesh Chakrabarty's passing comment that "the Irish woman Nivedita's love for India or Indians could not be called 'nationalist' in the simple sense" (2000, 151). On cross-national exchanges between Irish and Indian nationalists, see Boehmer 2002.

32. Elleke Boehmer (2002, 34–125) offers a fascinating analysis of the manner in which the Irish-born Margaret came to "self-identify" with India, especially with the militant nationalism that emerged in Bengal around the swadeshi movement. Indeed, it was in this context that she developed a complex "cross-border" collaboration with Aurobindo as well as other influential ideologues of the time. See also Roy 1999, 120–27, for insights on how Nivedita subjected herself to "a complete makeover" in colonial India as she channeled her affective and libidinal relationship with Vivekananda into "love" for India.

33. Quoted in Boehmer 2002, 90–91. The mother's song "Vande Mataram" was in-

cluded in the daily prayers of the school for girls that Nivedita opened (mostly out of her own savings) in her home in north Calcutta in 1903 (Roy 1999, 126), and she also urged the chanting of its opening words in public as a means of building political solidarity (Boehmer 2002, 107).

34. This remarkable text also ends with the statement, "For that which is dearer to us than self, we long greatly to throw away our life, and this defeated sacrifice transforms all our work with energy. The whole of life becomes the quest of death" (35).

35. Nivedita 1967, 2: 429–31. Such statements clearly influenced at least one other Indian—namely the poet Subramania Bharati in the Tamil country.

36. Boehmer suggests that these utterances on Kali were critical to the process by which Nivedita attempted to transform herself into Hindu and Indian through "the excesses of the Mother" (2002, 67–74). Several of Nivedita's reflections on Kali as the quintessence of the Hindu conception of deity were systematized in her first book, published in London in 1900, called *Kali the Mother*—a text that has been credited with inspiring Aurobindo to compose his *Bhawani Mandir* in 1905 (Tripathi 1967, 64–65, 135).

37. The essay from which this quote is drawn was originally published in *Modern Review* in 1907.

38. The brief note was originally published in the August issue of *Prabasi* in 1906.

39. Nivedita was taking a swipe at one of Ravi Varma's well-known paintings of the classical heroine Shakuntala that was printed and circulated widely as an oleograph.

40. Quoted in Pravrajika Atmaprana 1961, 194–95.

41. Pravrajika Atmaprana 1961, 194–95. All subsequent writings on Nivedita's views on the flag quote from this particular source. The November 1909 issue of *Modern Review* reproduces another version of the thunderbolt flag that Pravrajika Atmaprana and others credit to Nivedita.

42. As related in Singh 1991, 23 (emphasis mine). For a facsimile, see Singh 1991, figure 14. See also Sarkar 1973, 307; and Virmani 2008, 53–55. Over the next four decades as various efforts were made to fashion a suitable flag for India, the logo map of the country was only occasionally proposed as an emblem for the national banner (Virmani 2008, 130, 147, 161, 174, 273, 281).

43. For accounts of Cama's activities in Europe, see Kaur 1968, 107–14; and Visram 2002, 152–54. A critical biography of this fascinating woman remains to be written.

44. National Archives of India, Home Department. Political-A. Proceedings, July 1913, Nos. 1–3. Criminal Intelligence Office. History Sheet of Madame Bhikhaji Rustom K. R. Cama. Reprinted in HFMU, Vol. 2 B 94/2. Note that this document has her year of birth as 1875 instead of circa 1861.

45. Quoted in Singh 1991, 26. This part of Bhikhaiji's speech is not reported in the gov-

ernment's "history sheet," and Singh does not give a proper source for this statement, which I have been unable to verify. If indeed Bhikhaiji uttered these words, this would have been one of the earliest instances when the mother's slogan was drawn into an emergent discourse of martyrdom for her nation and territory.

46. National Archives of India, Home Department. Political-A. Proceedings, July 1913, Nos. 1–3. Criminal Intelligence Office. History Sheet of Madame Bhikhaiji Rustom K. R. Cama. Reprinted in HFMU, Vol. 2 B 94/2. Cama is here alluding to the arrest of Hemchandra in Bengal in May 1908 for his role in the killing of two Englishwomen there (Sarkar 1973, 307; Heehs 1998, 76–83).

47. National Archives of India, Home Department. Political-A. Proceedings, July 1913, Nos. 1–3. Criminal Intelligence Office. History Sheet of Madame Bhikhaiji Rustom K. R. Cama. Reprinted in HFMU, Vol. 2 B 94/2. See also Ker 1917, 195–196.

48. British Library (APAC), EPP 1/13 (Proscribed Publications). This card might have been printed in the United States. The words "Resistance to Tyranny Is Obedience to God. B. S. Cama" are inscribed on the back of the postcard under "This Space for Correspondence." Other "seditious" postcards published by or associated with Cama (with the inscription "vande mataram" or with hymns to Mother India) were also proscribed (see, for example, EPP 1/36 and EPP 1/46 in the British Library's proscribed materials collection from India). For evidence that such "Bande Mataram" postcards circulated beyond Europe and the United States, see a letter postmarked April 2, 1915, written by an alarmed British official from Basrah and placed in a confidential file (IOR/L/PS/11/91).

49. National Archives of India, Home Department (Political): confidential (Part A), No. 88–91, December 1909.

50. The earlier *Bande Mataram*, associated with such important figures as Bipan Chandra Pal and Aurobindo, did not carry any visual traces of the Mother in this manner.

51. National Archives of India, Home Department. Political-A. Proceedings, July 1913, Nos. 1–3. Criminal Intelligence Office. History Sheet of Madame Bhikhaiji Rustom K. R. Cama. Reprinted in HFMU, Vol. 2 B 94/2.

52. Quoted in M. Sinha 2006, 49. I am grateful to Mrinalini Sinha for sharing a copy of this image.

53. Sarojini's poetic reputation rests on three anthologies, *The Golden Threshold* (1905), *The Bird of Time* (1912), and *The Broken Wing* (1917), which were collated and published in 1928 as *The Sceptred Flute: Songs of India*. For a thoughtful assessment and critique of these works, see Alexander 1985. A series of male mentors played critical roles in her life, and her poetic turn to patriotic politics was inspired by the Maharastrian Congress leader Gopal Krishna Gokhale who, in her own words, invited her one evening to "stand here with me, with the stars and hills for witness, and in their presence consecrate your life and your talent, your song and your speech,

your thought and your dream to the motherland. O poet, see visions from the hill tops and spread abroad the message of hope to the toilers in the valleys" (quoted in Naidu 1925, 22). For an intriguing analysis of Sarojini as a "mimic woman," complexly negotiating between her bourgeois English and nationalist Indian inclinations, see Roy 1999, 128–51.

54. Quoted in Forbes 1996, 134.

55. See Naidu 1928, 58, 180–81, for reprints of these poems.

56. Quoted in Pattabhi Sitaramayya 1935, 290.

57. Quoted in Forbes 1996, 94.

58. I thank Anne Feldhaus and Meera Kosambi for translating the Marathi inscriptions in this photograph.

59. For other examples, see Neumayer and Schelberger 2008, 75–76. In many of these examples the Rani is shown carrying her young boy in a pouch on her back, almost as if his presence legitimizes her actions as female warrior battling the British to restore *his* privileges (see also Lebra-Chapman 1986, 137–41; and McLain 2009, 79–81).

60. See also Pinney 2004, figure 166. For a useful discussion of collages like the one featuring Lakshmi in figure 135, see Jain 2003. On the Rani of Jhansi Regiment, see Forbes 1996, 212–14; and Lebra-Chapman 2008. Lakshmi Sahgal's remarkable memoir was edited and published in 1997, and it provides some fascinating reflections on a woman's experience of being an expatriate militant patriot in the heady mid-1940s.

61. It is also worth noting that Lakshmi's visage here visually echoes that of the cartographed Bharat Mata, who looks down on the assemblage of her devoted "officers." A pre-modern precedent for Lakshmi's martial persona might be sought in the so-called *virangana* ideal of the woman who embodies the qualities of male heroism (*viryam*). Typically, as Kathryn Hansen (1992) has shown, the virangana adopted male attire and other symbols of male martial authority. Hansen has also rightly argued that because *viryam* or heroism is always already male, "the problematic of a heroics of womanhood in India is inseparable from language and representation" (2). Nevertheless she documents the persistence of this category of woman across a wide variety of sources (mythological, historical, folk, and cinematic) if only as a subversive alternative to the dominant emphasis on female self-sacrifice and submissiveness.

62. Sarkar 1984, 99. A contemporary colonial official in Bengal in fact appears to "have lived in great fear of the woman terrorist in particular, who seemed to him to be deadlier than the male of her species" (quoted in Bose 1996, 145).

63. Although "photographs of the two girls along with pamphlets were printed on a massive scale by the Benu Press and circulated amongst revolutionaries across Bengal" (Mandal 1991, 37), they do not appear to have been a popular subject in

either the mainstream media or in barefoot cartographic productions. Nor do they appear in later works such as the *Amar Chitra Katha* comic books which did not shy away from stories of martial women as long as they had lived heroically and died valorously in the distant past (McLain 2009, 79–86).

64. See Bose 1996; Forbes 1996, 138–41; Sarkar 1984; and especially Mandal 1991. The quote appears in Bose 1996, 160; and in Mandal 1991, 41.

65. Quoted in Mandal 1991, 4; for details of the event, 88–96. The young Preeti was dressed as a soldier in man's clothing for the attack on the club. Tanika Sarkar, however, observes, "The woman terrorist in Bengal seemed to claim equality in an act of sacrifice at an extraordinary crisis point, but did not extend this to a claim for equality in political choice and action. Neither did she explicitly link up her action with any corresponding leap in domestic or family relations, or with a change in her life-style and role outside politics" (1984, 100).

66. Contemporary Bengali notables, who had formerly celebrated the militant woman in their fictional works, were quick to condemn such acts, with Rabindranath Tagore even characterizing them as "nightmarism" (quoted in Sarkar 1984, 100).

67. Here I am borrowing from James Elkins 1998, 241–66. The un-representable is "whatever is forbidden or considered dangerous for the eye, as well as whatever is thought to be beyond technique at any given moment or any given medium. The unrepresented constitutes 'another visible,' as Derrida says . . . a visible that cannot be shown, but can be imagined, and specifically imagined as a picture" (252). The "inconceivable" is that "which does not present itself to the imagination at all" and is outside the bounds of what can be even thought (259).

68. Indira was prime minister of India from January 1966 until March 1977, and then again from January 1980 until October 31, 1984. Her assassination by her two Sikh guards is widely held to have been in response to the Indian army's offensive against the holiest of Sikh shrines, the Golden Temple in Amritsar, in June 1984. For a political biography of Indira Gandhi with the revealing title "Mother India," see Gupte 1992. An insightful feminist analysis of the politics of representation that surround Indira may be found in Sunder Rajan 1993, 103–29.

69. For other such prints from this period, see Neumayer and Schelberger 2008, 181–192.

70. See Uberoi 1999–2000, 27–28; Pinney 2004, 131; and Jain 2005, 327.

71. In her recent analysis of the popular comic book series *Amar Chitra Katha*, Karline McLain briefly considers the visualizing of historical queens who acted as autonomous agents, even warriors who led troops on to the battlefield, but notes that "nearly all of the martial women featured in these comics came into power as regents, ruling the kingdom upon their husband's or father's death and on behalf of a juvenile male heir" (2009, 81). Although they are pictured as embodiments of martial heroism, their resistance is almost always "characterized in a 'helpmate' way,

so that women's actions were shown to be valuable precisely because they ena[ble] men to resist to the very end" (84). She also notes that female protagonists o[f] heroic variety are limited to ancient mythological and medieval historical wor[ld] and draws our attention to the absence of modern heroines (85–86). In the ____ twentieth century, powerful female leaders—such as J. Jayalalitha and Mayawati (with intriguing biographies as putatively single women), Sonia Gandhi (Indira's Italian-born daughter-in-law), and Benazir Bhutto in neighboring Pakistan—have become quite visible in public art. (For emergent work on some of these figures, see Dadi 2007; and especially Jacob 1997.) On the eve of the 2004 national elections, I saw on the streets of New Delhi several hoardings of Sonia Gandhi occupying a map of India, but have yet to see any similar ones for these other powerful women.

72. Inder Malhotra, an astute chronicler of the times, observes that soon after the war in 1971, "her countrymen—led, interestingly, by sophisticated leaders of opposition parties—hailed her as Durga, the eight-armed, tiger-riding, invincible goddess in the Hindu pantheon . . . Women, especially in villages, started worshipping her also as an incarnation of Shakti or female energy" (1989, 171). Parama Roy writes that when in later years a prominent journalist compared her estranged daughter-in-law (Maneka Gandhi) to Durga, Indira was "enraged" (1999 213).

73. For another pictorial example of the likening of Indira to Durga, see Sinha 1999, 123. See also Uberoi 2006, 65–66, for a discussion of the morphing of Indira into Durga in calendar art.

74. This is effectively the same image that Husain resurfaced many decades later in his controversial nude Bharat Mata (figure 3) and that may have also been resurrected in another painting from the 1970s (figure 52).

75. See Pal 1994, 130–31. Sotheby's recently auctioned a one-page document in Husain's handwriting (and dated to 1975) in which he gives us a sense of what might have compelled him to paint his canvas that he calls *India June '75: The Triptych in the Life of a Nation*. Over the years since he painted the triptych, Husain has prevaricated about the identity of the female body represented in it, indicating at first that it was Indira, but insisting in a later interview that she is Durga and Mother India, and not Indira at all. For a further discussion of these issues, see Ramaswamy 2010b.

76. So an influential journalist, member of parliamant, and fellow Muslim, Shamim A. Shamim, issued the following telling indictment in the *Illustrated Weekly of India*, one of India's leading English-language magazines: "I could not believe my eyes, for instance, when I saw a huge painting by the reputed artist, M. F. Husain, depicting Mrs. Gandhi as Durga, born out of the divinity of Emergency. Here was our greatest modern painter reducing himself to a courtier and dedicating his art to the 'Queen Empress.' What had India come to for a Husain to applaud the suppression

[Handwritten marginal notes:]

the role of mirror-of-the-nation. ... (T)he truest deepest motive ... [T]he role of mirror-of-the-nation. ... (T)he truest deepest motive ... why the declaration of a State of Emergency was the ... incredible discombobulation, the pulverizing, the smashing, the destroying upon me?... of the children at midn...

Salman Rushdie's "Midnight's Children":

ital. → "Indira is India and India is Indira ... but might she not have read her own father's letters to a midnight child, in which her own sloganized Centrality was denied, in which of freedom of expression? Did he not realise that he was not only killing himself but all the artists who revered him as their mentor?" (Shamim Ahmed Shamim, "Emergency: Who Were the Guilty?" *Illustrated Weekly of India*, May 22–28, 1977, 11). Incidentally, Shamim's essay includes the only published reproduction of the controversial triptych that I have been able to find.

77. See also Thomas 1989, 29. I thank Rosie Thomas for facilitating the acquisition of this image from the photographer Behroze Gandhy.

78. See, for example, Pal 1991, 176–77; and Siddiqui 2001, 210. See also the image housed at the Peabody Essex Museum Salem Massachusetts (No. E301550).

79. For more details, see Blurton 1989; and for another example, see Jain 2002.

80. I thank Srinivasacharya Kandala for translating the Telugu inscriptions in this and the other hoardings I discuss here. I also thank Raghu Rai for discussing with me the contexts in which he took these photographs.

81. For another shot of the same hoarding, possibly from an earlier moment when only the two women on the right are looking up at Mother Indira/India, one of them pointing directly at the bleeding female body, see Rai 2004, 21.

82. This photograph has been included in a collection of the century's most remarkable photographs published by the London-based Phaidon in 2002 as *Century: One Hundred Years of Human Progress, Regression, Suffering and Hope*.

83. For other photographs of deployments of similar images, see Rai 2004, 129, 142–43.

EPILOGUE: PICTORIAL HISTORY IN THE AGE OF THE WORLD PICTURE

1. Mahasweta Devi 1995, 93 (italics in original indicate words in English in the Bengali text). The author, in a later conversation with her translator in 1991, reiterates that "the sale of girls for rape still goes on. 'Douloti' is still true, and true for the rest of India. That is why I have ended the story like that. Douloti's bleeding, rotting carcass covers the entire Indian peninsula" (1995, xx).

2. This illustration is reprinted in Venkataraman 2001, 39.

3. This image can be found in Baros 1949, no. 214. (See also chapter 5, n. 17.)

4. I am grateful to G. Sundar of the Roja Muthiah Research Library, Chennai, for bringing this to my attention.

5. Quoted in Ramaswamy 2003, 184. By the time he penned these lines, Bharatidasan had turned from a votary of Bharat Mata to an antagonist, under the force of Dravidian and Tamil nationalism (Ramaswamy 1997, 204–6).

6. See Bayly 1996, esp. 284–313; and Cohn 1996, 6–8.

7. In a memorable example drawn from LePérouse's visit to Sakhalin in the 1780s, Latour argues that whereas the map drawn in the sand by the Chinese mapmaker who the French explorer meets will be washed away, that inscribed on paper and

taken back home possesses qualities of mobility and immutability that have consequences for the production of knowledge in European centers of calculation, for presenting absent things, and ultimately for establishing global empires.

8. See also in this regard James Scott's discussion of the scientific map as a classic exemplar of "state simplification" (1998, 11–52).

9. He goes on to write that "immutable does not mean that information is transferred unproblematically but that some features have to be maintained *in spite* of the mobility provided to them." It is important therefore to track "constant features through shifts in representation" (425–26).

10. In this regard, this book attempts to complicate a sweeping insistence by the influential theorist Partha Chatterjee that "Indians . . . like many other people, are . . . prepared to fight over maps" (2003, 291).

11. For my understanding of Heidegger's complex critique of Western ocularcentrism, I have benefited from Bolt 2004, 13–23; Casey 2002, 233–46; and Jay 1994, 269–75.

12. I borrow the phrase "fields of care" from Tuan 1977.

13. The undated letter (in Bengali) begins with Bose's praise of Durga, segues into an invocation of God (the selection quoted here), and then goes into rapture over the rivers and terrain of India before calling upon God to "come and resurrect us" and save the piteous "motherland." His own birth mother morphs into mother of the nation over the course of the long letter (20–22). Leonard Gordon speculates that the young Subhas was influenced, among others, by Bankim's *Anandmath* (1990, 34–35). I thank Sugata Bose for discussing the context of this letter.

14. See also Pinney 2004, 8, for a discussion of Mitchell's question in the Indian context.

15. I thank Christiane Brosius for alerting me to this image and for sharing it. See also Brosius 2005, 162–68.

REFERENCES

Agulhon, Maurice. 1980. *Marianne into Battle: Republican Imagery and Symbolism in France, 1789–1880*. Translated by J. Lloyd. Cambridge: Cambridge University Press.

Alexander, Meena. 1985. "Sarojini Naidu: Romanticism and Resistance." *Economic and Political Weekly* 20 (43): 68–71.

Allen, Brian. 1990. "From Plassey to Seringapatnam: India and British History Painting." In *The Raj: India and the British, 1600–1947*, edited by C. A. Bayly. London: National Portrait Gallery Publications.

Alpers, Svetlana. 1983. "The Mapping Impulse in Dutch Art." In *The Art of Describing: Dutch Art in the Seventeenth Century*. Chicago: University of Chicago Press.

Amin, Shahid. 2000. "Remembering the Musalman." In *Fusing Modernity: Appropriations of History and Political Mobilisation in South Asia*, edited by H. Kotani. Osaka, Japan: National Museum of Ethnology.

Anand, Mulk Raj. 1989. *Amrita Sher-Gil*. New Delhi: National Gallery of Modern Art.

Anderson, Benedict. 1991. *Imagined Communities: Reflections on the Origin and Spread of Nationalism*. 2nd ed. London: Verso.

Appadurai, Arjun. 1996. *Modernity at Large*. Minneapolis: University of Minnesota Press.

Atherton, Herbert M. 1974. *Political Prints in the Age of Hogarth: A Study of the Ideographic Representation of Politics*. Oxford: Clarendon Press.

Axel, Brian. 2001. *The Nation's Tortured Body: Violence, Representation, and the Formation of a Sikh "Diaspora."* Durham, N.C.: Duke University Press.

Babb, Lawrence A. 1981. "Glancing: Visual Interaction in Hinduism." *Journal of Anthropological Research* 37:387–401.

Baecque, Antoine de. 1997. *The Body Politic: Corporeal Metaphor in Revolutionary France, 1770–1800*. Translated by C. Mandell. Stanford: Stanford University Press.

Bagchee, Shyamal. 1998. "Augmented Nationalism: The Nomadic Eye of Painter M. F. Husain." *Asianart.com*, June 19.

Bagchi, Jasodhara. 1990. "Representing Nationalism: Ideology of Motherhood in Colonial Bengal." *Economic and Political Weekly (Review of Women's Studies)* 24 (42–43): 65–71.

Banerjea, Jitendra Nath. 1956. *The Development of Hindu Iconography.* 2nd ed. Calcutta: University of Calcutta. (Orig. pub. 1941.)

Banerjee, Mukulika, and Daniel Miller. 2003. *The Sari.* Oxford: Berg.

Banerjee, Sumanta. 2002. "The Ambiguities of Bharat Mata: A Bhadralok Goddess in Colonial Bengal." In *Logic in a Popular Form: Essays on Popular Religion in Bengal.* Calcutta: Seagull Books.

Banerji, Himani, Shahrzad Mojab, and Judith Whitehead, eds. 2001. *Of Property and Propriety: The Role of Gender and Class in Imperialism and Nationalism.* Toronto: University of Toronto Press.

Baron, Beth. 2005. *Egypt as a Woman: Nationalism, Gender, and Politics.* Berkeley: University of California Press.

Baros, Jan. 1949. *Mahatma Gandhi: Pictorial History of a Great Life.* 2nd ed. Calcutta: Gossain and Co.

Barrier, N. Gerald. 1974. *Banned: Controversial Literature and Political Control in British India, 1907–1947.* Columbia: University of Missouri Press.

Bartholomew, Richard, and Shiv S. Kapur. 1972. *Maqbool Fida Husain.* New York: H. N. Abrams.

Baskaran, S. Theodore. 1981. *The Message Bearers: The Nationalist Politics and the Entertainment Media in South India, 1880–1945.* Madras: Cre-A.

Bayly, C. A. 1996. *Empire and Information: Intelligence Gathering and Social Communication in India, 1780–1870.* Cambridge: Cambridge University Press.

Benei, Veronique. 2008. *Schooling Passions: Nation, History, and Language in Contemporary Western India.* Stanford: Stanford University Press.

Berger, John. 1972. *Ways of Seeing.* London: Penguin.

Bhabha, Homi. 1994. *The Location of Culture.* London: Routledge.

Bhattacharya, Sabyasachi. 2003. *Vande Mataram: The Biography of a Song.* New Delhi: Penguin.

Biggs, M. 1999. "Putting the State on the Map: Cartography, Territory and European State Formation." *Comparative Studies in Society and History* 41 (2): 77–95.

Biltcliffe, Pippa. 2005. "Walter Crane and the Imperial Federation Map Showing the Extent of the British Empire." *Imago Mundi* 57 (1): 63–69.

Blurton, Richard. 1989. "Continuity and Change in the Tradition of Bengali PaTa-Painting." In *The Sastric Tradition in Indian Arts,* edited by A. L. Dallapiccola. Stuttgart, Germany: Steiner.

Boehmer, Elleke. 2002. *Empire, the National, and the Postcolonial, 1890–1920: Resistance in Interaction.* Oxford: Oxford University Press.

Bolt, Barbara. 2004. *Art beyond Representation: The Performative Power of the Image.* London: I. B. Tauris.

Bose, Purnima. 1996. "Engendering the Armed Struggle: Women, Writing, and the

Bengali Terrorist Movement." In *Bodies of Writing, Bodies in Performance*, edited by T. Foster, C. Siegel, and E. E. Berry. New York: New York University Press.

Bose, Subhas Chandra. 1912–1913. "Mother India." In *The Essential Writings of Netaji Subhas Chandra Bose*, edited by S. K. Bose and S. Bose. Delhi: Oxford University Press.

Bose, Sugata. 1997. "Nation as Mother: Representations and Contestations of 'India' in Bengali Literature and Culture." In *Nationalism, Democracy and Development: State and Politics in India*, edited by S. Bose and A. Jalal. Delhi: Oxford University Press.

Brading, D. A. 2001. *Mexican Phoenix: Our Lady of Guadalupe: Image and Tradition across Five Centuries*. Cambridge: Cambridge University Press.

Brennan, Timothy. 1990. "The National Longing for Form." In *Nation and Narration*, edited by H. Bhabha. London: Routledge.

Brosius, Christiane. 1997. "Motherland in Hindutva Iconography." *The India Magazine of Her People and Culture* 17 (12): 22–28.

———. 2005. *Empowering Visions: The Politics of Representation in Hindu Nationalism*. London: Anthem Press.

———. 2006. "'I am a National Artist': Popular Art in the Sphere of Hindutva." In *Picturing the Nation: Iconographies of Modern India*, edited by R. Davis. New Delhi: Orient Longman.

Casey, Edward S. 2002. *Representing Place: Landscape Painting and Maps*. Minneapolis: University of Minnesota Press.

Chakrabarty, Dipesh. 2000. *Provincializing Europe: Postcolonial Thought and Historical Difference*. Princeton, N.J.: Princeton University Press.

Chakravarti, Uma. 1990. "Whatever Happened to the Vedic Dasi? Orientalism, Nationalism, and a Script for the Past." In *Recasting Women: Essays in Indian Colonial History*, edited by K. Sangari and S. Vaid. New Brunswick, N.J.: Rutgers University Press.

Chakravarty, Amiya, ed. 1961. *A Tagore Reader*. Boston: Beacon Press.

Chatterjee, Gayatri. 2002. *Mother India*. New Delhi: Penguin Books.

Chatterjee, Partha. 1989. "Colonialism, Nationalism, and Colonialized Women: The Contest in India." *American Ethnologist* 16 (4): 622–33.

———. 2003. "The Sacred Circulation of National Images." In *Traces of India: Photography, Architecture, and the Politics of Representation, 1850–1900*, edited by M. A. Pelizzari. New Haven: Yale Center for British Art; Ahmedabad: Mapin Publishing.

Chatterji, Bankim Chandra. 1906. *The Abbey of Bliss: A Translation of Bankim Chandra Chatterjee's Anandamath*. Translated by N. C. Sen-Gupta. Calcutta: Cherry Press.

———. 1941. *Dawn over India*. Translated and adapted from the Bengali by Basanta Koomar Roy. New York: Devin-Adair.

Chaudhuri, Rosinka. 2002. *Gentlemen Poets in Colonial Bengal: Emergent Nationalism and the Orientalist Project*. Calcutta: Seagull Books.

Chirol, Valentine. 1910. *The Indian Unrest*. London: Macmillan.

Chowdhury, Indira. 1998. *The Frail Hero and Virile History: Gender and the Politics of Culture in Colonial Bengal*. Delhi: Oxford University Press.

Cohn, Bernard S. 1996. *Colonialism and Its Forms of Knowledge: The British in India*. Princeton, N.J.: Princeton University Press.

Cosgrove, Denis. 2001. *Apollo's Eye: A Cartographic Genealogy of the Earth in Western Imagination*. Baltimore, Md.: Johns Hopkins University Press.

———. 2005. "Maps, Mapping, Modernity: Art and Cartography in the Twentieth Century." *Imago Mundi* 57 (1): 35–54.

Dadi, Iftikar. 2007. "Political Posters in Karachi, 1988–1999." *South Asian Popular Culture* 5 (1): 11–30.

Dalmia, Vasudha. 1997. *The Nationalization of Hindu Traditions: Bharatendu Harischandra and Nineteenth-Century Banaras*. Delhi: Oxford University Press.

Dalmia, Yasodhara. 2001. *The Making of Modern India Art: The Progressives*. New Delhi: Oxford University Press.

———. 2006. *Amrita Sher-Gil: A Life*. New Delhi: Viking and Penguin Books India.

Das, Sisir Kumar. 1984. "The Story of a Song." In *The Artist in Chains: The Life of Bankimchandra Chatterji*. New Delhi: New Statesman.

Datta, P. K., ed. 2003. *Rabindranath Tagore's "The Home and the World": A Critical Companion*. Delhi: Permanent Black.

Dave, J. H., C. L. Gheewala, A. C. Bose, R. P. Aiyer, and A. K. Majumdar. 1962. *Munshi: His Art and Work*. Vol. 1. Bombay: Shri Munshi Seventieth Birthday Citizens' Celebration Committee.

Davis, Richard H. 1997. *Lives of Indian Images*. Princeton, N.J.: Princeton University Press.

Dehejia, Vidya. 1997. "Issues of Spectatorship and Representation." In *Representing the Body: Gender Issues in Indian Art*, edited by V. Dehejia. New Delhi: Kali for Women, in association with the Book Review Literary Trust.

Del Bonta, Robert J. 1989. "Calendar Prints and Indian Tradition." In *Shastric Tradition in Indian Arts*, edited by A. L. Dallapiccola. Stuttgart: Steiner Verlag Weisbaden GmbH.

Derrida, Jacques. 1976. "That Dangerous Supplement." In *Of Grammatology*. Baltimore, Md.: Johns Hopkins University Press.

Dhavan, Rajeev. 2007. "Harassing Husain: Uses and Abuses of the Law of Hate." *Social Scientist* 35 (1–2): 16–60.

Dhingra, Baldoon. 1965. *Sher-Gil*. New Delhi: Lalit Kala Academy.

Dimock, Edward C. 1971. "The Symbol of the Motherland in Tagore's Patriotic Songs." In *Studies on Bengal: Papers Presented at the Seventh Annual Bengal Studies Conference, University of Minnesota, Minneapolis, May 28–30, 1971*. East Lansing, Mich.: Asian Studies Center, Michigan State University.

Dresser, Madge. 1989. "Britannia." In *Patriotism: The Making and Unmaking of British National Identity*, edited by R. Samuel. London: Routledge.

Durga Das, ed. 1970. *Gandhi in Cartoons*. Ahmedabad: Navjivan Publishing House.

Dutta, Krishna, and Andrew Robinson. 1995. *Rabindranath Tagore: The Myriad Minded Man*. New York: St. Martin's Press.

Dwivedi, Sharda Shankar, and Direndranath Singh. forthcoming. "Shri Bharatmata Mandir." In *Rashtranirmaata Shri Shivprasad Gupta*. Varanasi: Gyan Mandal Limited.

Dwyer, Rachel, and Divia Patel. 2002. *Cinema India: The Visual Culture of Hindi Film*. New Brunswick, N.J.: Rutgers University Press.

Eck, Diana. 1981. *Darsan: Seeing the Divine Image in India*. Chambersburg, Pa.: Anima Books.

———. 1982. *Banaras: City of Light*. Princeton, N.J.: Princeton University Press.

———. 1999. "The Imagined Landscape: Patterns in the Construction of Hindu Sacred Geography." In *Tradition, Pluralism, and Identity: In Honour of T. N. Madan*, edited by V. Das, D. Gupta, and P. Uberoi. New Delhi: Sage.

Edney, Matthew H. 1997. *Mapping an Empire: The Geographical Construction of British India, 1765–1843*. Chicago: University of Chicago Press.

———. 2003. "Bringing India to Hand: Mapping Empires, Denying Spaces." In *The Global Eighteenth Century*, edited by F. Nussbaum. Baltimore: Johns Hopkins University Press.

Elkins, James. 1998. *On Pictures and the Words That Fail Them*. Cambridge: Cambridge University Press.

Enloe, Cynthia. 1989. *Bananas, Beaches and Bases: Making Feminist Sense of International Politics*. London: Pandora Press.

Falk, Nancy Auer. 2002. "Mata, Land and Line." In *Invoking Goddesses: Gender Politics in Indian Religion*, edited by N. Chitgopekar. Delhi: Shakti Books.

Fenech, Louis E. 2000. *Martyrdom in the Sikh Tradition: Playing the "Game of Love."* Delhi: Oxford University Press.

Forbes, Geraldine. 1996. *Women in Modern India*. Cambridge: Cambridge University Press.

Freitag, Sandria B. 2001. "Visions of the Nation: Theorizing the Nexus between Creation, Consumption and Participation in the Public Sphere." In *Pleasure and the Nation: The History, Politics and Consumption of Public Culture in India*, edited by R. Dwyer and C. Pinney. New Delhi: Oxford University Press.

———. 2007. "South Asian Ways of Seeing, Muslims Ways of Knowing: The Indian Muslim Niche Market in Posters." *Indian Economic and Social History Review* 44 (3): 297–331.

Gadgil, Amarendra Laxman. 1978. *Vande Mataram (The Song Perennial): Vande Mataram Centenary Special Publication*. Pune: Mangala A. Gadgil for Gokul Masik Prakashan.

Gandelman, Claude. 1991. "Bodies, Maps, Texts." In *Reading Pictures, Viewing Texts.* Bloomington: Indiana University Press.

Gandhi, Mohandas. 1958. "Speech at Bharat Mata Mandir, Banaras." In *The Collected Works*, 63:388–89. Delhi: Government of India, Publications Division.

Ghose, Aurobindo. 1999. *Sri Aurobindo: Translations.* Vol. 5 of *The Complete Works of Sri Aurobindo.* Pondicherry: Sri Aurobindo Ashram Publication Department.

———. 2002. "Bhawani Mandir." In *Bande Mataram: Political Writings and Speeches, 1890–1908.* Vols. 6 and 7 of *The Complete Works of Sri Aurobindo.* Pondicherry: Sri Aurobindo Ashram. (Orig. pub. 1905.)

Gole, Susan. 1983. *India within the Ganges.* New Delhi: Jayaprints.

Gordon, Leonard A. 1990. *Brothers against the Raj: A Biography of Indian Nationalists Sarat and Subhas Chandra Bose.* New York: Columbia University Press.

Goswami, Manu. 2004. *Producing India: From Colonial Economy to National Space.* Chicago: University of Chicago Press.

Groseclose, Barbara. 1995. *British Sculpture and the Company Raj: Church Monuments and Public Statuary in Madras, Calcutta, and Bombay to 1858.* Newark, N.J.: University of Delaware Press.

Guha-Thakurta, Tapati. 1992. *The Making of a New "Indian" Art: Artists, Aesthetics and Nationalism in Bengal, c. 1850–1920.* Cambridge: Cambridge University Press.

———. 1995. "Visualizing the Nation." *Journal of Arts and Ideas* 27–28: 7–40.

———. 2004. *Monuments, Objects, Histories: Institutions of Art in Colonial and Postcolonial India.* New Delhi: Permanent Black.

Gupta, Charu. 2002. *Sexuality, Obscenity, Community: Women, Muslims, and the Hindu Public in Colonial India.* New York: Palgrave.

Gupta, Shivprasad. 1983a. "Sankshipth Atma-Katha." In *Kashi Vidyapith Heerak Jayanthi: Abhinandan Granth.* Varanasi: Kashi Vidyapith.

———. 1983b. "Shri Bharatmata Mandir." In *Kashi Vidyapith Heerak Jayanthi: Abhinandan Granth.* Varanasi: Kashi Vidyapith.

Gupte, Pranay. 1992. *Mother India: A Political Biography of Indira Gandhi.* New York: Charles Scribner's Sons.

Gutwirth, Madelyn. 1992. *Twilight of the Goddesses: Women and Representation in the French Revolutionary Era.* New Brunswick, N.J.: Rutgers University Press.

Habermas, Jürgen. 1983. "Modernity: An Incomplete Project." In *The Anti-aesthetic: Essays on Postmodern Culture*, edited by H. Foster. Port Townsend, Wash.: Bay Press.

Habib, S. Irfan. 2007. *To Make the Deaf Hear: Ideology and Programme of Bhagat Singh and His Comrades.* Gurgaon: Three Essays Collective.

Hale, H. W., ed. 1974. *Political Trouble in India, 1917–1937.* Rev. ed. Allahabad: Chugh Publications.

Hamilton, Walter. 1820. *A Geographical, Statistical and Historical Description of Hindostan and the Adjacent Countries.* Vol. 1. London: John Murray.

Hansen, Kathryn. 1992. "Heroic Modes of Women in Indian Myth, Ritual and History: The Tapasvini and the Virangana." In *The Annual Review of Women in World Religions*. Vol. 2. Edited by A. Sharma and K. Young. Albany: State University of New York Press.

Hansen, Thomas. 1999. *The Saffron Wave: Democracy and Hindu Nationalism in Modern India*. Princeton, N.J.: Princeton University Press.

Hardgrove, Anne. 1999. "Sati Worship and Marwari Public Identity." *Journal of Asian Studies* 58 (3): 723–52.

Harle, James C. 1963. "Durga: Goddess of Victory." *Artibus Asiae* 26 (3): 237–46.

Harley, J. B. 2001. *The New Nature of Maps: Essays in the History of Cartography*. Baltimore, Md.: Johns Hopkins University Press.

Harley, J. B., and David Woodward. 1987. "Preface." In *Cartography in Prehistoric, Ancient, and Medieval Europe and the Mediterranean*, edited by J. B. Harley and David Woodward. Chicago: University of Chicago Press.

Harvey, William. 1868. *Geographical Fun: Humourous Outlines of Various Countries, with an Introduction and Descriptive Lines*. London: Hodder and Stoughton.

Heehs, Peter. 1993. *The Bomb in Bengal: The Rise of Revolutionary Terrorism in India, 1900–1910*. Delhi: Oxford University Press.

———. 1998. *Nationalism, Terrorism, Communalism: Essays in Modern Indian History*. Delhi: Oxford University Press.

Heidegger, Martin. 1977. "The Age of the World Picture." In *The Question Concerning Technology and Other Essays*. New York: Garland.

Helgerson, Richard. 1986. "The Land Speaks: Cartography, Chorography, and Subversion in Renaissance England." *Representations* 16:51–85.

Helmreich, Anne. 2003. "Domesticating Britannia: Representations of the Nation in *Punch*: 1870–1880." In *Art, Nation, and Gender: Ethnic Landscapes, Myths, and Mother Figures*, edited by T. Cusack and S. Bhreathnach-Lynch. Aldershot, U.K.: Ashgate Publishing.

Higham, John. 1990. "Indian Princess and Roman Goddess: The First Female Symbols of America." *Proceedings of the American Antiquarian Society* 100:45–79.

Hiltebeitel, Alfred. 1988. *The Cult of Draupadi*. 2 vols. Chicago: University of Chicago Press.

Honour, Hugh. 1975. "A Land of Allegory." In *The New Golden Land: European Images of America from the Discoveries to the Present Time*. New York: Pantheon.

Horkheimer, Max, and Theodor W. Adorno. 1972. *Dialectic of Enlightenment*. Translated by J. Cumming. New York: Seabury.

Hudson, Dennis. 1989. "Violent and Fanatical Devotion among the Nayanars: A Study in the Periya Puranam of Cekkilar." In *Criminal Gods and Demon Devotees: Essays on the Guardians of Popular Hinduism*, edited by A. Hiltebeitel. Albany: State University of New York Press.

Hunt, Lynn. 1992. *The Family Romance of the French Revolution*. Berkeley: University of California Press.

Ilavarasu, R. 1990. *Intiya Vitutalai Iyakattil Paratitasan*. Tiruchi: Marutam.

Jacob, Preminda. 1997. "From Co-star to Deity: Popular Representations of Jayalalitha Jayaraman." In *Representing the Body: Gender Issues in Indian Art*, edited by V. Dehejia. New Delhi: Kali for Women.

Jaffrelot, Christophe. 1996. *The Hindu Nationalist Movement in India and Indian Politics, 1925 to the 1990s*. New Delhi: Penguin India.

Jain, Jyotindra. 2002. "Folk Artists of Bengal and Contemporary Images: A Case of Reverse Appropriation." In *Contemporary Indian Art: Other Realities*, edited by Y. Dalmia. Bombay: Marg Publications.

————2003. "Morphing Identities: Reconfiguring the Divine and the Political." In *Body.City: Siting Contemporary Culture in India*, edited by I. Chandrasekhar and P. C. Seel. Berlin: House of World Cultures; New Delhi: Tulika Books.

Jain, Kajri. 1995. "Of the Everyday and the 'National Pencil': Calendars in Postcolonial India." *Journal of Arts and Ideas* 27–28:57–89.

————. 2005. "Muscularity and Its Ramifications: Mimetic Male Bodies in Indian Mass Culture." In *Sexual Sites, Seminal Attitudes: Sexualities, Masculinities and Culture in South Asia*, edited by S. Srivastava. New Delhi: Sage.

————. 2007. *Gods in the Bazaar: The Economies of Indian Calendar Art*. Durham, N.C.: Duke University Press.

Jay, Martin. 1994. *Downcast Eyes: The Denigration of Vision in Twentieth-Century French Thought*. Berkeley: University of California Press.

Jha, Sadan. 2004. "The Life and Times of Bharat Mata: Nationalism as Invented Religion." *Manushi* 142:34–38.

Juneja, Monica. 1997. "Reclaiming the Public Sphere: Husain's Portrayal of Saraswati and Draupadi." *Economic and Political Weekly* 32 (4): 155–57.

Kapur, Anuradha. 1993. "Deity to Crusader: The Changing Iconography of Ram." In *Hindus and Others: The Quest of Identity in India Today*, edited by G. Pandey. New Delhi: Viking.

Kapur, Geeta. 1978. "Maqbool Fida Husain: Folklore and Fiesta." In *Contemporary Indian Artists*. New Delhi: Vikas Publishing House.

————. 1989. "Ravi Varma: Representational Dilemmas of a Nineteenth-Century Indian Painter." *Journal of Arts and Ideas* 17–18:59–80.

————. 1993. "Revelation and Doubt: Sant Tukaram and Devi." In *Interrogating Modernity: Culture and Colonialism in India*, edited by T. Niranjana, P. Sudhir, and V. Dhareshwar. Calcutta: Seagull Books.

————. 2000. *When Was Modernism?: Essays in Contemporary Cultural Practice in India*. New Delhi: Tulika.

Kaur, Madanjit, ed. 1987. *Painter of the Divine, Sobha Singh*. Amritsar: Guru Nanak Dev University Press.

Kaur, Manmohan. 1968. *Role of Women in the Freedom Movement, 1857–1947*. Delhi: Sterling.

Kaur, Raminder. 2003. *Performative Politics and the Cultures of Hinduism: Public Uses of Religion in Western India*. Delhi: Permanent Black.

Kaviraj, Sudipto. 1993. "The Imaginary Institution of India." In *Subaltern Studies VII: Writings on South Asian History and Society*, edited by P. Chatterjee and R. Guha. Delhi: Oxford University Press.

———. 1995. *The Unhappy Consciousness: Bankimchandra Chattopadhyay and the Formation of Nationalist Discourse in India*. Delhi: Oxford University Press.

Kearns, Cleo McNelly. 2001. "The Scandals of the Sign: The Virgin Mary as Supplement in the Religions of the Book." In *Questioning God*, edited by J. D. Caputo, M. Dooley, and M. J. Scanlon. Bloomington: Indiana University Press.

Ker, James C. 1917. *Political Trouble in India, 1907–1917*. Calcutta: Superintendent Government Printing.

Kimmel, Michael. 2002. "Foreword." In *Masculinity Studies and Feminist Theory*, edited by J. K. Gardiner. New York: Columbia University Press.

Kinsley, David. 1987. *Hindu Goddesses: Visions of the Divine Feminine in the Hindu Religious Tradition*. Delhi: Motilal Banarsidass.

Kolodny, Annette. 1975. *The Lay of the Land: Metaphor as Experience and History in American Life and Letters*. Chapel Hill: University of North Carolina Press.

Kopf, David. 1989. "A Historiographical Essay on the Idea of Kali." In *Shaping Bengali Worlds, Public and Private*, edited by T. Stewart. East Lansing: Michigan State University.

Krishnaswamy, Revathi. 1998. *Effeminism: The Economy of Colonial Desire*. Ann Arbor: University of Michigan Press.

Kuppusamy Das, K. R. 1948. *Malait Tamil Vaacakam (Moonravatu Puttakam)*. Madras: C. Coomaraswamy Naidu and Sons.

Lahiri, Shompa. 2000. *Indians in Britain: Anglo-Indian Encounters, Race, and Identity, 1880–1930*. London: Frank Cass.

Landes, Joan. 1988. *Women and the Public Sphere in the Age of the French Revolution*. Ithaca, N.Y.: Cornell University Press.

———. 2001. *Visualizing the Nation: Gender, Representation, and Revolution in Eighteenth-Century France*. Ithaca, N.Y.: Cornell University Press.

Larson, Gerald James, Pratapaditya Pal, and H. Daniel Smith, eds. 1997. *Changing Myths and Images: Twentieth-Century Popular Art in India*. Bloomington: University Art Museum, University of Indiana.

Latour, Bruno. 1986. "Visualization and Cognition: Thinking with Eyes and Hands." *Knowledge and Society: Studies in the Sociology of Culture* 6:1–40.

———. 1988. "Opening One Eye While Closing the Other: A Note on Some Religious Paintings." In *Picturing Power: Visual Depiction and Social Relations*, edited by G. Fyfe and J. Law. London: Routledge.

———. 1990. "Drawing Things Together." In *Representation in Scientific Practice*, edited by M. Lynch and S. Woolgar. Cambridge, Mass.: MIT Press.

———. 1998. "How to Be Iconophilic in Art, Science and Religion?" In *Picturing Science, Producing Art*, edited by C. A. Jones and P. Galison. London: Routledge.

Lebra-Chapman, Joyce. 1986. *The Rani of Jhansi: A Study of Female Heroism in India.* Honolulu: University of Hawai'i Press.

———. 2008. *Women against the Raj: The Rani of Jhansi Regiment.* Singapore: Institute of Southeast Asian Studies.

Le Corbellier, Clare. 1961. "Miss America and Her Sisters." *Metropolitan Museum of Art Bulletin* (2nd series) 19:209–23.

Lewes, Darby. 2000. *Nudes from Nowhere: Utopian Sexual Landscapes.* Lanham, Md.: Rowman and Littlefield.

Lipner, Julius. 2005. "Introduction." In *Anandamath, or The Sacred Brotherhood.* New York: Oxford University Press.

Lloyd, David. 1993. "The Poetics of Politics: Yeats and the Founding of the State." In *Anomalous States: Irish Writing and the Post-Colonial Moment.* Dublin: Liliput Press.

Loftus, Belinda. 1990. *Mirrors: William III and Mother Ireland.* Dundrum, Ireland: Picture Press.

Ludden, David. 1993. "Orientalist Empiricism: Transformations of Colonial Knowledge." In *Orientalism and the Postcolonial Predicament*, edited by C. A. Breckenridge and P. van der Veer. Philadelphia: University of Pennsylvania Press.

Mahasweta Devi. 1995. "Douloti the Bountiful." In *Imaginary Maps: Three Stories by Mahasweta Devi.* Translated by Gayatri Chakravorty Spivak. New York: Routledge.

Malhotra, Inder. 1989. *Indira Gandhi: A Personal and Political Biography.* London: Hodder and Stoughton.

Mandal, Tirtha. 1991. *Women Revolutionaries of Bengal, 1905–1939.* Calcutta: Minerva.

Maqbool Fida Husain—Petitioner. 2008. New Delhi: SAHMAT.

McClintock, Anne. 1995. *Imperial Leather: Race, Gender and Sexuality in the Colonial Contest.* London: Routledge.

McClintock, Anne, Aamir Mufti, and Ella Shohat, eds. 1997. *Dangerous Liaisons: Gender, Nation, and Postcolonial Perspectives.* Minneapolis: University of Minnesota Press.

McDermott, Rachel. 2001. *Mother of My Heart, Daughter of My Dreams: Kali and Uma in Devotional Poetry of Bengal.* Oxford: Oxford University Press.

McKean, Lise. 1996. "Bharat Mata: Mother India and Her Militant Matriots." In *Devi: Goddesses of India*, edited by J. S. Hawley and D. M. Wulff. Berkeley: University of California Press.

McLain, Karline. 2009. *India's Immortal Comic Books: Gods, Kings, and Other Heroes.* Bloomington: Indiana University Press.

McLeod, W. H. 1991. *Popular Sikh Art*. Delhi: Oxford University Press.

Menon, Ritu, and Kamla Bhasin. 1998. *Borders and Boundaries: Women in India's Partition*. New Brunswick, N.J.: Rutgers University Press.

Mines, Mattison, and Vijayalakshmi Gourishankar. 1990. "Leadership and Individuality in South Asia: The Case of the South Indian Big-Man." *Journal of Asian Studies* 49 (4): 761–86.

Mitchell, W. J. T. 1994. *Picture Theory: Essays on Visual and Verbal Representation*. Chicago: University of Chicago Press.

———. 1995a. "What Is Visual Culture?" In *Meaning in the Visual Arts: Views from the Outside. A Centennial Commemoration of Erwin Panofsky*, edited by I. Lavin. Princeton, N.J.: Institute for Advanced Study.

———. 1995b. "Interdisciplinarity and Visual Culture." *Art Bulletin* 77 (4): 534–52.

———. 2005. *What Do Pictures Want? The Lives and Loves of Images*. Chicago: University of Chicago Press.

Mitter, Partha. 1994. *Art and Nationalism in Colonial India, 1850–1922: Occidental Orientations*. Cambridge: Cambridge University Press.

———. 1997. "Cartoons of the Raj." *History Today* 47 (9): 16–21.

———. 2007. *The Triumph of Modernism: Indian Artists and the Avante Garde, 1922–1947*. London: Reaktion.

Mittra, Mukti. 1961. *Asit Kumar Haldar*. New Delhi: Lalit Kala Akademi.

Montrose, Louis. 1992. "The Work of Gender and Sexuality in the Elizabethan Discourse of Discovery." In *Discourses of Sexuality: From Aristotle to AIDS*, edited by D. C. Stanton. Ann Arbor: University of Michigan Press.

Morgan, David. 1997. *Visual Piety: A History and Theory of Popular Religious Images*. Berkeley: University of California Press.

Morgan, Victor. 1979. "The Cartographic Image of 'The Country' in Early Modern England." *Transactions of the Royal Historical Society* (5th series) 29:129–54.

Mulvey, Laura. 1989. *Visual and Other Pleasures*. Bloomington: Indiana University Press.

Naidu, Sarojini. 1925. *Speeches and Writings*. 3rd ed. Madras: G. A. Natesan.

———. 1928. *The Sceptred Flute: Songs of India*. New York: Dodd.

Nair, P. Thankappan. 1987. *Indian National Songs and Symbols*. Calcutta: Firma KLM.

Nair, Rukmini Bhaya. 2001. "Singing a Nation into Being." *Seminar* 497:95–100.

Najmabadi, Afsaneh. 1997. "The Erotic Vatan [Homeland] as Beloved and Mother: To Love, to Possess, and to Protect." *Comparative Studies in Society and History* 39 (3): 442–67.

———. 2005. *Women with Moustaches and Men without Beards*. Berkeley: University of California Press.

Nandy, Ashis. 1980. *At the Edge of Psychology: Essays in Politics and Culture*. Delhi: Oxford University Press.

———. 1994. *The Illegitimacy of Nationalism: Rabindranath Tagore and the Politics of the Self*. Delhi: Oxford University Press.

———. 2001. *Time Warps: The Insistent Politics of Silent and Evasive Pasts*. New Delhi: Oxford University Press.

Naqvi, Akbar. 1998. *Image and Identity: Fifty Years of Painting and Sculpture in Pakistan*. Karachi: Oxford University Press.

Nehru, Jawaharlal. 1980. *An Autobiography*. New Delhi: Oxford University Press.

Neumayer, Erwin, and Christine Schelberger. 2008. *Bharat Mata: Printed Icons from the Struggle for Independence in India*. Delhi: Oxford University Press.

Nivedita, Sister. 1905. *Aggressive Hinduism*. Madras: G. A. Natesan.

———. 1967. *The Complete Works of Sister Nivedita: Birth Centenary Publication*, edited by Pravrajika Atmaprana. Calcutta: Sister Nivedita Girls' School.

Noorani, A. G. 2001. *The Trial of Bhagat Singh: Politics of Justice*. Delhi: Konark Publishers.

Nowrosjee, Barjorjee, ed. 1904. *Cartoons from the Hindi "Punch": Being the Political and Social History of the Country during the Year, Told in Humourous Cartoons, etc.* Bombay: Bombay Samachar Press.

Padmanabhan, R. A. 1984. *Subramnia Sivam*. Madras: Pooram Publications.

Pal, Bipin Chandra. 1911. *The Soul of India: A Constructive Study on Indian Thought and Ideas*. Calcutta: Choudhury and Choudhury.

Pal, Ila. 1994. *Beyond the Canvas: An Unfinished Portrait of M. F. Husain*. New Delhi: Indus.

Pattabhi Sitaramayya, B. 1935. *History of the Indian National Congress (1885–1935)*. Bombay: Padma Publications.

Pickles, John. 2004. *A History of Spaces: Cartographic Reason, Mapping, and the Geocoded world*. London: Routledge.

Pinney, Christopher. 1997. "The Nation (Un)Pictured: Chromolithography and 'Popular' Politics in India." *Critical Inquiry* 23 (3): 834–67.

———. 2004. *Photos of the Gods: The Printed Image and Political Struggle in India*. New Delhi: Oxford University Press.

———. 2005. "Things Happen; Or, From Which Moment Does That Object Come?" In *Materiality*, edited by D. Miller. Durham, N.C.: Duke University Press.

Pollock, Griselda. 1983. "Women, Art and Ideology: Questions for Feminist Art Historians." *Women's Art Journal* 4:39–47.

Pravrajika Atmaprana. 1961. *Sister Nivedita of Ramakrishna-Vivekananda*. Calcutta: Sister Nivedita Girls' School.

Purani, A. B. 1958. *The Life of Sri Aurobindo*. Pondicherry: Sri Aurobindo Ashram.

Radice, William. 2005. "Preface." In *The Home and the World* by Rabindranath Tagore. London: Penguin Books.

Rai, Raghu. 2004. *Indira Gandhi: A Living Legacy*. New Delhi: Timeless Books.

Raj, Kapil. 2006. *Relocating Modern Science: Circulation and the Construction of Scientific Knowledge in South Asia, 17th-19th Centuries.* New Delhi: Permanent Black.

Ramalingam, P. 1995. Bharatiyan Bharata Mata. *Tamilp Puduvai* 1 (1): 1, 8–9.

Ramaswamy, Sumathi. 1997. *Passions of the Tongue: Language Devotion in Tamil India, 1891–1970.* Berkeley: University of California Press.

———. 2001. "Maps and Mother Goddesses in Modern India." *Imago Mundi* 53:97–113.

———. 2002. "The Goddess and the Nation: Subterfuges of Antiquity, the Cunning of Modernity." In *The Blackwell Companion to Hinduism*, edited by G. Flood. Oxford: Blackwell.

———. 2003. "Visualizing India's Geo-body: Globes, Maps, Bodyscapes." In *Beyond Appearances? Visual Practices and Ideologies in Modern India*, edited by S. Ramaswamy. New Delhi: Sage.

———. 2004. *The Lost Land of Lemuria: Fabulous Geographies, Catastrophic Histories.* Berkeley: University of California Press.

———. 2006. "Enshrining the Map of India: Cartography, Nationalism, and the Politics of Deity in Varanasi." In *Visualized Space: Constructions of Locality and Cartographic Representations in Varanasi*, edited by M. Gaenszle and J. Gengnagel. Weisbaden, Germany: Harrassowitz Verlag.

———. 2007a. "Conceit of the Globe in Mughal India." *Comparative Studies in Society and History* 49 (4): 751–82.

———. 2007b. "Of Gods and Globes: The Territorialisation of Hindu Deities in Popular Visual Culture." In *India's Popular Culture: Iconic Spaces and Fluid Images*, edited by J. Jain. Mumbai: Marg Publications.

———. 2008. "The Mahatma as Muse: An Image Essay on Gandhi in Popular Indian Visual Imagination." In *Art and Visual Culture in India, 1857–1947*, edited by G. Sinha. Mumbai: Marg Publications.

———, ed. 2010a. *Barefoot across the Nation: Maqbool Fida Husain and the Idea of India.* New Delhi: Routledge.

———. 2010b. "Mapping India after Husain." In *Barefoot Across the Nation: Maqbool Fida Husain and the Idea of India*, edited by S. Ramaswamy. New Delhi: Routledge.

Rangarajan, V. 1977. *Vande Mataram (Homage to Mother).* Madras: Sister Nivedita Academy.

Rao, Sirish, V. Geetha, and Gita Wolf. 2001. *An Ideal Boy: Charts from India.* Stockport, U.K.: Dewi Lewis Publishing; Chennai: Tara Publishing.

Ray, Bharati. 2002. *Early Feminists of Colonial India.* Delhi: Oxford University Press.

Raychaudhuri, Tapan. 1988. *Europe Reconsidered: Perceptions of the West in Nineteenth Century Bengal.* Delhi: Oxford University Press.

Rennell, James. 1783. *Memoir of a Map of Hindoostan or the Mogul Empire with an Examination of Some Positions in the Former System of Geography; and some Illus-*

trations of the Present One: And a Complete Index of Names to the Map. London: M. Brown for the Author.

Richter, Gerhard. 2006. "A Matter of Distance: Benjamin's *One-Way Street* through *The Arcades*." In *Walter Benjamin and the Arcades Project*, edited by B. Hanssen. London: Continuum.

Roy, Srirupa. 2006. "A Symbol of Freedom: The Indian Flag and the Transformations of Nationalism, 1906–2002." *Journal of Asian Studies* 65 (3): 495–527.

Roy, Parama. 1999. *Indian Traffic: Identities in Question in Colonial and Postcolonial India*. Berkeley: University of California Press.

Sabnis, Milind. 2000. *Vande Mataram: Down the Memory Lane*. Translated by A. Thatte. Pune: Dnyanada Pratishthan.

Sahgal, Lakshmi. 1997. *A Revolutionary Life: Memoirs of a Political Activist*. New Delhi: Kali for Women.

Samanta, A. K., ed. 1995. *Terrorism in Bengal: A Collection of Documents on Terrorist Activities, 1905–1939*. 6 vols. Calcutta: Government of West Bengal.

Sarkar, Kamal. 1969–70. "100 Years of Indian Cartoons (1850–1950)." *Vidura* 6–7:37–41, 25–29, 33–39, 36–40.

Sarkar, Sumit. 1973. *The Swadeshi Movement in Bengal, 1903–1908*. New Delhi: People's Publishing House.

Sarkar, Tanika. 1984. "Politics and Women in Bengal: The Conditions and Meaning of Participation." *Indian Economic and Social History Review* 21 (1): 91–101.

———. 1995. "Heroic Women, Mother Goddesses: Family and Organisation in Hindutva Politics." In *Women and the Hindu Right*, edited by T. Sarkar and U. Butalia. New Delhi: Kali for Women.

———. 2001. *Hindu Wife, Hindu Nation: Community, Religion, and Cultural Nationalism*. New Delhi: Permanent Black.

———. 2006. "Birth of a Goddess: 'Vande Mataram,' Anandamath, and Hindu Nationhood." *Economic and Political Weekly* 41:3959–69.

Scarry, Elaine. 1985. *The Body in Pain: The Making and Unmaking of the World*. New York: Oxford University Press.

Schwartzberg, Joseph E. 1992. "South Asian Cartography." In *Cartography in the Traditional Islamic and South Asian Societies*, edited by J. B. Harley and D. Woodward. Chicago: University of Chicago Press.

Scott, James C. 1998. *Seeing Like a State: How Certain Schemes to Improve the Human Condition Have Failed*. New Haven, Conn.: Yale University Press.

Scott, Joan Wallach. 1988. *Gender and the Politics of History*. New York: Columbia University Press.

Sedgwick, Eve Kosofsky. 1985. *Between Men: English Literature and Male Homosocial Desire*. New York: Columbia University Press.

Sen, Amartya. 2005. "Tagore and His India." In *The Argumentative Indian: Writings on Indian History, Culture and Identity*. New York: Picador.

Sen, Geeti. 2002. *Feminine Fables: Imaging the Indian Woman in Painting, Photography, and Cinema*. Ahmedabad: Mapin Publishing.

———. 2002–2003. "Iconising the Nation: Political Agendas." *India International Quarterly* 29 (3–4): 155–75.

Sen, Prabodhachandra. 1972. *India's National Anthem*. Calcutta: Vishvabharati.

Sen Gupta, Nagendranath. 1974. *Repentant Revolutionary: Autobiography of Nagendranath Sen Gupta*. Aurangabad: Parimal Prakashan.

Shaw, Graham, and Mary Lloyd, eds. 1985. *Publications Proscribed by the Government of India: A Catalogue of the Collections in the India Office Library and Records and the Department of Oriental Manuscripts and Printed Books, British Library Reference Division*. London: British Library.

Sher-Gil, Amrita. 1942. "The Story of My Life." *Usha: Journal of Art and Literature, Organ of the Punjabi Literary League* (August): 93.

———. 1971a. "Evolution of My Art." In *Amrita Sher-Gil*, edited by Vivan Sundaram, Gulam Mohammed Sheikh, and K. G. Subrahmanyam. Bombay: Marg Publications.

———. 1971b. "Indian Art Today." In *Amrita Sher-Gil*, edited by Vivan Sundaram, Gulam Mohammed Sheikh, and K. G. Subrahmanyam. Bombay: Marg Publications.

Shetty, Sandhya. 1995. "(Dis)figuring the Nation: Mother, Metaphor, Metonymy." *Differences: A Journal of Feminist Cultural Studies* 7 (3): 50–79.

Siddiqui, Rashda. 2001. *In Conversation with Husain Paintings*. New Delhi: Books Today.

Singh, Amrit Kaur, and Rabindra Kaur Singh. 2003. *Images of Freedom*. New Delhi: Indialog Publications.

Singh, Bhagat. 2007. *The Jail Notebook and Other Writings*, edited by Chaman Lal, with annotations by Bhupender Hooja. New Delhi: LeftWord.

Singh, K. V. 1991. *Our National Flag*. New Delhi: Publications Division, Government of India.

Singh, Rana P. B., and Pravin S. Rana. 2001. *Banaras Region: A Spiritual and Cultural Guide*. Varanasi: Sacred Books.

Sinha, Gayatri. 1999. "Woman/Goddess." In *Woman/Goddess, an Exhibition of Photographs*, edited by G. Sinha. New Delhi: Multiple Action Research Group.

———. 2006. "Cult of the Goddess: Gender and Nation: From Bharati to Bharat Mata." In *Iconography Now*. New Delhi: Sahmat.

Sinha, Mrinalini. 2004. "Nations in an Imperial Crucible." In *Gender and Empire*, edited by P. Levine. Oxford: Oxford University Press.

———. 2006. *Specters of Mother India: The Global Restructuring of an Empire*. Durham, N.C.: Duke University Press.

Sircar, D. C. 1967. *Cosmography and Geography in Early Indian Literature*. Calcutta: D. Chattopadhyaya.

———. 1973. *The Sakta Pithas*. Banaras: Motilal Banarsidass. (Orig. pub. 1948.)

Smith, David. 2003. *Hinduism and Modernity*. London: Blackwell.

Solomon-Godeau, Abigail. 1997. *Male Trouble: A Crisis in Representation*. London: Thames and Hudson.

Spivak, Gayatri. 1992. "Woman in Difference: Mahasweta Devi's 'Douloti the Beautiful.'" In *Nationalisms and Sexualities*, edited by A. Parker, M. Russo, D. Sommer, and P. Yaeger. New York: Routledge.

Srinivasan, Doris Meth. 1997. *Many Heads, Arms, and Eyes: Origin, Meaning, and Form of Multiplicity in Indian Art*. Leiden, Netherlands: Brill.

Srinivasan, P., ed. 2000. *Varanasi*. Chennai: TTK Healthcare Limited.

Srinivasavaradhan, R. 1947. *Cuppiramaniya Civam*. Ramachandrapuram: Ripon Prasuram.

Stafford, Barbara Maria. 1995. *Good Looking: Essays on the Virtue of Images*. Cambridge, Mass.: MIT Press.

Strong, Roy. 1987. *Gloriana: The Portraits of Queen Elizabeth I*. London: Thames and Hudson.

Sundaram, Vivan, Geeta Kapur, Gulam Mohammed Sheikh, and K. G. Subrahmanyam, eds. 1972. *Amrita Sher-Gil*. Bombay: Marg Publications.

Sunder Rajan, Rajeswari. 1993. *Real and Imagined Women: Gender, Culture and Postcolonialism*. London: Routledge.

Tagore, Rabindranath. 1917. *Nationalism*. New York: Macmillan.

———. 2005. *The Home and the World*. Translated by S. Tagore. London: Penguin Books. (Orig. pub. 1919.)

Tarlo, Emma. 1996. *Clothing Matters: Dress and Identity in India*. Chicago: University of Chicago Press.

Thomas, Rosie. 1989. "Sanctity and Scandal: The Mythologization of Mother India." *Quarterly Review of Film and Video* 11 (3): 11–30.

Thongchai, Winichakul. 1996. "Maps and the Formation of the Geo-Body of Siam." In *Asian Forms of the Nation*, edited by H. Antlov and S. Tonnesson. London: Curzon Press.

Traub, Valerie. 2000. "Mapping the Global Body." In *Early Modern Visual Culture: Representation, Race, Empire in Renaissance England*, edited by P. Erickson and C. Hulse. Philadelphia: University of Pennsylvania Press.

Tripathi, Amales. 1967. *The Extremist Challenge: India between 1890 and 1910*. New Delhi: Orient Longmans.

Trivedi, Lisa. 2003. "Visually Mapping the Nation: Swadeshi Politics in Nationalist India, 1920–1930." *Journal of Asian Studies* 62 (1): 11–41.

Tuan, Yi-Fu. 1976. "Geopiety: A Theme in Man's Attachment to Nature and to Place." In *Geographies of the Mind*, edited by D. Lowenthal and M. Bowden. New York: Oxford University Press.

———. 1977. *Space and Place: The Perspective of Experience*. Minneapolis: University of Minnesota Press.

Tuli, Neville. 2002. *A Historical Epic: India in the Making, 1757–1950. From Surrender to Revolt, Swaraj to Responsibility*. Mumbai: Osian's Connoisseurs of Art Pvt. Ltd.

Uberoi, Patricia. 1990. "Feminine Identity and National Ethos in Indian Calendar Art." *Economic and Political Weekly (Review of Women's Studies)* 25 (17): 41–48.

———. 1999–2000. "Times Past: Gender and the Nation in 'Calendar Art.'" *Indian Horizons* 46–47:24–39.

———. 2000. *From Goddess to Pin-Up: Icons of Femininity in Indian Calendar Art.* Fukoka, Japan: Fukoka Asian Art Museum.

———. 2003. "'Unity in Diversity'? Dilemmas of Nationhood in Indian Calendar Art." In *Beyond Appearances? Visual Practices and Ideologies in Modern India*, edited by S. Ramaswamy. New Delhi: Sage.

———. 2006. *Freedom and Destiny: Gender, Family and Popular Culture in India.* New Delhi: Oxford University Press.

Urban, Hugh B. 2003. "'India's Darkest Heart': Kali in the Colonial Imagination." In *Encountering Kali: In the Margins, at the Center, in the West*, edited by R. F. McDermott and J. J. Kripal. Berkeley: University of California Press.

van den Broecke, Marcel, Peter van der Krogt, and Peter Meurer, eds. 1998. *Abraham Ortelius and the First Atlas: Essays Commemorating the Quadricentennial of His Death, 1598–1998*. Utrecht, Netherlands: HES Publishers.

Venkatachalapathy, A. R. 1995. *Bharatiyin Karuttup Patankal: Intiya, 1906–1910.* Madras: Narmada.

———. 2006. *In Those Days There Was No Coffee: Writings in Cultural History.* New Delhi: Yoda Press.

Venkataraman, V. 2001. *Suthantira Sangu: Karuthuppadangal, 1930–33.* Rajapalayam: Swatantira Publications.

Virmani, Arundhati. 2008. *A National Flag for India: Rituals, Nationalism and the Politics of Sentiment.* New Delhi: Permanent Black.

Visram, Rozina. 2002. *Asians in Britain: 400 Years of History.* London: Pluto Press.

Viswanathan, Seeni. 1998. *Kala Varisaippaduttappatta Bharati Pataippukal.* Chennai: Published by the author.

Vogel, J. Ph. 1931. "The Head-Offering to the Goddess in Pallava Sculpture." *Bulletin of the School of Oriental and African Studies* 6 (2): 539–43.

Warner, Marina. 1985. *Monuments and Maidens: The Allegory of the Female Form.* New York: Atheneum.

Wood, Denis, and John Fels. 1992. *The Power of Maps.* New York: Guilford Press.

Woolf, Virgina, 1998. *"A Room of One's Own" and "Three Guineas."* Oxford: Oxford University Press.

Zitzewitz, Karin. 2003. "On Signature and Citizenship: Further Notes on the Husain Affair." In *Towards a New Art History: Studies in Indian Art*, edited by P. D. Mukerji, S. Panikkar, and D. Achar. New Delhi: D. K. Printworld.

INDEX

Bazaar art (*continued*)

275, 278, 286, 295, 296–97, 309 nn. 26–27, 310 nn. 28–29, 311 n. 43, 313 n. 54, 315 n. 16, 338 n. 39. *See also* Calendar art; Visual patriotism

Bengal, 76, 83, 98, 103, 108, 113, 114, 117, 135, 140, 142, 206, 209, 218, 240, 255, 267–68, 273, 314 n. 3, 315 n. 16, 317 n. 44, 319 nn. 64–65, 321 n. 5, 323 n. 21, 325 n. 41, 326 n. 53, 327 n. 68, 328 n. 7, 329 n. 14, 334 n. 1, 338 n. 34, 347 nn. 62–63, 348 nn. 65–66; Bharat Mata and, 15–18, 21–22, 24, 44, 80, 81–82, 110, 145, 305 n. 1, 305 n. 3, 339 n. 42; partition of, 15–18, 118, 119–20, 127, 137, 149, 246, 248, 306 n. 6, 307 n. 8; swadeshi movement in, 15–18, 21, 26, 119–20, 145–46, 147, 246, 248, 305 n. 4, 344 n. 26, 344 n. 32, 346 n. 46

Bhagat Singh, 220, 222–23, 225, 229–30, 268, 316 n. 25, 336 n. 13, 340 n. 43, 340 n. 47, 341 n. 54; Gandhi and, 218, 227–28, 231; life of, 339 n. 41; map of India and, 219, 221, 224, 226, 236, 266, 275, 278

Bhagavad Gita, 165, 195, 217, 255, 308 n. 20

Bharat, 81, 182, 194, 196, 301 n. 1

Bharatavarsha, 105, 157, 330 n. 17

Bharat Bhiksha, 80–82, 315 n. 16

Bharati, Subramania, 18–23, 24, 33, 45, 58, 100, 107, 113, 114, 118, 121, 130, 147, 155, 307 n. 9, 307 n. 12, 345 n. 35

Bharatidasan, 21–22, 288, 292, 350 n. 5

Bharati Mata, 307 n. 12

Bharat Mata: as armed goddess, 17, 24, 26–32, 50, 58–60, 62, 64, 82, 85, 124, 162, 203, 209, 227–28, 255, 258, 306 n. 7, 312 n. 47, 336 n. 14; Bhagat Singh and, 219–24, 226–29, 236, 316 n. 25, 340 n. 47; Bose and, 183, 188, 189–90, 206–13, 311 n. 36, 338 n. 32, 351 n. 13; in chains, 44, 183–84, 196, 205, 219, 221, 340 n. 43; as clay image, 21–22, 45, 58; colonial state and, 17, 29, 31–32, 33, 100–101, 108–12, 118, 145, 148–49; with Gandhi, 3, 44, 60, 64, 66, 180, 181–82, 183, 186, 189–90, 190–98, 212–13, 227, 231, 312 n. 49, 323 n. 23, 333 n. 42, 337 n. 23; Indira Gandhi and, 272–73, 280–81, 348 n. 68, 349 nn. 74–76, 350 n. 81; globe and, 18,

24–25, 32, 43–45, 84, 120, 125, 189, 210, 212, 213, 221, 224, 311 n. 36, 334 n. 44; with halo, 15, 17, 37, 39, 44, 56, 58, 60, 70, 120, 122, 124, 162, 183, 190, 224, 306 n. 7, 333 n. 42, 338 n. 32; in Hindi media, 28, 30–31, 40, 41, 43, 44, 60–61, 162–64, 194, 203, 219, 221, 340 n. 43, 343 n. 14; as Hindu goddess, 3, 15–16, 18, 249, 293, 294–95, 318 n. 49, 319 n. 63; in Indian diaspora, 29–32, 33, 45, 58, 107, 120, 130, 132–33, 252–56, 308 nn. 20–21, 309 n. 23, 321 n. 8; Indian flag and, 3–4, 44, 47, 48, 50–51, 55, 60, 66, 108, 120, 122, 130, 164, 183, 193–94, 198, 203, 209, 212, 213, 224, 269, 272, 333 n. 42; lion and, 17, 31, 50, 63–64, 85, 120, 123, 130, 209, 228, 255, 264, 316 n. 25, 333 n. 42; in movies, 343 n. 14; with multiple arms, 3, 15, 20, 22, 26, 42, 47, 60, 62–63, 70, 104, 123, 124, 130, 189, 250, 255, 272, 306 n. 7, 333 n. 43, 333 n. 32; Muslim artists and, 5–6, 26, 70, 105, 244, 302 n. 7, 303 n. 11, 336 n. 13, 343 n. 14, 343 nn. 16–17; 349 n. 76; with Nehru, 114–15, 183, 189–90, 199–205, 219, 227, 228, 231–33, 242, 286–87, 292, 311 n. 36; as "new woman," 65–66, 74–75, 113–14, 238, 255–56, 258; as nude figure, 4–5, 272, 302 n. 8, 303 n. 10, 304 n. 11, 349 n. 74; in pain, 231–32, 233, 280; pictured with infants and children, 22–23, 24–26, 70, 80–81, 123, 212–15; in Punjabi prints, 30–31, 255, 309 n. 23; sari and, 3, 15, 18, 20, 22, 23, 24, 30, 31, 32, 47–48, 50, 65–66, 82, 85, 123, 198, 212, 213, 263, 306 n. 7, 341 n. 60; scholarship on, 30, 130, 305 n. 1; with spinning wheel, 47, 60, 66, 130, 189, 193, 194, 209, 212; students and, 37–38, 120, 123–24, 125, 128, 145–46, 171, 173–76, 251, 332 n. 35, 334 n. 45; in tableaux, 100–101, 317 n. 47; in Tamil country, 18–23, 37–38, 47–48, 107, 113, 118, 130, 146, 147, 174, 286, 310 n. 32, 343 n. 14; in tears, 29, 81, 181, 196, 198, 221, 325 n. 43; in temples, 13, 48–49, 133, 136, 149, 151–72, 333 nn. 42–43, 334 nn. 44–45; as widow, 24, 80–81

Bharat Mata Association, 26, 147–48

Bharat Mata Mandir (Banaras), 48–49, 133, 151–69, 170, 328–29, 328 n. 7, 331 nn. 27–

28, 332 n. 29, 332 nn. 31–32, 332 nn. 35–36, 333 n. 37, 333 n. 39, 334 n. 44

Bharat Mata Mandir (Haridwar), 169–71, 333 n. 40

Bharat Mata Society, 26, 339 n. 40

Bharat Mata temples, 155–56, 171, 333 n. 42, 334 n. 45

Bhattacharya, Sabyasachi, 99, 134, 324 n. 39

Bhawani, 107, 155, 156, 209, 329 n. 14, 343 n. 21

Bhawani Mandir, 136, 155, 329 n. 14, 345 n. 36. *See also* Aurobindo

Bhu Devi, 100–103, 137, 165, 245, 317 n. 45, 318 nn. 49–50, 332 n. 31

Bombay, 4, 24, 82, 113, 127, 129, 166, 167, 183, 184, 186, 192, 216, 217, 243, 253, 260, 270, 273, 274, 286, 303 n. 11, 309 n. 23, 316 n. 23, 322 n. 19, 329 n. 14

Brahmo Samaj, 137, 325 n. 41, 326 n. 51

Brijbasi, 50, 51, 200, 201, 337 n. 337

Britannia, 76, 93, 317 n. 41; Bharat Mata and, 50, 63–64, 73, 85; British Empire and, 63, 77–85, 94–97; with globe, 78, 79, 84, 94–95; in India, 79–85, 316 n. 23; map of England and, 92, 95–97, 317 n. 38; map of India and, 79–80

Brojen, 183, 212, 213, 214, 338 n. 32

Bose, Khudiram, 119, 145, 229, 319 n. 62, 339 n. 42

Bose, Subhas Chandra, 56, 295; Bharat Mata and, 183, 188, 189–90, 206–13, 311 n. 36, 338 n. 32, 351 n. 13; biographical note on, 337 n. 29; Gandhi and, 183, 186, 199, 205, 206, 207, 209–12, 336 n. 16, 337 n. 29; with globe, 206, 210, 212–13; with halo, 183; map of India and, 182, 183, 186, 189, 206–12, 213, 228–29, 264, 266, 275, 278, 311 n. 36; martyrdom of, 206, 228–29; Nehru and, 183, 205, 206, 207, 209–10, 311 n. 36

Buddha, 44, 190, 331 n. 22

Buddhists, 141, 142, 160, 294, 334 n. 45

Burma, 22, 41, 42, 125, 157, 166, 206, 224, 299, 330 nn. 17–18

Calcutta, 78, 82, 103, 110, 113, 118, 125, 128, 189, 248, 249, 251, 253, 307 n. 15, 313 n. 1, 314 n. 11, 325 n. 41, 325 n. 44, 329 n. 8, 336

n. 36, 344 n. 33; patriotic pictures and, 25, 44, 45, 46, 59, 66, 184, 187, 191, 197, 198, 204, 208, 210, 211, 213, 224, 225, 230, 267, 285

Calcutta Art Studio, 80, 81, 82, 315 n. 16

Calendar art, 13, 16, 26, 29, 34, 36, 39, 50, 57, 65, 68, 200, 272, 295, 297, 308 n. 19, 309 n. 26, 313 n. 56, 335 n. 4, 349 n. 73. *See also* Bazaar art; Visual patriotism

Cama, Bhikhaiji, 29, 33, 120, 128, 252–56, 258, 345 n. 43, 345 n. 45, 346 n. 46, 346 n. 48

Cartography: colonialism and, 8–9, 11, 34–37, 48–49, 52–53, 77–78, 79–80, 99, 135, 164, 171, 287, 291; in Europe, 87, 89, 90–91, 92, 350 n. 7; as state science, 37, 41, 52–53, 71, 76, 88, 91, 92, 133, 144, 236, 289–90, 302 n. 4, 304 n. 16, 351 n. 8. *See also* Barefoot cartography; Map of India; Scientific-geographic

Cartoons, 6, 36, 82, 83, 84, 130, 146, 231, 233, 306 n. 6, 314 n. 11, 316 nn. 23–24, 337 n. 21, 341 n. 60

Ceylon, 17, 132, 157, 166, 309 n. 23

Chakrabarty, Dipesh, 291, 305 n. 20, 311 n. 41, 326 n. 51, 344 n. 31

China, 37, 157, 251, 255, 312 n. 47, 350 n. 7

Chowdhury, Sudhir, 204, 209, 210, 212, 214, 228, 267

Christians, 56, 70, 86, 141, 142, 146, 160, 161, 165, 174, 214, 231, 260, 294, 295, 341 n. 60

Civil disobedience movement, 56–57, 180, 312 n. 44. *See also* Dandi salt march; Indian nationalism

Colonial surveys, 8, 36, 49, 52, 79, 133, 156, 157, 289, 310 n. 30, 315 n. 15, 329 n. 9, 330 n. 16, 331 n. 28. *See also* Cartography

Congress, 47, 60, 67, 82, 84, 152, 155, 181, 183, 186, 193, 199, 251, 253, 278, 316 n. 23, 323 n. 24, 325 n. 41, 333 n. 42, 337 n. 29; Gandhi and, 66, 180, 194, 209, 286, 312 n. 44, 336 n. 13; Naidu and, 259–61, 263, 346 n. 53; "Vande Mataram" and, 118, 144, 146, 246. *See also* Indian nationalism

Continents personified, 77, 86–89, 314 n. 10, 316 n. 30

Dandi salt march, 216, 260, 312 n. 44, 335
n. 10, 337 n. 20. *See also* Indian nationalism

Darshan, 158, 174, 196, 311 n. 43, 326 n. 51,
330 n. 20, 333 n. 37

Das, Yatindranath, 219, 227, 340 n. 45

Dayal, Prabhu, 180, 181, 213, 214, 221, 226,
227, 247, 335 n. 9

Derrida, Jacques, 52–53, 291, 311 nn. 40–41,
337 n. 19, 348 n. 67

Desai, Kanu, 193–94, 337 n. 20

Devanagari script, 21, 30, 50, 104, 121, 122,
125, 128, 129, 130, 251, 254, 255, 324 n. 31,
336 n. 18

Dhingra, Madan Lal, 120, 321 n. 8

Ditchley portrait (of Elizabeth I), 90–91

Dixit, J. B. 124, 322 n. 14

Dravidian movement, 47, 311 n. 37, 350 n. 5.
See also Tamil nationalism

Durga, 106, 109, 110, 112, 224, 329 n. 14, 343
n. 21; in Bankim's imagination, 108, 119,
123, 133; Indira Gandhi and, 271–73, 349
nn. 72–73, 349 nn. 75–76; Ghosal and, 247,
344 n. 28; in Husain's painting, 272–73; as
model for Bharat Mata, 58, 63, 107–8, 114,
117, 139, 249, 255, 305 n. 2, 318 n. 55, 339
n. 42, 351 n. 13

Durga Prasad, 154, 329 n. 9

East India Company, 76–77, 79, 315 n. 14

Edney, Matthew, 77, 290–91, 304 n. 17, 315
n. 14

Elizabeth I, queen of England, 90–93, 317
n. 33

Elkins, James, 235, 296, 302 n. 5

Erin, 76, 98, 317 n. 43

Flag of India, 99, 181, 283; Bharat Mata and,
3–4, 44, 47, 48, 50–51, 55, 60, 66, 108, 120,
122, 130, 162, 183, 193–94, 198, 203, 212,
213, 224, 269, 272, 338 n. 32; as Bharat
Mata's sari, 3, 47, 48, 50, 66, 122; evolution of, 60, 66–67, 128, 251–55, 313 n. 53,
323 n. 24, 345 nn. 41–42; Gandhi and, 66,
190, 193–94, 198, 212, 216, 338 n. 32; Indira
Gandhi and, 272, 274, 275; in Husain's
paintings, 3–4, 104, 272; map of India and,
3–4, 66–67, 104–5, 252–53, 269, 345 n. 42;

as saffron, 39, 60; "Vande Mataram" and,
122, 128, 251–55, 323 n. 22, 323 n. 24

Ganesha, 3, 214, 302 n. 17

Gandhi, Indira: assassination of, 268, 348
n. 68; Bharat Mata Mandir (Haridwar)
and, 169; as Durga, 271–72, 349 nn. 72–73;
Husain and, 245, 272–73, 349 nn. 74–76;
map of India and, 268–69, 272–73, 275,
278–81, 333 n. 42; martyrdom images of,
271–81, 350 n. 81; as Mother India, 272–
73, 280–81, 348 n. 68, 349 nn. 74–76, 350
n. 81

Gandhi, Kasturba, 192, 263, 335 n. 11

Gandhi, Mohandas, 26, 30, 56, 312 n. 44,
316 n. 25, 320 n. 2, 325 n. 41, 335 nn. 9–10,
336 n. 13, 336 n. 16, 336 n. 18, 337 n. 20,
339 n. 40; Bharat Mata and, 3, 44, 60, 64,
66, 180, 181–82, 183, 186, 189–90, 190–98,
212–13, 227, 231, 312 n. 49, 323 n. 23, 333
n. 42, 337 n. 23; at Bharat Mata temples,
151, 152, 155, 160, 167; Bose and, 183, 186,
189–90, 206, 207, 264, 337 n. 23, 338 n. 33;
with halo, 196, 199, 215–16, 336 n. 12, 338
n. 39; Husain and, 3; Indian women and,
198–99, 239, 246, 247, 259–60, 262, 263;
with map of India, 180, 181–82, 183, 186,
188, 189, 190–98, 213, 215–17, 218, 233, 264,
275, 278, 333 n. 42, 338 n. 39; martyrdom
and, 190–92, 194–95, 196, 198, 215–17, 218,
227, 336 n. 12, 337 n. 22, 338 n. 39, 341
n. 56; national flag and, 47, 66, 338 n. 32;
Nehru and, 183, 186, 189–90, 199, 200, 204,
264; spinning wheel and, 60, 66, 189, 337
n. 21

Ganga (Ganges), 3, 22, 40, 140, 141, 157, 168,
170, 332 n. 36

Geo-body, 304 n. 16. *See also* Map of India

Geography, 9, 11, 36, 38, 43, 68, 91, 115, 133,
135, 137, 139, 141–42, 143, 144, 154, 170, 178,
292, 294, 304 n. 14, 304 n. 16, 332 n. 35, 335
n. 3. *See also* Scientific-geographic

Geo-piety, 123, 140, 142–44, 159, 169, 321
n. 11

Ghadar movement, 30–32, 33, 40, 67, 218,
255, 308 n. 20, 308 n. 22, 309 n. 23, 324
n. 36

Ghosal, Sarala Devi, 246–48, 249, 256, 258, 261, 344 nn. 23–24, 344 n. 26

Globe, 33, 36, 83, 97, 182, 304 n. 13, 338 n. 38; Bhagat Singh and, 224; with Bharat Mata, 18, 24–25, 32, 43–45, 84, 120, 125, 189, 210, 212, 213, 221, 224, 311 n. 36, 334 n. 44; Bose and, 189, 206, 210, 210, 212, 213, 311 n. 36; Britannia and, 78, 79, 84, 95; Elizabeth I and, 90–91; Europe and, 86–87; Gandhi and, 189, 192, 196, 210, 213, 215–17, 338 n. 39; with Hindu deities, 100, 311 n. 35; map of India inscribed on, 18, 24, 32, 44, 84, 100, 120, 125, 196, 204, 210, 217, 221, 224; Mother Tamil and, 310 n. 32; Nehru and, 189, 201, 204, 210, 215, 311 n. 36. *See also* Cartography

Guadalupe, 76, 97, 317 n. 42

Gupta, Shivprasad, 152, 153, 157, 158, 159, 160, 162, 164, 165, 166, 168, 169, 328 n. 7, 329 n. 8, 332 n. 31

Haldar, Asit Kumar, 306 n. 7

Haldar, Harish Chunder, 307 n. 15

Halo, 86; Bharat Mata with, 15, 17, 37, 39, 44, 56, 58, 60, 70, 120, 122, 124, 162, 183, 190, 224, 306 n. 7, 333 n. 42, 338 n. 32; Gandhi with, 196, 199, 215–16, 336 n. 12, 338 n. 39

Har Dayal, 255, 309 n. 23

Heidegger, Martin, 293, 302 n. 3, 351 n. 11

Hemchandra Bhargava, 187, 203, 206, 338 n. 39

Hibernia, 76, 98, 317 n. 43

Himalayas, 140, 141–42, 157, 167, 169, 207, 284, 332 n. 32; Bharat Mata and, 3, 4, 17, 22, 37, 39–40, 67, 170, 213, 256–57, 272

Hind Devi, 82–84, 144, 263. *See also* Bharat Mata

Hindi Punch, 82–84, 306 n. 6, 316 nn. 23–24

Hindu goddess: with Bharat Mata, 24, 100–101; fierce devotion and, 224–50, 340 n. 50; Husain and, 4, 303 n. 11; as model for Bharat Mata, 2, 8, 20–21, 55–65, 98–112, 112–14, 122, 156, 198; map of India and, 7–8, 100

Hinduism: defined, 301 n. 2; image worship and, 70–71, 114–15, 137, 159, 161, 165, 313 n. 57, 333 n. 38; Indian nationalism and, 21,

139, 160, 167, 294, 295, 301 n. 1; sacrifice cult and, 109–11, 224–25, 340 nn. 50–51. *See also* Hindu goddess; Hindu nationalism; Sanskritic Hinduism

Hindu nationalism, 5–6, 38–39, 42–43, 57, 60, 121, 123, 136, 165, 169–73, 190, 196, 231, 269, 295, 298, 305 n. 1, 308 nn. 19–20, 311 n. 33, 313 n. 1, 320 n. 3, 322 n. 19, 332 n. 35, 334 n. 44, 335 n. 6, 341 n. 57, 341 n. 60

Home and the World (Tagore), 114, 139, 168, 178–79, 237–38, 247, 320 n. 67, 334 n. 1, 335 n. 2

Husain, Maqbool Fida, 13, 15, 22, 57, 303 n. 11, 304 n. 12, 310 n. 30; Bharat Mata and, 3–8, 66, 78, 303 n. 9, 349 nn. 74–75, 343 n. 16; Indira Gandhi and, 245, 272–73, 349 nn. 75–76; Hindu nationalists and, 3–6, 302 n. 8, 303 nn. 9–10; map of India and, 3–8, 104–6, 272–73, 304 n. 15; Parvati and, 104–6, 318 n. 54

India: in Bharati's cartoons, 20; in British art, 76–79; in colonial art, 76–79, 314 n. 11, 316 n. 23; creation of, 3; as motherland, 11, 15, 26, 28, 53, 69, 73–74, 99, 102–4, 107, 108, 113–14, 118, 125, 132, 134–35, 136, 139, 149, 155, 156, 166, 178, 236, 237, 238, 248, 250, 254, 256, 268, 293, 295, 298, 305 n. 3, 313 n. 1, 315 n. 19, 318 n. 53, 319 n. 63, 322 n. 18, 323 n. 29, 324 n. 38, 331 n. 22, 331 n. 27, 332 n. 31, 339 n. 42, 346 n. 53, 351 n. 13; as nude female, 78–79, 314 n. 11; territorial conceptions of, 8–9, 11, 51–55, 67–68, 99–103, 104–6, 115, 121, 133–35, 140–41, 157–58, 168, 171, 173–75, 287–88, 290–91, 292–93, 321 n. 11, 330 n. 16. *See also* Bharat Mata; Indian nationalism; Map of India

Indian National Army, 183, 188, 206, 263, 264, 266

Indian nationalism, 26, 38, 47, 56, 58, 60, 107, 112–15, 134, 181, 198, 209, 227, 228, 238–39, 247, 248, 251, 256, 258, 263, 307 n. 9, 314 n. 11, 326 n. 45, 328 n. 7. *See also* Civil disobedience movement; Congress; Quit India movement; Swadeshi movement; Visual patriotism

Mayo, Katherine, 241, 242, 342 n. 10, 343 n. 14

Mitchell, W. J. T. 127, 233, 235, 297, 302 n. 5, 309 n. 24, 351 n. 14

"Mother and motherland are greater than heaven," 73, 149

Mother Bengal, 15, 137–38, 306 n. 6, 318 n. 55, 322 n. 15

Mother Cow, 165, 307 n. 11, 318 n. 50

Mother Earth, 100–103, 137, 165, 245, 317 n. 45, 318 nn. 49–50, 332 n. 31

Mother India. *See* Bharat Mata

Mother India (Mayo), 241, 242, 342 n. 10, 343 n. 14

Mother India (movie), 243–45, 343 nn. 13–14, 343 nn. 16–17, 343 n. 21, 344 n. 22

Mother India (Sher-Gil), 239–43, 245, 342 nn. 5–6, 342 nn. 8–10, 343 n. 14

Mother India Awakened, 306 n. 7

Mother Iran, 76, 97

Mother Tamil, 310 n. 32

Mukhopadhyay, Bhudev, 103–4

Muslims, 2, 21, 70, 133, 139, 141, 160–61, 165, 174, 218, 224, 244–45, 252, 260–61, 294, 295, 302 nn. 1–2, 305 n. 1, 322 n. 15, 323 n. 22, 323 n. 35, 334 n. 45, 335 n. 5, 336 n. 13, 341 n. 60; Vande Mataram and, 122, 128, 144, 320 n. 2. *See also* Bharat Mata: Muslim artists and

Naidu, Sarojini, 258–63, 346 n. 53

Najmabadi, Afsaneh, 76, 97

Nargis, 244–45, 273, 343 n. 17, 344 n. 22

Nehru, Jawaharlal, 144, 244, 268, 297, 316 n. 25, 326 n. 55; Bharat Mata and, 114–15, 183, 189–90, 199–205, 219, 227, 228, 231–33, 242, 286–87, 292, 311 n. 36; Bose and, 183, 204, 205, 264, 311 n. 36; Gandhi and, 183, 186, 189–90, 199, 200, 204, 205, 264, 311 n. 36; globe and, 189, 201, 204, 215, 311 n. 36; map of India and, 182, 183, 186, 199–205, 215, 231–33, 264

Nehru, Kamala, 336 n. 11

Nepal, 22, 39

Nivedita, Sister, 15, 16, 18, 248–52, 256, 306 n. 5, 323 n. 24, 338 n. 36, 344 nn. 31–33, 345 n. 36, 345 n. 39, 345 n. 41

Noble, Margaret, 15, 16, 18, 248–52, 256, 306 n. 5, 323 n. 24, 338 n. 36, 344 nn. 31–33, 345 n. 36, 345 n. 39, 345 n. 41

Ortelius, Abraham, 86–87

Padmini, 305 n. 2

Pakistan, 2, 48, 49, 125, 231, 233, 271, 336 n. 13, 348 n. 71; as part of carto-graphed Bharat Mata, 37, 39

Pal, Bipin Chandra, 18, 107, 111, 113–14, 115, 135, 136, 137, 139, 325 nn. 41–43, 330 n. 17, 346 n. 50

Parliament, 64, 183, 199, 203, 272

Parsi, 29, 70, 141, 161, 253, 255, 260, 316 n. 23

Partition of Bengal, 15–18, 118, 119–20, 127, 137, 149, 246, 248, 306 n. 6, 307 n. 8. *See also* Swadeshi movement

Partition of India, 37–38, 123, 158, 204, 231, 233, 244, 341 n. 59, 342 n. 3; denial of, 37–38, 183, 188, 210–11, 244

Parvati, 58, 104–5, 318 n. 54. *See also* Sati

Patel, Vallabh Bhai, 181, 186, 199, 311 n. 36

Paul Picture Publishers, 204, 210, 211, 230

Pictorial history, 2–3, 6, 8, 30, 52, 54–55, 68–71, 93, 99, 120, 122, 143, 233, 235–36, 238, 239, 251, 283–99, 342 n. 4. *See also* Visual patriotism

Pilgrimage maps, 161–64, 168, 170

Pinney, Christopher, 80, 186, 190, 209, 218, 268, 277, 296, 309 n. 25, 313 n. 54, 324 n. 31, 341 n. 59; on corpothetics, 34, 57, 310 n. 29; recursive archive and, 14, 312 n. 44

Pondicherry, 18, 22, 130, 147, 307 n. 13, 325 n. 44

Prasad, Rajendra, 183, 311 n. 36

Prithvi, 100–103, 137, 165, 245, 317 n. 45, 318 nn. 49–50, 332 n. 31

Proscribed pictures, 17, 29, 31–32, 33, 41, 110–12, 129–31, 219, 308 n. 19, 309 n. 25, 335 n. 9, 339 n. 42, 346 n. 48. *See also* Visual patriotism

Pune, 123, 124, 127, 130, 153, 263, 322 nn. 13–14

*Purana*s, 102, 103–4, 106, 272

Tagore, Rabindranath, 144, 324 n. 36, 326
nn. 51–52, 342 n. 8, 348 n. 66; *Home and
the World*, 114, 168, 236, 237, 247, 297, 320
n. 67, 334 n. 1, 334 nn. 2–3; Indian national
anthem, 139–42, 143, 326 n. 55, 327 n. 57,
327 n. 62; life of, 321 n. 5; poems on Bengal,
137–38; "Vande Mataram," 118, 139, 246,
247, 344 n. 23

Tamil nationalism, 38, 47, 173, 310 n. 32, 350
n. 5

Tamiltttay, 310 n. 32

Textbooks, 36; carto-graphed Bharat Mata
and, 37–38, 174–75, 278; map of India and,
173–75, 290

Tilak, Bal Gangadhar, 28, 193, 308 n. 20, 317
n. 47

Uberoi, Patricia, 34, 200, 310 n. 30

"Vande Mataram" (hymn): as assumed national anthem, 118, 246, 320 n. 2, 321 n. 7;
Bankim and, 107, 117, 121, 132, 137, 139, 140,
144, 156, 320 n. 3, 326 n. 55; Bharati and,
118; colonial state and, 118, 120, 125, 129,
321 n. 9, 327 n. 64; Congress Party and,
118; in Indian diaspora, 119–20, 128; Indian
national anthem and, 122–23, 125, 139–41,
320 n. 2, 322 n. 12, 326 n. 55; martyrdom
and, 144–49; Muslims and, 128, 144; as national song of India, 117, 122, 123, 144, 320
n. 2, 322 n. 12; partition of Bengal and, 118,
120, 141, 246–47; in schools, 120, 123, 129,
146, 344 n. 33; as song, 24, 107, 117, 118–19,
120, 122, 132, 134, 137, 139, 141, 156, 160,
246, 320 n. 1, 320 n. 3, 320 n. 17, 344 n. 23,
344 n. 33; translation of, 118–19; visualization of, 123–32

Vande Mataram (lithograph), 47, 54, 212

"vande mataram" (slogan), 19, 113, 247, 320
n. 1, 320 n. 3, 323 n. 23, 323 n. 25, 323 n. 29;
Anti-Circular Society and, 125–26; 128,
323 n. 22; Bharati and, 19, 21, 118, 121–22;
Bharat Mata and, 24; carto-graphed Bharat
Mata and, 21, 29–30, 47, 50, 122, 130, 135,
255; Indian flag and, 50, 128, 251–52, 254,
323 n. 22, 323 n. 24; map of India and, 21,
121, 123–29, 130, 132, 133, 135, 215, 286, 334
n. 47; martyrdom and, 119–20, 145–49, 339
n. 40; Mother India temples and, 133, 160;
proscription and, 118, 120, 125, 145–46, 321
n. 9, 346 n. 48

Varaha, 100, 317 n. 45

Varanasi, 4, 48, 133, 224, 246

Vathy, T. B., 44, 311 n. 35

Velu, P. T., 55

Victoria, 81–82, 96–97

Vijaya, 20, 107, 343 n. 21

Vijaya, 20–21, 307 n. 13, 323 n. 25

Virgin Mary, 90, 92, 94, 98, 198, 214

Vishnu, 56, 100, 102, 103, 156, 190, 331 n. 22,
338 n. 39

Vishwa Hindu Parishad, 169

Visual patriotism, 8–9, 11, 13–14, 17, 33–
36, 52, 56–57, 291–92, 295–99; of Indian
women, 178, 181, 233, 238–81; martyrdom
images and, 217–36, 268, 273, 275–81;
men's bodies and, 178–236, 284, 286, 311
n. 36. *See also* Bazaar art; Calendar art

Vivekananda, 248, 311 n. 36, 344 nn. 30–31

Women's Indian Association, 256–58

SUMATHI RAMASWAMY is a professor of history at Duke University.
She is the author of *Lost Land of Lemuria: Fabulous Geographies,
Catastrophic Histories* (2004) and *Passions of the Tongue: Language
Devotion in Tamil India* (1997), and the editor of *Beyond Appearances?
Visual Practices and Ideologies in Modern India* (2003) and *Barefoot
across the Nation: Maqbool Fida Husain and the Idea of India* (2010).

Library of Congress Cataloging-in-Publication Data
Ramaswamy, Sumathi.
The goddess and the nation : mapping Mother India /
Sumathi Ramaswamy.
p. cm.
Includes bibliographical references and index.
ISBN 978-0-8223-4592-3 (cloth : alk. paper)
ISBN 978-0-8223-4610-4 (pbk. : alk. paper)
1. Group identity—Political aspects—India.
2. Postcolonialism—India. 3. Mother goddesses—India.
4. Symbolic anthropology—India. I. Title.
DS430.R363 2010
954.035—dc22   2009044003